Quotes about the Book:

"Wondrous nuggets of revisionist history at its best!"

Herodotus

"Too bad I hadn't read this before I set sail…"

Christopher Columbus

"Finally, credit given where credit is due!"

Sacajawea

"Lies, all lies—we were first in flight! But the rest of the book is really great…"

Orville and Wilbur Wright

"An intriguing insight into the deepest motivations and inner soul of homo touristicus."

Sigmund Freud

ON THE ORIGIN OF THE SPECIES
homo touristicus

The Evolution of Travel
from Greek Spas to Space Tourism

William D. Chalmers

iUniverse, Inc.
Bloomington

iUniverse books may be ordered through booksellers or by contacting:

iUniverse
1663 Liberty Drive
Bloomington, IN 47403
www.iuniverse.com
1-800-Authors (1-800-288-4677)

ISBN: 978-1-4502-8926-9 (sc)
ISBN: 978-1-4502-8927-6 (ebook)

Printed in the United States of America

iUniverse rev. date: 01/31/2011

Dedication:

To my sun and my moon...I love you Petra and Lucca.

Table of Contents:

Preface xiii

Introduction xvii

1. Pre-History & Ancient History (41,000 BCE – 0) 1
In the beginning...God takes a Day Off...Leviticus takes a Sabbatical...
Cro-Magnon's Summer Cave...Wheel moves man quicker...Bathing suits
are invented...The First Tourist attraction is built...Innkeepers lobby
Hammurabi...Moses gets Lost...Jason & the Argonauts Epic Voyage ...
The First Spa Springs up...Olympic ticket scalpers...Map makers begin
lying...The Great Wall keeps Tourists out...All Roads lead to Persepolis...
Tourists invade the Acropolis...No, All Roads lead to Roma...Compass,
Who needs a Compass?...Seven Wonders of the World... Scandal Rocks
a Roman Beach Resort...The Silk Road...Wine Tours & DUI's...No Vacancy in Bethlehem...

2. The Common Era (1 CE – 986) 18
Religious Pilgrims run amok...Toll roads...SRO crowds at the Colosse-
um...The Golden Age of Roman Travel...This Map is Wrong Ptolemy!...
Walking, Walking Everywhere...The Dark Ages...Buddhist Pilgrims...
The First Hajj...Japanese Inns...New Must-See Sites...As the crow flies...
La Ruta Maya...Vikings, Vikings Everywhere...

3. The New Millennium (1002 – 1414) 28
New Worlds...St. Bernard rescue dogs...Group Tourism begins (aka the
Crusades)...Pubs Around the World...The Seven Seas...Angkor Wat
opens...The Inca Trial...The Right to Travel...Marco—Polo...The Nine
Rings of Travel Hell...Spa Days...Bring out your dead... Travel Writ-
ers...Martini's for all my friends...Machu Picchu opens...Mapmaker
Mapmaker Make Me a Map...Zheng He conquers the world—Zheng He
goes home...Passport Denied ...Horses move man faster...

4. The Age of Discovery (1418- 1606). 40
Henry the Navigator...The Vinland Map...*terra incognita*...Dragons & El Dorado...The Grand Bazaar...The Book Fair...Spice Islands...Christopher Columbus lost as usual...Vasco da Gama ...Ain't that Amerigo, Home of the Free...Utopia—*not!*...The Legend of Magellan... *Conquistador, your stallion stands...The Brave New World...*The New & Improved Seven Wonders of the World...*Arr matee,* Pirates!...The Running of the Bulls...

5. The Era of *homo touristicus* Dawns (1608 – 1743) 55
Don Quixote...The Grand Tour...The Lost Continent—finally found...Thanksgiving...The Taj Mahal opens...Casinos-are-us...More Travel Writers...Life at Versailles...Museums, Museums ...The Armchair Traveler...*Robinson Crusoe*...The Traveler's Tax...*Gulliver's Travel*...What is the Bernoulli Theorem?...

6. The Era of Mechanized Transport Arrives (1744 – 1829) 68
Horse Trams...Berkeley Springs...Is your name Casanova?...The British Museum Needs Some Marbles...Cox & Kings Travel Agency...Ahh, Uffizi Gallery...The French Riviera...Traveller's Cheques...The First Epic Buddy Road Trip...The Greenbrier...Balloonmania Grips Europe...Grand Hotels ...Thank you Sacajawea...Trains are Faster than Horses...The Oktoberfest party... The Lost City of Petra is Finally Found...The Stendhal Syndrome...Gin 'n' tonics & the British Empire...The Santa Fe Trail...Baedeker Guidebooks...The Royal Geographical Society...

7. The Building of Tourism Infrastructure (1830 – 1898) 87
Alexis de Tocqueville discovers America...Let the Conventions Begin...A Niagara Falls Love Affair... Madame Tussaud's...Going on Safari...Astor House...Travel Photographs...*Mardi Gras*...Trans-Atlantic Steamships...Romance Romps...The Oregon Trail...Sir Thomas Cook... Tivoli Gardens...Blackpool Pleasure Beach...London Zoo opens...Macau: The Monte Carlo of the Orient...*The Excursionist* travel magazine...*Dr. Livingstone, I presume?*...New York's World's Fair...Vuitton Luggage...May Day...Lourdes & Coney Island...Mark Twain Takes to the Road...Travel *Tchotchkes*...The Atlantic City Boardwalk opens...The Bank Holiday Act... *Around the World in Eighty Days*...A Mercedes-Benz...The Oriental opens...Golf tourism... Venice Simplon-Oriental Express...Tijuana...National Parks...The Breakers...National Geographic Society...Behold *La Tour Eiffel*...Hillbilly Heaven...*Putting on The Ritz*...

8. The New Century and Industrial Tourism Takes Root (1900 – 1913) 122
The Paris *Métro* opens…Zeppelin, Zeppelin's Everywhere…Kodak's Box Brownie…Michelin Guides…Gustave's Flight…The First Lady of Waikiki…AAA…The Wright Brothers…Model T's Hit the Road…The Calgary Stampede…Youth Hostels & Spring Break…

9. The Era of Commercial Air Travel (1914 – 1951) 133
The First Passengers…Panama Canal opens…The Lincoln Highway…*If you see us rocking don't bother knocking!…You ever heard the one about the traveling salesman?…*Trans-Siberian (*not so*) Express…Mile High Club…Car Rentals…Mr. Hilton opens a Hotel…Booze Cruises …The Lost Generation…Boeing, Douglas & Lockheed….Hospitality Management University …Lenin's Tomb & other morbid sites…Pan Am, TWA & American Airlines…*Get your Kicks on Route 66…*The Winter Olympics…Hollywood & Celebrity Tourism…*The Adventures of Tintin*…The Concierge Mantra: *Yes, of course I can! Now what would be your question?…*SUX = Sioux City, Iowa…The Traveler v. Tourist Controversy…*Take me to Cuba baby!…*Travel Agents Unite!…*I want to be alone…*Petite Airhostesses arrive—On Time Too!…DC-3's…The Negro Motorist Green Book…Fodor's, Frommer's & Let's Go…Tiger Balm Gardens…Holidays with Pay Act…The Mystery Spot & other Roadside Wonders…*The Road to Singapore*…The King David Hotel explosion…Bugsy opens the Flamingo…Air Rage & Duty Free—A Connection?…The Bermuda Triangle…Club Mediterranée…Ché hits the road… Mexican Riviera…Diners Club & Holiday Inn…The Cold War Blues…

10. The Era of Hyper-Mobility (1952 – 1986) 179
The Jet Age, The Jet Set & Jet Lag arrive…Japanese Love Hotels…Wife Swapping or House Swapping…Culture Shock…Dramamine, DEET & Melatonin…Nation Inflation & The Century Club…Travel Writers get a Tax Deduction…The Happiest Place on Earth opens…Land Yachts … *An Affair To Remember*…Tipping Points Across the Ocean…Hyatt, Sheraton & Westin… Sputniks & Squirrel Monkeys in Space…Magic Fingers…A Little Intercourse & Intoxication… Time Shares, Bullet Trains & Shamu…The Gap Year & the Hippie Trail…*Coffee, Tea or Me?…*Men on the Moon…Hi-jacking Hell…The *Real* Cannonball Run…World Heritage Sites …ATM's, Eurail Passes & Discos…7 frickin' forty 7's…The Thing about Cars…The Lonely Planet Effect & The Loving it to Death Syndrome…I think I'm going to Kathmandu…The Love Boat & Fantasy

Island... *I ain't gonna play Sun City!*...CNN, USA Today & Walkman's... Graceland...*Tiananmen Massacre & the Chinese Travel Boycott*...

11. Post-Modern Tourism (1987 - 1996) 253
No matter where you go, there you are...Been there, done that, what's next... Space Tourism... The Travel Channel...Flying the *not* so Friendly Skies & Economy Class Syndrome...Tourist Ghettos, War Zones & Wynn's Las Vegas...Guidebook Personality Disorder... Cell phones & Happy Endings...The Traveler's Bribe Paying Index...CAAPS I & the No-fly List... The World's Greatest Travelers"

12. The Advent of Travel 2.0 (1996 - 2001) 277
Hotmail, Yahoo! & You...Blogging *ad nauseam...GPS, Hotel Porn Bills & Hotels.com*...The Dark Side of Airline Alliances...That's a *Really BIG Wave Dude*...Paradise Island, Shangri-La & Dubailand...William Shatner's Revenge—Priceline.com...*Where in the World is Matt Lauer?*... Heavenly Beds, Bed Bugs & Tummy Tuck Tourism...Millennium Madness... TripAdvisor.com...The Global Scavenger Hunt"... Kumbh Mela, Burning Man & iPods...*What Me Worry?*

13. Travel in the Post-9/11 World (2001 – 2010) 294
Barbarians are at the Gate...Fear Inc...Flying While Muslim...The Amazing Race...It's a Wi-Fi World...A Blind Date with the World™...America's Geographic Illiteracy...The World's Greatest Travelers...Debauchery Tourism, part *deux*...TSA, CAPPS II & the Shoe Bomber ...WikiTravel...Road Warrior Fact & Fiction...Google & Virtual Tourism...Nano-Vacations, Staycations & Vocation Vacations...Guests Behaving Badly... *Rights, you don't got no stinking rights!*...United Airline's present to America—$5 billion pension debt... *Lifestyles of the Rich and Famous*...Private Jets, Super Jumbos & the Dreamliners...*The Confessions of a Rogue Travel Writer*...Jetlag, Viagra & Body Scanners...Arrested while Kissing in Dubai...Rick Steves Go Home—Oh, you are Home?...

14. The Future of Travel, the Tourism Industry, and *homo touristicus* is Unwritten. 334
The Tourism Time Bomb...*The Asians are Coming, the Asians are Coming*...Everestland, Hydropolis & Biodiversity Farms...Singapore Girls for all my flying friends...Mega-Projects... Global Weather Weirding... *Boy are these skies crowded or what?*...Welcome to the Hotel Disconnect... Airline Passenger Bill of Rights passes in United States—*just kidding!*...

The Scarcity of Place...High-Speed Rail in United States—*just kidding!*...
Finally, Star Trek's Tele-transporter arrives—Too Late...

Acknowledgements...................................... 347

About the Author 349

Bibliography 351

Chronological Index 359

A-Z Index 363

Preface:

This project started almost a decade ago as a smaller chapter within a larger book about travel and tourism, and has evolved into this single subject volume. What to include, and what *not* to include within these pages was my single biggest challenge. There have been giants for sure: visionaries and inventors, explorers and mapmakers, missionaries and mercenaries, entrepreneurs and market innovators to consider. Indeed there are thousands who have moved the arrow of travel history forward.

It is recognized that history is a cumulative science; specialists in other fields have helped assemble that knowledge database, and we are deeply indebted to them. A big collective "they" created and recorded the vast mine of knowledge that we are able to dig deeper into and uncover interesting nuggets and significant gems. As Isaac Newton knew all too well with his own discoveries: *"If I have seen further than others, it is by standing upon the shoulders of giants."*

Alas, *everything* cannot fit into a 350-page manuscript. And rightfully so, this manuscript is by no means complete; it is a work in progress—indeed all works of history are works in progress from the moment the typeface is set. We certainly hope to hear from fellow scholars, historians, adventurers, corporate publicists, and aviation-junkies alike, about some omission, error, or outright misrepresentation of facts, printed somewhere within. We sincerely hope we do hear from you, and please contact me directly at homotouristicus@worldsgreatesttravelers.com to help make the second edition of this volume bigger and better, and a more complete and accurate work of history. And to those errors we have made, we humbly apologize in advance—*Sorry about that folks!*—next time we will get it right.

As a history book, out of deference to the majority of the world's citizens who are *not* Christian, the use of Common Era (CE), and Before Common Era (BCE), as chronological signposts will be utilized throughout this book. The use of the lower case "c" after any year—1950c BCE—means it is the historical best guessed time period by the experts about the event in question. Some dates are certain, but frankly, some are really not known—they are guesstimates at best.

Since George Carlin advised that it is better to use the metric system, with his informative and factual line, *"Kilometers are shorter than miles. Save gas, take your next trip in kilometers."* We have used the internationally recognized metric system of measurements throughout this book and convert only when it serves for a better understanding for all our North American readers.

Throughout this book you will also notice the free and unfettered use of aka—as in Music Hall (aka Radio City Music Hall), where added alternative names (aka also known as), nicknames, or slang terms of endearment, are liberally exploited without restraint or conscience.

The word "discover" is a rather complicated expression when you think about it. What does "discover" really mean? Sure, a nuclear physicist can discover a new element in a particle accelerator experiment. And yes, the judges on *American Idol* can discover a new singing sensation. But it is hard to "discover" a mountain or a river; or for that matter a continent and a whole race of people, as if by some heuristic *Eureka!* moment to behold that something new was *ipso facto* suddenly found! I would submit to you that other folks may have seen them first—in fact, those *other* folks may live within a stone's throw away of some of those said discoveries—but it just never occurred to them to "discover" them for themselves. *Nuff* said...

A note about "terrorism" also needs to be qualified. What is a "terrorist"? A terrorist is a person or group of people fighting for a cause they believe in—rightly or wrongly—in an *asymmetric* fashion against a larger, better armed controlling ruling class. The folks who fought for our freedom in the American Revolution were "terrorists" to the English ruling elite, as are the Tibetan Buddhist seeking freedom from the Communist Party tyrants in Beijing. Clearly, terrorist acts of violence, no matter who does it, and for whatever reason or cause is bad, ugly, immoral and unjustified when noncombatant civilians are threatened, hurt or killed—as is war itself many would argue. The truism that asserts that, *"One man's terrorist is another man's freedom fighter," is relevant.* So, whether these acts are indeed high crimes or just misdemeanors is for someone else to decide, and only "terrorist" incidents that affect the history of travel and tourism or *homo touristicus* directly are included within this text.

> *"History is always written wrong, and so always needs to be rewritten."*
>
> - George Santayana (1863-1952) Spanish philosopher

This book is *not* presented in a traditional narrative style, but rather in bite-sized tender morsels of fact (and fiction) by means of chronologically categorized citations. The reason for this is simple: there are simply too many diverse topics within this field of travel and tourism, over 5,000 years worth, to be both comprehensive in any coherent manner, or to be put in any relevant context—which is kind of important for any historical narrative! Having said that, there are indeed patterns, themes and unified theories that are revealed within the presentation of these especially interesting and salacious nuggets of knowledge, that are later subtly explained.

Lastly, we have chosen *not* to footnote this edition. This pragmatically made decision tormented the serious scholar in us. But, with over 900 individual citations and literally thousands of unique facts that we felt were pertinent to the history of travel and the evolution of *homo touristicus* enclosed within these pages—the footnoting of all those citations and facts would have taken up more space than the actual entries themselves. (Plus we love trees, the bigger the better!) So, please forgive us, and know that credit is appropriately given as much as possible.

In the final analysis, this book is filled with a plethora of factual, interesting, and downright entertaining citations that are all just little nuggets of history, small picture postcards of time as it were—but oh how cumulatively they add up! It was a gratifying task digging in the vast data dump to assemble these juicy tidbits. Each one taking into account some travel or tourism milestones that furthered the evolution of *homo touristicus* along; they include: the development of geography, historical firsts, famous voyages, the adventures of infamous travelers, the building of tourist infrastructure, the pop culture connection to travel, along with scores of other remarkable and amusing related happenings and events—and it must be said that the science of superlatives is tricky business indeed! Obviously, if any citation captures your interest, please research it by visiting the library, hitting the book stores, or surfing the net, to indulge that curiosity.

And like everything in life, we readily admit to some biases. The Los Angeles Lakers *are* the world's best professional basketball franchise in the history of the sport. There, I said it! There are a few other biases that you will inevitably notice in your coming read. In spite of our personal peccadilloes and biases, we hope that you enjoy the book and find it factual, enlightening, opinionated, and extremely entertaining. It is an irreverent look at the history of travel and the evolution of tourism and hopefully offers you a fresh take on just who *homo touristicus* is…enjoy the adventure.

> *"The big question is whether you are going to be able to say a hearty yes to your adventure."*
>
> - Joseph Campbell (1904-1987) an American mythologist

Introduction:

On The Origin of the Species *homo touristicus*:
The Evolution of Travel from Greek Spas to Space Tourism

> *"Very deep, very deep is the well of the past. Should we not call it bottomless?"*

- Thomas Mann (1875–1955) a German Nobel Prize laureate

Putting together the history of anything is a daunting task. Writing the history of travel is no less daunting due to the fact that there is no real beginning of travel. People have always traveled for one reason or another. Indeed, the travel gene is clearly embedded deep within the mysteries of our DNA. We humans are made to move—check out your own two legs. Our most basic and fundamental human nature seems to require it. Cavemen traveled as hunter-gatherers to eat. Babylonian kings traveled to escape the summer heat. Pilgrims traveled to find answers to unknowable things. Merchants and traders traveled over the horizon to make a buck. Warriors traveled to conquer and protect their known way of life. Normal everyday folks traveled in search of a better life for themselves and their families.

What I discovered as my research progressed on this book was that the history of travel was if truth be told, nothing less than the history of man—and that is indeed a daunting scope.

As travelers, man has always looked for more convenient, comfortable, and efficient ways to transport himself. Transportation is the way we move from place to place, and the evolution and history of travel runs parallel with the evolution and history of our methods of transportation. It is certainly breath-taking that modern-man can visit any remote corner of our now known world safely in a few short hours; whereas just s few hundred years ago it might have taken many perilous years—if they made it at all! Man's vision of the world has also expanded, yet paradoxically gotten smaller at the same time. All of mankind has grown, developed, and dare I say it, evolved since our earliest days—*homo touristicus* included.

Within the pages of this book, you will see our glorious cultural, technological, and creative evolution unfold before your very eyes. Evolving from man's more primitive technological state and from literally walking but a few steps a day; to our current hyper-mobile 24/7 world of perpetual movement and instant communications. We have in fact evolved, and that evolution—each baby step forward, and each step backwards too—is documented within these pages.

The history of travel assembled here shows the profound growth and breath-taking development of the travel and tourism industry. It is, chronology speaking, a list of the good, the bad, and at times downright ugly moments, that have occurred over the millennium as we have discovered, and rediscovered each little corner of our world—and now the heavens above too—and in doing so have slowly evolved into the species we are today—*homo touristicus.*

> *"To boldly go where no man has gone before..."*
> - Star Trek TV show theme tagline

As a traveler, who loves to travel, the anticipation of going over the hill to see what was on the other side, has always thrilled me—no matter how near or far I roam. That thrill of adventure and potential discovery is always with me wherever I go, however far I travel. Man too is a curious lot—we want to know—and yes, curiosity has killed the cat on more than a few occasions as we shall see. Yet that fundamental curiosity that each of us holds deep inside has always pushed us out that door, down the street, and over the mysterious horizon to distant unknown lands—*terra incognito.*

Think for a moment what it would have been like for an ancient man, before any technology, before any communications, before anyone he knew had ever told stories about it, to have walked for days across some vast forbidding stretch of land—be it an intense tropical jungle, swampy wetland, vast desert, menacing mountain pass, or dark forest—to somehow have survived the journey itself, and come out on the other side of the horizon and find a new land with new people awaiting you! Absolutely exhilarating, absolutely frightening, and yet absolutely what defines man as *homo touristicus.*

That, I think, is what traveling is all about. Admittedly it is harder to achieve in this day and age of known known's and well-beaten paths, but that is fundamentally why people still do travel—to see what they have not seen before with their own eyes and to experience what they have not experienced before, personally and authentically.

Yet other motivations move people too. Denis Diderot (1713–1784), the French social critic and editor of the *Encyclopédie,* argues persuasively that early discovers and explorers, were driven not by humankind's nobler instincts but by some of its basest: "…tyranny, crime, ambition, misery," and only occasionally, curiosity. And that is all too true as we shall see.

Aside from the wanderlust gene in many of us (all of us I would submit), the *why* people have traveled is a somewhat easier nut to crack. People travel because they have an inclination to go. And once that is established, a few other conditions allow them to do so—firstly they must be healthy enough to go; secondly they must enjoy the leisure time in which to go; thirdly, they must have the resources to go (money); and finally, there must be the basic facilities (aka tourist infrastructure) available for the traveler that allows them to go (modes of transportation, places to stay and eat, things to do, etc.). Of course, many travelers have more will than wallet, and nowadays, time pressed modern travelers have more money than time ironically; but, it is always necessary to have an appropriate mixture of time, resources—and inclination—to go.

Individual motives aside, man has been empowered to travel because the infrastructure has both followed his needs and pushed his desires and wants to new levels. Yes, many travel industry developments have arisen out of the basic economic principle of solving man's problems—and making a few bucks at the same time. (One should never forget that travel and tourism, no matter for what purpose or motivation, is, and always will be, just another consumer good.) That is why inns and taverns developed over time—modern day hotels and restaurants—to feed and house road weary travelers. That is why inter-city thoroughfares and water ways developed—modern day highways and shipping lanes—to move goods and people quicker and more efficiently. And that is why ports, rail stations, bus stations and airports developed—to more efficiently and safely move the masses along. The travel tourism infrastructure has been in a constant state of flux, innovation, invention, and development since about 5,000 BCE.

Technology has changed the way we travel too, from boats to railway systems to automobiles and now jet planes. What's more, it has shrunk the globe. This evolution has continued to show a declining relevance of distance between places and destroyed any physical constraints of geography that had earlier bound mankind. Traveling today takes hours—not weeks or months. Our new technologies of movement, along with the immediacy offered 21st century travelers with the evolution of the truly amazing global Internet system, has revolutionized the travel tourism business as much as any other industry, and has helped empower the independent traveler with a mouse click or a real-time face-to-face Skype video call—"Dad, send money, *please!*"

On the flip side, man is always ingenious in the development of new, interesting, and unique human diversions, and the Field of Dreams *"If you build it, they will come,"* mantra is alive and well in the tourism industry. Someone opened a warm and soothing spa in ancient Greece—and they came. Someone opened a zoo thinking city folks might be interested—and they came. Walt Disney opened Disneyland to make kids laugh—and they came. The tourism industry is filled with these radical acts of inspiration, genius and greed—and yes, they did come most of the time. How else can you explain the world's largest ball of twine?

It also seems clear that the infrastructure of tourism as we know it today, has constantly developed in ebbs and flows, that are directly related to political stability and the dynamic of economic imperatives that eventually led directly to the new and improved markets and new and improved travel-related infrastructure including: safer and faster modes of transportation systems and communication technologies; be it Rome's *Via Appian* (aka the queen of the long roads), or the advent of Internet travel sites. Simply put, markets helped move people.

It is also true that over the eons travel has evolved and grown with our political liberties, material affluence and technical prowess. Technology has compressed distances; indeed it has almost transcended them as any jet-setter can attest to—having a traditional Japanese breakfast in Kyoto, a dim sum lunch in Hong Kong, and then enjoying a tandoori dinner in Delhi, India.

Globalization, for good or bad, has changed the very nature of how we perceive travel in the 21st Century. The travel industry is BIG business. Individuals and villages rely on it for sustenance. Ministers of Tourism promote it as an economic savior, and whole nations depend on it for their economic stability. Indeed, our lives grow more and more intertwined and interdependent each and every day as a result of these travel-related exchanges of people, cultures, and smiles. No ideology can change the historic inevitability of this dynamic, a function of both increased disposable income and leisure time—though some forces continue to try; be they wars, pandemics, acts of nature, boycotts, terrorism, or parochial-minded nationalism. Mostly in times of economic prosperity and development people go, and more importantly in the absence of war, *homo touristicus* was usually on the move. (People stay close to the campfire in times of war and uncertainty—as the events of September 11th have proven.) For whether the travel gene exists or not, throughout history as incomes rose, man's movements inevitably followed, hand in hand.

So then…inclination, resources (both time and money), infrastructure, and diversions—along with freedom of movement; that in a nut shell is the driver, the lubricant, the machine, and the road itself for travelers that help explain the travel tourism industry as a functioning entity. But my, oh my, has it evolved and grown!

As early as 1990, the *Los Angeles Times* was touting the travel industry as the "largest single industry on Earth," (31 July 1990); and the *New York Times* followed suit a little later, claiming that, "tourism is the world's largest industry." (26 May 1991) Indeed it has continued to grow in the twenty years since, and according to the World Tourism Office (WTO), the travel tourism industry is the Global Golden Goose of the US$58 trillion global economy. Tourism is not only arguably the world's largest industry today, but it also remains one of the fastest growing industries in the world despite current economic conditions *circa* 2010.

And we travelers keep moving too—between 1950, what are called international arrivals (people crossing borders from one country to another) exploded from just 25 million globally to over 920 million international tourist arrivals by the end of 2008—and that is expected to grow to over 1.6 *billion* by 2020, as developing nations break that magic middle class economic ceiling and start fulfilling their own travel desires! This exchange of people to and fro, has been—and will hopefully continue to be—the largest peaceful movement of people across national borders since human history began.

In fact, financially and economically speaking, the development of the travel tourism industry is staggering: One out of every 9 people around the world, representing over 300 million jobs, is directly created by the industry! The direct and indirect impact of the industry generated an estimated US$5.47 trillion—almost 10% of the world's entire gross world production (GWP) in 2009! In the U.S. alone, the industry contributes US$640 billion to the economy, or 5.4% of GDP and employs almost 10 million people. (Now think for a moment the impact the industry has on tourism-dependent nations like Egypt, Mexico, Thailand, or the Bahamas!) And with the expected continued growth of the industry pegged at over 4% annually for the next several decades—as demographics (both social and economic) change globally—the industry will double in as little as 16 years from today!

"*The future is unwritten,*" as Joe Strummer so eloquently foretold, but to sum up the travel tourism industry's future in one word would be—*more*! *More* people coming and going, *more* mega infrastructure projects are coming, *more* flights flying, *more* high-speed rail systems, *more* cruise ships, *more* taxicabs, *more* hotel rooms, resorts and spas, *more* amusement parks, music venues, museums and theatres, and *more* convention centers, country clubs, and casinos. More, more, more…in corporate-think bigger is better and more creates demand.

The structure of this book is simple, it shows the chronological development of travel and evolution of what we call *homo touristicus,* since the beginning of recorded history. Yep, real simple! And although this book has been constructed as a chronological timeline, patterns of development and eras have revealed themselves and were neatly put into sub-chapters within the whole text.

Here is what your read will look like:

The first few chapters deal with pre- and ancient history, along with the first millennium of the Common Era. Critters, mammals, and humans have always traveled, but it had to start somewhere at sometime; and these myths, legends, and scientific archeological facts point to these early well-documented signposts in the evolution of *homo touristicus*. But when the Cro-Magnon moved from their summer cave to their winter cave—the rest as they say, is history.

> *"Man can learn nothing except by going from the known to the unknown."*
>
> - Claude Bernard (1813-1878) a French man of science

Anthropologists tell us that man roamed the world from Africa to Europe to Asia and over the ice bridge to North America followed by South America. Archeologists tell us that watercraft was used to travel to New Guinea, Australia, and all those little specks of rocks in the vast Pacific Ocean. Humans evolved from nomadic hunters and gathers to an agricultural-based people. Some early tribes in Babylon left for parts unknown looking for a better life. The Pharaohs enjoyed the dry desert air of the Sahara in the winter along with the cool waters of the River Nile in the summer. And we all know how Moses loved to wander! Already we see religious travel as the original reason to travel, for essentially non-essential purposes, as they searched for enlightenment and the legendary lost worlds of either the Garden of Eden or for loved ones in Hades.

That wise man Plato referred to them as "breathing spells" and the Greeks mandated over 50 public holidays a year. The Roman Empire was built over many centuries on the legacy—and roads and sea routes—of the Greeks before them. One can easily imagine toga-clad Roman tourists milling about the Great Pyramids at Giza, checking out the Acropolis, or even taking side trips up to Ur to catch a glimpse of an ancient ziggurat—with the touts in tow! And as the story goes, Mary and Joseph traveled to Bethlehem for the census and all they saw were *"No Vacancy"* signs. It took a while to catch on, but Christian pilgrims begin traveling to those same Holy Land sites centuries later, as did their Muslim contemporaries a few centuries after that during the Dark Ages; which somewhat stunts the evolution of *homo touristicus* after centuries of wandering and growth.

Man's second millennium, and our third chapter opens with the New World being "discovered" and populated for a time—by Vikings! Missionaries from all the great and not so great religions have traveled in search of converts, enlightenment and to achieve other divinely inspired goals.

But Holy sites remained the focus of elective travel—and mass medieval tourism (aka religious crusades). While on the other side of the world (aka the Orient or Far East) their *terra incognito* shrinks as travelers from the West visit for trade and commerce and their amazing treasure fleets visit destinations far and wide. Islamic scholarship in the arts, sciences, and navigation flourishes—soon to be just as quickly lost.

The next chapter opens with the explosive and profound *Age of Discovery* in which a confident and wealthy man begins to literally expand his horizons. Experts and historians disagree on many things, but they do agree on a few things, one being that an early Renaissance-era man named Henry the Navigator, almost single-handedly pushes his little sea-faring Nation of Portugal—and other nations *de facto*—further than it ever imagined going with both his moral and financial support. This great *Age of Exploration* lasts for roughly 350 years between 1418 and1779, but really takes off in 1453 when the Turks seized Constantinople which effectively blocks off all eastern Mediterranean travel and Eastern trade routes significantly increasing the prices of goods. There is now an economic incentive to roam and tread on paths less beaten. This act more than any other, gives rise to the conditions for the advent of Europeans to seek out alternative routes to the Far East.

Mercenaries begin traveling, where others would not, in order to make a buck. The great men of adventure during the *Age of Exploration* traveled mostly for the profit of king and country. They ended up being great explorers in spite of themselves—because on the whole, they traveled for profit, not curiosity. But they did expand trade routes in a drive for resource rich colonies, and later for the slave trade. Many of the great "explorers" actually had only a mild thirst for knowledge and traveled with a missionary zeal to convert heathens and enrich themselves; but the scientists and cartographers, who did travel with them, acquired great knowledge in the hopes of filling in some of the many gaps of human knowledge. And soon adventurers had traveled the so-called "four corners of the world" (because they were always looking at a rectangular map) for the sheer joy and challenge of doing something or visiting someplace that no one else (sic) ever had. Or more likely, no one that ever wrote about it!

In any event, *homo touristicus* begins a grand new era of discovery after centuries of religion dominating his parochial travels; traveling for the purpose of exploration, discovery, wealth and fame.

By 1605, and our fifth chapter, the dawning of *homo touristicus* officially arrives with man now traveling for the sake of travel (aka leisure travel). This evolution of *homo touristicus* takes a huge leap when incomes rise as a result of the Industrial Revolution giving would-be travelers both the time to travel freely and the money to do so. Man begins traveling for personal development and growth—not just for commerce or religion.

Up until this age of leisure travel, the cycle of travel history went pretty much like this: kings and queens wanted more land and traders looked for new markets, which pushed explorers to find new places, which led mapmakers to make new maps showing how to get to those places; and finally, which led to technological innovators to help find safer and faster modes of transportation to get there.

And as more travelers hit the terrestrial byways and ocean sea lanes, beginning around 1744, man's great transportation inventions, from steamboat and railways, firmly takes root in helping expand man's traveling abilities. The *Era of Mechanization* of transport arrives in our sixth chapter, and shows how each new mode of transportation developed usually took about 50 to 100 years to fully saturate its desired niche. And as each new machine assists man in significantly surpassing his limited five kilometers per hour of mobility by foot— a progressive evolution of *homo touristicus* territorial range expands and man travels more freely and confidently.

Some historians label the 1830's as the *Golden Age of Travel*, and by this time and our seventh chapter, travel becomes a technical pursuit for *homo touristicus*; in that man starts building machines to rest his limbs and get from place to place faster and *en mass* as wealth spreads. The revolutionary age of the steam engine is upon us and man starts building the modern-day infrastructure that keeps the whole transportation system—and man— moving along. Be it by constructing bigger ships, canals and ports for water travel; or rail lines, byways and intercity systems for inland ground travel; or hotels for staying the night. Tourist attractions start popping up also to entertain the now mobile *homo touristicus*, and in turn, travelers also begin to chronicle their travel adventures, sharing their thoughts, reflections, observations, impressions and war stories.

Modern tourism firmly takes root in our eighth chapter and the dawning of the 2nd millennium. By 1900, inter-city and intra-city transportation systems are now complete, grand hotels are flourishing around the world, things-to-do tourist attractions grow by leaps and bounds, travel cameras and guidebooks are sold to the masses, travel clubs and tourist bureaus are formed. The terrestrial world is known and travelers can go anywhere— and getting there is half the fun. And with the advent of automobiles in 1908, a revolutionary paradigm shifts man away from mass transit as personal transit begins—especially in the United States, that gives travelers new unencumbered transportation freedoms. But an even more dramatic development in the evolution of *homo touristicus* is literally ready to take off...

Having mastered land and sea, our next chapter welcomes the advent of commercial air travel in 1914 that of course takes *homo touristicus* to new heights. No place on earth is unapproachable despite two world wars, a terrible global pandemic, and a long lasting economic depression.

Despite all these terrible, albeit temporary setbacks, the arrow of history aims upward again for *homo touristicus* and in the tenth chapter, the *Era of Hyper-Mobility* arrives with man's ability to travel much greater distances with ease and frequency on jet planes. But, creative destruction being what it is, the glory and predominance of ocean liners begins to wane when larger and larger, and faster and faster passenger airplanes began whisking more and more passengers across the ocean in less and less time. For obvious reasons, the speed of crossing the ocean became more popular than the style of crossing it, whether by Boeing 747 Jumbo, supersonic Concorde, or 21st century double-decker Airbus A380. A new era of travel evolves when the journey itself is secondary to arriving at the destination—getting there is *no* longer half the fun. And between 1950 and 2010, international arrivals grow from 25 million to over 920 million—*a year!*

The next evolutionary step of *homo touristicus* arrives in our next chapter and 1987, with the reality of *Post-Modern Tourism*. Daniel J. Boorstin (1914–2004), an American historian, so easily explains it: "*The modern American tourist now fills his experience with pseudo-events. He has come to expect both more strangeness and more familiarity than the world naturally offers. He has come to believe that he can have a lifetime of adventure in two weeks and all the thrills of risking his life without any real risk at all.*"

Theoretically the post-modern era of tourism intellectualizes that man's travel tendencies are now irrevocably intertwined with his progressive instincts and civilized modernity; and that our consumption patterns by now are thoroughly jumbled together within our concepts of wealth and consumerism, as well as our attitudes about leisure—and ourselves—along with technological innovations, and pop-culture. Simply put, travel is no longer undertaken just to travel or to just go on a vacation—it must mean something to us and add to our modern sense of cultural identity.

One definitely see's a pattern develop during this era as travel is now somehow less than the "*way it used to be.*" The average travel consumer is swimming in a sea of 24/7 media data and images in an everything-all-the-time world. A somewhat cynical edge about travel evolves. "We're not tourists—ugh, bite your tongue!—*we are travelers!*" protest many people on the go. Tourists become jaded with a "*...been there, done that, what's next*" attitude that evolved somewhere between the upper-crust's Grand Tour and the 1980's jet-setters.

And so the commercialization of travel adventure begins to accelerate as people anchored to desk jobs dream of getting away from it all—for two weeks at least (if they are lucky!)—and become more thrill-seeking in their leisure pursuits. Robert Young Pelton, a North American adventurer and travel commentator, may have said it best, "*The more civilized a society is, the more outrageous their adventures.*" The advent of space tourism proves the point.

We arrive in 1996 and our chapter on the advent of the new and improved era of *Travel 2.0*. Pre-packaged tourism evolves into dynamic tourism with more and more travel consumers, especially independent travelers, now empowered by the technological advances of the *Digital Age* of computers and Internet era of direct sales. Travelers and tourists alike, now have at their fingertips—just a mouse click away—a truly remarkable breath of online research potential with the proliferation of websites offering travel information and goods to be purchased and consumed; be it for planning a trip, using GPS mapping sites, buying goods via e-commerce, checking fellow user-generated peer reviews, reading blogs, participating in collaborative community bulletin boards and forums, using and contributing to wikis and professionally-written guidebooks, eye-balling video-sharing sites, writing moblogs, along with a multitude of social media platforms—mostly being offered in real-time at your convenience from anywhere. It seems quaint to say it now as we take it all for granted, but it remains nonetheless true—never before has so much been available to so many!

Until finally our collective bubbles are burst with the tragic events of 9/11 that changes everything in the American mindset—indeed the *barbarians are at the gates.* And so we cautiously enter our next to last chapter and the Post-9/11 era with rightfully fearful, scary paranoia (and willful ignorance) that ushers us into an era of collective national insecurity and creates a whole new set of challenges facing travelers, both domestically and internationally. It is an era that *homo touristicus* is still trying to figure out (witness the aggressive TSA pat-downs and peek-show body scanners of late 2010); one that not only includes the safety factor, but with all his newfound awareness and concern of the environment challenges before him and the changes it has brought—and will bring. Let alone traveler's potentially adverse social and economic impact on fragile cultures and "simpler" peoples.

Homo touristicus' very essence is called into question as some wonder aloud whether travel is indeed even necessary anymore in a hostile world with shrinking resources. Not only is getting there not half the fun anymore, but the actual going part may become morally and ethically taboo for socially conscious citizens!

Which brings us to our final chapter, and the future of the travel and tourism industry and *homo touristicus.* Man, having evolved a long way from hunter-gathers, to city folk and traders, warriors and conquerors, and into an adventurous and now thoughtful traveler, has to go somewhere to continue to feed his endless appetite for curiosity and meaningfulness—but where? Will it be real or virtual?

The era of discovery, terrestrially speaking, is clearly over because man has pretty much uncovered and discovered everything there is, physically at least. Maybe that's why we went to the moon? Certainly the depths of the oceans still hold some promise of discovery and satellites continue to amaze us with those x-ray eyes of distant worlds. And maybe, for that reason, we are back where we started with in *homo touristicus's* evolution ironically with the growth of religious tourism; which according to the World Tourism Organization, is moving an estimated 300 to 330 million pilgrims a year to visit the world's key religious sites.

Against that trend, today's wealthy Baby Boomers and Generation X'ers are busy hatching new firsts to quench their adventure gene; like windsurfing solo across the Pacific Ocean, or snowboarding the Antarctic icecaps. Humans have always been silly, egocentric beings, and I suspect just like conquering the Seven Summits, self-anointed adventurers (and high income earners) of the future will always find new and different ways to amuse themselves—like spending US$20 million to go into space.

Yes, *the future is unwritten*. Yet one thing remains certain, that our historical timeline so significantly and continuously shows, travel *is* important and relevant to *homo touristicus* and that simply because of that fact, he will continue to evolve with the coming changes to the environment, political realities and new transportation challenges before him. He will survive as long as man himself survives, because the twin species of *homo sapiens* and *homo touristicus* are irrevocably intertwined. But, what is the next wave for man the builder, problem-solver extraordinaire? Indeed, the future is unwritten...but, the past is prologue.

CHAPTER ONE

Pre-History and Ancient History (41,000 BCE – 0):
It had to start somewhere at sometime, myths and legends abound; and scientific archeology point to the following signposts in the early evolution of *homo touristicus.*

-The Biblical God takes a day off resting after allegedly creating the universe (See: 4,004 BCE) and everything in it over six days…he/she takes the first vacation day ever!

-Man, constantly evolving, walks upright and utters, "*…meat better over there.*" The original *walkabout* begins.

-Leviticus and friends, demand a periodical hiatus called a *sabbatical* from work (aka a *shmita*) of between a couple months and a year.

-Man, continuing to follow his basic instincts, makes a raft and uses poles to cross a mighty river. Many sadly fall overboard and float downstream; those that make it order-in at their clans cave and enjoy an *al fresco* celebration of survival.

41,000c BCE
Homo sapiens have successfully scattered throughout the world—the initial migrants.

40,000c BCE
Ocean going vessels are used by wanderers heading to New Guinea and Australia.

29,000c BCE
Cro-Magnon's move semi-annually between their summer and winter caves—how civilized!

16,500c BCE
The caves in Lascaux, France show signs of stellar maps. One shows a crude arrow with the remark, *"You are here"*!

12-15,000c BCE
Spanish cave paintings at Altamira indicate that Early Man wore boots made of fur called *Uggs*.

10,500c BCE
The Bering Land Bridge is officially closed after being inundated by rising sea levels due to global warming. This effectively halts all land travel between Asia and North America for the next 13,500 years.

9,000c BCE
The city of Jericho (aka City of Palm Trees) along the Jordan River is founded and remains the world's oldest continually inhabited city.

7,000c BCE
Ancient wall paintings in Çatalhöyük, Turkey seem to indicate signs of a regional map. Some experts dispute the findings.

6,000c BCE
Egyptian rock drawings show primitive wooded river boats. Sailing ships would appear about a millennium later around 5,000 BCE.

5-6,000c BCE
The oldest surviving attempt at a world map, created by an early Indus Valley civilization, is painted on a cave wall in India. Some experts dispute the findings.

5,000c BCE
Ancient Finn clans utilize animal bones as a sort of primitive ice skate—making them the earliest to use a man-made tool to get around. Metal skates would have to wait until about 200c...when a French-Canadian invites ice hockey.

4,004 BCE

Sunday, October 28th - On this day in history, Adam and Eve were created according creationists, and are soon thrown out of the Garden of Eden by their vengeful God. Travelers have been in search of Paradise Lost ever since…

4,000c BCE

The Sumerians build the earliest known health spas, around geothermally-heated hot water springs bubbling from the ground, that by now include grand temples with flowing pools.

3,806 BCE

The Sweet Track, a 2,000 meter (6,600-feet) causeway built by Neolithic farmers out of timber-poles through a bog in the Somerset Levels of England, is claimed to be the oldest road in the world.

3,500c BCE

The first vehicles in history are used when fixed wheels are attached to carts pulled by oxen or donkeys.

Wild horses are domesticated and used for man's transportation needs for the first time along the fertile plains (aka steppes) of the Black Sea area. This increases man's daily travel distance capabilities significantly.

3,000c BCE

The general ideas of navigation begin to be developed along the rivers of the Indus Valley where the word "navigation" comes from the Sanskrit word *navagati*, meaning "to travel by boat." And so they must have been—traveling by boat!

2,850c BCE

The earliest known religious pilgrimages occur when Egyptians journey to Sekket's shrine—the Egyptian goddess of magic—at Bubastis. Later, Herodotus (See: 462 BCE), the great Greek writer, gives the Bubastis site a formal review with this eye-witness account: *"Barges and river craft of every description, filled with men and women, floated leisurely down the Nile. The men played on pipes of lotus. The women on cymbals and tambourines, and such as had no instruments accompanied the music with clapping of hands and dances, and other joyous gestures. Thus did they while on the river: but when they came to a town on its banks, the barges were made fast, and the pilgrims disembarked, and the women sang, playfully mocked the women of that town and threw their clothes over their head. When they reached Bubastis, then held they a wondrously solemn feast: and more wine of the grape was drank in those days than in all the rest of the year. Such was the manner of this festival: and, it is said, that as many as seven hundred thousand pilgrims have been known to celebrate the Feast of Bast at the same time."*

2,750c BCE
Hannu (aka Hennu), an Egyptian functionary, takes the earliest recorded exploration trek from Egyptian. He makes stops that include: the Red Sea, Ethiopia and Somalia, before returning safely…but with a nasty bout of traveler's diarrhea.

2,600c BCE
Public baths are built in Mohenjo-Daro (aka Mound of the Dead) the largest settlement along the Indus River valley in present day Pakistan. Bathing suits are required…and don't forget the sun block!

2,560c BCE
Khufu (aka Cheops) (-2566 BCE), an ancient Egyptian Pharaoh, commissions the building of the Great Pyramid of Giza in Egypt. It remains the world's oldest man-made tourist attraction. The original touts evolve—and thrive!

The age-old tourist Pyramid routine.
(Author Photo)

2,500c BCE
An unaccredited Sumerian makes one of the earliest known Mesopotamian maps that illustrate the military operations of Sargon of Akka. Experts dispute the findings.

2,000c BCE
Snow sleds pulled by domesticated animals begin being used in Scandinavia. Primitive skis quickly follow…although the après ski tradition takes some time.

The Pyramid of Djoser (aka Step Pyramid) in Egypt, Stonehenge in England, and the Sumerian city of Ur, are all well-established around this time. People now have a reason to hit the road and start visiting man-made sites.

1,900c BCE
The first tell-tale signs of the rise of tourism can be found with graffiti etching on the Great Pyramid of Giza (See: 2,560 BCE) carbon-dated around now…"*Marduk was here.*"

1,829c BCE
The world's oldest organized sporting competition, the Tailteann Games, takes place in what is presently County Meat in Ireland. Greek experts dispute the findings.

1,792 BCE
Hammurabi (aka the paternal kinsman) (-1750c BCE), a Babylonian king, conceives the *Hamurrabi's Code of Laws,* and embedded within it lies a reference to innkeepers—as opposed to tavern-keepers—in Rule 111: "*If an innkeeper furnish sixty ka of usakani-drink to (?), she shall receive fifty ka of corn at the harvest.*" One can only assume fifty ka of corn was the ancient rack rate?

1,600c BCE
Single-rider horse drawn chariots come into use for the well-to-do.

1,480 BCE
Hatshepsut (1508–1458 BCE), a teenage Egyptian Queen, journeys to the lands of Punt, on what may be the earliest official diplomatic junket ever made for the purpose of promoting peace and tourism to Egypt?

1,390c BCE
By this time, Ammon's Oracle, located at the desert oasis of Siwa some 500 kilometers west of Cairo in the Libyan Desert, and is a well established New Age spot (aka New Age tourism). World renown, in February 332 BCE, Alexander the Great (See: 330BCE) takes a side trip to Siwa to discuss his future destiny with a few buddies (aka a mancation).

1,350c BCE
With Moses roaming around the Sinai desert for an extended time, the word *holiday*, which is a contraction of the words *holy* and *day*—representing religious holy days—is originally coined. Or, maybe not!

1,200c BCE
The Amber Road, linking the Baltic Sea shores—an area rich in amber—to the Adriatic and Mediterranean Seas, is well established by now. It may be the world's oldest international road, err, trial. The young Egyptian pharaoh Tutankhamen had Baltic amber among his burial goods and amber was also used as offerings to Apollo at Delphi by the Greeks (See: 900 BCE).

1,160c BCE
Amennakhte, the son of Ipuy and an Egyptian tomb artist, produces the Turin Papyrus map that helps prepare Ramesses IV's the Egyptian pharaoh for his eastern desert foray. It is considered by some experts to be the oldest surviving topographical map in the world—others disagree.

1,100c BCE
Jason and the Argonauts set sail on their epic mythical voyage—or did they? A book and movie deal quickly follows.

950c BCE
The Chinese are said to have invented kites which actually carried men—lightweight boys—to scout out enemy troop locations...Marco Polo

corroborates the kites carrying humans story in 2,000 years later. (See: 1298)

900c BCE
The Greeks begin taking spiritual pilgrimages seeking the counsel of the god Apollo at the Delphic oracle.

850c BCE
Homer, an epic Greek poet, pens his legendary masterpiece the *Odyssey*, about the travels of the Greek hero Odysseus, on his rather long voyage home from Troy. It's always about the girl.

800c BCE
Aachen (aka *Aix-la-Chapelle*), located in the North Rhine-Westphalia area, is a well established spa city (aka spa tourism) that was supposedly visited by Neolithic-era wanders, then by the Celtics, the Romans, and then the Franks. King Charlemagne (742-817), would later build his vacation home there.

776 BCE
The original Olympiad is held in ancient Greece...innkeepers begin instituting a three night minimum stay requirement for booking guests!

770c BCE
The invention of iron horseshoes immediately improves transportation by horse...and the off-track betting business too!

610c BCE
Under the reign of the Lydian king Alyattes (619c-560BCE), coins are said to have been invented which were made of electrum, a natural alloy of gold and silver—and a godsend to merchants and travelers alike. The business of travelers collecting foreign coins begins.

600c BCE
By now there are over six hundred well-established Phoenician developed sea routes across the Mediterranean, Red Sea, and Indian Ocean. Historians claim that the Phoenicians understood celestial navigation, although they probably stayed within sight of land whenever possible. Smart.

The below clay tablet (aka the Babylonian World Map), remains the earliest surviving map of the world. It now sits in the British Museum…having been stolen fair and square.

The Babylonian World Map
(© Trustees of the British Museum)

600 BCE
Necho II (-595BCEc), an Egyptian pharaoh, hires an experienced Phoenician seaman to undertake an expedition to determine the size of *his* Kingdom of Egypt. Mapmakers begin lying to appease their benefactors. It's bigger than you think sire…

595 BCE
Anaximander (611-546 BCE), an ancient Greek mapmaker, draws one of the earliest world maps. Greece, as we all know, is shown to be the center of the world.

540 BCE
The Chin's of China, begin construction on the 1,782 kilometer (1,107-mile) Grand Canal of China to ease travel inland. It is finally finished 1,800 years later in 1327…talk about a Full Employment Act!

510 BCE
Scylax of Caryanda, a Greek explorer, who worked for Persian Emperor Darius, surveys the Middle East and Indus River on a long 30-month journey. He draws one of the earliest known pilot books (aka navigation journals), called a *periplus*, to help in future navigation. Legend has it that Alexander the Great used his map and reconnaissance centuries later.

500c BCE
Laozi (aka Lao-Tzu), an ancient Chinese philosopher of note, gives us that famous travel truism: *"A journey of a thousand miles must begin with a single step."*

Greek pilgrims begin visiting Epidaurus, the legendary birthplace of Asclepius (the god of medicine and healing) for exotic healing cures (aka medical tourism).

Homer (See: 850 BCE), among other writers, describes how the Greeks favored a variety of hot water tubs and hot air baths (*laconica*), that could denote some of the first real destination spas.

Confucius (557-479 BCE), a Chinese deep thinker, offers us these words of wisdom about checking into a hotel, *"When you go to an inn let it not be with the feeling that you must have whatever you ask for."*

500 BCE
Hanno the Navigator, a Phoenician native of Carthage, explores the west coast of Africa…and comes back alive to the amazement of many!

Darius I (aka Darius the Great) (550-486 BCE), a Persian king, begins construction of the Persian Royal Road, a great network of traveler thoroughfares, that has at its center, the 3,219 kilometer (2,000-mile) well-worn road from Susa (near Persepolis, Iran) to Sardis (present day Izmir, Turley). Mounted couriers could travel this route road in seven days; on foot it took 90 days!

462 BCE

Herodotus (485-425 BCE), a wise Greek historian, pens his much-celebrated book *Histories*. This old scholar documents various Egyptian travel rituals, like the visiting of their many legendary shrines. He also reveals for the first time, the inspiration behind the concept of the so-called *wonders of the world*—different from today's travel porn hot "it" lists—these are the timeless *must see* ancient sites (aka heritage tourism) that every traveler really ought to experience at least once during their lifetimes.

460c BCE

Himilco, a traveling Carthaginian, sails through the Straits of Gibraltar, turns right and heads up around the western coasts of Spain and France—and allegedly all the way to the southern coast of England.

450c BCE

Nehemiah, an official serving King Artaxerxes of ancient Persia, meekly asks permission in requesting a safe passage document of sorts for traveling to Judah to visit relatives. The king agrees, and gives Nehemiah a letter, "...*to the governors of the province beyond the river.*" Maybe, quite possibly, the earliest travel document on record?

438 BCE

The Greek Parthenon, that prominent white marble temple atop the Athenian Acropolis, opens to stunning success and fabulous architectural reviews. One local ancient Pláka-area critic gives it a four-broken plate review—the highest in the land! By 2010, over 500,000 tourists a year come to see it—although now just an illustrious ruin.

One unlucky tourist among many on the Acropolis.
(Author Photo)

405 BCE

Aristophanes (446–386 BCE), a notorious Greek comic playwright—who apparently did not like local inns—tells the world about his inner feelings in his work known as *The Frogs,* his version of an epic buddy road trip comedy. Metaphorically speaking, he makes Hades the inn *"with the fewest bedbugs."*

330 BCE

Alexander the Great (356-323 BCE), the Great Greek—who needs no introduction, begins his great walkabout and global conquests reaching as far as Central Asia and India.

Did You Know? Yes, Alexander the Great died young at 33… but that was the norm back then when the average Greco-Roman life expectancy was just 25 years. Forensic cultural anthropologists tell us also that each woman produced an average of five children and that the 'wisdom of age' was bestowed upon only about 4% of the population who were lucky enough to live past their forties!

326c BCE
Dicaearchus (350-296 BCE), a Greek philosopher, makes the innovative orienting line on a map, a west-to-east line (aka lines of latitude) through Gibraltar and Rhodes, on his world map.

320c BCE
Pytheas (*aka* Phtheas) (380-300 BCE), a Greek explorer, travels the North Atlantic and then circumnavigates the islands of Britain. He visits the North Sea, and possibly travels as far north as Norway. Some say he may have even visited Iceland (aka Ultima Thule), where he states, *"the summer sun never sets."* Experts disagree, claiming that the term *ultima Thule* defines areas beyond the borders of the known world and not the Latin literal meanings *Ultima Thule* = Greenland, and *Thule* = Iceland.

312 BCE
The Romans begin building their famed network of roads, including the Appian Way, a 212 kilometer (132-mile) road from Rome to Capua. When complete, the system allows for safer and more efficient mobility for all travelers, traders, and of course the military—and the spinoff creation of road-side restaurants and inns. The Romans built their paved roads well, with an average width of about 9 meters and a meter or more deep, of carefully constructed layers. Thank you Roma…too bad no one in Italy ever learned to drive sanely!

310 BCE
Ptolemy I Soter (367-283 BCE), a Greek general, founds the world's earliest known simply as The Museum (aka *musaeum* or *mouseion*) in Alexandria next to the royal palace. Admission is free!

300c BCE
The Greeks further expand their medical resort industry as therapeutic Asclepius-inspired temples, hot baths and gymnasiums, based on the original in Epidaurus (See: 500c BCE), begin springing up (no pun intended) all over the realm. Some say they were the original travel-related franchises…

285c BCE

It is believed that the Chinese build the earliest known suspension bridge over a difficult to traverse water way. Experts remain unsure of the claim—but happy not to have to swim the rushing river.

280c BCE

Devanampiya Tissa (?-267 BCE), a Buddhist monarch of Sri Lanka, establishes one of the world's earliest wildlife sanctuaries on his Garden of Eden-like island.

279 BCE

Timosthenes of Rhodes, the Captain-in-Chief to Ptolemy II Philadelphus, adds two winds to the ten already named by Aristotle; thereby creating directions that have become the 12-points of the original compass. (See: 1190)

275c BCE

An ancient canal built between the Red Sea and the Nile River opens to ease shipping travel.

225c BCE

Apollonius (262-190 BCE), a Greek astronomer, presents the astrolabe projection, an astronomical instrument that helps locate planets for either astrology or navigation—depending on your cup of tea. However, it was the influential Hipparchus (190-120 BCE), the Greek mathematician, who later in 160c BCE, uses it to finally solve complex astronomical problems that opens its use for truly navigation purposes.

Romans, catching on quickly to the Greek traditions, begin visiting *balneum* (aka hot springs) *en masse* and ritually.

225 BCE

Philo of Byzantium (aka Philo Mechanicus) (280-220 BCE), a well-known Greek writer, initially notes the "*seven prominent sights of the ancient world.*" And the travel-related lists making has never stopped!

The Wonders: Although lists vary, the generally accepted original *Seven Wonders of the Ancient World*, included: the Great Pyramid of Giza; the Hanging Gardens of Babylon; the Statue of Zeus at Olympia; the Temple of Artemis at Ephesus; the Mausoleum of Halicarnassus; the Colossus of Rhodes; and the Lighthouse of Alexandria.

221 BCE
Qin Shi Huang (259–210BCE), the king of the Qin, needing better protection from the neighboring Xiongnu's (aka Huns), begins the building of the Great Wall. It continues to be a major tourist attraction to this day—although Frisbee playing on the Great Wall is banned in 1972, following American cartoonist Garry Trudeau's diplomatic *faux pas*.

215c BCE
During the Qin Dynasty (221-206 BCE), the Chinese are said to invent the world's earliest compass after Imperial Court scientists discover magnetic forces. Some experts question this claim. (See: 1088)

205 BCE
Eratosthenes (276-196 BCE), a Greek man of science, coins the word "geography," and is the first to understand the notion behind the circumference of the earth. He also creates his own map of the world (aka Eratosthenes' map).

190c BCE
Baiae, located in the Campania region of southern Italy near the western end of the Bay of Naples, becomes a fashionable Roman beach resort. A truly Italian scandal-ridden hot spot—where Nero murdered his mother Agrippina; where Hadrian died; where Caligula built his notorious bridge of boats; where Claudius built his great villa; and where Cleopatra was sunning when Julius Caesar her *amour* brutally died. In 65 BCE, the resort area became infamously known as a "vortex of luxury," according to Seneca the Younger's *Baiae and Vice* op-ed piece; as well as a "harbor of vice," and "den of licentiousness," according to Sextus Propertius. Basically, it was kind of vulgar mix of Daytona Beach meets Vegas meets the Hamptons albeit Roman-style; complete with the usual licentious and depraved

behavior of youthful flesh, corrupted power and bling. Sadly, never been there myself…

150c BCE

Crates of Mallus, a Greek linguist and philosopher, constructs the earliest known globe of the Earth—that clearly shows the spherical surface of the planet.

138-124 BCE

Zhang Qian (aka Chang Ch'ien) (?-114 BCE), a Han Dynasty explorer, travels to Pamir (aka the Roof of the World) mountains, and may be the earliest Chinese on record to have heard about the existence of Tien-chu (aka India). He also visits Central Asia and Russia during his walkabout— and maybe even Persia; as he establishes what we know today as the illustrious Silk Road, a major east-west trade route that would later link, among others destinations: Antioch, Babylon, Ray, Erzerum, Hamadn, Bukhara, Tashkent, Samarkand, Kashgar and Xian.

> **Did You Know?** The Silk Road was not given its name until the 1870's, when Baron von Richthofen (1833-1905), a German geographer, named it *seidenstrasse* (aka Silk Road).

127 BCE

Hipparchus (190–120 BCE), a Greek academic, was the earliest to apply mathematical rigor to the determination of the latitude and longitude of places on the earth; he literally wrote the book on it, called *Against the Geography of Eratosthenes* (See: 205 BCE).

119 BCE

Eudoxus of Cyzicus, a Greek explorer, investigates the Arabian Sea for the king of Egypt Ptolemy VIII.

118 BCE

The first truly international road opens with the completion of *Via Domitia,* a Roman highway that connects Italy to Spain via France.

101 BCE

The Tower of the Winds is built in Athens as a public "wind" compass, along with a variety of sundials and water clocks.

100 BCE

Alexandria, Egypt is said to have a population of over one million inhabitants. Some experts do not agree.

75c BCE

Historians begin reporting that wealthy Romans are taking late summer journeys called *turismo enologico* (aka wine tours). My guess is that the Romans had not yet fashioned the notion of DUI's yet?

The Travel gods: Hermes was the Greek god responsible for treaties, commerce and free travel. Mercury, the Roman god of trade and commerce, as well as the messenger of the gods, is known as the Roman god of travel. Tara, the Hindu goddess, is the protectress of navigation and earthly travel. *St.* Christopher is the patron Saint of safe travel.

---

45 BCE

Rome officially adopts the Julian calendar—a solar year divided by 365 days into 12 months with a leap day added to February every four years—heralding in the first ever New Year's Eve party as thousands of patricians, plebs and country folk alike, descend upon Rome's city-center Forum to watch the giant candle get blown out...

33 BCE

An enterprising Bethlehem inn keeper tries out his new "*No Vacancy*" sign on some rather humble weary travelers. Word has it that he helps them locate alternate lodging in a nearby manger.

25 BCE

Marcus Vipsanius Agrippa (63–12 BCE), a Roman statesmen and court luminary, builds the original *thermae* (aka hot baths); and thus began the building of Roman baths all over the Empire from England to Africa.

One bath, the Baths of Diocletian, is said to have been able to hold 6,000 bathers. *Yuck!*

23c BCE

Not done yet, Agrippa's most remarkable legacy might have been his world map, albeit a Roman-centric one at that, carved into marble and set up in the Porticus Vipsania along *Via Flaminia* for all of Rome to see. The road map is now gone, but has been reconstructed with the help of Pliny the Elder (23-79), a Roman historian's famed description in his *Natural History*, in what is known as *Tabula Peutinger* (aka the Peutinger map).

Coin collecting (aka numismatics) probably began the first time someone traveled to the Lydian kingdom and saw their shiny coins (See: 610c BCE). Collections have grown ever since and some fellow travelers have amazingly unique collections. Suetonius, a Roman historian, tells the story of Emperor Augustus regaling his friends and foreign visitors alike with his collection of exotic coins, in his book *De vita Caesarum* (aka *The Lives of the Twelve Caesars*) written in 121.

CHAPTER TWO

The Common Era (1 CE – 986):
The Roman Empire was not built in a day, but over many centuries on the legacy of the Greeks (and Persians) before them; but the roads and conditions of this era are ripe for travelers. Wealthy Romans begin taking *peregrinatio*—holiday trips. Some just head for coastal resorts, while others ventured further to Homer's Greece and Mother Egypt—with Alexandria being a hot Roma destination. Christian pilgrims in small numbers begin traveling to Holy Land sites, as do their Muslim contemporaries a few centuries later. (We all remember Ambrose Bierce's *Devil's Dictionary* definition of a pilgrim: "PILGRIM, n. A traveler that is to be taken seriously.") The evolution of *homo touristicus* takes on a new form under Rome, but his progress is somewhat stunted a little later after centuries of wandering and growth by the coming Dark Ages. But still, man's travel propensities grow…

14
Marcus Gavius Apicius, a Roman nobleman (and iron chef of his day), writes *Of Culinary Matters*, the first book containing worldly recipes. Mediterranean fusion has never been the same.

19
Strabo of Amasia (64-21CE), a Greek geographer, produces *The Geography*, a hand-drawn collection of maps of the known, and mostly Roman, world.

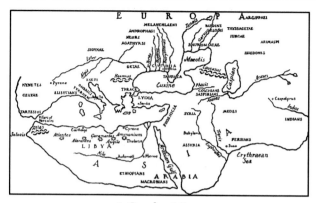

A Strabo Map.
(A reconstruction)

47

Roman legions build the *Fosse Way*, a raised road with a ditch on either side stretching from Lincoln to Exeter in modern day England.

64

The Sulpicius family of Moregine (near Pompeii), convert a Nero-built imperial pavilion into a public spa-like travel stop...it may be the world's first chic boutique hotel too? It closes after just fifteen years of successful operations as a result of a rather unwelcome volcano eruption!

73

General Ban Chao (32-102), a Chinese general, becomes the official protectorate of the Silk Road. That means that a toll must be paid from now on to you know who...

80

The Colosseum of Rome opens to spectacular reviews and standing room only crowds.

85c

A fashionable Roman shop just around the corner, called *Secundus,* begins selling a novelty item of sorts, a *parachment codex* (aka a book)...that are said to be a hit with travelers who hated lugging around all those cumbersome scrolls, clay tablets, and papyrus rolls in their over-nighters!

90c

The Periplus of the Erythraean Sea, a mysteriously written document created by an unknown Greek merchant-cum-author living in Alexandria, describes the trading (and traveling) routes as far east as India. Ptolemy would later use it as a source for his innovative atlas. (See: 150) By the way, the *Erythraean Sea* literally means Red Sea.

100c

This era is known as the Golden Age of Roman Travel (aka *Pax Romanus*); as Europe sees over 200 years of relative peace with safety prevailing across the Empire—unprecedented in world history up to this point in time. The ports are busy, the coastal resorts over-sold in high season, and museums of antiquity brimming with wayfarers.

133

Rome becomes a city with over one million inhabitants. Romulus and Remus would be proud!

150

Claudius Ptolemaeus (aka Ptolemy) (100-170), an Egyptian scientist, uses mathematics and centuries of old Greek learning to create a collection of 27 maps for his book *Geographike Syntaxis*. Sadly, he underestimates the Earth's circumference by just a degree here and there.

160c

Pausanias, a Greek geographer (and well known traveling man), pens his magnum opus *Description of Greece*; thus becoming the Baedekers of his day and one of the earliest true travel writers, with his critical evaluations and wry prose of the facilities and destinations he encounters along the way.

250

Pei Hsiu (224-271), a Chinese cartographer, designs a series of official government maps of China and surrounding lands; and is considered the father of scientific geography by many. By now, Chinese junk ships can travel vast distances in the open ocean, and have expanded known Chinese knowledge significantly.

333

The renowned Bordeaux Pilgrimage—not for the wine!—begins taking place as an effort to map out all the significant Christian sites of the gospels in the Holy Land (aka Christian tourism). There is a historic mention of Bishop Alexander visiting the Holy Land a few decades earlier however—it could be that he was the first real Christian pilgrim (aka theological tourist). Can you believe that theologians disagree?

350c

The first travel journals began appearing as many religious pilgrims start writing what were known as *Peregrinationes*, or day-to-day descriptions of the countries through which they journeyed. In the 1960's and 70's they were called travel diaries—and they were boring; nowadays they are called travel blogs…ditto, the boring part.

> **Did You Know?** An average person traveling by foot covers about 5 km/h—kilometers an hour—about 3 miles). So, a 10-hour day would take someone walking 50 kilometers (30 miles) a day…a week's journey would take a traveler 350 kilometers (about 220 miles)…a 30-day month of traveling by foot would yield 1,500 kilometers (900 miles). The walk from the English Channel town of Calais to Rome (about 1,800 kilometers) would take 36 days. Assuming of course they avoided trouble like: bad weather, floods, bandits, festivals, blockades, war, food-borne illnesses and any and all diseases!

384c

The *Tabula Peutingeriana* (aka Peutinger Table) (See: 23 BCE) shows the *cursus publicus*, the road networks of the Roman Empire. Amazingly, it includes over 100,000 kilometers (62,137 miles) of roads from India to Britain; all of course leading to Rome, hence the phrase, *"All roads lead to Rome."* The map was later found in the 15th century by Conrad Peutinger (See: 1598), who got it published posthumously making it, and him, famous.

394c-414

Faxian (aka Fa-Hsien) (337c-442), a Chinese Buddhist pilgrim, writes *Record of Buddhist Countries* after traveling far and wide—known today as the *Travels of Fa-Hsien*.

416

Rutilius Claudius Namatianus, a Roman writer, famously chronicles his sea voyage along the Mediterranean Sea's coast from Rome to Gaul in *Concerning His Return*.

425c

Augustine of Hippo (aka Saint Augustine) (354-430), a Christian theologian, produces what may be the best travel quote of all-time, "*The world is a book, of which those who stay in one place, read only one page.*"

489

By this time Christian pilgrimages had begun to trickle into the Holy Land, especially to the sacred stones located in Bethlehem.

530

St. Bernard (aka the Navigator, the Voyager, or, just the Bold) (484-578), an Irish abbot, whose mysterious Dark Age legend is long and controversial, maintains that he actually came aground in Newfoundland, Canada during one of his many Atlantic voyages in search of the mythical island (aka Isle of the Blessed, or St. Brendan's Island) where the dead live in paradise. We'll never know…because he died!

532

The Church of Hagia Sophia (aka *Aya Sofya*) opens, in what is then known as Constantinople (aka Istanbul) Turkey. It remains both an internationally-celebrated architectural and spiritual wonder. (But just a small word of advice: don't stick your finger in the hole!)

542

In Madaba, Jordan on the floor of the Saint George church, lays the *Madaba Map,* an extraordinarily colorful mosaic of Jerusalem (maybe the first and oldest ever found) that includes parts of the Holy Land, created by unknown artist(s) of the day.

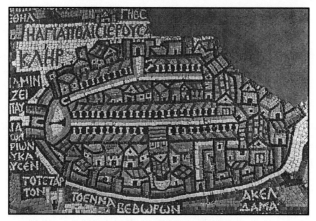

The Madaba Mosaic Map:
(Author Photo)

550

Cosmas Indicopleustes, a Greek from Alexandria, visits the Indian sub-continent region several times and pens the beautiful *Christian Topography* map. His name literally means, "*he who sailed to India.*"

589

The earliest known reference for the use of toilet paper is made, in China of all places, when Yan Zhitui (531–591), an official Chinese scholar, wrote: "*Paper on which there are quotations or commentaries from Five Classics or the names of sages, I dare not use for toilet purposes.*" Hmm, bad writing used as toilet paper...they may have something there.

630c

Muhammad (571-632), Allah's prophet and the founder of Islam, wisely says: "*Don't tell me how educated you are—tell me how much you have traveled.*"

633c

The initial *Hajj*'s, which literally means, "*to set out for a place,*" begin to Mecca. Being the fifth pillar of Islam, it is a religious obligation that must be carried out at least once in their lifetime by every able-bodied Muslim who can afford to do so (aka Hajj tourism). Sort of mandatory tourism! According to the Saudi Press Agency, as recently as 1950 the number of pilgrims during *Hajj* was less than 100,000, but that number doubled by

23

1955, and by 1972 it had reached 645,000. In 1983, the number of pilgrims coming from abroad exceeded one million for the first time, and in 2001, over 2.5 million Muslims descended on Mecca.

645
Hsuan-tsang (aka Xuan Tsang) (602-644/664?), a Chinese Buddhist, travels widely and to Buddha's Indian holy spots (aka Buddhist tourism) spreading the word, and eventually writes *Record of Western Regions* chronicling his travels out of China.

608c
A remote Scottish abbot named Adamnan (625-704), recounts the Holy Land travels of Bishop Arculf in *De locis sanctis* (aka *Concerning the Sacred Places*), that was presented to King Aldfrith of Northumbria.

717
According to the *Guinness Book of World Records*, the oldest hotel still in operation today, the *Hoshi ryokan*—a traditional Japanese inn—in Awazu, Japan, opens. It features hot springs and excellent hand-made towels.

725c
The Santiago de Compostela (aka El Camino de Santiago, or the St. James' Way) a Christian pilgrimage begins. It grows and grows in importance until the 18th century.

742c
Chang'an, the ancient capital of China, becomes a city of one million inhabitants.

776c
Beatus of Liébana (730-798), a theological geographer—in a time when science and religion apparently mixed—from what is today Spain, draws the Beatus Map.

778c
Sailendra King Vishnu (aka Dharmatunga), a Hindu-cum-Buddhist local Javanese ruler, begins construction of the impressive Temple of Borobudur (aka Candi Borobudur). Relatively unknown even today, this central Java,

Indonesia site is maybe the greatest—certainly the biggest—Mahayana Buddhist monument in Southeast Asia. A must see...

790c
Abu abdallah Muhammad ibn Ibrahim al-Fazari (?-806), a Muslim astronomer, makes an astrolabe (aka star key) —*astro* means star and *labe* translates as to take or to find—to help identify the times of sunrise (for morning prayers called *salat*) and sunset, and to more easily locate the direction of Mecca for praying Muslims. The Islamic Golden Age begins.

828
Japanese Buddhist's begin their holy pilgrimage, called the 88 Temple Pilgrimage, on the Japanese Island of Shikoku, Japan.

> **The Great Buddhist Pilgrimages:** Believers of all religions have sacred sites that call to the them, these are the top Buddhist sites:
> Lumbini Nepal – Buddha's birthplace
> Bodh Gaya, India – the site of Buddha's enlightenment
> Sarnath, India – where the Buddha gave his first sermon
> Kushinagar, India – where the Buddha died
> *Lesser pilgrimage sites include:* Yungang Grottoes, China; Potala Palace, Tibet; Mount Kailash, Tibet; Shwedagon Pagoda, Burma; Boudhanath, Nepal; Sri Dalada Maligawa, Sri Lanka; Wat Phra Kaew, Thailand; Borobudur, Indonesia; and Todai-ji, Japan.

832
Al-Khwarazmi (790-840), a Muslim scholar, produces *Face of the Earth*. On the side he invents algebra too!

835c
Abbas Ibn Firnas (810–887), a Moroccan Muslim engineer, is known for an early attempt at aviation. Records are limited.

847

Ennin (aka Jikaku Daishi) (794-864), a Japanese priest, chronicles his Chinese adventures in *The Record of a Pilgrimage to China.*

851

Sulaiman el-Tagir (aka the Merchant), a Muslim man of commerce, visits India and China on repeated business trips opening the door for future visitors, like Marco Polo's clan.

857

The world's earliest university, Al-Karaouine in Fez, Morocco, opens...and kids have been taking trips home ever since. (Al-Azhar University in Cairo (973) and Baghdad's Nizamiyyah College (970), also claim to be the world's first universities, as does Bologna (See: 1088). You pick who's right?

870c

Floki Vilgerdarson (aka Raven-Floki), a Norseman navigator, who kept starved ravens aboard his vessels and released them when he thought he was close to land (*or lost?*) and watched their flight direction—hence the term, *"as the crow flies"*—discovers Iceland.

900c

La Ruta Maya, the 2,400 kilometer (1,500-mile) system of roads connecting the great Mayan cities of current day Mexico, Belize, Honduras, and Guatemala is built.

910c

Baghdad becomes a city of one million inhabitants.

930c

Ahmad ibn Fadlan, an Arab diplomat turned writer, writes his account of his travels (including wild Viking rituals) as a member of the embassy of the Caliph of Baghdad on visits to the King of the Volga Bulgars, called, *Voyage chez les Bulgares de la Volga.*

940c

Abul Hasan Ali al Masu'di (895-957), a noted Muslim scholar, attempts to visit every Islamic nation while writing a journal of his travels.

956

Public inns had been doing business since the Roman era, but the earliest inns, in which a weary traveler could obtain refreshment, began to appear in Europe. By the time the Romans left, the beginnings of the modern pub had been well established and they became so commonplace, that in 965 King Edgar decreed that there should be no more than one alehouse per village. Now that's a monopoly!

970c

The novel idea of menus begin to appear in Chinese guest houses during the Song Dynasty, to help traveling businessmen order food in other non-native lands. The farmer's daughter takes the order.

980c

The Vikings word "*hjunottsmanathr*" means to go into hiding with your woman, we take that as the first honeymoons—although it could mean the woman was just abducted?! The OED again tells us that the notion of a honeymoon being "the idea that the first month of marriage is the sweetest" came about in 1546. So, that first month is the honeymoon (aka honeymoon tourism). In Biblical writings, in Deuteronomy 24:5 states that a 'newly wed' man should get a year off to *build* his family—wink, wink, nudge, nudge…and the taking of honeymoons in the traditional sense that we know it today begins in the *Belle Époque* era around 1870ish. But we give the Norsemen the benefit of doubt here because they all suffered from IWD (aka Icelandic woman disease) a common affliction!

985

Eiríkur the Red (950-1001), the Norse chieftain, discovers Gronland (aka Greenland). Later, Herjólfr, another Viking Age seaman, eventually colonizes Greenland in an effort that lasts about five centuries.

986c

Bjarni Herjólfsson, son of Herjólfr, tells us in the *Grænlendinga* saga (aka *Greenlanders Saga*), that he is blown off course and eventually sights an unknown land (Canada?), but then returns to Iceland and tells a fellow explorer named Leifr (son of Eiríkur the Red) of his discovery…the rest is history.

CHAPTER THREE

The New Millennium (1002 – 1414):
The Dark Ages begin to lighten up a little, and the New World beckons to be "discovered" and populated. Holy sites remain the focus of elective travel—and mass medieval tourism (aka religious crusades). While the East (aka the Orient) opens to adventurous travelers for trade, commerce, and curiosity. Islamic scholarship in the arts, sciences, geography and navigation flourishes. Man's urge to go has never been stronger with a pent up demand to see the unknown.

1002c
Leifr Eiríksson (970-1020), son of Eiríkur, who according to the *Book of the Icelanders* by Ari the Learned (1067-1148), reaches North America, and names what he sees as Vineland (Newfoundland); Helluland (aka the land of the flat stone, or maybe Baffin Island?), and Markland (aka forest land, or maybe Labrador?). His men make a settlement at *L'Anse aux Meadows* and winter in Newfoundland, Canada. This was all of course about 500 years *before* Columbus discovers America! (See: 1492)

1046
Nasir Khusraw (1004–1088), a Persian poet and philosopher, recounts his Middle East travels in *Safarnama* (aka *The Book of Travels*.)

1049
Bernard of Montjoux (aka Saint Bernard of Menthon) (923-1008), a Saxony priest, founds the earliest known hospice for travelers in the Valais Alps on the road between Italy and Switzerland. Welcoming St. Bernard rescue dogs met all guests at the door.

1061

Our Lady of Walsingham, the first of many to come (indeed countless today), spiritual shrines devoted to the Virgin Mary, is created and generates a tourism boom of sorts in Walsingham, England.

1064

Thirty years before the Crusades began came what is known as the Great German Pilgrimage, when as many as 12,000 pilgrimages (aka group tourism), sometimes complete families, left Germany lead by Archbishop Siegfried of Mainz. It took two years, but they eventually did get to Jerusalem after passing en mass and surviving harsh conditions and ill-treatment through Hungary, Bulgaria, Patzinakia and Constantinople, Antoli, Latakia, Tripoli, Caesarea Palestine, Ramla and then Jerusalem. And then they all went home. It remains a great story that no one seems to know about.

1068

Alleged to be the world's oldest adult beverage serving inn, *Ye Olde Trip to Jerusalem*, is established as brew house at the foot of Nottingham Castle; so named as the place the knights fortified themselves before their crusades (aka ye olde trip to Jerusalem).

1070c

William the Conqueror (aka William I of England) (1028-1087), a Norman king, introduces the custom of long summer breaks to facilitate the grape harvest by members of the law courts, and later, universities attendees… these may in fact be the earliest truly government mandated vacations?

1088

Bologna University opens and young folks from all over Europe travel to attend it. Could the invention of spring break be far behind? (See: 857)

Shen Kuo (1031–1095), a Song Dynasty Chinese scientist, writes about his discovery of the true north and magnetic compasses in his *Dream Pool Essays*. (See: 215cBCE)

> **The Seven Seas:** When ancient mariners often referred to sailing the *Seven Seas* they included: the Indian Ocean, the Persian Gulf, the Mediterranean, the Red, Black, Caspian and Adriatic seas.

1096

Those nasty Crusades begin in earnest—maybe the first organized group tours to visit the Holy land (See: 1064)—and lead to more travel in general following a period of prolonged chaos and infrastructure decay that followed the fall of Rome in 476 (aka the Dark Ages). At least people are moving again and seeing how others live, eat, work and pray.

1104

Records show that bottled sweetened lemon juice is served in Cairo to road weary travelers.

1125c

Angkor Wat, the giant Hindu temple complex that may have been as big as 3,000 square kilometers in size and located near the modern day city of Siem Reap, Cambodia, opens.

1130

Aimeri de Picard, a French monk, writes what may be the world's first guidebook for pilgrims following the Way of St. James (aka St. James' Way) to Spain called, *Codex Calixtinus.*

1154

Al-Idrisi (1100-1166), an Arab geographer in the court of the Norman king Roger II of Sicily, creates a world map influenced by Ptolemy (See: 150) in his *The Book of Roger* (aka *Tablula Rogeriana*). It contains 70 rectangular sheets taken from various travelers' reports. Maps become state secrets at this point in time.

1174

The Leaning Tower, located in Pisa, Italy opens. Oddly, according to numerous historical photos of it, tourists continually attempt to straighten out the lean?

1185

Ibn Jubayr (1145-1217), an Arab geographer, publishes his aptly titled travel memoir, *The Travels of Ibn Jubayr*. And so, ego travel writing begins.

1190

Alexander Neckham (1157-1217), an Englishman, is the earliest recorded instance of the mariner's compass being used by a European. (See: 215c BCE & 1088) We are indeed, slow but sure!

1191

Gerald of Wales (1146–1223), a medieval blogger type, chronicles his local trail blazing as a crusade recruitment officer in *Itinerarium Cambriae* (aka *Journey Through Wales*).

1193

Abu Ishaq Ibrahim ibn Muhammad al-Farisi al Istakhri (*aka* Estakhri), a Persian geographer, makes an Islamic atlas and map of the world with his Balkhi School of Geography colleagues.

1195c

Hangzhou, China becomes a city of one million inhabitants.

1200c

Qhapaq Ñan (aka The Great Inca Road), running 6,000 kilometers (3,700 miles) along the spine of the Andes of South America from Quito, Ecuador to Mendoza, Argentina, is regularly used. Relay messengers, (aka *chasquis*), stationed at intervals of six to nine kilometers apart, and carried both messages and objects, such as fresh marine fish or other refreshments, for the rulers in the sierra. It is claimed that these *chasquis* could cover some 250 kilometers (160 miles) per day—chewing coca leaves of course!

1200

Genghis Khan (1165-1227), the leader of the Mongol tribe, conquers the lands from Mongolia and China all the way to Hungary. The father of Kublai Khan (1215-1294), he also issues *Paiza* (*aka* passports?), made out of iron to allow for the safe conduct of his royal emissaries during their travels to enemy lands.

1207

Mersey Ferries, operating between Liverpool and Birkenhead run regularly. There is evidence that ferry service over the river has been running for over 800 years by this time, but in the 1207 Liverpool city charter, it officially specifies, *"rights of passage across the river payable by a toll"*. More tolls…

1215

The Great Charter of the Liberties of England (aka the *Magna Carta)* codifies the right to travel with the following provision:

"All merchants shall have safe and secure exit from England, and entry to England, with the right to tarry there and to move about as well by land as by water, for buying and selling by the ancient and right customs, quit from all evil tolls, except (in time of war) such merchants as are of the land at war with us."

1219

Ch'ang-ch'un, a Chinese recorder of history, is ordered by Genghis Khan to explore Asia; and begins his 14-month journey at the age of 71! Using his AARP card he received senior discounts at every stop thus saving Genghis Khan on travel *per diem* expenses.

1245

Giovanni da Pian del Carpini (1180-1252), an Umbria native, travels from Lyon to Russia, and then onward to Karakorum in Mongolia, and then writes *Historia Mongolorum.*

1250c

Matthew Paris, a Benedictine monk and cartographer, quills the *Chronica majora*, a set of road maps and pilgrim's itinerary routes from England to various Holy Land sites.

1253

William of Rubruck (1210-1270), a Franciscan missionary, is sent on, err a mission, by the Pope to visit Khan—and maybe suggests to him that he (Kahn) not attack the Christian world?—and later writes about his exotic travels east in *A Journey to the Eastern Parts of the World.*

1260

Niccolo and Maffeo Polo, two Venetian traders and the father and uncle of Marco Polo (See: 1298), take the ancient Silk Road to visit China on a trade mission business trip (aka road warriors). Marco catches the travel bug after hearing their tales of adventure in exotic places.

1269

Petrus Peregrinus (1220-?), a French scholar, does his ground-breaking work on magnetism and reveals the European notion of the compass in his study *Epistola de Magnete*.

Toll roads begin popping up in England. No fast-track lanes though...

1270

The first noted use of a map on a ship is recorded when Louis IX (aka Saint Louis) (1214 –1270), the French king, sails on his crusade—the seventh edition! It could have been the oldest surviving *portolan*, the *Carta Pisana*, which was created by Pietru Visconte. (See: 1275)

1275

The earliest known *portolan*, the *Carta Pisana* (aka Pisan Chart), appears with no known predecessors. It is perhaps the earliest modern scientific map ever made and contrasts sharply with the *Mappa Mundi* (See: 1290).

1290

Mappa Mundi, a medieval map of the world with Jerusalem as the center is drawn. (Sometimes known as the Hereford Cathedral World Map, because that is where it lays in trust.) It mixes the idea of *portolan* charts and the medieval theoretical maps. It is a colorful map with unrecognizable geography, fantastic creatures, and legendary places. It bears no resemblance to any of the mathematician methods employed by Ptolemy, nor does it use any measurements of longitude and latitude—science, who needs it! The *Mappa Mundi* is a so-called T and O map, meaning that it is a flat map, shaped like a wheel. (I had a photo of this map in the original manuscript inserted here, but the church that "protects this work of art" wanted £20 to use it. I said no thanks. Imagine that, a church asking for money?! So, if you want to see a hundred images of it for free—just Google Image it!)

1298

Marco Polo (1254-1324), a Venetian merchant, releases his celebrated book, *Travels: The Book of Marco Polo* that he wrote while sitting in a Genoese jail. Some scholars now question the veracity of his tales.

1307

London's Tabard Inn is built, and seems to be the original hotel to offer "*minny barres*" in rooms containing: pints of ale, drumsticks and holy water blessed by St. Thomas! One wonders the cost of drumsticks back then? It is later mentioned by Geoffrey Chaucer in his prologue of the *Canterbury Tales*, as the starting point of Chaucer's pilgrims. A bar is always a good place to begin an adventure.

1317c

Dante Alighieri (1265–1321), an Italian poet, writes the *Divine Comedy* which cites the nine rings of hell.

The Nine Rings of Travel Hell (circa 2010):

Ring One: Suffering from *dromomania* (aka wanderlust) and Vacation Deficit Disorder.

Ring Two: Suffering pre-trip planning overload and booking anxiety.

Ring Three: Suffering from Economy Class Syndrome and possible bouts of Air Rage.

Ring Four: Suffering from Culture Shock and overcoming Internet Addiction Disorder.

Ring Five: Suffering from Guidebook Personality Disorder and Holiday Heart Syndrome.

Ring Six: Suffering from Away From Home Syndrome and possible bouts of *turistas*.

Ring Seven: Suffering from Cultural Emulation Syndrome (aka Going Native).

Ring Eight: Suffering from Vocation Amnesia and possible bouts of Temple Burnout.

Ring Nine: Suffering from Jet Lag and Post-Holiday Depression.

1325

Ibn Battutah (1304-1369), a Morrocan-born Arab, travels over 120,000 kilometers (75,000 miles) through 40 countries after originally visiting Mecca, and then off to all the Muslim holy places from Mombasa to Sumatra over the next 29 years! He writes *Travels (Rihala) of Ibn Battuta* in 1355. It is a remarkable trip…and adventure told!

1326c

Ville d'Eaux (aka Town of Waters), a small French village, becomes well-known for its iron-rich hot springs. Future visitors would include: Peter the Great and Victor Hugo. The word "spa," derived from the Roman term *"salude per aqua"* (health through waters), was initially used here.

1330

The Arabic Maghreb, is the first known *portolan* (aka chart) of north-western Africa. *Portolans* comes from the Italian word *portolani*, which were medieval pilot books and navigational charts, whose main function was to record, usually on parchment, the distances, hazards and notable landmarks for the guidance of mariners.

1332

Charles VI (1368–1422), the king of France, was known to play card games with court members during the "intervals of melancholy" he suffered while on long trips. I feel your pain Chuck, and we all know a good game of gin (or hearts) helps make the road less wearisome.

1340

Francesco Balducci Pegolotti (1310-1347), a Florentine merchant, working for the Bardi family-run trading firm, compiles what many consider the first ever guidebook designed for medieval road warriors plying their trade along the now ancient Silk Road. Loosely titled *The Book of Descriptions of Countries* embedded within his *Pratica della mercatura* (aka Practice of Marketing), it gives traders of the day valuable details as to the best rest stops along the route, local customs, costs, travel rip-offs to avoid, and local food issues. The *Lonely Planet* of the day!

1342

Levi ben Gersohn (1288-1344), a Jewish scholar based in Catalan, first describes the use of a cross-staff (aka *balestilla),* that he described as a being made from a "square stick" with a sliding transom that is used as an astronomical and navigation tool. The cross-staff shares the same principles as the ancient Arabic navigational tool called the *kamal*.

1348c

The Black Death (aka bubonic plague) wreaks havoc in Europe killing between 30 and 60% of Europe's population (over seventy five million!) and is said to have been transmitted by travelers returning from Mongolia or Central Asia. One wonders how quickly such a serious slate wiper would spread nowadays after infecting just a few international airport passengers.

1350

Charles IV (1316–1378), a Czech king and Holy Roman Emperor, officially opens the mineral hot springs Karlovy Vary spa resort that developed around its 12 springs.

1360

The palace fortress complex known as Alhambra (aka the red one) is completed in Granada by Muslim sultans. It is a remarkable example of Islamic architecture that took about a century to finally build after being inspired in 1238. By 2010, so many people come to visit Alhambra that they had to limit access to just 7,700 a day!

1366

John Mandeville (1322-1372), an Anglo-Christian writer, who after concluding his 34-year pilgrimage, writes *The Travels*.

The world's first public library opens in Prague—although the libraries of Ashurbanipal (650c BCE), Alexandria (380c BCE), Pergamum (290c BCE), Celsus (135), Constantinople (350c), Fez's Al-Karaouine Mosque Library (857), and Hanoi's Temple of Literature (1070); may beg to differ!

Pray Pay: According to Catholic scholars, three weeks were set aside each year to enable believers to visit shrines within their own kingdoms. But, to go abroad and visit say the tomb of St. Denis—seven weeks of absence was allowed; 8-weeks to visit the body of St. Edmund at Pontigny; and 16 weeks to go to Rome or to St. James at Compostella; and a full year was granted to visit the Holy Lands near Jerusalem. We're sure it was not a paid leave!

1370c

The Guild of the Resurrection at Lincoln begins granting "pilgrimage pay" (aka vacation pay) for guild members that head off to the Holy Land shrines.

Also around this time, the term "day-tripper" is coined for religious pilgrims going on a day trip to visit nearby shrines of significance. With the advent of railway excursions (See: 1841) the distance traveled by day trippers grew. Nowadays, day trippers jet from New York City to Washington D.C. for lunch; or from Vancouver to Los Angeles to attend a Laker basketball game.

1375

The word *travel* is used for the first time, according to the OED; "The word travel has a common origin with the word *travail*. Once upon a time, travel was exceedingly uncomfortable and often dangerous. Indeed, the ultimate source of the word *travel* is a medieval instrument of torture - the *trepalium* - a contraption would pierce its victim's flesh with three sharp stakes (*tres* 'three' and *palus* 'stake'). The *trepalium* became a verb, *trepaliare*, which meant any form of torture. From torture to the Old French concept of *travailler* – or, putting oneself to pain or trouble. *Travailler* came to mean 'work hard' in French. English borrowed the word as 'travail' and this, in turn, was used to describe a wearisome journey - travel." Hmm, I know that sitting in a cramped economy seat flying across the Pacific Ocean for 14 hours is torturous, so that makes sense. Now you know!

Cresques Abraham (1326-1387), a Mallorcan cartographer, crafts the *Catalan Atlas* at the Majorcan Cartographic School, which shows the earth's spherical shape for the first time. This breakthrough owes its prominence to the contributions of both Arab and Jewish scholars.

1391

Construction begins on a canal from Lübeck south to the Elbe; thus linking the Baltic and the North Sea for easy of transportation.

1398

Henry Sinclair (aka Earl of Orkney) (1345-1400), a Scottish landowner, may have traveled to North America. Experts disagree.

1400c

Finally, the word *vodka* is recorded for the first time in 1405 in the court documents from the Palatinate of Sandomierz in Poland, and utterly loudly thereafter as, *"shaken, not stirred"* by a grand succession of acclaimed rouges and fellow travelers at Trader Vic's. (See: 1862)

Machu Picchu, the Quechua/Inca city in the Peruvian highlands (aka Old Mountain), is said to have been founded.

1402

Gim Sa-hyeong (1341-1407), a Korean mapmaker, produces the Kangnido Map (aka Integrated Historical Map of Countries and Cities) from a collection of Chinese source materials. The map describes Old World pre-European and Chinese voyages of exploration suggesting great geographical knowledge. This map assumes that Chinese explorers were busy travelers even before the great Zheng Ho (See: 1405).

1405

Admiral Zheng He (1371-1434), a Chinese seaman, was the illustrious commander of the Chinese Treasure Fleets (1405-1436) of the Dragon Throne of Ming Youngle Emperor. The fleet was enormous and consisted of at least 63 large ships and 100+ other support vessels. Some scholars claim that between 1421 and 1423, Admiral Zheng He even circled the world—75 years before Magellan's voyage—and that he may in fact have even visited the New World—70 years before Columbus! Yet still 400 years after Leifr Eiríksson's settlement at *L'Anse aux Meadows* in Newfoundland.

(See: 1002c) Historians argue, fuss and fight. Some of the Admiral's *Speed Junks* were shown to have traveled as much as 200 kilometers (125 miles) a day.

1414

One of the earliest references to an English passport comes during the reign of King Henry V (1387–1422), where in an Act of Parliament there is mention of *Safe Conducts* for travelers on official business. With these, the King asked for his official subjects to freely and safely travel abroad; and in return that no subjects of the King should injure or rob a foreigner who carried a *Safe Conduct*.

> **Did You Know?** Most traveling was made on foot until about 1800 when horses gained widespread popularity. More a reflection of wealth versus utility, horses did little for human mobility. Faster than the average 5 km/h (3 mph) walk distance covered, with speeds of 6.4km/h (4mph) for a walking horse, and 13 km/h (8 mph) for a trotting horse; yet horses really did not much improve human transportation for the masses. In fact, around 1815, Sweden topped the world in horse ownership with about 1 per 6 people, while Great Britain had about 1 per 10 and Belgium about 1 per 16.

CHAPTER FOUR

The Age of Discovery (1418 – 1606):
Experts and historians disagree on many things, but they do agree that an early Renaissance-era man named Henry the Navigator (See: 1418), almost single-handedly pushed his little sea-faring nation further than it ever imagined going, with both his moral and financial support. And thus begins the Great Age of Exploration (aka the Age of Discovery), that lasted roughly between 1418 and 1779. But the era really begins to take off in 1453 when the Turks seized Constantinople (Istanbul), Turkey which effectively blocks off all eastern Mediterranean travel and trade routes, and significantly increases the prices of goods being imported from the East. This act more than any other, gives rise to the conditions for the advent of Europeans to seek alternative routes to the Far East. *Homo touristicus* begins a grand new era of discovery after centuries of religion dominating his travels. Traveling for the sake of exploration, discovery, gold and fame begin…

1418
Henry the Navigator (1394-1460), a prince of Portugal, profoundly impacts the explorers of the day with his personal patronage. With his visionary support, the far reaches of the Portuguese coast and the Azores are charted. He also builds the *Institute at Sagres*, which becomes the earliest known places for the advanced study of cartography in 1450. And owning to his direct financial support, Portuguese ships sailed to the Madeira Islands (1420), to Cape Blanc (1441), the Gambia River (Cadamosto in 1455), and Cape Palmas (Gomes in 1459-1460).

1424

Zuane Pizzigano, a Venetian cartographer, produces the *Pizzigano* map, that has made some scholars of the 20th century speculate that maybe the Chinese under Zheng He (See: 1405), may have indeed traveled to America—68 years before Columbus! (See: 1492)

1434

Gil Eannes, a sailor supported by Henry the Navigator (See: 1418), is the first to sail past the mythical and dreaded *Green Sea of Darkness* beyond Cape Bojador...and return! (Cape Bojador is off the coast of Africa just below latitude 27° north.)

1450

The earliest known use of a navigational mariner's quadrant—a quarter of a circle—made of wood or brass that easily locates latitude using the sun was used by a Portuguese sailor. (Some historians' date the use back to at least the 1200's, though no records exist.)

1453

The Turks seize Constantinople (Istanbul), Turkey, which effectively blocks off all eastern Mediterranean trade routes.

The infamous *Vinland Map* is said to be created. Long declared a forgery, but still insured for over US$20 million, this Yale University-held map if authentic, would be the oldest known map of North America and Canada's northeastern coast. It was supposedly created with Viking insight in the early 1400's. (See: 1002c)

1455

Alvise da Cadamosto (1432-1511) a Portuguese sailor, travels to the mouth of Gambia River and discovers the Cape Verde Islands.

> **Think About It!** Old sailors would venture off to *terra incognita* where bizarre and mythical (but real to them) creatures lurked, like: devils, gryphon's, dragons, Bonnacon, and giants with eyes on their chests, Hydras, Garudas, Leviathans, along with giant octopuses...to places previously unknown and unseen by any man, undocumented terrestrial places like: Atlantis, Cockaigne, El Dorado, Shangri-La, Eden, or even hell itself... One never knew when they went beyond.

1457

Fra Mauro, a Venetian monk and mapmaker, designs a six-foot circular map of the world commonly called the *Fra Mauro map*, which for the first time includes Japan (aka Zimpangu). By the way, Fra Mauro was the landing site named for the Apollo 14 lunar mission.

1461

Istanbul's Grand Bazaar (aka Kapalıçarşı), essentially a giant covered shopping center, opens as a major attraction. The era of mall tours (aka shopping tourism) officially begins. Nowadays, places like the Mall of America in Bloomington, Minnesota, attract tour groups from over 32 nations! Shopping in exotic (sic) destinations continues to be one of travels greatest allures.

1466

Afanasy Nikitin (?-1472), a Russian businessman and writer, becomes one of the earliest Europeans to document his visit to India in a narrative known as the *Voyage Beyond the Three Seas*. They named a beer after him in his hometown of Tver—a really good beer!

1472

João Vaz Corte-Real (?-1496), a Portuguese explorer, is granted the lands on Terceira Island of the Azores because he had located *Terra do Bacalhau* (aka Newfoundland) during an earlier cod fishing expedition. Speculation exists that after his original North Atlantic expedition and his locating of *Terra Verde* (aka Greenland), he also visited Newfoundland. He returns later, with among others, Gaspar Corte-Real (See: 1500). Corte-Real claims to also have been to America before Columbus...and the list is growing!

1480

The initial Frankfurt book fair takes place on the Römerberg and becomes a yearly tradition of international bookmakers (aka bookstore tourism).

1486

Bartholomeu Diaz (1450-1500), a Portuguese explorer, discovers and names the Cape of Good Hope. Rounding the treacherous Cape marks the beginning of a great leap forward for world exploration that takes place over the next 50 years.

1490

Afonso de Albuquerque (1462-1515), a Portuguese explorer, becomes the earliest European to visit the Spice Islands (aka the Maluku Islands/ Moluccas of Indonesia).

1492

Martin Behaim (1459-1537), a German scientist, constructs one of the first modern round terrestrial globes (aka *erdapfel* or earthapple), called the *Nürnberg Terrestrial Globe*...although it is not yet generally accepted that the world is round.

Isabella I (1451-1504), the Queen of Castile and León and wife of Ferdinand II of Aragon, becomes the patron of Christopher Columbus's voyage west to the Indies and Spice Islands seeking trade routes to enrich the Spanish Crown.

Christopher Columbus (1451-1506), an Italian-born freelancer, working for the Spanish Crown and looking for the Spice Islands, sails the ocean blue and gets seriously lost and ultimately discovers the West Indies for Spain. Columbus didn't know about the giant land mass between Europe and Asia. He also miscalculated the circumference of the earth by just a tad— 6,000 miles in fact—because he used Roman miles in his calculations, instead of nautical miles. In four voyages to the New World, Columbus claims: Bahamas, Hispaniola, Cuba, Dominica, Jamaica, Guadeloupe, Central America and South America. Lost, he originally thought he had found the Orient by heading west. To this day, U.S. citizens celebrate this tarnished lost traveler with a national holiday!

1494

Pope Alexander VI (1431–1503), the Spanish-born pope, mandates the *Treaty of Tordesillas,* that divides the new world between Spain and Portugal along a simple meridian 370 leagues west of the Cape Verde islands, to help spread Christianity more efficiently—and some would say arrogantly. That is why Brazil is the only Portuguese-speaking nation in the New World; all the nations to the west of it are Spanish-speaking.

1497

Giovanni Caboto (aka John Cabot) (1450-1498), an Italian mariner, who settled in England, becomes the first explorer to search for the Northwest passage via Greenland & Baffin Island, and one of the earliest to make landfall on the Atlantic coast of Canada.

Vasco da Gama (1460-1524), a Portuguese sailor, who followed Dias' route around the Cape of Good Horn (See: 1486), visits the coast of Africa while making a route to India.

1499

Hotel de los Reyes Catolicos at Santiago de Compostela, built as a hospital and hostel catering to Christian pilgrims along the Way of St. James (See: 1130) opens and later becomes a legendary five-star hotel—and one of the oldest still in operation too.

1500c

The *Jerusalem Syndrome,* a form of hysteria that is known to occur among pilgrims visiting the Holy Sites of Jerusalem (aka Jerusalem squabble poison, or *fièvre Jerusalemmiene*) is expressed. It is finally clinically described in the 1930s by Jerusalem psychiatrist Heinz Herman (See: 1930c). As Peter Høeg the Danish writer says, *"Traveling tends to magnify all human emotions."*

1500

Juan de la Cosa (1460–1510), a Spanish explorer, draws a *portolan* chart, the first surviving *old* world map to show the *new* world—that is if the Vinland map (See: 1453) is in fact a fraud?—that may indeed be the earliest true map of North America.

Gaspar Corte Real (1450-1501), a Portuguese explorer, visits Greenland, and maybe Labrador with João Vaz Corte-Real (see: 1472).

Pedro Álvares Cabral (1467-1520), a Portuguese explorer, is the earliest European to see Brazil; he claims it—and all the millions of indigenous people already living there—for Portugal.

Martin Alonso Pinzon (1441-1493), a Spanish explorer, visits the mouth of the Amazon River.

Vasco Nunez de Balboa (1475-1519), a Spanish explorer, sees the Pacific Ocean via the Panama isthmus on September 25th.

Diogo Dias, a Portuguese sailor and the brother of Bartolomeu Dias (See: 1486), is the first European to visit Madagascar.

1502
The *Cantino Map* is the earliest to show the Tordesillas Line, a north-south line dividing the world between Spain and Portugal. (See: 1494)

1503c
The Lenox Globe (aka Hunt-Lenox Globe), highlights the unsafe water patches of the world and is the only known map to have the Latin phrase "*Hic sunt dracones*" (*Here be dragons*) on it! But, maybe he was just referring to those Komodo dragons on an Indonesian BBQ?

1506
The famed otherworldly Vatican Museum opens, and traces its origin to one marble sculpture from Greece—ironically, the statue's quote warns of Greeks bearing gifts!

1507
Amerigo Vespucci (1454-1512), all-around good-guy and Italian explorer, was sent to follow up on Columbus's claims and who after his epic 1497 voyage decides that it is not the West Indies of Spice Islands fame, but really a New World—both continents—and gets the whole area of the New World named after him, *Amerigo* (aka America)! And before dying of malaria five years later, he wrote about it in *Four Voyages*.

Martin Waldseemüeller (1470-1522), a German cartographer, draws the Waldseemüeller map (aka *Cosmographiae Introdcutio)*, which is the original New World map calling *America* after Amerigo Vespucci. Some have labeled it as, "America's birth certificate," although alternative names and theories abound. It is owned by the Library of Congress—*we the people*—and was acquired for US$10 million in 2003.

1510

The Portuguese set up shop in Goa on the west coast of India under Afonso de Albuquerque (See: 1490) and their *Índia Portuguesa* (aka *Estado da Índia*) terms of colonial rule. The beach parties have never stopped…

1513

Juan Ponce De Leon (1460-1521), a Spanish explorer, searching for the fountain of youth, discovers Florida on April 2nd. Realizing that there are too many retirees and mosquitoes, he quickly leaves!

Piri Reis (aka Hadji Muhammad) (1465-1554), an Ottoman admiral, draws a world map, the appropriately named but not so well-known Piri Reis map within his maps and charts collection entitled *Kitab-i Bahrieh* or the *Book of the Navy*. It is special because of its uncanny depiction of areas only recently discovered, which has led researchers to believe that others had already been there, done that, and moved on to what's next…

1514

The Worshipful Company of Innholders becomes one of the first incorporated entities under a Royal Charter in the City of London. The innholders were originally known as Hostellers, but their name had been changed by the time it was incorporated under a Royal Charter.

1515

The *Hostal San Marcos* in Leon, Spain, opens its doors as a commercial entity.

1516

Sir Thomas More (1478–1535), an English humanist, pens his much celebrated must read work of genius *Utopia,* about an imaginary island nation (aka Bob's dock).

1518

Pedro Reinel (1485-1522), a Portuguese mapmaker charts the Indian Ocean, and drew the innovative, but now-standard 32-point compass rose with the *fleur-de-lis* indicating north.

1519

Ferdinand Magellan (1480-1521), a Portuguese explorer, along with his crew and ship *Victoria* leave for their legendary round-the-world sea voyage, finally closing the gap between the 123rd and 124th degree! Despite his crew circling the globe for the first time ever, he was not so lucky and does not return.

Lopo Homem (1497-1572), a Portuguese cartographer, creates a map of Brazil then gets a Royal Charter (Read: monopoly) on certifying the calibration of all compass needles aboard Portuguese ships. He was the Map*Quest* of his day.

Hernando Cortes (1485-1547), a notorious Spanish *conquistador,* discovers the Aztec empire and visits the island capital of Tenochtitlan—the world's second largest city at the time behind only Constantinople. The rest as they say is savage history. (Interesting, Cortes passes by

Tikal the great Mayan city later in 1525, by just a few short kilometers, but never actually lays eyes on it.)

Aztec Pyramid of the Sun.
(Author Photo)

1522

Juan Sebastian de Elcano (1476-1526), Magellan's Spanish pilot, returns Magellan's flagship*Victoria* back to Spain on September 6th. Antonio Pigafetta (1491-1534), also returns to Spain aboard the Victoria, his journal was later published in 1525 called, *The Report on the First Voyage Around the World.*

The First—Technically Speaking: Magellan's slave boy, Enrique of Malacca (aka Henry the Black), (1493c- ?), who was bought in Malacca some years prior to Magellan's voyage, was in fact the first person to circle the globe. He may have been from the Philippines, as he spoke the local dialect in Cebu. At his return to Cebu, Sumatra, or even later to Malacca, that would have made him the first person to circumnavigate the globe, well before any of Magellan's ships returning to Spain. History is filled with these messy and inconvenient facts!

1527

Alvar Nuñez Cabeza de Vaca (1490-1557), a Spanish explorer of the New World, sees bison for the first time.

1529

Diego Ribero, a Portuguese explorer, puts together the *Ribero World Chart* (aka Padrón real), which is the earliest known world map based on empiric latitude observations and includes Magellan's information about the true extent of the Pacific Ocean.

1530

Peter Martyr d'Anghiera (1457-1526), an Italian explorer and historian, pens his little known *De Orbe Novo* (aka On the New World), a book about his travel adventures to the New World and what the locals and locales where like. Travel reportage at its earliest and best.

1531

Francisco Pissarro (1470-1541), a Spanish conquistador, founds the city of Lima and later conquers the Incan Empire. It is but another sad chapter in history.

1535

Jacques Cartier (1491-1557), a French explorer and master navigator, sails to Newfoundland and up the St. Lawrence River to present day Montreal. Claims what he found—Canada—for the French.

1539

Fray Marcos de Niza (1495-1558), a Spanish missionary, who describes the fabled *Seven Golden Cities of Cibola* after visiting Central America, Mexico and New Mexico, as well as the Zuni Indians area.

1540

Francisco de Orellana (1490-1546), a Spanish conquistador, sails up—*or is it down?*—the Amazon.

1542

Juan Rodriguez Cabrillo (1499-1543), a Portuguese explorer, becomes the first European to explore what is now the west coast of the United States, and proved that California was not an island. (Although many still believe that is indeed and island of insanity!)

Fernão Mendes Pinto (1509-1583), a Portuguese explorer, who after traveling through Sumatra, Malaysia, Siam, Cochinchina (*aka* Vietnam), China, and possibly Korea, becomes one of the earliest Europeans to visit Japan.

Jean Rotz, a French artist-cum-cartographer, helps create the Dieppe Map series, a wonderfully decorative set of world maps.

1543

Luca Ghini (1490-1556), an Italian botanist, opens the imaginatively innovative public botanical garden, *Orto botanico di Pisa*, in Pisa.

1544

Sebastian Cabot (1476-1557), the son Giovanni Caboto (1450-1498) and general explorer at large and accomplished cartographer in his own right, publishes an engraved map of world.

1547c

The so-called *Harleian Map* is the first to use the name Canada for the upper part of North America.

1547

An anonymously produced colorfully illustrated map of the Arabian Sea, Red Sea and Persian Gulf, known as the *Vallard Atlas* is published in the *Portolan Atlas.*

1554

Andrea Palladio (1508-1590), a Venetian architect, publishes twin guidebook-type books to the *"City of Wonders."*

> **The New Seven Wonders:** Somewhere in the mid-16th century a new list, a list that is commonly referred to as the *Seven Wonders of the Middle Ages* is created that includes: the Colsseum, the Taj Mahal, the Leaning Tower of Pisa, Hagia Sophia, Chartres Cathedral, the Porcelain Tower of Nanking, and the Great Wall of China. Experts of course disagree.

1559

Mateo Prunes, a Majorcan mapmaker, is shown an old portolan chart, a nautical map of the Mediterranean and Black seas that is inked onto the skin of a single sheep! It represents one of the world's greatest and most enduring mysteries: Where and how did medieval mapmakers, armed with no more than a compass—if that!—an hourglass and sets of sailing directions, create such stunningly accurate maps of southern Europe, the Black Sea, and North African coastlines? It was as if they were looking down from at earth from a satellite? When of course, no one had ever been higher than a treetop or nearby hill?

1565

The pencil is invented giving writers a mobile writing instrument that prevails until 20th century blogging begins.

1568

Gerhardus Mercator (1512-1594), a Flemish cartographer, establishes the Cartographical Institute, and invents the flat map concept (2D) of viewing the world (3D), also known as the Mercator projection map.

1570

Abraham Ortelius (1527-1598), a Flemish cartographer, produces *Theatrum Orbis Terrarum*, the original real atlas with fifty-three maps. He is considered the father of modern cartography.

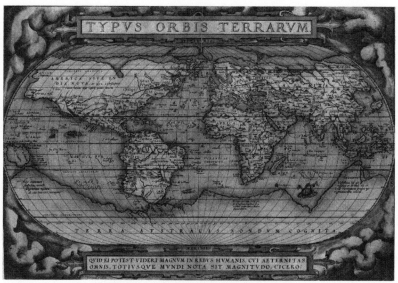

Theatrum Orbis Terrarum page.
(Courtesy Regional Archives Leiden)

1574

Said to be the world's first public park, *la Alameda de Hércules,* opens to allow weary travelers visiting the town of Seville, Spain to picnic and relax. Budapest's *Oxmeadow* (aka Városliget) city park shows signs of being open to the public (and not just the monarchy) around 1241. Other urban parks open thereafter, including the famous: Peel Park in Manchester, England in 1846; New Orleans' City Park in 1853; Central Park located in Manhattan, New York City in 1857; and Stanley Park in Vancouver opens in 1888. Disputes abound.

1580

Sir Francis Drake (1540-1596), an English explorer and maybe pirate, actually becomes the first Englishman to successfully circumnavigate the globe.

1583

The world's earliest amusement park with water springs, gardens, entertainers, and hawkers, Dyrehavsbakken (aka The Deer Park Hill and better known as Bakken), opens to the public in Klampenborg, Denmark, 13 kilometers (eight miles) from Copenhagen.

1589

Richard Hakluyt (1552-1616), an Englishman, known for promoting immigration to the New World, publishes *Principall Navigations*.

1590

John Davis (1550-1605), an English explorer, who after several unsuccessful Northwest Passage journeys, invents the backstaff that helps navigators figure their position by keeping his back to the sun, working with its shadow.

1591

The now annual *Fiestas San Fermín* (aka the Running of the Bulls) is established. Later popularized by Ernest Hemingway's 1926 the novel *The Sun Also Rises*, tourists flock to show their honor, bravery and sometimes, stupidity, by running with mad bulls.

1592

Juan de Fuca (aka Ioánnis Fokás) (1536-1602), a Greek-born pilot working for Spain, sails up the west coast of North America from Mexico to Vancouver Island looking for a passage from the Pacific Ocean to the Atlantic Ocean. He may have been the first European to visit some parts of this area.

1593

Admiral John Hawkins (aka John Hawkyns) (1532-1595), an English naval commander and profiteer (aka slave trader), first suggested the use of citrus juice to ward off sailor scurvy.

1594

Martin Frobisher (1535-1594), an English pirate, made one of the first searches for what is known as the Northwest Passage through the Arctic Circle, and later publishes his journals, *Three Voyages*.

Thomas Nashe (1567–1601), an English poet, pens his famously wicked satirical novel *The Unfortunate Traveller*, and gives us these words of travel advice:
"A traveler must have the back of an ass to bear all,
a tongue like the tail of a dog to flatter all,
the mouth of a hog to eat what is set before him,
the ear of a merchant to hear all and say nothing."

1596

According to the OED, the word luggage enters the vocabulary, meaning to lug as in *"to drag"*; as in when a husband asks his wife, *"Honey, do you to have drag all this stuff everywhere we go?"*

1598

Jodocus Hondius (1563-1612), a Flemish artist-cum-cartographer, becomes a significant mapmaker during the Dutch Golden Age of Cartography.

Conrad Peutinger (1465–1547), a German humanist, who found The *Tabula Peutingeriana* (aka Peutinger Table) (See: 384c) mysteriously, gets it published posthumously making it somewhat famous.

1602

Matteo Ricci (1552-1610), an Italian missionary, who worked in China for 27 years, draws the *Kunyu Wanguo Quantu* (aka the *Pekin map*), that means "A Map of the Myriad Countries of the World", and becomes the earliest known European map of China.

1603

Walter Raleigh (1552-1618), an English ne'er-do-well, spy, and tobacco exporter, writes his tour de force *History of the World*.

1605

Miguel de Cervantes (1547-1616), a Spanish dreamer, writes the world's earliest novel, *Don Quixote,* and begins it with this great travel line, *"Somewhere in la Mancha, in a place whose name I do not care to remember..."* Haven't we all been there?

1606

Willem Janszoon (1570-1630), a Dutch explorer, becomes the first European to sail to Australia.

CHAPTER FIVE

The Era of *homo touristicus* Dawns (1608 – 1743):
By this point of our social evolution, man has discovered, and re-discovered, almost every significant terrestrial region on planet Earth. Thus begins a new era of travel, a big step forward, travel for travel's sake (aka leisure travel)! This evolution of *homo touristicus* takes an even larger leap when incomes begin to rise as a result of the still to come Industrial Revolution (1750c-1850c), giving would-be travelers both the time to travel freely as well as the money to do so. Elizabethan era man begins traveling for personal development and growth—not just for commerce or religion.

1608

Thomas Coryat (aka Coryate) (1577-1617), an intrepid English courtier, walks across Europe and miraculously manages to return home in one piece! Thus conceiving what will be later known as the *Grand Tour* (See: 1670); whereby young, aristocratic men, upon completion of their schooling, take a few years off traveling Continental Europe as a sort of rite of passage from youth to adulthood, and was once considered an essential part of any gentleman's education. The deeper-meaning goals of the Grand Tour—and of traveling itself—begin to evolve into self-development, perceptive expansion, and serving as a roving ambassador to their countries. In 1611, Thomas writes a first-person travelogue, known as *Coryate's Crudities* describing his 3,200 kilometer (1,970-mile) walk to the city-state of Venice.

1610

Henry Hudson (1565-1611), an English navigator, who while looking unsuccessfully for the Northwest Passage to the Orient, discovers—what a coincidence—Hudson Bay, and then the Hudson River too!

1613

Galileo Galilei (1564-1642), an Italian man of science, who while employed by the Spanish Crown is tasked to provide Spanish navigators with eclipse tables for their armadas. It never works, but a few others things he worked on did get noticed a little bit!

1614

Fernão Mendes Pinto (1509–1583), a Portuguese explorer who was also a writer, finally gets a little respect with his posthumously published *Peregrinação* (aka *Pilgrimage*), that described his travels to the Middle and Far East, Ethiopia, India, and also becomes one of the earliest known Europeans to reach Japan by the mid 16th century.

1615

Samuel de Champlain (1567-1635), a French explorer and hardy seaman, who helped found the original French colony in North America called Quebec; also discovers Lake Champlain and the source of the St. Lawrence River. Most remarkably he survived 27—yes twenty-seven!—trans-Atlantic ocean crossings!

1616

Terra Australis (*aka* Australia), the sadly lost continent, is finally located by Dutch sailors.

1617

Fynes Moryson (1566–1630), an English gentleman, who after traveling for the better part of ten years, pens his travel opus, *An Itinerary: Containing His Ten Years Travel Through the Twelve Dominions of Germany, Bohemia, Switzerland, Netherland, Denmark, Poland, Italy, Turkey, France, England, Scotland and Ireland.* Long trip, long title...

1620

Jean Nicollet (1598-1642), a French *coureur des bois* (aka runner of the woods), is the earliest to visit the Great Lakes—not counting of course the thousands, maybe millions of First Nation Indians that have already lived there for eons.

1621

The original Thanksgiving weekend takes place when the Native American Indians feed the down-on-their-luck hapless Pilgrims…and it's off to grandmother's house we go from then on. Thanksgiving weekend, remains the busiest travel week in America history.

1625

Hugo Grotius (aka Hugo de Groot) (1583-1645), a Dutch jurist, becomes the father of international law by creating the very foundation for the concept of international law, with his magnum opus, *On the Law of War and Peace.*

1626

Peter Minuit (1580-1638), a German administrator from Westphalia, buys Manhattan for the equivalent of US$24, and calls it New Amsterdam. A bargain at half the price!

1628

Wu Pei Chih, Chinese historian, redraws Zheng He's sea charts (See: 1405), into what becomes known as the Wu Pei Chih map.

1630

The Taj Mahal masterpiece opens to widespread critical acclaim in Agra, India. The Taj is a must see visit for anyone, and is not only one of the world's most recognizable buildings and most beautiful buildings, it also ranks among the *Wonders of the Medieval World* (See: 1554); and by 2007, not only was the Taj receiving over 3 million visitors a year, but was also named a member of the New Seven Wonders of the World in an international poll. But be forewarned, the road trek from Delhi to Agra is a real killer—literally.

Taj Tourists.
(Author Photo)

1633
In a setback for Asian tourism, Japanese Shogunate Iemitsu (1604-1651) establishes an outright ban on any overseas travel for all Japanese. In 1639, he then expels all foreigners from Japan, with the only exceptions made for a handful of Dutch and Chinese traders. In an unrelated story, Fuji film has their worst year on record...

1635
The Hackney Carriage Act passes in British Parliament, becoming the first legislation to control vehicles for hire. Inter-city stagecoach service begins operating out of London in 1640.

1638
Pubblico Ridotto, a legalized public gambling (aka casino), opens in the city-state of Venice. Always a progressive and rather permissive city-state, by 1755 the canals of Venice are said to have housed over 73 *casini* (*aka* casinos) in active operation. Las Vegas and Macau had nothing on these guys.

1640c
Evliya Çelebi (1611–1682), a Turkish writer, publishes his *Seyâhatnâme* (aka Book of Travel), that chronicles his journey exploring the far reaches of the Ottoman Empire.

1640

Nicolas Sauvage, a French entrepreneur, begins his hackney carriage services (*aka* horse-drawn for-hire) in both Paris and London. He called his vehicles *fiacres*—because his main vehicle depot was opposite a shrine to Saint Fiacre.

1641

Jean Bourdon (1601-1668), a French land-surveyor, is the probable creator of the *Nouvelle France* map used by France in Upper Canada.

During the reign of Henry V, passports begin being used in the form of a "safe conduct" letter. (See: 1414) The Privy Council had granted these passports from at least 1540 with one of the earliest found issued on 18 June 1641 and signed by Charles I.

1642

Abel Janszoon Tasman (1603-1659), a Dutch merchant, sails around Tasmania his namesake, along with Australia and New Zealand.

Joan Blaeu (1642-1665), a Dutch cartographer, produces *Grooten Atlas* and *Atlas Blaeu-Van der Hem*, a few of the most beautiful atlases ever produced.

1647

Johannes Janssonius (aka Jan Jansson) (1588-1664), a Dutch mapmaker, releases Martino Martini's (1614-1661) *Novus Atlas*.

1650

The first public ice slides open in St. Petersburg, Russia.

1653

François de La Boullaye-Le Gouz (1623–1669), an aristocratic French traveler, writes what some consider one of the earliest travel guide-like books with useful information, *Les voyages et observations du sieur de La Boullaye Le gouz*.

1656

The Hotel *de Beauvais* holds its grand opening in Paris.

1661

The art collection of the estate of Basilius Amerbach (1533-1591), is purchased by the city of Basel, thereby creating the world's earliest public municipal museum—Kuntsmuseum Basel (*aka* Öffentliche Kunstsammlung).

London's New Spring Gardens (aka Vauxhall Gardens in 1785), a pleasure garden for all visitors opens.

1662

Blaise Pascal (1623-1662), a French scientist, designs the original public bus—a horse-drawn scheme with regular routes, schedule and fare system.

1665

Samuel Pepys (1633-1703), an English naval administrator and perpetual diarist, records seeing in London, "a fine rarity, of fishes kept in a glass of water, that will live so forever, and finely marked they are, being foreign." The fish observed by Pepys were likely to have been the paradise fish (aka *macropodus opercularis*), a familiar garden fish in Canton, China, where the East India Company was then trading. It may be the earliest known aquarium? (The self-anointed Wardian case, created by Robert Warrington and the inspiration for the glass aquarium, was not invented until 1829.)

1669

René-Robert Cavelier (aka Robert de LaSalle) (1634-1687), a French explorer, after extensive exploration of the Great Lakes area, he discovers the mouth of the Mississippi River via the Ohio River. La Salle claimed the entire Mississippi River basin for France and names it Louisiana after Louis XIV—smart move.

1670

According to the OED, the term "Grand Tour" was coined by Richard Lassels (1603-1668), an expatriate Roman Catholic priest who wrote *The Voyage of Italy*, which was published posthumously in Paris.

1671

Adriaen van Ostade (1610–1685), a Dutch painter, produces his *Travellers Resting* painting.

1672

Louis Jolliet (1645-1700), a French-Canadian explorer, is the first white man to see the Mississippi River.

King Louis XIV (1638-1715), a French monarch, begins signing "letters of request," that become popular among his court favorites. These letters were dubbed *"passe port"*, literally meaning, "to pass through a port," because most international travel was by sailing ships, hence the term *passport*. (See: 1414 & 1641)

1675

John Ogilby (1600-1676), a Scottish mapmaker, publishes what is dubbed a "road book;" a collection of road maps for England and Wales called, *Britannia: A Geographical and Historical Description of the Principle Roads Thereof.* Rumor has it he could not refold it once opened though...

1678

Jean Gailhard, an English author on the proper training for the English nobility, writes in his *Compleat Gentlemen* handbook, that a three year Grand Tour, with stops in France, Italy, Germany, Switzerland and the Low Countries, is a customary requisite for any wannabe noble gentlemen. Indeed, sir, please pass the gin...

1681

The *Canal du Midi*, a 240 kilometer (149-mile) long canal that connects the Atlantic Ocean with the Mediterranean Sea opens in France. The canal was built as a shortcut between the Atlantic and the Mediterranean, while avoiding an additional month long sailing around sometimes hostile Spain, and marauding Barbary pirates.

1682

Luis XIV (aka the Sun King) (1638 –1715), the King of France—and all he could set his eyes on—opens his *magnum opus château* Versailles to his court—and tourists everywhere.

1683

Elias Ashmole (1617-1692), an English art collector and astrology buff, leaves his entire collection to Oxford University under the condition of public viewing and access. And so the Old Ashmolean Building on Broad

Street in Oxford thus lays claim to be the "oldest surviving purpose-built museum building in the world" open to the public. (See: 1753 and 1787)

Spanish missionaries begin establishing a series of religious outposts throughout present-day state of California and the Mexican state of Baja California. To facilitate missionary work into these previously unsettled areas, missions put were approximately 48 kilometers (30 miles) apart— one long day's ride on horseback—all along the 966 kilometer (600-mile) long *El Camino Real* (aka The Royal Highway).

1684
Vincenzo Coronelli (1650-1718), a Venetian globe maker and geographer, founds the initial geographic society–the *Cosmographic Academy of the Argonauts.*

1687
Matsuo Bashō (1644–1694), a renowned Japanese poet and sometimes traveler, pens *Kashima Kikō* (aka A Visit to Kashima Shrine), followed by *Oi no Kobumi* (*aka* Record of a Travel-Worn Satchel) in 1688, both commentaries on his travels.

1688
Aphra Behn (1640-1689), one of England's earliest female writers, publishes *Oroonoko.* She quite possibly becomes the world's first armchair traveler, started the whole idea of travel memoir. Critics contended that, "*She started the tradition of European travelers grossly exaggerating and lying about what they'd done. They've been fictionalizing ever since.*" And so they do; or, as Benjamin Disraeli so eloquently stated, "*Like all great travelers, I have seen more than I remember, and remember more than I have seen.*"

1693-98
Giovanni Francesco Gemelli Carreri (1651–1725), an Italian adventurer and traveler, may be the first known commercial around-the-world traveler using public transportation, because between 1693 and 1698 the Italian is said to have sailed to Mexico, crossed by land to the Pacific then returned to Italy on other ships via Asia. His memoirs, *Giro Intorno al Mondo* (aka *Voyage du Tour du Monde)* in 1699 may have been the inspiration behind *Around the World in Eighty Days* by Jules Verne. Giovanni was a man after my own heart...

1697

William Dampier (1651-1715), an English buccaneer, scientist and one great traveler, publishes *A New Voyage Round the World*. Oh yea, he also lays claim to being the first person to have circumnavigated the globe on three separate occasions! Records are made to be broken though…

> **Did You Know?** During the so-called Golden Age of Pirates (1680-1730), there was a difference between pirates and privateers, buccaneers and corsairs. Pirates were lawless cats who raped and pillaged whenever and whatever. Privateers were entrepreneurs who were sanctioned to rob and pillage the merchant goods of rival nations by enemy officials. Buccaneers were actually butchers who banded against Spanish interests in the Caribbean—and stole their livestock! While corsairs were mostly Muslim pirates or privateers operating exclusively in the Mediterranean Sea from the shores of North Africa. (aka the Barbary Coast) .

1699

Isaac Newton (1643-1727), a noted smart guy, probably invents the sextant a double-reflecting instrument that helps in navigation. He comes up with a few other good thoughts too.

1700

Ayutthaya, Thailand, the ancient capital of Siam, is said to have over one million inhabitants.

Guillaume Delisle (1675-1726), a Parisian cartographer, draws the first highly accurate map of the world, called interestingly enough, *The Map of the World*. His great later maps include, *Carte de la Louisiane et du cours du Mississippi, which* was the first detailed map of the interior of the United States of America.

1701

Antonie Laumet de La Mothe de Cadillac (1658-1730), a French New World explorer, founds Fort Pontchartrain du Détroit—the beginning of the city of my birth.

Saxony Hall (aka Grandhotel Pupp), a hotel in Karlovy Vary (aka Carlsbad), Czech Republic opens to the public.

1704

Alexander Selkirk (1676 –1721), a Scottish sailor, after taking a three-hour tour (...*a three hour tour*) the weather started getting rough, that tiny ship was tough, but off the coast of Chile he becomes marooned on an uninhabited island—likely the Juan Fernandez Islands—for four years until rescued by William Dampier. On 1 January 1966, Selkirk's island was officially renamed Robinson Crusoe Island—and Century Club members had a new place to visit!

Antonio Maria Valsalva (1666–1723), an Italian ears-nose-throat specialist, presents his ideas for clearing the blockage of your Eustachian tubes caused by deep water diving or by pressure changes from air flight—300 years before man actually fly's! Called the *Valsalva maneuver* it forces pressure on ear and sinus cavities to help equalize the pressure. And now you know... gum works wonders too!

1705

Eusebio Francisco Kino (1645-1711), a Jesuit missionary, produces an accurate map of the California, Baja regions.

1709

Bartolomeu de Gusmão (1685-1724), a Brazilian naturalist and priest, is said to have worked on a lighter-than-air airship, and according to some historians, may have even attempted (or actually did?) fly his experimental machine over Lisbon landing in Terreiro do Paço. It is said that church officials became alarmed, and that the insiders of the Portuguese Inquisition forbade him to continue his aeronautic investigations, as they offended God's natural order. So, in the name of God once again, we will never know?

1719

Daniel Defoe (1660-1731), an English writer and novel enthusiast, publishes his famed work *Robinson Crusoe*, which was maybe, probably, most-likely, inspired by the true story of the Scottish castaway Alexander Selkirk (See: 1704).

1720

Originally introduced in France, the *postchaise*, a two-or-four wheeled simple horse-drawn carriage, provides the first chance of reasonably comfortable travel by land.

Because of a high volume of visitors and sweet travelers' tax to be collected, Bath became the first city in England to receive a covered sewage system, way ahead of London by several years. The city also received technological, financial, and social benefits as a result of fat public coffers; roads were paved, streets had lights, the hotels and restaurants were beautified—all because of early medical tourism.

1721

Tokyo (aka Edo) becomes a city with over one million inhabitants.

1722

Jacob Roggeveen (1659-1729), a Dutch explorer, lost and looking for something else in the wild blue Pacific, locates *Isla de Pascua* (aka Easter Island, now *Rapa Nui*). He found more than three thousand inhabitants—and 887 monolithic stone statues—on this, one of the world's most isolated inhabited islands.

1723

Entrudo, which originally was a prank, brought over by the Portuguese from the Azores, whereby people threw flour and water in spitball fashion at each other, first appears in Rio de Janeiro, Brazil. This annual tradition turns into the initial *Carnaval Masquerade* in 1840. By 1855, the first *Carnaval* clubs are formed—called Great Societies—with the earliest official parade taking place in 1935.

1726

John Swift (1667-1745), a quick-witted Irish poet, publishes *Gulliver's Travel*. Always a childhood favorite; yet some explorers are still looking for Lilliput.

1727

The first railway viaduct, the Causey Arch in northern England, is built. Which means there must have been a railway one could assume—most likely a horse-drawn carriage on rails.

1730

Edward Wright, an English writer, publishes *Travelling through France and Italy in the years 1720, 1721 and 1722*. It was ten years in the making—due to the heavy hand of an editor no doubt!

1731

Edward Cave (1691–1754), an English publisher, begins offering *The Gentleman's Magazine,* not only the first general interest magazine, but one that also had a few articles here and there about travel and how it related to life abroad, doing business abroad and intelligence from afar.

Thomas Godfrey (1704-1749), an American inventor, builds an important navigational instrument he calls an octant—as did John Hadley (1682-1744), an English mathematician, that very same year. Hmm, talk about synchronicity! Hadley calls his the reflecting quadrant as per his fellows at the Royal Society, including Isaac Newton.

1735

Charles Marie de la Condamine (1701-1774), a French explorer, is sent by the King of France and the French Royal Academy of Sciences, to Ecuador to measure the equator. He later does an extended trip to Levant—the Holy Land.

1736

John Harrison (1693–1776), an English clockmaker, invents the marine chronometer, a simple yet complex device that allows sailors to establish their East-West position (aka longitude) while out at sea. And in so doing he collects a tidy prize of £20,000—that would be equivalent to winning a small lottery jackpot of about US$5 million today!—that the British government had posted twenty years earlier in 1714 as an incentive for inducing such creative genius. Harrison's solution turns out to be an accurate clock which could compare any local time to another fixed time as a reference point—what today we know as Greenwich Mean Time (GMT)! Needless to say, this development revolutionizes sailing and travelers just don't get as lost as much they used to. It is the modern day GPS system. (By the way, the U.S. does not use that clock in Greenwich, but rather uses the official time kept at the U.S. Naval Observatory in Washington, D.C. for national security reasons.)

1738

Daniel Bernoulli (1700–1782), a Dutch math wiz, publishes his ground-breaking book *Hydrodynamica,* declaring in the now-called Bernoulli Theorem stating that " $$\frac{v^2}{2} + \Psi + \frac{p}{\rho} = \text{constant}$$ " (aka a calculation for lift force), that makes flight possible! Now you know.

1743

Admiral George Anson (1697-1762), a wealthy aristocrat-cum-British Admiral, circumnavigates the world, but is later ship wrecked in Chile, writes *Narrative of Great Distresses on the Shores of Patagonia* in 1748.

C H A P T E R   S I X

The Era of the Mechanized Transport Arrives (1744 – 1829):
The Industrial Revolution unleashes man's true talents—building stuff! And so it goes that around now man's great transportation inventions, from steamboat, locomotive—and later motor vehicles, air planes, and high-speed rail networks—firmly take root and expand man's traveling abilities. Each new mode of transportation developed takes from 50 to 100 years to fully saturate its desired niche and help accelerate man's movement and open new doors. And as each new machine assists man in significantly surpassing his leisurely five kilometers per hour of mobility by foot—a progressive evolution of *homo touristicus* territorial range expands and man travels more freely and confidently.

1744
In one of the first mass transit systems ever built, Santa Teresa's horse trams cross Rio de Janeiro's Lapa Arches Carioca Aqueduct.

1747
The earliest North American spa, located in West Virginia and known as the Medicine Springs, shows up on a map drawn by Thomas Jefferson's father. Today it is known as Berkeley Springs.

1749
Thomas Nugent (1700-1772), a British writer, publishes *Grand Tour*, a popular travelogue in two volumes. He uses the artistic device of writing letters to an imaginary friend to get his commentary across. We all know the feeling of being friendless…because we traveled so much.

1750c

By this time *Grand Tour* visitors from England and France commonly visit the ancient archaeological ruins (aka archaeological tourism) of Pompeii just across the bay from Naples, Italy since its accidental rediscovery in 1599. By 2008, the site now a museum is attracting almost 2.5 million visitors—and most don't see the famous erotic frescoes scandalously hidden away in a dusty Naples museum.

Giacomo Girolamo Casanova de Seingalt (aka Casanova) (1725–1798), a Venetian playboy, takes his womanizing ways on the road (aka Don Juanism) and begins an extended Grand Tour of Europe (aka Sex Tour). With quotes like, *"Cultivating whatever gave pleasure to my senses was always the chief business of my life..."* and *"Cheating is a sin, but honest cunning is simply prudence. It is a virtue. To be sure, it has a likeness to roguery, but that cannot be helped. He who has not learned to practice it is a fool."* What more can be said...

1751

The British Calender Act passes, making January 1ˢᵗ the official day of hangovers—and a day off too!

1752

Daniel Bernouilli (1700-1782), a Swiss mathematician, conceives the idea for screw propellers for ships.

An early and rather primitive version of a public zoological garden is opened in Vienna when the Habsburg Emperor decides to grant public access to his former privately-owned Schönbrunn Palace menagerie, now called Tiergarten Schönbrunn.

1753

Established in a 17th-century mansion, Montagu House in Bloomsbury (aka the British Museum) opens on an invitation-only basis in London, becoming one of the world's first national—public or secular museums. It eventually opens its doors to the masses on the 15ᵗʰ of January 1759. (See: 1683 and 1787)

The English seaside town of Brighton begins to become popular with the city folk after Dr. Richard Russell publishes his pseudo-scientific dissertation on sea bathing and the beneficial health effects of the salt water. Must be the foam? The now popular Palace Pier, later named Brighton Pier, opens more than a century later in May 1899.

1755
The non-existent St. Brendan's Isle lying off the northwest coast of Ireland is taken off maps. (See: 530)

Frederic Louis Norden (1708-1742), a Danish explorer, who after twenty years of regaling his family and friends with his tales of high adventures, finally produces *Voyage d'Egypte et de Nubie,* that records some of the very first realistic drawings of Egyptian monuments.

1758
Richard Cox (1718-1803), a London businessman, forms Cox & Kings, allegedly the first official travel company ever formed. Getting his start by housing and feeding some of the Grenadier Guards, and currying favor with the British military establishment—he then becomes a civilian contractor for wealthy bank clients. Cox & Kings is said to be the oldest travel agency in the world still in existence.

1760
Horace de Saussure (1740-1799), a wealthy Swiss mountain climber, invents the sport of Alpinism, by offering a cash prize for the first to successfully climb Mont Blanc. A French climber later claims the money in 1786 and the adventure and extreme tourism market is born—extreme tourism meaning traveling to do something you could die doing…as in mountain climbing!

1763
Charles Mason & Jeremiad Dixon, two English surveyors, fashion the infamous Mason-Dixon Line between Pennsylvania and Maryland. Let the culture wars begin.

1764
Pierre Tresaguet (1716-1796), a French engineer, becomes the designated "father of the modern road," when he introduces three-tiered road marking—which lessens traffic jams due to road hazards.

1765

John Harrison (1693-1776), an English clockmaker, who over a 35-year career finally makes an accurate marine chronometer, that solves longitude problems for sailors at sea.

The earliest known North American fair is held in Windsor, Nova Scotia, Canada.

The Uffizi Gallery (aka Palazzo degli Uffizi), already a well-regarded display place for paintings and sculpture collected by the Medici family at private functions, is officially opened to the public. It remains one of the great cathedrals for art in the world.

Tobias Smollett (1721-1770), a Scottish novelist, visits the area of Nice, France in 1763, still an Italian city in the Kingdom of Sardinia, and writes about the "fresh sea air and warm winter climate" in his book *Travels through France and Italy,* that catches the attention of members of the British upper crust....it popularizes the soon-to-be-called *French Rivera* and *Côte d'Azur* as a new play-ground for wealthy aristocrats.

The first winter hotel (aka snow chalet, or inns) opens in the Chamonix, France, so that grand tourists can visit the Alps, see the glaciers, and enjoy some après-ski festivities.

1766

Nestled in the Allegheny Mountains of Western Virginia, the Homestead Hot Springs is established. Spa resorts have come to America with pampered guests "taking the waters."

1767

Father Junipero Serra (1713-1784), a Spanish Franciscan, who had earlier traveled threw Mexico in 1749 to do missionary work, travels further north to what is now California—converting native Americans zealously, sometimes forcibly! He founds many of the missions in California, including the Mission of San Diego in 1769, and eight others.

St. Joseph of Cupertino (aka the Flying Friar) (1603-1663), is canonized by Pope Clement XIII as a saint. He later becomes the patron saint of aviators and air travelers everywhere. On a side note: there are no less than

24 other patron saints for various types of travel, from St Christopher to Raphael the Archangel.

1768

James Cook (1728-1779), an English naval officer and surveyor, publishes his *Journals*. Cook, who while looking for the mysterious southern continent sailed the Pacific extensively. Always the innovator, he is the first sea captain to help prevent scurvy with citrus juice and carries a chronometer.

Gaspar de Portolá (1767-1784), a Spanish-born soldier and explorer, founds San Diego and Monterey, while enjoying his walk along the California Coast. PCH (aka Highway 1) would later follow his trail and Malibu's Sunset Grill is soon to follow...

1769

David Garrick (1717-1779), an English actor-cum-producer, establishes the first secular tourist trap by producing Stratford's initial annual Shakespeare Festival (aka cultural tourism).

Nicolas Cugnot (1725-1804), a French engineer, invents the earliest known steam powered self-propelled car, a true horse-less carriage, albeit a military tractor.

Louis Antoine de Bougainville's (1729 –1811), a French explorer, circles the globe on orders of Louis XV becoming the first Frenchman to do so and the "14th sea Captain" to do so, and he pens *Voyage autour du monde* in 1771.

Jeanne Baré (1740–1803), a kept Frenchwomen, becomes the first woman to circumnavigate the world as a passenger aboard Louis Antoine de Bougainville's expedition of ships *La Boudeuse* and *Étoile*. Truth be told, the expeditions botanist, Philibert Commerçon, simply could not live without his love and dressed her up as his boy valet, keeping her hidden until the gig was finally up when they reached Tahiti. Frenchmen may not know the difference between men and women—but the Tahitians surely did!

1770

Juan Bautista de Anza (1736-1788), a Spanish explorer, founds Los Angeles, San Francisco and San Jose.

1772

The Brenner Pass, the road that connects Italy and the Austrian frontier at a height of 1,370 meters (4,495-feet) opens. It is one of the most important passageways across the Alps, and in 1867 the railroad link between Innsbruck, Austria and Bolzano, Italy, finally completed.

What are nicknamed "traveller's cheques", begin being offered on the 1st of January by the London Credit Exchange Company for use in ninety European cities. Later, in 1874 Thomas Cook (See: 1841) began issuing "circular notes" that operated in the same manner of traveler's checks. In 1891, American Express developed a large-scale traveler's check system and is still the largest issuer of traveler's checks today by volume—although creative destruction being what it is, ATM machines have almost zeroed out that market.

1775

Samuel Johnson (1709–1784), an English moralist and poet, takes his pal James Boswell on a road trip of epic proportions and publishes *A Journey to the Western Islands of Scotland*. (See: 1996) Johnson and mate also become the first to discuss the now time-honored institution of tipping, according to the OED, as the term tip first appears as slang for "to give a gratuity" (aka To Insure Promptness (TIP). The modern-era traveler knows all too well the *Avenue of Palms* that must be lubricated while traveling (aka the tourist tithe). Personally, I like Sam's travel quote: *"The use of traveling is to regulate imagination by reality, and instead of thinking how things may be, to see them as they are."* Travel does open your eyes to reality…

1778

La Scala (aka *Teatro alla Scala*) the world renowned opera house in Milan, Italy, opens.

1779

After the merging of Bavaria and Palatinate, many smaller municipal German art collections are centralized in Munich, and the *Alte Pinakothek* opens to the public.

1780c

Peking (*aka* Beijing), becomes a city with over one million inhabitants.

The Russian hot springs/mineral baths area between the Black Sea and the Caspian Sea, and around Kislovodsk, Pyatigorsk, Essentuki and Zheleznovodsk (known collectively as the Russian Baden-Baden), becomes fashionable for the wealthy with *dachas* are seen as healthy places for those who are ill.

1780

A steel pen point is created to replace quill feathers, thus further empowering travel writers everywhere!

The White Sulphur Springs resort (aka The Greenbrier), opens in West Virginia. In 1857, a hotel was built on the property for wealthy clients. Following the Civil War in the Chesapeake & Ohio Railway purchased the resort, building additional amenities and The Greenbrier Hotel itself in 1913.

Russia's Bolshoi (both ballet and opera) company was founded in 1776 and held performances in private homes until 1780 when it finally acquired the Petrovka Theatre. The current *Imperial Bolshoi Theatre of Moscow* (*aka* the Bolshoi Theater) building was built on Theatre Square in

1824. (The St. Petersburg edition, called the Saint Petersburg Imperial Bolshoi Kamenny Theatre was built in 1783.)

1783

Joseph and Jacques Montgolfier (aka the Montgolfier Brothers), two French inventors, who on November 21st, send Jean François Pilâtre de Rozier and the Marquis François-Laurent d'Arlandes on the first ever tether-free Montgolfier hot air balloon (aka *globe aérostatique*) flight—a 22-minute ride in Paris. Various historians claim that more than one Frenchman took to the skies in a balloon in 1783, but for my book, the Montgolfier Brothers get mentioned.

Marquis Claude Francois de Jouffroy d'Abbans (1751–1832), French inventor, demonstrates the earliest practical steamboat named the

Pyroscaphe down the Saône—a paddle wheel steamboat. Twenty years later, Robert Fulton (See: 1807) sailed a larger steamship on the Seine.

1784

The 43 kilometer (27-mile) long Eider Canal (aka *Eiderkanal*), linking the North Sea with the Baltic Sea opens. It would later join up with the larger Kaiser-Wilhelm-Kanal (aka Kiel Canal) in

1895.

The *Le Grand Véfour* restaurant, one of Paris's earliest grand eateries, opens in the culinary promised land of France. It quickly becomes one of Napoleon's favorite.

The first healing water springs are discovered in Leamington Spa, an English village appropriately named. In 1814 the *Royal Pump Rooms and Baths* were properly opened.

1785

Dr. John Jeffries & Jean-Pierre Blanchard, an American and Frenchmen, make the first aerial crossing of the English Channel in a hot air balloon. The two and a half hour flight took place on the 7th of January. (It may have been a New Year's resolution?) Balloon mania overtakes Europe.

William Cowper (1731-1800), English poet and wannabe traveler, invents the idea of being an "armchair traveler." While relishing in the delights of other's adventures (Captain Cook's in particular), he pens the poem *The Task*, of which he says, *"My imagination is so captivated upon these occasions, that I seem to partake with the navigators, in all the dangers they encounter."*
He writes:
"He travels and I too. I tread his deck,
Ascend his topmost, through his peering eyes
Discover countries, with a kindred heart
Suffer his woes and share in his escapes,
Runs the great Circuit, and is still at home."

1786

James Boswell (1740–1795), a Scottish abolition movement lawyer, takes up travel writing when he published his *The Journal of a Tour to the Hebrides*—proving anyone can do it!

1787

John Fitch (1743-1798), an American inventor, builds the first passenger steamboat for use on the Delaware River. Fitch was granted a patent 1791. But again, it was twenty years later when Robert Fulton (See: 1807) makes a living out of it...

Catherine II (aka Catherine the Great) (1762-1796), the Empress of Russia, opens the Hermitage, one of the world's earliest public art museums in St. Petersburg, Russia—or so it is claimed! One could ask: What about Oxford (See: 1683), London's British Museum (See: 1753); Florence's Uffizi (See: 1765); or, Munich's *Alte Pinakothek* (See: 1779).

1788

Admiral Arthur Phillip (1738-1814), a British colonial administrator, founds Sydney, New South Wales (aka Australia), as a penal colony.

William Symington (1763–1831), a Scottish engineer, builds the first practical steamship.

1789

Elizabeth Craven (*née* Lady Elizabeth Berkeley) (1750–1828), English tabloid scandal queen, publishes *A Journey through the Crimea to Constantinople,* while in exile.

1790

Vice Admiral William Bligh (1753-1817), an infamous British captain, surviving the mutiny itself, and years of exile on Tonga and Timor, publishes *Mutiny on the Bounty.* Many believe that Anthony Hopkins was the real William Bligh!

1792

John Lovett opens the City Hotel on Broadway in New York City with 73 rooms on five floors. It is the first publicly held hotel.

1793

Heiligendamm (aka the White Town by the Sea), the German seaside resort is founded. Once the Baltic Sea playgrounds of Europe's aristocracy, it is the oldest seaside spa in Germany where topless Teuton's can still be found.

The Museum Français (aka *Musée du Louvre),* opens in Paris on the 10th of August.

1794

Catherine the Great (See: 1787), founds the Russian Black Sea resort city of Odessa.

1795

Located along the banks of Europe's largest thermal lake—Lake Balaton— the oldest, and maybe the most celebrated, Hungarian spa called *Hévíz,* is opened.

1796

A little known attempt to revive the ancient Olympic games is started in France called *L'Olympiade de la République.* It only lasts three years and doesn't seem to catch on—maybe the reputation of the guillotine had something to do with the lack of enthusiasm? (See: 1862; and 1896)

1797

Andre Jacques Garnerin (1769–1823), a French eccentric, completes the first manned parachute jump after leaping from a balloon approximately 600 meters (2,000-feet) in the air; begging that eternal question: Why would anyone voluntarily jump out of a perfectly fine-functioning aircraft?

1798

The tradition of annual exhibitions begins in Paris with France's Marquis d'Aveze held on the grounds and interior of the Maison d'Orsay on Rue de Varennes. These annual events took place as a showcase to the world of France's wonderful achievements until the British held their own Great Exhibition at the Crystal Palace in 1851 (See: 1851)

Samuel Taylor Coleridge (1772–1834), a romantic English poet, pens his critically-acclaimed *The Rime of the Ancient Mariner* poem; exploring the perils of sea life, with lines like: *"Water, water, everywhere, Nor any drop to drink."*

1799c
The box-spring is finally invented, making mattresses more comfortable, consistent and less lumpy in hotels—but creating a whole new sound coming from the next room.

1799
Mungo Park (1771-1806), a Scottish explorer, and the earliest known white person to see the Niger River in 1796, publishes *Travels in the Interior of Africa*. The Royal Scottish Geographical Society continues to award the Mungo Park Medal in his honor.

1800
Mariana Starke (1762-1838), an English author, best known for her later works, *Travels on the Continent*, and #1 Bestseller follow-up *Information and Directions for Travellers on the Continent* in 1824, publishes her original travel book, *Letters from Italy*. Her books become must-haves for would-be Continent beboppers. She is indeed the Rick Steves of her day...

1801
Alexander Mackenzie (1764-1820), a Scottish explorer, who while employed as a fur trader, looks really hard for the Northwest Passage in Canada, and locates many new rivers—all disappointing for him. He is the first person (white person that is) to cross the North American continent from sea-to-shining-sea in 1789; and writes *Journal of the Voyage to the Pacific*. They name a great river after him, the Mackenzie River—the longest river in Canada at 1,738 kilometers (1,080 miles).

Zadok Cramer, an American writer, publishes *The Navigator*, a guidebook of sorts to help westward settlers find their way with some timely tips about what they were in for long the primitive byways and waterways of America's west.

1802
The Grand Union Hotel in Saratoga Springs, New York opens; thus beginning a new era of grand hotels in America—and later becomes a good reason for wives to attend horse races with their husbands when the track opens in 1863.

1803

Samuel Pegge (aka the Younger) (1733-1800), an English poet and lexicographer, posthumously publishes a rather serious but ultimately funny-titled book called the, "Funny Story of English Language." In it, some claim he becomes the earliest to coin the phrase "tourist" —along with it I am sure, the when and where of the original tourist versus traveler debate too! —with this sentence: *"A traveler is now-a-days called Tourist."* The Oxford English Dictionary (OED) agrees that he was the first, others don't. (Later, in 1811, the authoritative OED establishes the first negative use of the word "*tourism*," as in "*subime Cockney tourism*," that appears in England's *Sporting Magazine*. Tourism already connotes a bad reputation.)

Thomas Jefferson (1743 -1826), an American politician, as President he establishes the Corps of Discovery to a scientific and military expedition to explore the uncharted West of America and the newly acquired Louisiana Purchase. Lewis and Clark get a job. (See: 1806)

William Jessop (1745-1815), an English civil engineer, opens England's first public tramway, The Surrey Iron Railway (SIR), a 15 kilometer (9-mile) line between Croydon and the River Thames at Wandsworth.

1804

Richard Trevithick (1771-1833), a British mining engineer, builds a road carriage and the first steam engine railroad locomotive he endearingly called *Catch Me Who Can*, near Merthyr Tydfil, South Wales.

George Cayley (aka the father of Aerodynamics), (1773–1857), an English engineer and inventor, after tinkering with various flying machines, he builds and actually flies the world's first successful model glider.

Meriwether Lewis (1774-1809) & William Clark (1770-1838), two American soldiers and explorers, conduct the famed Lewis and Clark Expedition of 1804–1806. Returning unsuccessfully—they failed to locate an east-west waterway across North America—from their long twenty-eight month walk through more than 8,000 miles of woods, and write *Journals*. They survived on luck, outdoor acumen, and the help of their Shoshone guide, Sacajawea.

1806

The earliest known reference to the term "cocktail," finally appears in The Balance and Columbian Repository, a New York City newspaper. The editor defined a cocktail as, *"...a stimulating liquor, composed of spirits of any kind, sugar, water and bitters."* Many travelers simply ask: What took so long!

America's first grand "city" hotel opens in Boston when the 200-guest Boston Exchange Coffee House opens. It burns down in an insurance fraud scheme some 12 years later after bedbugs stories proliferate.

1807

The first railroad takes passengers between Swansea and Mumbles, South Wales. It moved limestone from the quarries earlier. (See: 1825)

Robert Fulton (1765-1819), an American engineer and inventor, builds his first commercial steamboat on the Hudson River, operating from New York's Christopher Street to upstate Albany, and called it the *North River Boat* (later the *Clermont*). In 1811, Fulton's steamboat, the *New Orleans,* is built in Pittsburgh, and then sails down the Ohio and Mississippi rivers to New Orleans. It is the first steamboat in western waters. Passage on the *New Orleans* cost US$30.

Samuel Latham Mitchill (1764-1831), an American politician, publishes *Picture of New York*, a guidebook of sorts, promoting the natural beauty, history, cultural attractions, and recreational activities that the state has to offer.

1810

The first Oktoberfest is held on the occasion of the marriage of the Crown Prince Ludwig to Princess Therese of Sachsen-Hildburg-hausen. Around 40,000 people attended the event at a horse race track in Munich, Germany. The era of Party Tourism (aka annual Festival Tourism) begins.

1811

The National Road *(aka* Cumberland Road), a 1,000 kilometer (620-mile) long road between Maryland and Illinois begins being built. Completed in 1824, it is the USA's first interstate road and later becomes known as the National Pike and Interstate 40.

John Stevens (1749-1838), an American inventor, who earlier, in 1809 builds a screw-driven steamboat, the *Phoenix*, that sailed from Hoboken to Philadelphia, becoming the first steamship to successfully navigate the open ocean; builds a ship called *Juliana*. *Juliana* becomes the first steam-powered ferry operating between New York City and Hoboken, New Jersey. New York City is never the same.

1812

Johann Ludwig Burckhardt (1784–1817), a Swiss explorer and renown Arabic scholar, rediscovers the ruins of the Lost City of Petra (in present day Jordan) that is hidden behind an almost impenetrable barrier of rugged mountains. He is disenchanted with his find and heads to Cairo.

The Mivart's Hotel (aka Claridge's) a traditional grand hotel opens near Buckingham Palace in central London, England.

1814

Henry Shreve (1787-1880), an American inventor, builds the steamboat *Enterprise*, and makes two successful voyages transporting passengers and cargo to ports between Brownsville, Pennsylvania and Louisville, Kentucky. In 1816, he builds the *Washington* at Wheeling, West Virginia, and this 150-foot-long two-deck 400-ton side-wheeler ship sets the pattern for all future steamboats (aka showboats). He names his passenger cabins after states of the union, calling them "staterooms."

1815

In what may be the earliest travel advertisement, an ad appears in an Edinburgh, Scotland, weekly paper seeking out *tourists* for a journey to the Faeroe Islands and Iceland. No word on whether or not the *cruise* ever sailed.

Pierre Andriel, a French entrepreneur, is the first to cross the English Channel aboard the steam ship named *Élise*—it took 17 hours!

1816

Johann Wolfgang von Goethe (1749–1832), a great German thinker, takes his concept of *Weltliteratur* (aka world literature) far and publishes his travel diaries as *Italian Journey*. This inspires thoughtful Germans everywhere to take their own Grand Tours. Interestingly enough, the *Italian Journey* only discuses Goethe's first year in Italy, leaving the other time spent their largely undocumented, with this now infamous "gap in the record," has been the source of much speculation, research, and grant requests over the years. Haven't we all had a lost year in Italy—or dreamt of it anyway?

The year 1816 is also known in the Northern Hemisphere as the well-known *Year Without a Summer* when average global temperatures dropped 0.7 °C (1.3 °F) causing crop harvests to be disrupted. Why? Two reasons, one, the lack of solar activity that year, but more importantly the 1815 eruption of Mount Tambora in Indonesia.

By this time, it is estimated that as many as 150,000 English residents annually cross the Channel headed to various Continental destinations.

1817
Marie-Henri Beyle (aka Stendhal) (1783-1842), a French writer, depending on who you read, Stendhal was either enraptured by a performance of Rossini's opera *La Donna del Lago* at the Teatro San Carlo in Naples, or overwhelmed by the frescoes in the Church of Santa Croce when he ordains a new psychosomatic travel-related disorder called Stendhal Syndrome (aka Monument Burnout). What is certain is that he faints with some sort of art attack (aka *hyperkulturemia, or* too much culture*)*. Universal symptoms include: rapid heartbeat, dizziness, confusion and hallucinations brought on by an overdose of beautiful art, old paintings, artistic masterpieces or stage performances—combined with a lack of food and suitable adult beverages. I know the feeling well!

The Black Ball Line begins scheduled trans-Atlantic service with four so-called packet ships, the *Amity, Courier, Pacific* and the *James Monroe,* running between Liverpool and New York City. This service proves popular among banks shuttling between London and Wall Street cutting normal travel time to just *23-days heading east and 40-days heading west!* Yikes! Thank you Boeing for your 747's!

Pierre Joseph Pelletier (1788–1842) and Joseph Bienaimé Caventou (1795–1877), two French scientists, discover a method for extracting quinine (aka Jesuits Powder) from the bark of the cinchona tree (aka the fever tree, and named after the Spanish Countess of Chinchon in the 1630's) that the Quechua Indians of Peru and Bolivia had long ago discovered as a helpful remedy against malaria. By 1825 the British East India Company introduces it to company men throughout Asia in the form of tonic water by adding water, sugar, lime (aka Indian tonic water) and gin (aka the classic gin-and-tonic) as an ounce of prevention for travelers from the bite of killer mosquitoes. We know it well...

1818

Karl Drais von Sauerbronn (1785–1851), a German inventor, constructs and exhibits in Paris on the 6th of April, his *Laufmaschine* (aka Running Machine) a type of pre-bicycle. The steerable Laufmaschine was made entirely of wood and had no pedals; a rider would push his/her feet against the ground to make the machine go forward. (Frenchman Comte Mede de Sivrac created a *celerifere*, an early bicycle precursor that had no steering capabilities in earlier in 1790. And it was not until Ernest Michaux (1813-1883), a Parisian blacksmith, created the modern bicycle pedal and cranks in 1861 that we had a real modern bicycle.)

1819

The magnificent *Museo Nacional del Prado* located in Madrid, Spain, is opened to the public for all to see in November.

Stamford Raffles (1781–1826), a British statesman, founds the former Malaysian Peninsula area known as the Lion City as Singapore for *God and Country* (aka England) to counter growing Dutch interests in the region.

1821

The Santa Fe Trail, a transportation route between Missouri and Santa Fe, New Mexico, that ran straight through native American Comanche territory, begins serving as a vital commercial and military highway—that is until the introduction of the railroad in 1880.

Theodore Dwight (1796–1866), an American author, publishes a guidebook entitled, *Tour in Italy*. Later in 1825, he compiles the travelogues of his uncle Timothy at Yale, and publishes *The Northern Traveller*.

1822

Gideon Miner Davison (1791-1869), an American writer, publishes the first tourist guidebooks for North America; called *The Fashionable Tour:*

A Guide to Travellers Visiting The Middle and Northern States and the Provinces of Canada. It was followed up in 1825 with *The Fashionable Tour: An Excursion to the Springs, Niagara, Quebec and Boston.* Guidebooks had indeed become fashionable.

1824
The National Gallery of Britain was formally opened to the public on the 10th of May, at 100 Pall Mall in London.

1825
The Erie Canal opens for business connecting Albany, New York on the Hudson River in the east, with Buffalo, New York on Lake Erie and the Great Lakes in the west. At 584 kilometers (363 miles), it saved passengers and traders time and money. Infrastructure is good for business!

George Stephenson (aka the Father of Railways) (1781-1845), an English civil engineer, establishes what is reputed to be the world's first public railway using steam engines, called the Stockton & Darlington in England on the 27th of September (See: 1807). It moved a lot of coal, quicker and cheaper than ever before along its 40 kilometer (25-mile) line. His rail gauge of 1,435 millimeters (4 feet 8½ inches) has becomes the world's standard railway track gauge.

> **Did You Know?** The mosquito is the world's biggest killer infecting approximately 250 million people a year and causing about 700 million cases of severe fever. Malaria, fully preventable nowadays, kills between one and three million people annually—this represents at least one death every 30 seconds.

The term "*visa*" first appears in English legislation. More paperwork and additional fees for us travelers is assured.

Henry Dilworth Gilpin (1801-1860), an American lawyer and future Attorney General of the United States, kills time in his youth over-achieving at university writing a guidebook entitled: *A Northern Tour: Being a Guide to Saratoga, Lake George, Niagara, Canada, Boston.*

1826

Nicéphore Niépce (aka Joseph Niépce) (1765-1833), a French inventor and voyeur, takes the first known photograph—an eight hour exposure—in France. (And by the way, later, he also invents the world's first internal combustion engine (aka *Pyréolophore*), with his brother Claude in 1807.)

Stanislas Baudry (1777-1830), a retired French army officer and enterprising man, who had earlier built public baths on the edge Nantes, France—run from the surplus heat from his flour mill—sets up a short stage line between the center of town and his baths. He calls it the omnibus, and it is the earliest organized urban public transit system. It moves 6-passengers at a time. His idea spreads to Paris in 1828 and the beginning of *Le Metro* in 1900 is established.

1827

Abraham Brower (1761-1855), an American entrepreneur from New York City, builds the first U.S. public transportation system, operating a twelve-seat stagecoach (aka omnibus) along Broadway from the Battery to Bleecker Street.

Joseph Ludwig Franz Ressel (1793-1857), a Czech inventor, produces the iron-built screw-driven propulsion system (*aka* propellers), that greatly enhances sailing. The first trans-Atlantic journey of a ship powered by a screw-propeller took place in 1839.

New Orleans' first casino (aka saloon) opens with the south becoming the early gaming capital of America with its open attitude towards gaming, reflecting the Spanish, French, and early Virginian traditions, and before the outbreak of the Civil War in 1861, over 6,000 gambling locations operate in America mostly in San Francisco, Chicago, New York and Boston. (Bar historians reveal that legend claims the very first western-style saloon, serving trappers, settlers and cattlemen alike, was established at Brown's Hole, Wyoming in 1822.)

1828

René Caillié (1799-1838), a French explorer, gets the recognition for being the "first European to return alive from the town of Timbuktu," and winning the Paris-based Société de Géographie prize of 10,000 francs for being the first European to visit it—and return alive! An amazing story too…

1829

Karl Baedeker (1801–1859), a German publisher, publishes J. A. Klein's guidebook, under the title *Rheinreise von Mainz bis Köln* (aka Travelling the Rhine from Mainz to Cologne) on onionskin paper. The original *Baedeker* in English guidebook, *The Rhine* is published in 1861. Baedeker's company becomes synonymous with travel guides prints. One of Karl's most understated quotes was: "*The traveler's ambition often exceeds his power of endurance.*" How true…

The Coney Island House Hotel opens in New York.

Tremont House (aka Tremont Hotel), opens in Boston becoming maybe the earliest five-star hotel by 1829 standards! The 170-room hotel is often referred to as the beginning of First Class Service, including indoor plumbing, toilets and baths, free soap, a reception area, doors that locked and bellboys.

The Welland Canal, a 42 kilometer (27-mile) canal that connects Lake Ontario with Lake Erie allowing ships to avoid that troublesome Niagara Falls, opens.

CHAPTER SEVEN

The Building of Tourism Infrastructure (1830 – 1898):
At this juncture in time, travel becomes a technical pursuit for *homo touristicus*; in that man starts building bigger and better more efficient machines to rest his limbs and get him from place to place faster—and *en mass*. The revolutionary age of the steam engine is upon us and man starts building the modern-day infrastructure that keeps the whole transportation system—and man—moving along; by constructing bigger ships, canals and sea ports for water travel; or rail lines, giant train stations, byways and intercity systems for inland ground travel; or grand city hotels for staying the night. Tourist attractions start popping up to entertain the now more mobile *homo touristicus*, and in turn, travelers also begin to chronicle their travel adventures more, sharing their thoughts, impressions and war stories.

1830
George Stephenson (See: 1825), begins operating the 51.5 kilometer (32-mile) Manchester-Liverpool line, the first modern railway line that consists of a double track and a regular schedule.

The *Geographical Society of London* (aka Royal Geographical Society) is founded in England for the expressed purpose of the "advancement of geographical science." A long list of luminary members include: Charles Darwin, David Livingstone, John Hanning Speke, Henry Morton Stanley, Ernest Shackleton and Sir Edmund Hillary, among others. (www.rgs. org)

1831

Sir James Clark Ross (1800-1862), a British explorer and naval officer, takes missions to both the Arctic and Antarctica polar regions, performing magnetic surveys. He locates the true north magnetic pole on Boothia Peninsula, and later charts much of the Antarctica coastline, and in 1841 he discovered the—what else should we name it, but, err, the Ross Sea!—and the Victoria Barrier, which is later renamed the Ross Ice Shelf. He is a cold-hearted man.

Alexis de Tocqueville (1805–1859), a witty Frenchmen, explores the New World and the United States for an extended period, and reports his famous observational findings in *Journey to America*.

The *Trail of Tears* was the so-named route of the forced relocation of the First Nation Cherokee people from their Georgia and Alabama area homes west to the Oklahoma Territory...over 4,000 of the 15,000 relocated Cherokee died while traveling to their promised land (sic) during the dead of winter.

1832

The Democratic Party (*formerly* the Democrat-Republicans), held their first convention (aka convention tourism) in Baltimore, Maryland, to nominate Andrew Jackson as their candidate. The good times roll in Baltimore as ladies of the evening are shipped in from nearby New York City. Convention fever catches on in America.

John G. Stephenson (1809-1893), an Irish-American inventor, builds the first horse-drawn streetcar in America, called the New York and Harlem Railroad that ran along the Bowery between 14th Street and Prince Street and in New York City. The second city to operate a streetcar system is New Orleans in 1835.

1833

America's first steam railroad, the South Carolina Canal and Rail Road Company, begins running scheduled service over its 219 kilometer (136-mile) line from Charleston to Hamburg. When opened, it was also the longest railroad in the world.

The Clifton Hotel, built on the Canadian-side of Niagara Falls opens at the base of Ferry Road, becoming the first hotel at the scenic spot—making Niagara Falls maybe the first ever U.S. roadside attraction. The hotel was destroyed by fire in 1898, but with the increased use of automobiles by the 1920s, Niagara Falls saw considerable growth as a tourist destination.

1834

Otokichi (aka John Matthew Ottoson) (1818–1867), a Japanese sailor, is lost at sea and sails adrift for 14-months floating from Japan's coast all the way to Washington State's Olympic Peninsula. After surviving that harrowing journey, attempts are made to repatriate him to Japan and he circles the globe only to be unable to ever actually return to his native land due to the happenstance of his life. *Ah*, bitter-sweet serendipity…

1835

Anna Maria Tussaud (aka Madame Tussaud) (1761-1850), a morbid French artist, establishes her first permanent wax (aka *cabinet de cire)* exhibition in London's Baker Street at the Baker Street Bazaar.

William Wordsworth (1770–1850), the romantic English poet, oddly pens a guidebook entitled, *A Guide Through the District of the Lakes in the North of England*….yet he later complains about the tourist lot, "*…the railway with its swarms of pleasure-seekers, most of them thinking that they do not fly fast enough through the country which they have come to see.*"

1836

John Murray III (1808–1892), heir to a British publishing house, starts printing *Murray Handbooks*, a series of travel guides from which all modern-day guides are directly descended. The successful firm was acquired in 1915 by the Blue Guides.

William Cornwallis Harris (1807-1848), an English officer and hunter, this Victorian-era traveler is said to be the first to begin the tradition of "going on safari" during an extended trip to Africa. He writes about his efforts in *The Wild Sports of Southern Africa* (1839). Back then they had the Big Seven unlike the Big Five they have today…sadly, the Missing Two are evidently extinct!

Drachenfels (*aka* Dragon's Rock), a mountain 321 meter (1,053-feet) high in the Siebengebirge mountain range outside Bonn, Germany, is credited as being the world's first real nature reserve. Although that is disputed and scant evidence proves it so—but maybe a fact nonetheless?

Charles Robert Darwin (1809–1882), a tormented English scientist, returns from his five-year global tour on the HMS *Beagle*—with a severe case of *mal de debarquement* syndrome (aka boat sway sickness) triggered by a few years at sea! He pens not only *The Voyage of the Beagle* in 1839, but another kind of important book—*On the Origin of Species* in 1859! He rocks the world.

John Jacob Astor (1763–1848), America's first multi-millionaire, holds the grand opening of his Park Hotel (aka Astor House) on Broadway between Vesey and Barclay Streets in New York City. It was a huge place with 309 rooms in its six story building, and becomes the standard of things to come.

1837
Louis-Jacques-Mandé Daguerre (1789-1851), a French chemist, invents a method of taking photographs he calls *daguerreotypes* and were the first clear and permanent photographs. John Herschel (1792 –1871), an English chemist, later coins the term photograph in 1839. While even later, William Henry Fox Talbot (1800-1877), a British inventor, who while on holidays at Lake Como, Italy, advances photography even further in 1841 with what was designated as the *calotype* process. And camera-toting Japanese tourists have been ever thankful!

The Brantly hotel (aka St. James Hotel) opens in Selma, Alabama. Still there, the 42-room hotel is the only surviving ante-bellum riverfront hotel in Selma. It is also haunted according to some, with the ghost of Jesse James—a frequent guest—still roaming the halls.

A small group of costumed revelers, funded by a wealthy plantation owner, walk the streets of New Orleans, United States, in the earliest documented *Mardi Gras* parade—and nothing says having fun at a great party like getting thrown up on and groped at all-American *Mardi Gras* festivities, *circa* 2000.

1838

Isambard Kingdom Brunel (1806-1859), a British civil engineer, builds England's Great Western Railway (GWR) (*aka* God's Wonderful Railway, Great Way Round, and the Holiday Line), a 36 kilometer (22.5-mile) line from Paddington Station in London to Maidenhead Bridge station. (He really intended to go all the way to Bristol to enhance his shipping empire, but was stopped short.) Isambard later builds the *Great Western,* which at the time was the longest ship in the world at 72 meters (236-feet) with a 76-meter keel, which crosses the Atlantic in record time—just 15-days!

1839

Samuel Cunard (1787-1865), a Canadian entrepreneur, establishes the British and North American Royal Mail Steam-Packet Company moving mail and passengers on the Liverpool–Halifax–Boston route when Cunard's first steamship, the *RMS Britannia,* sets sail with 63-passengers. In 1879, he reorganizes under the Cunard Steamship Company, Ltd for his trans-Atlantic steamship empire to begin.

1840c

Horace Mann (1796-1859), an American educational reformer and huge proponent of universal public education, successfully lobbies the U.S. Congress to alter school calendars—out of concern that rural schooling was insufficient and that over stimulating young minds in the city could lead to nervous disorders or insanity—and invents what is today known as summer vacation. American families have never been the same. You couldn't say that family road trips began occurring, because station wagons and SUV's hadn't been invented yet!

Built on the exotic romantic notions and the mystic of foreign lovers, British women of means and of a certain age are known to take "romance romps" to Rome, Italy.

1840

RMS Britannia, the first ship under the British and North American Royal Mail Steam Packet Company (aka Cunard Steamship Company), left Liverpool on the 12.5-day transatlantic crossing to Halifax, Canada. She travels fast as speed was about 16 km/h (8.5 knots)—but faster with favorable winds! They take a cow to supply fresh milk to the passengers. Charles Dickens (1812-1870), later takes the voyage in 1842.

The world's first adhesive postage stamp, the so-called *Penny Black,* begins getting licked in England on May 6th. A simple portrait of the young Queen Victoria launches the great hobby of stamp collecting (aka philatelists) for travelers everywhere.

1841

The earliest large wagon trains organized at Independence hit The Oregon Trail that by this time zigzags some 3,220 kilometers (2,000 miles) from Independence, Missouri to Portland, Oregon. The legendary U.S. West is open for business and emigration.

Thomas Cook (1808-1892), an English-Baptist entrepreneur, originates the first railway tour by taking 570 fellow temperance campaigners aboard an 18 kilometer (11-mile) train at Leicester Station for a day of relaxation at a Temperance Society rally in England. Thus begins the idea of "inclusive package" tours from these humble beginnings; one wonders how Cook would feel about the Sex Tour business? The Archbishop of Canterbury, Baron Runcie (1921-2000), once said of Cook: *"I sometimes think that Thomas Cook should be numbered among the secular saints. He took travel from the privileged and gave it to the people."* Indeed he did…

1842

Charles Dickens (1812–1870), a British novelist, pens the mocking and unflattering *American Notes for General Circulation*, his travelogue detailing his trip to North America where he mostly visited prisons and mental institutions.

1843

Blackgang Chine cliff-top park is established on the Isle of Wright as a rather odd theme park, with simple gardens, and steps built for beach access; with the real fascination seeming to be a huge whale skeleton on display for the morbid curiosity of all. A gift shop followed with great success—and "The Blackgang Experience" had begun as hordes of Victorian and Edwardian families arrived.

The joyous Tivoli Gardens, amusement park and pleasure garden is opened in Copenhagen, Denmark.

George Borrow (1803-1881), a precocious English writer, pens the engrossing *The Bible in Spain* recounting his adventures roaming that country—with side trips to Portugal and Morocco—as a Bible salesman! He really wants for cultural immersion and becomes obsessed with the Romani people (aka Gypsies), and later writes a novel called *The Romany Rye*. The Romany of Spain make him an honorary *Gitanos*.

1844

The advent of pleasure cruises is linked to Peninsula & Oriental Steam Navigation Company (P&O), taking passengers from Britain to Spain and Portugal in 1822, and then to Malaysia and Hong Kong in 1844. A new travel industry begins as people begin to travel to "see and do," not just for the necessity of transit.

Samuel Morse (1791-1872), an American engineer, invents the telegraph and revolutionizes communications. Direct travel is no longer required— using boats, horses, trains, walking, etc...—in communicating something between Point A and Point B. Real time communications becomes a reality. His initial telegram delivered on the 24th of May, read: "*What hath god wrought!*" Aside from telephones, e-mail, and Skype video, this is a big paradigm shift.

William M. Tacherary (1811-1863), an English satirical writer, pens his *Notes on a Journey From Cornhill to Grand Cairo* under the name Mr. M.A. Titmarsh, after visiting Egypt. Thinking travelogues were lowbrow, he decided to protect his fame with a pseudonym!

The French Industrial Exposition takes place in Paris, marking the beginning of regular international expositions. (See: 1798)

1845

John Franklin (1786-1847), an English navigator and Arctic explorer, sets out on his ill-fated North-West Passage search. The mystery lingers and stories of cannibalism abound.

Thomas Cook (See: 1841), publishes his original travel book entitled, *A Handbook of the Trip to Liverpool*. Cook's first guidebooks, *Switzerland* and *Holland, Belgium & the Rhine*, were later published in 1874.

Richard Ford (1796-1858), an English writer, who became a frequent visitor of Spain, publishes *Handbook for Travellers in Spain*.

1846

The Lake Compounce amusement park is opened in Briston, Connecticut, when a local scientist announced he was going to "blow something up" in an experiment. His experiment failed, but this being America, thousands showed up to see and hear the blast. He decided right then and there to cash in and build the amusement park! It is the oldest continuously operating amusement park in North America.

The earliest looping gravity railway (aka a roller coaster), is exhibited at Frascati Gardens, in Paris, France. The French called the device *Chemin du Centrifuge*, others call it nauseating.

Town and Country, the general interest lifestyle magazine launches with a regular travel-related feature. Let the travel writer query letters begin.

Launched originally as a ferry boat taking travelers from the American side to the Canadian side, the first edition of the famous *Maid of the Mist* begins service and in 1854 begins awing tourists fulltime who are willing to get wet and get a close up and personal look at the Niagara Falls, taking adventure tourism to a different level.

Peter Felix Richards (1808-1868), a Scottish expatriate entrepreneur, opens Richards' Hotel and Restaurant (aka Astor House Hotel, and then Pujiang in 1959) on The Bund in Shanghai, China. It is the first foreigners' hotel built in China.

With a railway line completed, Blackpool, England booms and becomes maybe the world's first popular seaside resort town (See: 1793). The Blackpool Pleasure Beach amusement park crops up later in 1896. The town elders not wanting to miss out on a good thing quickly employ the world's earliest tourism tax on visitors. Exorbitant hotel taxes, car rental taxes, and airport taxes would quickly follow in the coming century!

Sophia Lane Poole (1804-1891), an English writer, authors *The Englishwoman in Egypt,* in which she tells of her exploits veiling as a local to gain access to harems, bathhouses, and other "women-only" areas in the Islamic country. Rumor has it that she later works as a reporter for *60 Minutes*.

The forerunner of the Associated Press is founded in New York City, as a news pool formed by five New York City daily newspapers in order to share the expenses of covering the Mexican War. It establishes an international reporting community.

1847
The London Zoo opens to the public and is the world's first scientific zoo allowing public visitors. It was originally opened in 1828 as a collection for scientific study by the Zoological Society of London established by Stamford Raffles (See: 1819).

Gambling becomes legal in the Portuguese enclave of Macau that quickly became known as "Monte Carlo of the Orient".

1848
Maxime Du Camp (1822–1894), a French writer, pioneers publishing by publishing the earliest known travel photographs in *Souvenirs et paysages d'orient* (See: 1837) Since the market for armchair travelers is good, he follows it up with his *Egypte, Nubie, Palestine, Syrie* in 1852.

Antonio Manguino, a French showman, introduces a primitive Ferris wheel called a wooden pleasure wheel, at his start-up fair in Walton Spring, Georgia. "Pleasure wheels" may have been earlier invented in the Ottoman-controlled area Bulgaria, with the idea being brought to Vienna later (See: 1897).

1849
The New World Coffee Stand (*aka* The Tadich Grill) on Clay Street opens for business in San Francisco, California. Crab Louis's have never been the same!

Rufus Porter (1792-1884), an American painter and wannabe inventor, founds *Scientific American* in 1841 and advertises a scheme to fly Gold Rush prospectors to California in an "800-foot steam-powered airship with accommodations for 50 to 100 passengers." It never happens—mechanical difficulties!

1850c

The original transatlantic telegraph cable links North America with Europe directly in real time for the first time—actually it is between two islands, Newfoundland and Ireland.

1851

The 1851 Great Exhibition of the Works of Industry of all Nations is held in London, unveiling the Crystal Palace, a 33 meter high exhibition hall made of iron and glass temporarily built in Hyde Park by Joseph Paxton. It is recognized as the first World's Fair.

The Excursionist magazine (1851-1902) is launched by Thomas Cook (See: 1841 & 1845), and is widely regarded as the first travel-focus magazine. It was later followed by *The Traveller's Gazette* magazine (1902-1939).

1852

Jean Bernard Léon Foucault (1819-1868), a French physicist, invents the gyroscope as a navigational aid as it helps offset the effect of the Earth's rotation.

The State Hermitage museum in St. Petersburg, Russia founded in 1764 by Catherine the Great, finally opens to the public.

The New Street (aka Birmingham New Street) railway station is built, and is thought to be the first ever inter-city train station, that links the London and Birmingham Railway. (Although records indicated that the old Madrid Atocha station opened earlier in 1851, but burned down a few years later?) New Street was the beginning of many great railway terminals being built around the world, including: Zürich Hauptbahnhof in 1847; St. Petersburg's Vitebsk Rail Terminal in 1853; Paris's Gare du Nord in 1864; New York City's Grand Central Terminal (GCT) in 1871; Istanbul's Haydarpaşa Terminal in 1872; Bombay's great Victoria Terminus opens in 1887; New York's Pennsylvania Station in 1919; Chicago's Union Station in 1925; and Los Angeles Union Station in 1939. Railways stations always make me think about E.M. Forster's great line, *"Railway termini are our gates to the glorious and the unknown. Through them we pass out into adventure and sunshine, and to them, alas! we return."* Yes we do…

1853

David Livingstone (1813-1873), a heroic Scottish explorer, discovered Victoria Falls and writes *Missionary Travels* in 1857. Livingstone, upon meeting up with the lost H. M. Stanley, gave us the popular quotation, *"Dr. Livingstone, I presume?"* David later dies of hemorrhoids, so much for sexy adventuring! But he did leave us with this wonderful travel truism saying, *"I am prepared to go anywhere, provided it be forward."*

Richard Burton (1821-1890), an English explorer and master linguist, who is best known for his travels to Mecca disguised as a Muslim and then writing *Pilgrimage to Mecca*; also writes *First Footsteps in E Africa*. He is said to have mastered about 30 different languages!

The London Zoo (See: 1847) creates the first public aquarium, the popular attraction became known as the "Fish House" with its popularity. P.T. Barnum (1810– 1891), an American businessman, quickly followed with the first American aquarium that he opened on Broadway in New York.

The first of three of the well-documented New York's World's Fair takes place within the small confines of Bryant Park in downtown Manhattan, New York City. The fair's theme was called the Exhibition of the Industry of All Nations. (See: 1939 & 1964)

Edward Stanford (1827-1904), an English armchair traveler and map seller, opens his flagship Stanford's in London and specializes in travel books. It moves to its current location, maps and all, in 1901. (www.stanfords.co.uk)

The "flower park" known as Hanayashiki, opens to the public in Tokyo, Japan. It expands over the years and is Asia's first theme park.

1854

Louis Vuitton Malletier (aka Louis Vuitton) (1821-1892), a French designer, opens the doors of his initial store on *Rue Neuve des Capucines* in Paris and builds up his legend around travel by creating fashionable lightweight luggage.

1855

James Gall (1784-1874), a Scottish clergyman, designs what is christened as the Orthographic Equal-Area Projection map in the *Scottish Geographical Magazine*.

The German encyclopedia *Brockhaus Conversationslexikon* finally defines what a *tourist* is: "*...a traveler who does not link the journey with any e.g. scientific purpose, but only travels to have made the journey and be able to describe it subsequently.*" Indeed.

Visitors out west were already coming to see the nature in all its glory in the Yosemite Valley, United States (See: 1872), the Indian encampment, the Giant Sequoias, the rock formations, waterfalls and critters that make it special. The Wawona Hotel was built near the Mariposa Grove in 1879, and the large tunnel cut through the even larger tree had tourists taking pictures by 1881.

1856

Alexander von Humboldt (1769-1852), a German naturalist, develops the first weather map, an isotherm map that contains lines of equal average temperatures. The Weather Channel would be soon to follow—okay a hundred years or so!

Although celebrated for many reasons in many places, Australia establishes the modern era May Day, a "workers holiday," on the 1st of May. May Day is regarded world-wide as International Workers' Day (aka Labor Day).

Walt Whitman (1819-1892), an American poet, pens *Song of the Open Road* bringing travelers everywhere these words:
"A foot and light-hearted I take to the open road,
Healthy, free, the world before me,
The long brown path before me,
Leading wherever I choose."

1857

Samuel Sharp, a Canadian, invents the earliest true railway sleeper car; although George Pullman (See: 1865), would get all the credit and fortune.

1858

Henry Ruttan (1792–1871), a Canadian inventor, designs a system for heating and cooling railway coaches (aka air-conditioning). Thank you!

John H. Speke (1827-1864), a British army officer, who after three expeditions traveling the African Nile writes *Journal of the Discovery*. He is credited with locating the source of the Nile coming from Lake Tanganyika and Lake Victoria. Now we know.

An eraser is fitted to the end of a pencil to help travel writers correct their spelling errors and ~~longish~~ meandering prose.

The first cruises offered by P&O Cruises, a British company, on the ship *Ceylon* begin taking place. Launched the same year, the *Great Eastern*, at 692 feet long, becomes the world's longest cruise ship. Samuel Johnson's (See: 1775) apt quote comes to mind, *"Being on a ship is being in a jail, with the chance of being drowned."*

John Murray (See: 1836) publishes *A Handbook Of Travel-Talk: A Collection Of Dialogues And Vocabularies Intended To Serve As Interpreter To Travellers In Germany, France, and Italy*, is the first practical book to help with translations for travelers.

A Hamburg-America company liner, the *RMS Austria*, making a North Atlantic crossing to Halifax catches fire and sinks with all 471 aboard dying on the 13th of September.

Bernadette Soubirous (1844 -1879), a miller's daughter and 14-year-old French girl, claims to have witnessed a series of visions in a cave of the Virgin Mary, outside a town called Lourdes, France. Tourist creep being what it is, the masses started coming in 1867 and the simple grotto now receives over 6 million pilgrims a year, covers 51 hectares (126 acres), has twenty-two places of worship, dozens of on-site chaplains, and permanent and seasonal staff numbering in the hundreds. Religious shrines are big business and are a big part of the travel industry.

Prior to the radio being invented, the only real means of communication across the Atlantic Ocean was to physically connect North America to Europe, and the first transatlantic telegraph cable was installed and operating this year between Heart's Content, Newfoundland, Canada and Valentia, Ireland.

1860c

Benjamin Disraeli (1804–1881), a former British Prime Minister and quotable guy, sums up the travel writing genre to come: *"Like all great travelers, I have seen more than I remember, and remember more than I have seen."*

Historic documents reveal that a sanctuary dedicated to *Our Lady of Travel* exist in Rio de Janeiro, where the pious people of Brazil seek the protection of the Blessed Virgin on their journeys. It certainly wouldn't be the first, or last…

1860

The *SS Great Eastern*, sailing between Southampton, England and New York City, makes its inaugural voyage. Nicknamed "Leviathan," it was the largest, grandest sailing vessel of her day and had a 4,000 passenger capacity!

1861

Henri Mouhot (1826-1861), a French naturalists, discovers—was it ever lost?—the Khmer people's Angkor Wat ruins. Angkor may have been the "largest preindustrial city in the world" and the Cambodian ruins rivals in size the 125 square kilometer Mayan city of Tikal in Guatemala. By 2010, about one million visitors a year from around the world come to visit it.

Tourist visiting Angkor.
(Author Photo)

An internal type of passport is introduced to all American's as a result of the Civil War in the United States.

1862

With the completion of the first railroad to Coney Island, it quickly becomes a popular day-visit seaside resort.

No. 4472 *Flying Scotsman* (*formerly* No. 1472), is a named passenger rail service operating between Scotland and England. The 10AM departure from London Kings Cross station to Edinburgh, Scotland's Waverley station (the down service), and its compatriot from Edinburgh to London (the up service), have traditionally been known by this name since June 1862. In

1862, the journey time was ten and a half hours; today, it takes just over four hours.

A second attempt (See: 1796) at reviving the ancient Olympic Games takes place in Liverpool, England, with the Grand Olympic Festival. It lasts five years. (See: 1896)

It is said that the first gin martini (aka a Martinez), was created when Jerry Thomas, the "Principal Barman" attending San Francisco's Occidental Hotel bar, created the so-called *Martinez* daily for a client who took a ferry to Martinez, California. As in most bar stories, counter claims are also made that the barkeep at New York City's Knickerbocker Hotel named Martini di Arma di Taggia, created the concoction in 1911...Maybe, *maybe* not?

Did You Know? Hotel bars seem to be a breeding ground for new cocktail inventions—could it be the diverse clientele? A few famous cocktails created at hotels:

Singapore Sling	- Raffles Hotel (1915)
Margarita	- Rancho La Gloria Hotel (1938)
Old Fashion	-Waldorf-Astoria Hotel (1881c)
The Cosmopolitan	-The Strand (1984)
Tom Collins	- Plater's Hotel (1851c)
Piña Colada	- *Caribe* Hilton (1954)
Black Russian	-Hotel Metropole (1949)
Bloody Mary	-St. Regis Hotel (1934?)
Long Island Ice Tea	-Oak Beach Inn (1976)

1863

Cook Tours, always the travel industry innovator, offers prepaid international package tours to Switzerland for the first time.

The London Underground (aka The Tube) opens as the world's first underground railway with six stations: London Bridge, Euston, Paddington, King's Cross, Bishops gate and Waterloo. The initial section of the London Underground—the Metropolitan Line—running between Paddington and Farringdon was the world's first urban underground passenger-carrying railway. After initial delays in the scheme's adoption in 1854, public traffic eventually began on January 10th. By 2010, *the Tube* had 270 stations and over 400 kilometers (250 miles) of track.

Francois Blanc (1806-1877), a French promoter extraordinaire, accepts an invitation from the Crown Prince of Monaco to open and operate the newly built Monte-Carlo Casino.

1864

Johannes Badrutt, a Swiss hotelier, makes St. Moritz, Switzerland, popular with the British aristocracy as winter holidays hot spot by proposing a bet to a few well-to-do summer guests: "…that they should return in winter and if it was not to their liking, he (Johannes) would pay for the cost of their journey from London and back. If they found St. Moritz attractive in winter, he would invite them to stay as his guests for as long as they wished." A *win-win* for any traveler! Needless to say, winter tourism takes off for the scenic Swiss spot.

Sir John Kirk (1832–1922), a Scottish explorer, publishes "*Hints to Travellers*" in *Journal of the Royal Geographical Society* (1864), 34, 290-2.

Jules Verne (1828-1905), a French sci-fi author, creates volcano tourism with his epic novel *Journey to the Center of the Earth,* and when his Professor Lidenbrock descends into the crater of Iceland's Snæfellsjökull volcano (See: 1866).

1865
Founded in Paris as the International Telegraph Union becomes the world's first specialized international agency. The International Telecommunication Union (ITU) took its present name in 1934.

George Pullman (1831-1897), an American industrialist, begins building a luxurious sleeping car named *Pioneer* (aka the Pullman Sleeper cars). (See: 1857)

Sofia and Julius Gerhardt, a Russian animal-loving couple, found the St. Petersburg zoological gardens (aka Leningrad Zoo) located in Alexander Park. It closes in 1909.

The Grand Pier (aka Teignmouth Pier) with a 212 meter (696-feet) in length pier, and now an amusement park, opens in Teignmouth, England.

1866
Cook Tours, keeps innovating by offering prepaid hotel vouchers (aka hotel coupons) for travelers booking in England and traveling abroad. It helps take the guesswork out of finding accommodations.

Pandit Nain Singh Rawat, an intrepid North Indian *pundit* (aka surveyor, and what lesser gentlemen would call a spy), takes his epic 1,900 kilometer (1200-mile) trek from Leh in Kashmir to Lhasa in Tibet, where he meets the Dalai Lama.

Samuel Langhorne Clemens (aka Mark Twain) (1835–1910), a real American humorist, visits Kilauea located in Hawaii's Volcanoes National Park and admires the potential of volcanic action, and creates what is now known as volcano tourism. Tourists really start going in 1983 after a little eruption and hundreds of volcano tourists flock to see the show at Iceland's Eyjafjallajokull in the spring of 2010 (See: 2010)

1867

Sylvester Howard Roper (1823-1896), an American inventor, constructs a two-cylinder steam-engine motorcycle—powered by coal!—called a Roper steam velocipede. This can be considered the original motorcycle.

Charles Feltman (1841–1910), a German-American chef, starts selling the German version (*frankfurter*) and the Austrian version (*wiener*) in Coney Island to visitors and calls it a hot dog!

John Muir (1838 –1914), a Scottish-born naturalist, begins his years as an advocate for Mother Earth and her beauty when he embarks on a long hike from Indiana to Florida that is chronicled in his book *A Thousand-Mile Walk to the Gulf* published in 1916. Muir later establishes the uniquely special John Muir Trail (JMT) through California's Sierra Nevada Mountain range and the Yosemite Valley area; he becomes a life-long advocate for protecting our natural beauty and is a key voice in the creation of the U.S. National Park system (See: 1872). John was also a conscientious objector and spent time in Canada (beginning a long tradition that would last until the mid-1970's) during the Civil War to avoid all the killing. John told us how he really felt about urban traveling with this quote: *"Only by going alone in silence, without baggage, can one truly get into the heart of the wilderness. All other travel is mere dust and hotels and baggage and chatter."*

The now famous Catacombs of Paris (aka *Catacombes de Paris*) open to the public creating a whole new type of urban exploration tourist (aka creepers or urban spelunkers), who seek out the unseen and off-limits parts of urban areas, usually tunnels, crypts, old ruins, alleged haunted house, and abandoned buildings (industrial archaeology) of note.

1868

The initial publication of the ABC Alphabetical Railway Guide (aka the *Official Guide of the Railways*, and now known as the *Official Railway Guide* (ORG), is printed to assist business travelers with their schedules—and keep trains from crashing into each other! Which somehow reminds one of the great American sociologist Thorstein Veblen's famous line, "... *No one traveling on a business trip would be missed if he failed to arrive.*" Well, now they do arrive, and on time too!

1869

The first transcontinental North American railroad is completed when tracks of the Union Pacific met those of the Central Pacific at Promontory, Utah, on the 10th of May. Travel was simple, two trains, one train from the east and one from the west run each week; it sufficiently met the travel demands at that time.

Mark Twain (See: 1866), who after a series of international trips writes *Innocents Abroad*, followed by *Roughing It* in 1872. He is quoted as saying, among a million other things, that, "*Travel is fatal to prejudice, bigotry, and narrow-mindedness.*"

The 164 kilometer (102-mile) long Suez Canal, linking the Mediterranean Sea with the Red Sea, opens on November 17th. The project took 2.4 million Egyptian workers—of which it is claimed that more than 125,000 lost their lives!—14 years to construct. The Italian musician Verdi composes *Aida* to celebrate its grand opening.

Postcards are allowed to be posted by the Austro-Hungarian postal service and the first card is sent in 1870. It is a historical card, produced in connection with the Franco-German War. The United States would begin permitting postcard usage in 1873. It is said that the first postcards being saved as souvenirs (aka travel *tchotchkes*), began in 1893 at the Columbian Exposition in Chicago. Thus begging the fine tradition employed by *deltiologists* everywhere. (On the other hand, Theodore Hook of England may have sent a hand-painted card in 1840? And John P. Charlton of USA, patented a postal card—with no pictures on the other side?—in 1861? Semantics being what it is—who knows?)

1870

New York City's first elevated railway, the *El* (versus subway), begins operating regular service on February 14 and runs along Greenwich Street and Ninth Avenue in Manhattan.

The Atlantic City boardwalk is built. It was originally designed to keep the sand out of hotel lobbies. The idea catches on and before the Great Atlantic Hurricane of 1944, the boardwalk stretched almost 11 kilometers (seven miles)! The Traymore Hotel begins as a small boarding house in 1879. Ocean Pier (See: 1882) then opens. In 1976, voters approved a gambling referendum and the casinos came and re-vitalized the area.

Cedar Point opens as an amusement park in Sandusky, Ohio. Formerly just a scenic lake-side picnic area, that during the Civil War house a confederate prisoner of war camp, the area is developed into a real fun zone.

Man-powered rickshaws (aka *jin-riki-sha*, or man-power carriages) first appear in the streets of Japan. There is a big dispute as to who actually invented them: an American blacksmith in 1848, an American missionary to Japan in 1869, or a restaurateur in Tokyo in the same year, especially when a 1707 painting by French painter Claude Gillot, shows them on the streets of Paris? I don't know—you decide...

Les Deux Carrosses **by Claude Gillot, 1707.**
(A reproduction, the original sits in the Musée du Louvre)

George Francis Train (1829–1904), a larger-than-life American businessman, completes his second circumnavigation of the globe in just 80 days, going from San Francisco to Japan, Hong Kong, Saigon, Singapore, Suez, Marseilles, Liverpool, ending in New York City—George would circle the globe four times during his life—and is said by a few to have been the real life inspiration for Jules Verne's *Around the World in Eighty Days* (See: 1873). In 1890, Train traveled around the world in just sixty-seven days (to beat Nellie Bly's record time of seventy-two days (See: 1889-90); and in 1892 he circled the globe again in just sixty days! His autobiography, published in 1902 entitled *My Life in Many States and in Foreign Lands*, stands as a testament to life well-traveled.

1871

Fréjus Rail Tunnel (aka Mont Cenis Tunnel), a 13.7 kilometer (8.5-mile) tunnel connecting the towns of Mondane, France and Bardonecchia, Italy, cutting through the Alps is open.

British Parliament passes the Bank Holiday Act creating official days off that include: Easter Monday; Boxing Day, New Year's Day; Good Friday; the First Monday in May; and Christmas Day, among others. Although there is no legal right to time off on these days, the majority of workers not employed in essential services receive them as holidays. Bank holidays are days when banks are closed.

1872

The Metropolitan Museum of Art (aka The Met), opens in New York City. Today its collection has over two million pieces.

Yellowstone National Park becomes America's first national park, when Congress reserves the Wyoming and Montana territories "as a public park or pleasuring-ground for the benefit and enjoyment of the people." By 1916, the Interior Department was responsible for 14 national parks and 21 national monuments and implements wise-use policies. Today the National Park system comprises 384 areas. People everywhere grab onto that Victorian-era tradition of admiringly gazing-upon the landscape...

Thomas Cook does it again, and begins a 222 day around-the-world trip with nine friends.

Rand McNally & Company, a well-established Chicago-based printing company, publishes there first map in the December 1872 edition of its *Railroad Guide.*

Jules Verne does it again (See: 1864), and pens *Le tour du monde en quatre-vingts jours (aka Around the World in Eighty Days),* his fantasy around the world novel. Adventurous and inspiring, this work has led many to follow the footsteps of Fogg's fictional circumnavigation. This writer included, (See: www.GlobalScavengerHunt.com).

1873
Andrew Smith Hallidie (1836 –1900), a London-born mechanical genius, patents and operates the first cable car as the Clay Street Hill Railroad, in rolling San Francisco—ultimately sparing many horses the excruciating work of moving people over San Francisco's steep roadways takes passengers from Leavenworth up Clay Street to Kearny.

Weltausstellung 1873 Wien (aka The Vienna World's Fair), is held in Austria.

1874
America's first zoo, the Philadelphia Zoo is opened on July 1st.

Thomas Cook's company does it again, and began issuing "circular notes" to travelers that operated in the same manner of traveler's checks. (See: 1772)

1875
The Palace Hotel, built at a price of an incredible five million dollars as one of the most ornate and expensive hotels of its days, opens in San Francisco, California. With 800 rooms and covering 2.5 acres in the heart of The City, it sadly burns down in 1906 when someone tries to warm himself from the severe cold in the lobby with a small bonfire—in August! The New Palace Hotel remains one of my favorites…

The Grand Hotel Europe opens as a luxurious five-star Saint Petersburg, Russia hotel.

1876

Fred Harvey (1835-1901), an American restaurateur, is the first to begin a large-scale restaurant chain called Harvey Houses after he opens a successful lunchroom in Topeka's Santa Fe depot. He focuses on train stations and at his peak he ran 84 restaurants.

Alexander Graham Bell (1847 -1922), a Scottish-Canadian innovator, on March 10th makes the first phone call to his assistant, *"Mr. Watson, come here; I want you."* He changes communications.

Franz Sacher (1816 -1907), an Austrian confectioner, bakes the Sachatorte, after his son, Eduard Sacher (1843-1892) opens Hotel Sacher as a *maison meublée* in Vienna. The tortes on Franz...

1878

Henry Morton Stanley (1841-1904), a Welsh explorer-journalist, recounts his infamous journey in *Through the Dark Continent.*

Karl Friedrich Benz (1844-1929), a German designer, invents a motorized 3-cycle vehicle and a 4-wheel car in 1893. Expensive Mercedes-Benz's, stop signs and parking meters are sure to follow.

1879

The Oriental hotel opens as a 40-room inn along the Chao Phraya River in Bangkok, Siam (Thailand). The legend begins...

David Starr Jordan (1851–1931), an American educator, who after taking the helm of Indiana University (at the tender age of 34!) begins taking groups of students on an extended European field trip to advance their study of natural history, language, and culture. The semester study abroad program is born and by the 1920's is well-respected right-of-passage *ala* the Grand Tour (See: 1608) for young adults in North America.

1880c

The urban area population of London, England exceeds five million for the first time.

1880

The Hotel Del Monte opens in Carmel, California, a nine-iron shot away from Pebble Beach. The Old Del Monte golf course opens 20-years later. Back then, Pebble Beach could be visited by coach from the Del Monte Hotel. Golf tourism begins.

The Good Roads Movement begins to gain steam in America advocating the improvement of roads—for bicycles! It grows to later include the advocating of trans-national roads, east-west and north-south. Too bad everything old isn't new again!

Gala Amusement Park (aka Bowery Bay Beach), a New York City amusement park, also known as the "Coney Island of Queens," opens with carousels, picnic grounds and beer halls. Never heard of it? Well, it turned into LaGuardia Airport (IGA) in 1939.

William Gilpin (1813-1894), a wide-eyed American futurist, develops the idea of the so-called Cosmopolitan Railway linking all continents (except for Australia and Antarctica) in travel and commerce, which would "break down barriers and bring the world's civilizations into harmony." Now, if we could just deal with that Bering Sea issue…

1881

Oscar II (1829-1907), the King of Norway and Sweden, opens the world's first open air museum exhibiting his Royal collection at his summer residence near Christiania (aka Oslo). The original plans comprised 8 or 10 buildings intended to show the evolution of traditional Norwegian building types since the middle ages.

1882

Ocean Pier, the world's first ocean side amusement pier opens in Atlantic City, New Jersey, as the coastal city becomes celebrated for its boardwalk, casino gambling, sandy beaches, shopping centers, and view of the Atlantic Ocean. It is the inspiration for the board game *Monopoly*.

John Michael Lyons, a Canadian ticket-taker, creates the first "separable coupon ticket" in Moncton, New Brunswick, Canada. That means you get a stub to claim your baggage—simple, but effective!

The Orient Express (aka Venice Simplon-Oriental Express, (VSOE), begins service between Paris and Constantinople on October 4th. Service is later added to Budapest and London. The legendary lines operate until 1977. The original route, while not so seamless, had passengers travel from Paris to Giurgiu in Romania via Munich and Vienna, at Giurgiu, passengers were ferried across the Danube to Ruse in Bulgaria and then to pick up another train to Varna, from where they completed their journey to Istanbul by ferry.

1883

The *Normandie,* a French ocean-going ironclad battleship, becomes the first ship to have indoor plumbing. Thank you, finally, no unidentified organic matter floating in ports.

Standard time zones are introduced by the American Railway Association internationally in order to overcome the utter chaos that the existing 100+ time zones in current use cause to railway schedules. In 1885 the International Prime Meridian Conference held in Washington, D.C., finally codifies 24-international time zones. Holdouts and contrarians like: China, Nepal, India and Newfoundland, continue to confound travelers with the quirks of time-space continuum. And don't ever forget AFT— *African Flexible Time!*

1884

LaMarcus Adna Thompson (1848–1919), an American businessman, engineers the world's first roller coaster that debuts on Coney Island, New York, called the Switchback Gravity Pleasure Railway. The device is recognized as the first true roller coaster in America.

Nord Express (aka The Northern Express), was introduced in Compagnie Internationale des Wagons-Lits (CIWL), a Belgian train company. It left Paris via Brussels, Cologne, Hanover, Berlin, Konigsberg (aka Kaliningrad) and Daugavpils to Moscow and St. Petersburg. The company's vision was to see trains run from St. Petersburg, Russia to Lisbon, Portugal, in order to catch trans-Atlantic South American ocean liners. (See: 1887)

The Sarkies Brothers (Martin, Tigran, Aviet and Arshak), four brothers of Persian-American descent, open their earliest luxury hotel, the Eastern Hotel, on the island of Penang in what is now Malaysia. Later they would open and operate some of the world's great hotels in Southeast Asia including: the Oriental Hotel, in Malaysia; the Raffles Hotel in Singapore; Kartika Wijaya on Java, Indonesia; the Strand Hotel in Rangoon, Burma; and Hotel Majapahit (aka Hotel Oranje) in Surabaya, Indonesia.

John Lawson Stoddard (1850-1931), an American academic, who quits his day job to become a fulltime travel lecturer, pens his inaugural travel-related work *Red-Letter Days Abroad*.

Helen Hunt Jackson (1830–1885), an America writer and Indian activist, publishes the novel *Ramona*. The popularity of the novel inspires people to see some of the novels backdrops and starts a sort of tourism boom in Tijuana, Mexico. And then with the opening of the race track Agua Caliente in 1916, things took off for TJ, which has led to many photos of tequila infused "excursionists" wearing sombreros on the backs of black and white painted donkeys. Been there, done that! It remains the only global destination where the First World meets the Third World…

1885
Eduard Spelterini (aka King of the Skies) (1852-1931), a Swiss balloon man, who after having successfully made 17 ascents by himself in a hot air balloon, began offering commercial rides with passengers and catering to the rich and adventurous. It is said that 1,000 meter high club was created on one of his early flights!

The Banff National Park becomes the first of Canada's 39 national parks. The park encompasses over 6,640 square kilometers (2,564 square miles) of amazing mountainous terrain. Banff Springs Hotel opens later (See: 1888).

The Kiel-Canal becomes the most frequented artificial waterway in the world (See: 1784 Eider Canal).

Lee Meriwether (1863-1966), an iconic American, and maybe America's first backpacker, publishes his fantastic read, *A Tramp Trip: How To See Europe on Fifty Cents a Day*. Frommer's (See: 1957) had nothing on this guy!

The last spike is driven in the first Canadian transcontinental main line at Craigellachie, British Columbia, in the Eagle Pass on the 7th of November. Cornelius Van Horne (1843-1915), the Canadian Pacific Railway (CPR) president, makes his famous fifteen-word speech, *"All I can say is that the work has been well done in every way."* A special CPR train arrives in Port Moody, British Columbia at the Pacific Tidewater making it the first railway train ever to travel across Canada from sea-to-shining-sea.

Karl Benz (See: 1878), the famed German engineer, designs and builds the world's first practical automobile to be powered by an internal-combustion engine. Benz built his earliest four-wheeled car later in 1891, and by 1893, the Benz-Velo became the world's first mass-produced inexpensive car.

1887

James Gordon Bennett (1841–1918), the innovative New York publisher, founds *The Paris Herald*, the forerunner of *The International Herald Tribune*, the world's first international newspaper. In 2002, the IHT had a global circulation of over 263,000, of which 40% was bulk buys by major international hotel chains and air carriers. The Internet has made its ultimate demise a slow and painful death.

Thomas Stevens (1854-1935), an eccentric English cyclist, becomes the first person to bicycle around the world—very loosely defined—after a two year and eight month journey that began in San Francisco on 22 April 1884. It took him 103 days just to get to Boston!

Thomas Stevens, circa 1887.
(Harper's Weekly - 30 August 1884)

Walter T. Brownell, an American businessman, forms the oldest travel agency in North America creating the Brownell Travel Company, by personally leading ten travelers on a European tour, setting sail from New York on the *SS Devonia*. Now that is service!

The Sarkies (See: 1884), open the 10-room colonial bungalow at Beach Road in Singapore known as The Raffles Hotel. The Singapore Slings begin flowing in the Long Bar sometime around1915.

The Sud Express becomes the name of a well-known night train connection between Paris and Lisbon—the trip takes two nights. The direct link between St Petersburg and Lisbon is now complete. (See: 1884)

The Grand Hotel on Michigan's Mackinac Island is opened. The grand front porch of the hotel, at 200 meters (660-feet), is said to be the longest in the world.

Hotel Ponce de Leon opens in St. Augustine, Florida, and ushers in the novel idea of wintering in Florida! Other Gilded Age grand hotels, like the lavish 1,150-room Hotel Royal Poinciana in 1894, and the Palm Beach Inn in 1896 (aka The Breakers), solidifies the idea. The term *Snow Bird* is popularized.

Electric trolleys begin being used in Los Angeles, California and the Pacific Electric Railway (aka Red Car system) begins operating routes from downtown to Pasadena and Santa Monica and by 1911 the system had 1,600 kilometers (1,000 miles) of track "*from the mountains to the sea.*" In 1925 in a great sell-out, Red Car lines began being converted to cheaper buses. Freeways followed and gridlock has prevailed ever since! (See: 1990)

1888
Following the completion of the trans-Canada railway link (See: 1885), the Canadian Pacific Railway (CPR), opens the Hotel Vancouver and begins a cross country link of grand hotels in Canada from sea-to-shining-sea, including: Banff Springs Hotel (1888), Chateau Lake Louise (1890) and the Chateau Frontenac (1893).

The National Geographic Society is established in the United States. It was created by a group of august explorers and influential men of leisure, who, after swapping war stories at their favorite watering hole, the Cosmos Club in Washington D.C., thought it would be a grand idea to share their collective ideas with the world. Or maybe, they have a bad case of Euro-envy? (See: 1830 – Royal Geographic Society) The *National Geographic* Magazine is first published nine months later in October, and those wonderful yellow magazines that brought the whole world into my tiny bedroom have been piling up ever since. (NationalGeographic.com)

Palace Amusements, in Asbury Park, New Jersey opens with a Victorian pavilion. It expanded with a steam powered Ferris wheel in 1895—some claim the first of its kind (See: 1848). The hall of mirrors called The Crystal Maze was added in 1903. The park closed in 1998 after years of neglect—and lack of *Bruuuuuce* concerts!

George Eastman (1854–1932), an American industrialist and founder of the Eastman Kodak Company, introduces the Kodak Box Camera to the world that makes picture taking simple for the masses, with a slogan no one could resist: "*You press the button – we do the rest.*"

Frank Sprague (1857-1937), an American businessman, runs Richmond's (Virginia) entire system of streetcars using electricity.

The Prospect House hotel on Blue Mountain Lake in New York is said to be the first U.S. hotel with electric lights! (Although Thomas Edison would argue that it was the Hotel Ponce de Leon (See: 1887).

The Hotel del Coronado (aka the Del) opens in a beachside community outside San Diego, California. The Victorian-beach resort opened as the world's largest hotel and has hosted Rudolph Valentino, Charlie Chaplin, Thomas Edison, Babe Ruth, and that famous crew from the movie *Some Like It Hot*—Marilyn Monroe, Jack Lemmon and Tony Curtis, which was filmed there in 1958.

1889

Richard D'oyly Carte (1844–1901), a London-based talent agent, opens his Savoy Hotel in London. The hotel, with profits from his Gilbert and Sullivan operas, is the first luxury hotel in England that offers, among other amenities: electric lights, elevators, in room bathrooms, and hot and cold running water. Carte, always an eye for talent, hires César Ritz as the manager (See: 1898)

La Tour Eiffel (aka the Eiffel Tower) is opened at the Paris Expo. At about 81-stories in height, 324 meters (1,063-feet), it becomes a must see and is widely regarded as one of the most recognizable structures in the world. (A little know fact, until the Chrysler Building in New York City was built 40-years later, *La Tour Eiffel*, was the tallest man-made structure in the world. Over 6 million people a year visit it!

1889-90

Elizabeth Jane Cochran (*aka* Nellie Bly) (1864-1922), an American journalist—the world's first undercover reporter—re-enacts Jules Verne's book *Around the World in Eighty Days* (aka retro tourism). On November 14, 1889 she left New York on her 40,000 kilometer (24,899-mile) journey, and 72 days, six hours, eleven minutes and fourteen seconds later, she returns on 25 January 1890. She traveled by steamship, on existing railway lines with the re-enactment sponsored by New York newspaper *Cosmopolitan*. This was an amazing world record for circling the earth, which would stand until 1929, when the *Graf Zeppelin* did it in 20 days, four hours and fourteen minutes.

1890c

Sebastian Kneipp (1821-1897), a Bavarian priest, develops holistic herbal and water therapies (aka Kneipp Cure) in the Bavarian Alps village of Bad Worishofen. The spa town never looks back.

The word hobo appears to financially-challenged homeless vagabond looking for work along the way. Hobo's are *not* bums—who don't work and are often beggars, or tramps (aka gentlemen of the road)—who only work when they have to in a scavenger-like manner; and are somewhat romantized in American lore as freight-hoppers after the Civil War. The National Hobo Convention takes place each August in Britt, Iowa.

1890

The first souvenir spoons in the United States were made by Galt & Bros., Inc. of Washington D.C., featuring the profile of George Washington… only in America! I have ten.

1891

The Sheridan Hotel opens in Telluride, Colorado. The city is infamous, not only for its natural beauty and *après* skiing nightlife, but also for being the home of Butch Cassidy's 1st bank robbery, and after 1972 when the ski lifts open, for its wicked black diamond runs.

Otto Lilienthal (aka the Glide King) (1848-1896), a German aviation pioneer, makes the first of his over 2,000 gliding flights in winged hang glider-like contraptions—until his untimely death in a 1896 crash.

John William Lambert (1860–1952), an Ohio businessman, produces the first American gas-powered car, a three-wheeled buggy.

Marcellus F. Berry, an American Express lawyer, is granted four copyrights for what he called "the travelers cheque"—even though they didn't really invent them (See: 1772 & 1874). In the initial year, American Express sold just US$9,120 worth of traveler's checks. The amount has risen every year, and in 2000 sales of American Express Travelers Cheques reached US$24.6 billion. Today, in 2011, they are all but obsolete for travelers.

1892
The Brown Palace Hotel, the first atrium-style hotel ever built, opens in Denver.

Isabella Lucy Bird (1831–1904), a prolific English adventurer and travel writer, becomes the first woman inducted into the Royal Geographical Society. Her works include: *The Englishwoman in America* (1856), *The Hawaiian Archipelago* (1875), *Unbeaten Tracks in Japan* (1880), *Journeys in Persia and Kurdistan* (1891), among others.

1893
John Joseph Wright (1847-1922), a Canadian electrical engineer, builds Toronto's electric streetcar.

Cunard Line's *RMS Campania* becomes the first ship to offer *en suite* berths—private bathrooms.

Katharine Lee Bates (1859–1929), an American songwriter, who after traveling west and seeing the beauty that can be seen from the top of Pike's Peak in the Colorado's Rocky Mountains, pens the famous American anthem *"America the Beautiful"*…
"O beautiful for spacious skies,
For amber waves of grain,
For purple mountain majesties
Above the fruited plain!"

Chicago's Columbian World's Fair Exposition introduces the legendary George Ferris Giant Wheel; that weighs in at over 4 million pounds and was 264 feet high. It is said to inspire the birth of Coney Island's Ferris wheel (See: 1848). And with 27 million paid admissions to the fair that year, you can't fault success!

The *Le Château Frontenac*, the grand hotel, opens in Quebec City. Catie, Boston's Copley Plaza Hotel's canine ambassador and loveable lobby lab, now has a place to visit in her books.

The *art-deco* Waldorf-Astoria opens in New York City.

1894

Paul Boyton (aka Fearless Frogman) (1848-1924), an American showman, opens the Paul Boyton Chutes Park in Chicago and dry and aquatic park—the first amusement park to be enclosed and charge an admission. A year later he opens Sea Lion Park (aka Luna Park) on Coney Island. After relocating the Chicago park in 1896, the Chutes Park closes in 1908.

When William Henry Lynch, an budding-American entrepreneur, buys the self-anointed Marble Cave (aka Marvel Cave) and charges local visitors to see it—it is a sinkhole cave with no marble!—the first tourist attraction in the hillbilly-Mecca Ozark Mountain town of Branson, Missouri. (See: 1959)

1896

Guglielmo Marconi (1874-1937), an Italian inventor, makes his first wireless transmission in England. In 1899 he established wireless communication across the English Channel between France and England. And in 1901, Marconi sends signals across the Atlantic between England and Canada, a distance of 3,500 kilometers (2,200 miles). The era of instant global communications has begun.

The Budapest Metro subway system opens, the renowned Line 1, a 3.7 kilometer route and becomes the first underground urban metro line on the European Continent. (See: 1863)

The first Modern Day Olympics are held in the Panathenaic stadium in Athens, Greece. Fourteen nations participate.

Henry Flagler (1830-1913), a New York railroad tycoon, trying to expand his domain, officially incorporates the city of Miami, basically a giant orange grove, on July 28th with a population of just over 300—all soon to be maître de's, waiters, hoteliers, and chefs. Miami becomes the first city in the world created solely of leisure.

1897

Streetcar congestion in downtown Boston—they started operating in 1856—leads to the opening of the Tremont Street Subway, the oldest subway tunnel in North America.

Mary Henrietta Kingsley (1862-1900), an intrepid English writer, publishes her opus *Travel In West Africa* about her many trips to the African continent and sympathies for the indigenous peoples. Cultural empathy in travel begins to take form.

The Prater (aka *Wiener Riesenrad* or Viennese giant wheel), opens in Vienna, Austria, in a public park to celebrate Emperor Franz Josef I's Golden Jubilee. *The Third Man*, a film shot in 1948 post-war Vienna immortalizes the wheel—and Vienna. (See: 1848)

The *SS Kaiser Wilhelm der Grosse*, a German-built pre-World War One cruise ship launches, the first of the fourteen four-stackers ever built, and the original of the coming super liners.

Elias Burton Holmes (1870-1958), American film-maker, coins the term travelogue, and begins making and showing his, well, *travelogues* by integrating his film and slides together into his travel lectures—and now we have Power Point! A great traveler in his own right, Burton sometimes disguised himself as a diplomat while traveling to every continent, going six times around the world—all before airplanes had been invented. (Who will be the first to do it seven times?)

The National Gallery of British Art (aka the Tate Gallery, and now just Tate), opens to the public in London, England. It was the site of a former prison.

1898
César Ritz (1850-1918), a Swiss hotelier who manages London's Savoy (See: 1889), opens his Ritz Paris hotel. The key amenity, aside from the great Ritz-service, is having a private bathroom in each room! He later opens the Ritz in London in 1906. (By the way, the Parisian fashion darling Coco Chanel lived in the Hotel Ritz Paris for more than 30 years.)

Alberto Santos-Dumont (1873-1932), a Brazilian aviation enthusiast, begins building and flying the first gas-powered lighter-than-air balloon aircraft (aka dirigible balloons). His original ship is called *Brésil*.

Captain Joshua Slocum (1844-1909), a legendary Canadian sailor, becomes the first person to sail solo around the world after a three year 74,000 kilometer (46,000-mile) journey on his ship called *Spray*. His book *Sailing Alone Around the World* is published in 1899.

The Fourteenth Amendment (Amendment XIV) to the U.S. Constitution was adopted in 1868 in order to give African Americans born in slavery in the United States full U.S. citizenship. By this time citizens of other countries (especially "guest workers" from China) want their children born in the United States. Nowadays, it claimed that pregnant women from numerous nations, including Korea, Hong Kong, Taiwan and Mexico, attempt to enter the U.S. (aka Birth Tourism) to give birth and claim those rights.

The Takarazuka Onsen (aka Takarazuka Family Land), opens outside Osaka, Japan. This hot spring area was intended for family-use, and was called "Paradise," where luxurious big marbled bath rooms and amusement facilities such as music rooms were included and nearby inns were built. Takarazuka Family Land is now Takarazuka Garden Fields.

Ewart Scott Grogan (1874–1967), a British explorer, becomes the first to traverse (walk) the African continent south-to-north from the Cape to Cairo, white-umbrella and all. His extraordinary journey is chronicalized in Chalmers Robert's *A Wonderful Feat* (no pun intended) *of Adventure* in 1901.

Valdemar Poulsen (1869-1942), a Danish electrical wiz, invents the magnetic wire recorder (aka telephone answering machine)…so that people can travel more.

CHAPTER EIGHT

The New Century & Industrial Tourism Takes Root (1900 -1913):
Both inter-city and intra-city transportation systems are now complete, grand hotels are flourishing around the world, wholly-contrived and natural *things-to-do* tourist attractions grow by leaps and bounds, cameras and guidebooks are sold to the masses, travel clubs and tourist bureaus are formed. The world is known and travelers can go anywhere they desire—and getting there is still half the fun of traveling! But with the advent of automobiles in 1908, a revolutionary paradigm shift away from mass transit to personal transit begins anew—especially in the United States—that gives travelers new unencumbered transportation freedoms. Yet an even newer development in the evolution of *homo touristicus* is literally just over the horizon ready to take off…

1900
By this time, the number of people crossing the English Channel from England to France, or Belgium, passes 500,000 per year.

The Paris *Métro* (*aka* Métropolitain) opens on July 19th during the *Exposition Universelle* world's fair. In 100 years to grow to the sixteen lines employed by 2000, with current total track length of 214 kilometers (133 miles) and 300 stations.

Ferdinand Graf von Zeppelin (1838-1917), a German engineer, builds the first rigid airship at 126 meters (420-feet) that on July 2nd takes five passengers on a 17 minute test run. The first airship to provide commercial air service for passengers, the *Deutschland* was later launched in 1910. Between 1910 and World War I in 1914, *zeppelins* flew over 107,000 miles carrying over 34,000 passengers and crew without injury or accident.

The Kodak Box Brownie camera starts selling for a single buck and the film sells for 15 cents a roll. These types of simple point-and-click box cameras would sell well into the 1960's.

Wilbur Wright (1867-1912) & Orville Wright (1871-1948) (aka The Wright Brothers), two American aviation pioneers, make their first glider flight. It would be two years until their three-axis control system is fully incorporated. (See: 1903)

The first scheduled long distance "bus" service (aka horse-drawn transport) takes place in England between the cities of London and Leeds. The 317 kilometer (198-mile) route takes three days!

The *Prinzessin Victoria Luise,* operated by the Hamburg-America Line, becomes the first ship built for the sole purpose of pleasure cruising—versus a destination-only focus. It was used to take Europeans to the waters of South American during the harsh winter months.

André Michelin (1853-1931), the French industrialist of Michelin Tires fame, begins publishing his red *Michelin Guides.* In 1926 they launch originally blue restaurant books implementing their now widely used culinary rating system—much to the dismay of short order cooks everywhere!

The first international motor car race takes place between London, England and Lyon, France. Just five cars enter the race and the winner averages a speed of just 62 km/h (38 mph).

1901

Gustave A. Whitehead (aka Weisskopf) (1874–1927), a German aviator, allegedly flew a four-cylinder two-cycle powered-batwing monoplane on August 14th in Bridgeport, Connecticut. It reportedly flew about a mile and a half! *The Bridgeport Herald* further reports that Whitehead and his power-driven plane made three other flights that same day. Supporters further claim that he made cruder, steam-driven flights as early as1899 in Pittsburgh. Who's first? The Wright Brothers in 1903, or Gustave in 1901, you decide. My money's on Gustave, he didn't have a press agent!

Travel magazine (aka the Four-Track News) is first published by the New York Central Railroad and then merges with *Holiday* (See: 1928) in 1977 to make *Travel Holiday*…that sadly goes belly-up in 2003.

The Moana Hotel (aka First Lady of Waikiki) opens in Honolulu and becomes Hawaii's earliest large resort hotel. The Shriners become the hotel's first paying guests—US$1.50 rack rate!

Annie Edison Taylor, a dare-devil school teacher, becomes the first person to ever *deliberately* want to go over Niagara Falls—she survives the fall in a wooden barrel—thus creating the world's first adrenaline-junkie tourism sport (aka extreme tourism). The *type T* personality (thrill seeker) is born.

1902
The Circumnavigators Club is established in New York as "a club composed of those adventurous individuals who had actually experienced the crown jewel of travel"—circling the globe. They continue to have rather silly and cumbersome membership rules for wannabe members. (Circumavigators. org)

The American Automobile Association (AAA) is formed.

The *20ᵗʰ Century Limited* begins offering express service (20-hours) between New York and Chicago. The self-proclaimed *"Most Famous Train in the World,"* ceases operations in 1967 after Amtrak subsidies were slashed. (Personally, I only know this line because of the popular 20ᵗʰ Century Cocktail (1 1/2 ounces of gin, 3/4 ounce of Lillet Blanc, 3/4 ounce of light *creme de cacao*, 3/4 ounce of fresh lemon juice…shake in an iced cocktail shaker, and strain into a cocktail glass. Garnish with a lemon twist!)

The Berlin U-Bahn (*aka* Berlin subway) opens. By 2010, the U-Bahn serves 173 stations on nine lines with 147 kilometers (91 miles) of track.

The Hollywood Hotel opens in Hollywood, California on Hollywood Boulevard among the lemon groves and eucalyptus trees. Rudolph Valentino lives in room 264. The hotel was destroyed in 1956.

In a *New York Times* article, you can find the first use of the term "airport" in a quote by Alberto Santos-Dumont (See: 1906). He states that he fully expected New York City to be the principal "airport" of the world very soon. This is an odd citation—because planes weren't really flying yet, airships yes, but planes no!

1903

Mario Calderara (1879-1944), an Italian aviator, is said to take a glider flight in Italy. He later becomes Wilbur Wright's first flight student in 1910.

Horatio Nelson Jackson (1872-1855), an East Coast American physician, bets US$50 that he could travel from San Francisco to New York City in a "horseless carriage" within 90-days. On July 26th he successfully completes the first American road trip and first transcontinental automobile trip at a personal cost of over US$8,000—a huge sum back then. It should be noted that at this time there were less than 240 kilometers (150 miles) of paved road in the entire United States!

The Wright Brothers (See: 1900) fly! Wilbur wins the coin toss and makes history in the appropriately named Wright Flyer and becomes the first recorded controlled, powered and sustained heavier- than-air flight—on their fourth attempt of the day—when Wilbur stays aloft for 59 seconds and travels 260 meters (852-feet). Man can actually fly! Two years later, Wilbur stays aloft again, this time for a full 39 minutes circling a field and traveling some 39 kilometers (24 miles) in their Wright Flyer III. There do remain some disputes (See: 1901).

The Hawaii Tourist Bureau is formed.

The Taj Hotel group opens their first property in Bombay (aka Mumbai), India—the Taj Mahal Palace & Tower. In 2010, the Taj Group had sixty hotels in forty-five locations in India alone.

Henry Simpson Lunn (1859–1939), an English travel agent, organizes the first packaged ski holidays (aka ski tourism) to Adelboden, Switzerland under the guise of the Public Schools Alpine Sports Club. Lunn establishes Lunn Poly, one of the largest chains of travel agents in Britain today.

1904

New York City's Interborough Rapid Transit Subway (IRT), a privately-run company, begins operating its subway between 145th Street at Broadway and City Hall on the 27th of October. The City of New York purchases the company in 1940.

The Explorers Club is established in New York City, "dedicated to the advancement of field research and the ideal that it is vital to preserve the instinct to explore." (Explorers.org)

1905

The Chelsea Hotel, originally built as a 12-story apartment building in 1884—and the tallest building in New York City until 1902—opens for business. No celebrity dies there until Dylan Thomas opens the flood gates in November 1953.

The first reported bird strike (aka avian ingestion) on a flying machine, is reported by Orville Wright according to the Wright Brothers' diaries, *"Orville … flew 4,751 meters in 4 minutes 45 seconds, four complete circles. Twice passed over fence into Beard's cornfield. Chased flock of birds for two rounds and killed one which fell on top of the upper surface and after a time fell off when swinging a sharp curve."* Bird strikes are no small matter for planes as we know, to date, the greatest loss of life directly linked to a bird strike was on October 4, 1960, when an Eastern Air Lines flight, flying from Boston, flew through a flock of common starlings during takeoff and damaged all four engines. The plane crashed, with 62 fatalities out of 72 passengers. Subsequently, minimum bird ingestion standards for jet engines were developed by the FAA. Countermeasures include the use of falcons, dogs, human stick wavers, pyrotechnics, radio-controlled airplanes, decoys, and guns.

1906

Alberto Santos-Dumont (1873-1932), a Brazilian aviator, flies for 8 seconds on September 13th, marking the first South American flyer—in Paris.

César Ritz (See: 1898), opens The Ritz Hotel London in Piccadilly, adding a whole new verb to the English language, as heard in Irving Berlin's 1929 pop hit, *"Puttin' on the Ritz."*

Theodore Roosevelt (1858 –1919), an American outdoorsy President, becomes the first U.S. president to get an official travel expense account—US$25,000 a year—after a nasty eye-gouging, name-calling, and partisan fight in the U.S. Congress—some things never change!

The Great Northern Railway, formed in 1889, adopts the *"See America First"* slogan to help promote their budding resort facilities in northern Montana. The slogan quickly catches on, and turns into a national tourism campaign (aka patriotic tourism) that captivates Americans and helps create a national identity. Natural wonders including: Yellowstone, Glacier National Park, and the Grand Canyon grew in popularity.

1907
Edward W. Scripps (1854–1926), an American newspaperman, forms the United Press International (UPI) international news service.

Paul Cornu (1881-1944), a French bicycle-maker, takes the first rotary wing aircraft flight (aka helicopter) on November 13th.

Gertrude Margaret Lowthian Bell (1868–1926), an English writer, archaeologist, explorer and generally fabulous woman of her day, publishes *Syria: The Desert and the Sown;* which opens up the desert regions of the Middle East for future travelers.

The *Art Nouveau*-styled Hotel Metropol opens in Moscow. The Russian hotel is nationalized by the Bolshevik's in 1918 and renamed *Second House of Soviets,* but converted back to a 365 room hotel in the 1930's.

1908
Albany International Airport (ALB), located on a former polo field on Loudonville Road outside Albany, New York becomes the first public use international airport—and remains the oldest, municipal airport in the United States. In 2010, the CIA states that there are approximately 44,000 functioning airports or airfields globally—including exactly 15,095 in the U.S.

Henry Ford (1863-1947), an American industrialist, produces the Model T automobile that originally sells for just US$950. Over 15-million Model T's are eventually sold helping herald in the beginning of the Motor Age;

and by 1930 this game changing technology was owned by over 23 million Americans. Road trips become as American as mom, baseball and apple pie, as hotels, motels, and campgrounds began popping up like weeds across the land.

Henri Farman (1874-1958), a French industrialist, claims to be the first airplane passenger (aka aviation tourism), flying in an aeroplane with Léon Delagrange (1873–1910), a French aviator, at Issy, France on March 28th. Later, on September 9th, well-known American aviator Lt. Frank P. Lahm (1877-1963), takes a six minute flight with Wilbur Wright in the *Wright Flyer.*

The first cable to pull skiers—and tobogganers too—up a hill, is built at Germany's Black Forest Schwarzwald area.

Thérèse Peltier (1876-1923), a French aviator, becomes the first woman to pilot an aircraft solo.

Gideon's International, an American Christian group, begins placing Bibles in the Superior Hotel in Montana, USA. By the year 2000, they are disbursing Bibles at the rate of 107 per minute!

The London Underground (aka *The Tube*) (See: 1863), prints the first system-wide map.

1909
Louis Blériot (1872-1936), a French aviator, becomes the first to fly across the English Channel in his *Blériot XI*—it takes him 37 minutes.

Robert E. Peary (1856-1920), an America explorer, claims to be the first person to visit the magnetic North Pole. Some have wondered aloud if any of the indigenous Inuit's who have lived in the region for thousands of years might have already visited it?

Herbert Lang (1879-1957), a German taxidermist, leads the American Museum of Natural History's famed Congo expeditions. On a previous trip to Africa, Lang returned with over 400 critter samples (aka dead carcasses).

The first *Grande Semaine d'Aviation (aka* International Aviation Competition) is held in Rheims, France. The top speed among flyers is 75 km/h (46.5 mph).

Deutsche Luftschiffahrts-Aktiengesellschaft (DELAG) is founded in Germany, becoming the world's first passenger aviation enterprise—they plan to use airships manufactured by the Zeppelin Corporation, not airplanes!

1910
The first American air meet is held at Dominguez Field in Los Angeles, California. Over 250,000 amazed spectators attend. Louis Paulhan (1883–1963), a celebrated French pilot, dominates the event setting a record by taking a passenger on a 177 kilometers (110 miles) flight. And a new air speed record is set by Glenn Curtiss (1878 –1930), the father of U.S. aviation, of approximately 89 km/h (55 mph).

The first recorded ski lift in America, a drag tow, opens at Truckee, California. (See: 1908)

Jesse Shwayder (1882-1970), an American businessman, establishes the Samsonite luggage company in Denver, Colorado. The firm is named after the Biblical strongman and is oddly known to use apes in ads—or was that American Tourister?

Calbraith "Cal" Perry Rodgers (1879–1912), an American aviator, becomes the first to fly coast-to-coast in 30 days or less, and claims the US$50,000 prize offered by William Randolph Hearst. Rodgers' plane, the *Vin Fiz*, was plagued with problems from the outset, but his endurance and fortitude through five—*yes five!*—major crashes, only endeared him to the American public.

The notorious Hāna Highway (aka the Road to Hāna) that wild six-hundred and twenty curve 109 kilometer (68-mile) road between Kahului and Hāna, on the Hawaiian island of Maui, opens.

1911
Roald Amundsen (1872-1928), a Norwegian polar explorer, becomes the first person to reach the South Pole on December 14th, traveling by dog sled. Amundsen was also the first person to sail around the world through

the Northeast and Northwest passages, from the Atlantic to the Pacific in 1906. Roald was also the first person to reach Earth's two poles, North and South, as well as the first person to fly over the North Pole in a dirigible in 1926. A busy guy who really liked the cold.

Hiram Bingham (1875–1956), an American archaeologist, locates the "lost" Inca city of Machu Picchu. Today over 500,000 annually visit the site.

Tourists pose for the Machu Picchu money shot.
(Author Photo)

The Danish ship *MS Selandia* becomes the first diesel-engine driven ocean-going ship.

The Quebec-Miami International Highway, an auto trail that runs from the Canadian border north at Fort Kent, Maine all the way south some 3,800 kilometers (2,400 miles) to Key West, Florida, is established. In 1915, the trail is renamed the Atlantic Highway, and even later it becomes U.S. Route 1.

1912

The Calgary Stampede, an annual 10-day rodeo and farmer's exhibition, takes place for the first time in Calgary, Canada.

The unsinkable *RMS Titanic* sails…and sinks. See the movie.

Martin Sixt (?-1945), a German businessman, founds the *Sixt Autofahrten und Selbstfahrer* Company (aka a rent-a-car company) with seven cars—four Mercedes and three Luxus-Deutz-Landaulets. Sixt specializes in day-trips and custom tours with many of his clients being members of the British nobility as well as dollar-rich Americans.

The first diesel-electric motor coach is manufactured in Sweden.

The famous Morse code SOS distress signal is universally (well, at least on planet Earth) adopted as: ...---... (aka dot-dot-dot-dash-dash-dash-dot-dot-dot).

The Beverly Hills Hotel opens on Sunset Boulevard in Beverly Hills, California. The hotel façade is used on The Eagles' 1976 LP *Hotel California*.

The first working holiday dude ranch, the Bar B C Dude Ranch (aka Rural Tourism), was established outside Jackson Hole, Wyoming, for city folk suffering from *nature-deficit disorder* can do chores in the great outdoors. Get along little doggies...

Richard Schirrmann (1874–1961), a German schoolteacher, originates the youth hostel concept (aka student travel) at Altena Castle, Germany—after sleeping outside a bar one night as a traveling starving student. As every student knows, in every hostel you're treated like royalty, but don't forget to flush! In 1919, Richard founds the nation-wide youth hostel association. Thanks Dick!

Ludwig Borchardt (1863–1938), a German Egyptologist, locates the gorgeous *Nefertiti Bust,* and then illegally exports it to a German Museum, where it has stayed ever since...much to the dismay of the Egyptians and cultural repatriationists everywhere.

1913
Dissatisfaction among Grand Tour participants begins appearing in several travel publications. Tourists it seems are getting annoyed traveling great distances only to then run into hometown acquaintances, as well as encountering price gouging by local operators. And tourist angst is born.

The first American intercity bus service takes place on a seven-passenger nicknamed *Hupmobile,* built by Hupp Motor Company, between the towns of Hibbing and Alice, Minnesota.

The Buenos Aires Subway (*SUBTE*) (aka *subte*rráneo), begins operation in Argentina, becoming Latin-America's first subway system.

The East–West Lincoln Highway is finally pieced together from coast-to-coast—from Times Square in New York City, to Lincoln Park in San Francisco. At 5,454 kilometers (3,389 miles), it becomes the first road across the United States.

CHAPTER NINE

The Era of Commercial Air Travel Begins (1914 - 1951):
Having now mastered land and sea transportation methods, the advent of commercial air travel takes *homo touristicus* to new heights. No place on earth is unapproachable. Although a few global events impact the traveler: World War I, the Spanish flu pandemic, the Great Depression, World War II—man still remains eager to travel. Due to the rapid rise of globalization, governments start getting involved in the travel plans of would be travelers, retail travel businesses begin to thrive and airlines begin marketing their wares.

1914

On January 1ˢᵗ, the first scheduled commercial passenger flight begins operating in the U.S., taking one person at a time for a US$5.00 fee, on the eighteen-mile Airboat Line between St. Petersburg and Tampa, Florida. They use the *Benoist XIV* flying boat.

The U.S.-built Panama Canal opens, linking the Pacific Ocean with the Caribbean, and ultimately, the Atlantic Ocean. The first complete Panama Canal passage is made by a self-propelled, oceangoing vessel and it took place on January 7ᵗʰ. The US$375 million project—US$23 million under budget!—cost over 5,600 workers lives due to disease and accidents.

The first radio message is sent from the ground to an operating airplane, allowing for mid-flight changes and communications…a good development in anyone's book.

The first U.S. transcontinental telephone call takes place, *"Hello, mom!"*

The W.J. Brown Hotel opens as the first hotel in Miami Beach, Florida.

The *Rutschbanen* (aka roller coaster) built for the Baltic Fair, is sold to Copenhagen's Tivoli Gardens, and has claims as the world's oldest roller coaster. Coney Island's famed *Cyclone* later began taking brave customers in 1927.

Due to the outbreak of World War One (1914-1918), the U.S. State Department begins issuing public notices (aka travel advisories) for travelers visiting or going to visit near war-torn areas of Europe. As time and world events evolve, these advisories and stronger "travel warnings" began to include the safety and security of U.S. citizens in regards to all travel abroad including: severe weather, crime, natural disasters, civil unrest, pandemics and disease, war, and terrorism. The U.S. State Department started posting these public notices online in 1996. (State.gov)

1915
American Express established a Travel Division within the company, and soon establishes its first travel agencies.

A German U-boat sinks the *RMS Lusitania*, and of the 1,153 passengers aboard, only 200 survived.

An Executive Order of December 15th requires that every person entering or leaving the United States to have a valid passport. That will keep those Commie Reds out!

As part of the continued growth of the National Auto Trail system in the U.S., the North–South Dixie Highway, inspired by the example of the slightly older East-West Lincoln Highway (See: 1913), comes into official operation. The main route runs from Chicago and Northern Michigan, south to Miami, Florida.

1916
Robert Frost (1874-1963), an American poet, pens his one of many works of art, the famous poem *A Road Less Taken* that includes the inspiring independent traveler lines:
"Two roads diverged in a wood, and I –
I took the one less traveled by,

And that has made all the difference."

When Roland and Mary Conklin of Huntington, New York, finish building their house-car (aka Gypsy Van), the first recreation vehicle (RV) hits the road. With a homelike interior "similar to their mansion, which was styled after English manor houses", Roland and Mary immediately throw a bumper sticker on the back reading: *If you see us rocking don't bother knocking...*

Joe Saunders, a Nebraskan businessman, is the first person to start a rent-a-car business in the U.S. (See: 1912), when he lent out his Model T to a traveling salesman for a date with a local gal, for a cent-a-mile. And so begins America's penchant for bad traveling salesmen jokes!

The Trans-Siberian Express, a railway, opens between Moscow and Vladivostok, Russia...all 9,440 kilometers (5,866 miles) of it! Trans-Siberian Express is a tad of an oxymoron.

William Boeing (1881-1956), an American businessman, forms the Pacific Aero Products Company, his airplane manufacturing business. One year later, he changes the name to the Boeing Airplane Company when he gets his first government contract for 50 planes for the United States Navy—and Boeing has been sucking that tit ever since.

Mrs. Waldo Polk, a New York socialite, and Mr. Lawrence Sperry, an early daredevil pilot, supposedly become the first members of the infamous *Mile High Club*. Technically, they were only flying at about 500 feet at the time (we want details please?) not the legitimate height of 5,268 feet! As a side note, this is also the first time an "auto pilot" system was engaged! Now you know.

1917
The American State of Wisconsin becomes the first state to use a highway numbering system, starting at 11 and going up to 199, to identify its many highways and byways. The glorious names of the Old Spanish Highway, the Oregon Trial, and Lincoln Highways begin going out of fashion—it becomes Route 66 all the way baby! (See: 1926)

1918

Blue Guides, a series of authoritatively detailed high-brow travel guidebooks that focus almost exclusively on history, art and architecture—with just a smattering of actual practical information—begins publication. *London and its Environs*, becomes the first Blue Guide published by the Scottish brothers James and Findlay Muirhead—the former English language editors of the German *Baedeker*. (See: 1836)

The U.S. Air Mail Service commences operations with single-engine biplanes on May 15th. Mail planes help pushed the aviation industry forward in the U.S. in a big way—and who says governments can't assist private business?

Ross & Keith Smith, Australian brothers, win the amazing London to Australia Air Derby covering 18,500 kilometers (11,000 miles) in twenty-nine days in a Vickers Vimy, G-EAOU bi-plane (affectionately known as *"God 'Elp All Of Us"*), claiming a prize of £10,000.

Walter L. Jacobs, an American entrepreneur, opens a car rental business in Chicago, Illinois with about a dozen Model T Fords. He repairs the cars himself, and by 1923 his car rental business was generating over US$1 million in annual revenues. The Yellow Cab and Yellow Truck and Coach Manufacturing Company, owned at the time by John Hertz (1879-1961), a Slovakian-American businessman, acquires Jacobs' business in 1923. General Motors then bought out Hertz's Yellow Truck Company in 1926, with that car-rental business becoming better known as the Hertz Drive-Ur-Self System.

1919

On February 22nd the first sustained and regular domestic civilian airline service was begun by the German airline *Deutshe Luft Reederi* (DLR), using AEG biplanes. The daily flights operated between Berlin and Leipzig, and Weimar.

Conrad Hilton (1887-1979), a Texas-based entrepreneur, purchases his first hotel, The Mobley Hotel in Cisco, Texas. He keeps buying hotels in Texas and surrounding states; and in 1946 Conrad forms the Hilton Hotels Corporation, that eventually owned 188 hotels in thirty-eight U.S. cities.

Hilton's most well-known legacy nowadays remains—his granddaughter Paris Hilton!

On August 25th, the first sustained and regular international civilian airline service was begun by the British airline Air Transport and Travel (AT&T), between London's Hounslow airport (aka London Heathrow Airport (LHR) and Paris's Le Bourget Airport (LBG), using a *de Havilland DH-49*. The daily flight took two and a half hours and cost 21 Pounds Sterling. (Some argue that the first international commercial flight took place a month earlier between Paris and Brussels.)

A British Air Force flight in a *Vickers Vimy* bi-plane bomber, flies between St John's, Newfoundland, Canada and Clifden, Ireland, some 3,630 kilometers (1,960 nautical miles), to become the first non-stop transatlantic flight. It takes sixteen hours and twelve minutes.

The Tin Can Tourists club is formally organized at Desoto Park in Tampa, Florida for budding RVer's—then called *auto campers*.

Royal Dutch Airlines (KLM) is created in The Netherlands, and remains the oldest airline still flying under its original name. In 1920, KLM begins international service between Amsterdam and London. There is no truth to the rumor that cannabis was found aboard, but they did provide the first in-flight meal—a basket lunch of sandwiches, coffee and tea—on an October 11th flight!

The new Bolshevik regime in Russia, wanting to emphasize the culture of the country, creates the Society for Proletarian Tourism (OPT RFSFR).

The first version of the International Air Traffic Association (IATA) is founded in The Hague, as an international industry trade group of airlines.

The U.S. Congress funds the creation of the Intracoastal Waterway, a north-south inland waterway system long the Atlantic Coast; which is later connected to the Gulf Intracoastal Waterway, an east-west navigable waterway along the Gulf Coast. The two systems create a 4,800 kilometer (3,000-mile) navigable inland waterway route that when joined with the Mississippi River in 1949, creates The Great Loop that allows small vessels (aka boating/water tourism) easy access up north to the Great Lakes, and then back east over to the Eastern Seaboard. Although doing it counter-clockwise is the wiser choice due to tides and prevailing currents.

1920's

During the Prohibition Era (1920-1930), so-called "booze cruises" began taking drinkers on trips to nowhere. *Nowhere* being three miles out of the U.S. territorial limits, to indulge in a legal drink. Longer weekend cruises became popular as well and called on the nearest offshore ports of Havana and Bermuda for the same purpose. (Nowadays, "booze cruises" take place between England and either Belgium or France in order to take advantage of lower alcohol prices on the Continent (aka cross-border shopping).

America's self-styled *Lost Generation* of writers, artists and bohemians, begin traveling to Paris, France on an extended creative pilgrimage of sorts. This post-World War I expatriate generation stays until the Great Depression begins to force economic reality on them. Cultural luminaries included: Henry Miller, Ernest Hemingway, F. Scott Fitzgerald, T. S. Eliot, Ezra Pound, Gertrude Stein, Edith Wharton, Josephine Baker, and Langston Hughes, among others. Fitzgerald may have said it all with, "*The best of America drifts to Paris. The American in Paris is the best American. It is more fun for an intelligent person to live in an intelligent country. France has the only two things toward which we drift as we grow older--intelligence and good manners.*"

The advent of ski tourism becomes particularly pleasing to the Austrians, with well-known resorts like Kitzbühel, St. Anton and St. Moritz, becoming popular travel destinations. Snow skiing also catches on in America following the 1932 Winter Olympics held at Lake Placid, New York.

With the building of Buck Hill Falls, Pocono Manor, and the Skytop resort hotels in the Pocono Mountains, located in northeastern Pennsylvania, a new era of vacationing begins with city-folk yearning to enjoy the great outdoors. By this time, nature-starved travelers from New York City, Philadelphia, Pittsburg, Cleveland, and Buffalo, employ cars, buses, and trains, to escape the city and "get away from it all," heading for the Poconos. Later, in 1945, the Farm in the Hill Hotel is opened as the areas first "honeymoon hotel." The rest is Pocono lore...

1920

Marks the peak of North American railway ridership, with over 48 billion passenger miles a year. U.S. railway ridership begins a long and painful decline as private automobiles firmly take hold within the American national identity.

1921

It is regarded by most historians as the beginning of the end of the storied British Empire (aka *Pax Britannia)* which at this time at the height of its power, ruled over 25% of the world's population (458 million people) and controlled 35% of world's geographic landmass; up until now it was indeed *"The Empire on which the sun never sets."*

Donald Wills Douglas, Sr. (1892–1981), an American plane manufacturer, moves his company, the Douglas Company, to Santa Monica, California and builds the popular *Cloudster* model.

White Castle opens in Wichita, Kansas and becomes the first U.S.-based hamburger chain.

Roy Chapman Andrews (1884-1960), an American explorer, who after his travels to Outer Mongolia and the Gobi Desert, pens *The Business of Exploring* in 1935.

Capturing the imagination of Hollywood, Oliver Hardy (aka half of Laurel and Hardy) stars in the black and white silent film called *The Tourist.* Apparently it was a swell movie with a bad box office reception, so Fatty Arbuckle stars in the 1925 remake!

The first in-flight movie called *Howdy Chicago* was shown on Aeromarine Airways amphibious airplane during the Chicago Pageant of Progress exposition in August of 1921, as it flew *around* Chicago. Was this a real flight, or just an in-flight entertainment (IFE) publicity stunt? (See: 1925)

Early In-flight Entertainment.
(Aerial Age Weekly - 29 August 1921)

1922
Howard Carter (1873-1939), a British archaeologist and Egyptologist, excavates Tutankhamen's Tomb in the Valley of the Kings. The *Treasures of Tutankhamun* tour (1972-1979) becomes one of the most popular international traveling tours in history.

The National Geographic Society officially adopts the Van der Grinten Projection map, one that projects the entire Earth into a circle, over the outdated and distorted Mercator projection map that shows the Earth as a cylindrical map projection. Just details to novices, but big stuff to serious geographers—and spies alike. This map stays the standard until 1988.

On April 7th a de Havilland DH.18A, *G-EAWO*, collides with a Farman F.60 Goliath, *F-GEAD*, over Thieulloy-St. Antoine, France killing all seven people on both aircraft, becoming the first mid-air collision of airliners in aviation history. Due to bad weather, the pilots of both machines were using the local roads as route markers, and collided at an airborne intersection in poor visibility.

Cornell University's School of Hotel Administration opens and specializes in what is called "hospitality management," and becomes the first four-year intercollegiate school devoted to the field. Later in 1927, the School of Hospitality Business at Michigan State University opens the nation's first business-based Hotel Training Course. The Hilton College (aka Conrad N. Hilton College of Hotel and Restaurant Management) of hospitality management is later established on the University of Houston, Texas grounds in 1969. Hospitality management studies (aka travel and tourism courses) are today offered in more than 40 major international institutions of higher learning.

The first airborne bathrooms show up on a few British flights.

1923
Aeroflot, the Russian national airlines, is established, and would later become the world's largest airline, *albeit* with a complete monopoly on flying in the Soviet Union. In 1992 before the breakup of the Soviet Union, Aeroflot claims to have over 600,000 people operating over 10,000 aircraft.

Hôtel la Mamounia opens in Marrakech, Morocco. Some claim it to be the most exotic hotel in the world at the time. Alfred Hitchcock's *The Man Who Knew Too Much* was filmed there in 1956.

A U.S. Air Force single-engine T-2 makes the first nonstop transcontinental flight across the United States. It takes the crew of two, 26 hours and 50 minutes to fly from Roosevelt Field, Long Island, New York to San Diego, California.

The Pan America Highway idea, a 25,750 kilometer (16,000-mile) road linking Alaska to Argentina, is born. Today it is a reality, except of course for that little 87 kilometer (54-mile) Darién Gap stretch between Panama and Columbia.

The Bronx River Parkway opens in New York City and is said to be the world's first expressway. A traffic jam instantly arises brining cars to a slow creep—and it has been that way ever since!

1924

AT&T introduces the Teletype machine, a real-time printing telegraph system. It helps reduce the time news takes to travel from one part of the world to another. The Global Village is upon us.

The first ever flight from Lisbon, Portugal to its Macau, China colony takes place.

Alexandra David-Néel (1868–1969), French anarchist, explorer and writer, sneaks into the forbidden region of Tibet. Always a rebel and ahead of her time, her daring exploits and book, *Voyage d'une Parisienne à Lhassa* in1927, would later influence Jack Kerouac (See: 1951).

Footprint Handbooks, a British guidebook, introduces itself to the world with the publication of *South American Handbook*. Today, we know Footprint as the world's longest running guidebook in the English language.

The Topkapı Palace Museum in Istanbul, Turkey opens as a museum after serving over 400 years as the primary residence of the Ottoman Sultans. An amazing inside view of the colorful Ottoman Empire awaits anyone willing to buy a ticket.

The first around-the-world flight, traveling from Seattle, Washington all the way around and back to Seattle, Washington, is completed over a 175 day period! It took a small squadron of four *Douglas Cruiser* biplanes operated by the U.S. Army Air Corps, to make the 42,389 kilometer (26,345-mile) circuitous route. In 1980, a military B-52 circled the globe in 42 hours 23 minutes—non-stop! It was refueled in the air.

The politically-charged Lenin Mausoleum (aka Lenin's Tomb), situated in Red Square in the center of Moscow, Russia is opened...opening up a whole new vein (sorry!) of travel called Graveyard Tourism, albeit with political and patriotic bent . How many travelers have visited the *trifecta* of interned—maybe an inappropriate word selection, maybe not—former leaders: Lenin, Mao and Ho?

1925

Records show that by now an estimated one million people a year cross the Atlantic Ocean by ship—markets being what they are, that is about to change.

The U.S. Air Mail Act of 1925 (aka the Kelly Act) passed handing the nation's airmail service over to private airmail operators for four-year periods under a bidding scheme. This is truly the start of the United States airline industry as we know it today. The Morrow Board, which was the FAA's predecessor, is also established to regulate the new business.

Richard Halliburton (1900-1939), an American adventure traveler and adrenaline junkie, pens his inspirational *"The Royal Road to Romance."*

The Grand Ole Opry opens in Nashville, Tennessee and folks from around the world have been coming ever since.

The Motel Inn of San Luis Obispo opens and is called "the first roadside motel." The San Luis Obispo, California hotel charges US$2.50 a night. The concept behind motels—as opposed to city hotels—which allowed for easy highway access for cross country travelers, was started by Arthur Heinman. These family-run mom and pop motels quickly spread across the United States and between 1939 and 1960 over 35,000 motels were built. Today, it is said that as many as 60% of all mid-sized motels and hotel properties in the U.S., are owned and operated by people of Indian origin. Of this, nearly one-third have the surname Patel—a popular name among Indian Gujarat's.

Western Air Express, and what would later be called Trans World Airlines (TWA), is founded. Western Air Express would later merge with Transcontinental Air Transport in 1930, to become the Transcontinental and Western Air, the early TWA.

The first in-flight movie, a media-invited publicity stunt by Imperial Airways in a WWI converted twelve-passenger Handley-Page bomber, shows Sir Arthur Conan Doyle's black and white silent film *The Lost World,* during a 30-minute flight between London and Paris. Maybe it is the first in Europe, or maybe it was the first in-flight entertainment (IFE) shown on an actual scheduled flight? (See: 1921)

The International Congress of Official Tourist Traffic Associations (ICOTT) is formed in The Hague, as an international body to coordinate travel-related issues between nation-states, trade groups, and consumers. It becomes the aptly titled International Union of Official Tourist Propaganda Organizations in 1934; and then in 1974 the World Tourism Organization (WTO).

1926

Aeromaritime Airways begins flying tourists from Miami to Havana and Miami to Nassau, so that passengers can avoid the dry Prohibition era laws. The 297 kilometer (185-mile) trip to Nassau is priced at US$85 and conducted by flying boats.

Lufthansa Airways is formed out of *Deutsche Luft Hansa Aktiengesellschaft*, and is renamed simply Lufthansa in 1933. Always looking for new markets, the airline partakes in a flying expedition to China.

The Motor Bus Division of the American Automobile Association (AAA) is formed. It is reorganized in 1930 as the National Association of Motor Bus Operators, and in 1977 becomes the American Bus Association.

Route 66, the 3,540 kilometer (2,200-mile) highway linking Chicago to Los Angeles opens...although it is patchy in most urban areas. (See: 1938)

William Matson (1849–1917) a Swedish-born American shipping magnet, whose company Matson Navigation Company, that specialized in Pacific Coast to Hawaiian Island shipping runs, takes over the Oceanic Steamship Company, and begins successfully taking passengers to Hawaii. This opens the door wider to Hawaiian tourism growth.

The U.S. *Air Commerce Act*, allowing the Federal regulation of air traffic and backed by the aviation industry, passes the U.S. Congress. The industry strongly believed that without the governmental action to improve air passenger safety, that the commercial potential of the airplane would not be fully realized. Air traffic control needed standards and the Postmaster General took control over the industry...think about that: the Post Office running airlines!?

The Mesaba Transportation Company, a bus transportation company operating out of Minnesota, becomes Greyhound Lines. By 1941, the company had 4,750 stations and nearly 10,000 employees.

1927

Charles Lindbergh (1902-1974), authentic American hero, makes his successful solo non-stop transatlantic flight in the *Spirit of St Louis* from New York City to Paris on May 21st and collects the US$25,000 Orteig Prize. He traveled 6,667 kilometers (3,600 miles) in 33 hours and 30 minutes with a few sandwiches, a thermos and paper cup to pee in.

Allan Loughead (1889–1969), an American industrialist, forms the Lockheed Aircraft Company, and builds the Lockheed Vega, the company's first craft to the skies.

The 22-storey Detroit-Leland Hotel opens its doors on 400 Bagley Street in downtown Detroit, Michigan boasting "800 rooms - 800 baths" and all air-conditioned—the first hotel to do so. I knew it well…

The Royal Hawaiian Hotel (aka Pink Palace of the Pacific) opens in Waikiki, Honolulu, Hawaii. Without it, the kid-friendly Shirley Temple cocktail would not exist!

A cable car for winter skiers (and summer hikers) is built at Chamonix, France, the home of the site of the 1924 Winter Olympics—the first Winter Olympics. The Swiss constructed the first cable car built expressly for the skiers at Trübsee, above Engelberg, a year later. And the first cable car in America opened in 1938 at Franconia, New Hampshire.

Juan Trippe (1899-1981), an American airline visionary, founds the Pan American Airways (aka PAA, then Pan Am) company on March 14th out of his Aviation Corporation of America (AVCO). By October PAA makes its first flight, flying a Fairchild FC-2 floatplane, between Key West, Florida and Havana, Cuba. Trippe, a true pioneer--some called him "Pan Ambitions", continued to make markets and knock down aviation business barriers his whole life. Later he purchases the China National Aviation Corporation (CNAC) in order to open the door to China with Pan Am becoming the first airline to cross the Pacific Ocean. Trippe always believed in air travel for all, so he invents the *tourist class*. In 1946 he forms the InterContinental hotel group creating a vertical travel empire.

Everyone's Favorite Airline, Pan Am.
(Author Photo)

The American Hotel Association merges with the Hotel Red Book, first printed in 1886, lists over 20,000 properties.

The Huntington Hotel in San Francisco, California installs the first Olympic-size hotel swimming pool.

The Hotel New Grand opens in Yokohama, Japan.

The first Gypsy Tour motorcycle rally takes place with 40 bikers from Melbourne to Sydney, Australia. Motorcycle tourism is born.

Grauman's Chinese Theatre (aka the Egyptian Theater), a Hollywood, California movie theater known for showing the world premières of feature films, adds celebrity footprints to the forecourt of the theater entrance and becomes a must-see Hollywood attraction creating celebrity tourism. The Hollywood Walk of Fame was later created in 1960 and by 2010 celebrated 2,365 media stars.

There is mention of an Oakland Airport hotel in conjunction with the inaugural 1927 air race over the Pacific to Hawaii; which if true, would have to be considered the first of its kind in the country—an airport hotel.

But according *Encyclopedia Britannica*—I know quaint) the first airport hotel did open in Oakland on July 15, 1929. As usual, claims and counter-claims abound. (See: 1957)

The *Delta Queen*, a sternwheeler steamboat, begins sailing—no, not the mighty Mississippi River—the Sacramento River between San Francisco and Sacramento!

Ellsworth Milton Statler (1863–1928), an American hotelier, opens the Statler Hotel in Boston, Massachusetts, and is the first U.S. hotel to offer radio reception. His empire, the Hotels Statler Company, is sold to Hilton Hotels in 1954 with its 11 significant hotels in major U.S. cities for US$111,000,000—in what was then the world's largest real estate transaction!

The Ahwahnee Hotel opens in the heart of the picturesque Yosemite Valley in California. The amazing hotel was built with 5,000 tons of rough-cut granite and over 9,140 meters (30,000-feet) of hard wood timber. Many babies are later conceived there, including one special moon/rock in 1994!

1928
The legendary Peninsula Hong Kong opens her doors on Nathan Street in Kowloon, Hong Kong, and is immediately recognized as "*the finest hotel east of Suez.*" *Ahh*, I know it well!

The *Graf Zeppelin* (aka LZ 127), the famously large passenger-carrying hydrogen-filled airship is launched (See: 1900). We only know of her sister ship the *Hindenburg*'s (aka LZ 129) terrible fireball accident of 1937; and not the LZ 127's glorious nine year history of flying over 1.5 million kilometers on almost 600 safe and successful voyages, including 145 ocean crossings. These giant airships were the equivalent of the trans-Atlantic steamers, but would quickly go the way of the dinosaur towards extinction.

Amelia Earhart (1898-1937), an American pilot, becomes the first women to cross the Atlantic Ocean. She did not pilot the craft, and is quoted after the landing, saying, "*Stultz did all the flying—had to. I was just baggage, like a sack of potatoes. Maybe someday I'll try it alone.*"

Charles Edward Kingsford Smith (aka Smithy) (1897–1935), an Australian aviator, who made the first trans-Pacific flight from the United States to Australia, taking just over 83 hours to cover the 11,822 kilometers (7,388 miles) from Oakland, California to Brisbane, Australia—with fuel stops in Hawaii and Fiji.

The *Zagelmayer* pop-up tent camper is introduced.

Thomas and Paul Braniff, two American brothers, one an insurance salesman, the other an aviation dreamer, form the company known as Braniff airlines, after securing some plum airmail routes, including routes between Oklahoma City-Tulsa, Chicago-Dallas, and Chicago-Mexican border.

Pan Am publishes the first airline timetable/schedule, reading, *The air-way to Havana, Pan American Airways.*

Dixie Trucker's Home (aka Dixie Travel Plaza and Dixie Truck Stop) may be the first truck stop in the United States opens on old *Route 66* outside McLean, Illinois. Whole little towns and industries would evolve along Route 66 supporting truckers, traveling salesmen, and families on vacation.

Western Air Express, previously incorporated in 1925, begins offering passengers boxed lunches from Los Angeles's Pig 'n Whistle restaurant.

The American Automobile Association (AAA) begins publishing a travel magazine known as *Holiday* that continues until 1977. (See: 1901)

1929
Modeled a tad after the Chateau Amboise in France's Loire Valley, Hollywood's Chateau Marmont opens originally as an apartment complex, and later becomes a legend. The 8221 Sunset Boulevard hotel becomes a celebrity haven and legendary rock n' roll hotel. Stories abound, from Jim Morrison hanging around, Led Zeppelin members riding motorcycles in the lobby, Judy Garland singing for drinks in the bar, James Dean sneaking in and out, Howard Hughes living in the attic, F. Scott Fitzgerald suffering a heart attack, and John Belushi dying—if walls could talk!

The *Graf Zeppelin* (See: 1928), circles the globe in 20 days, four hours, and fourteen minutes breaking the old around the world (RTW) world record of 72 days in 1890 by Nellie Bly.

Cesare Cardini (1896–1956), an Italian-Mexican chef, invents his now well-known Caesar Salad in his popular Prohibition-era downtown Tijuana, Mexico, hotel called Hotel Caesar's on Revolution Avenue. You can't miss the place—there is a black and white striped burro parked outside. It also may be true that no tourist trap tops the first and oldest grand daddy of them all, the Egyptian pyramids (See: 2,560c BCE), but TJ becomes a close second by the 1970's...

Georges Rémi (1907–1983), a Belgian artist, draws *The Adventures of Tintin* comic strip with the lead character involved in many swashbuckling international adventures. Kids in 50 languages learned about America, the Pharaohs, Tibet, Red Sea Sharks, the Congo and the Soviets too. We owe a lot to *Tintin*.

Richard Halliburton (See: 1925), swims the length of the Panama Canal—paying his thirty-six cents toll as requested—and writes his most well read travel book *New Worlds to Conquer.*

The *Les Clefs d'Or* (aka the Golden Keys), a professional association for hotel concierge's is established in Paris, France. Look for the double golden keys on your concierge's lapels as membership by 2010 included over 3,000 members in over fifty countries. Their unofficial mantra: *"Yes, of course I can! Now what would be your question?"* By the way, in Latin concierge means *conserves* (aka fellow slave)!

The first resort-based ski school in the United States was opened in Sugar Hill, New Hampshire, by Katharine "Kate" Peckett and her husband Sig Buchmayer.

General James Doolittle (1896–1993), aeronautical engineer and Medal of Honor recipient, invents the gyroscope that allows planes to fly blind on instruments. Bad weather be damned—sort of...

The Warsaw Convention (aka *The Convention on the Unification of Certain Rules Relating to International Carriage by Air*) is signed. It forms the foundation of the international system that is currently in force in over 130 jurisdictions, making it the most widely adopted international agreement affecting private law in the history of mankind. It introduces such concepts as: airport codes, *limited liability* for compensation of passengers, and *quid pro quo* for which there is a rebuttable presumption of liability on the part of every passenger—a reversal of the traditional burden of proof—that favors air carriers in court cases. The death limit was set at 125,000 French francs (about US$10,000) per passenger, and among other things, it also limits air carriers' liability for losing your bags! A sweetheart deal if ever there was one and well before the time of Consumer Protection Agency.

Airport Codes *De*-Coded A to Z:
AAE = Annabe, Algeria
FAT = Fresno, California
HEL = Helsinki, Finland
SUX = Sioux City, Iowa
MAD = Madrid, Spain
MOM = Moudjeria, Martinique
DAD = Da Nang, Vietnam
BUG = Benguela Deslandes, Angola
GUM = Guam
BOO = Bodo, Norway
CPR = Casper, Wyoming
CIA = Ciampino, Rome
EZE = Buenos Aires, Argentina
ZTH = Zakinthos, Greece

Paul Galvin (1895-1959), a self-educated, self-made American businessman, introduces the 5T71 car radio to the world, thus opening the era of the much celebrated road trip with tunes! At a cost US$110 each, and owners had to install it themselves, he calls it the "Motorola", and names his company the same. In 1933, Ford was offering preinstalled radios, and Motorola is still innovating today!

First publication of the *Official Aviation Guide of the Airways* comes out in February. It lists the schedules of all thirty-five airlines operating—a total of 300 flights. It is now known as the *OAG Flight Guide*.

Delta Air Service (aka Delta Airlines), named because they offered flights in the Mississippi Delta region, begins operating its first passenger flights over a route stretching from Dallas, Texas to Jackson, Mississippi, via Shreveport and Monroe. A year later, Atlanta, Georgia became its home.

On June 7th, the sovereign nation-state—and some would say newest theme park—the Vatican City, came into existence when copies of the Lateran Treaty were exchanged in Rome, Italy. As mini-states go, it is the smallest.

Transcontinental Air Transport begins offering passengers playing cards—because their flights were late more often than not some would argue!

"It was the best of times and the worst of times…", to steal a Dickens phrase; airplane transportation was taking off and people were loving it, but there were fifty-one commercial airline crashes in 1929, that killed 61 people—statistically, it remains the worst year on record at a death rate of about one for every 1,000,000 miles (1,600,000 kilometers) flown. That would equate to about 7,000 fatalities a year in 2010! Not good…

The world's first airline alliance—some would say first bout of industry collusion—takes place when Pan American-Grace Airways (aka Panagra) and parent company Pan American World Airways, agree to exchange routes to Latin America. Oh, that Juan Trippe (See: 1927).

Howard Deering Johnson (1897–1972), an American businessman, open's his first Howard Johnson's (aka HoJo's) restaurant in Boston to feed theater goers. By 1961, 605 franchised restaurants existed across America.

1930c
Heinz Herman, a Jerusalem-based psychiatrist, acknowledges a few clinical case-studies of "Jerusalem squabble poison" (aka *Jerusalemmiene* or Jerusalem Syndrome), a form of religious delusion and hysteria that pertains to the behaviors exhibited by some religious visitors to Jerusalem. It parallels the early-diagnosed cultural-oriented Stendhal syndrome (See: 1817 – Marie-Henri Beyle), but is specifically acute in places like Jerusalem, Mecca, Varanasi and Rome. (According to the Kfar Shaul Mental Health Centre in Jerusalem, during a 13-year period between 1980 and 1993,

analyzed admissions records revealed that 1,200 tourists were admitted with severe Jerusalem Syndrome symptoms—mostly U.S. residents!)

Gilbert Keith Chesterton (1874–1936), an English writer, sets off the first ever traveler versus tourist semantic debate, when he his quoted saying, *"The traveler sees what he sees, the tourist sees what he has come to see."* It has been hotly and tiresomely debated since.

The Ten Common Characteristics of Tourists and Travelers using Reductionist Methodology (aka stereo-typing):

A Tourist:	*A Traveler:*
-calls a travel agent	-prepares and researches
-buys a round trip ticket	-buys a one-way ticket
-a sight-seer	-a sight-doer
-takes a vacation	-goes on an adventure
-stays for a week	-stays for as long as they want to
-usually travels in a group	-usually travels alone
-hangs with folks from home	-hangs with folks from here and there
-stands outs	-blends in
-consumes	-experiences
-casual	-snobby
-follower	-adventurer
-Nervous Nellie	-Mister Wing-it
-brings home photos	-brings home memories
-seek out comfort	-seek out authentic
-trusts travel industry employees	-trusts strangers in strange lands
-eats at their hotel	-eats somewhere else
-pack expectations	-pack an open-mind
-talk a lot	-listen a lot
-money means freedom	-time means freedom
-travel is an ends	-travel is a means
-them	-us

1930

The Hotel Nacional de Cuba opens in Havana, Cuba. It is Havana's first grand hotel and was a hot spot to visit for almost 30 years before the revolution, with patrons of the hotel including: Winston Churchill, John Wayne, Marlon Brando, Gary Cooper, Ernest Hemingway, Frank Sinatra, Ava Gardner, Mickey Mantle, Johnny Weissmuller, Buster Keaton, Rocky Marciano, Tyrone Power, Errol Flynn and Marlene Dietrich to name a few. The hotel is also infamous for hosting the notorious self-anointed "mob summit" in December 1946 that included: Lucky Luciano, Meyer Lansky, Santo Trafficante, Jr., Frank Costello, Albert Anastasia and Vito Genovese. By the mid-1950's, mobster Meyer Lansky had control of the property (See: 1957).

The Western Hotel partnership is formed in Washington State when seventeen separately-owned hotel properties are combined under one corporate roof. It would eventually evolve into Westin Hotels & Resorts in 1980, operating over 120 hotels in twenty-four countries, and is a today a member of the Starwood chain.

Ellen Church (1904-1965), an Iowan nurse who wanted to be a pilot, becomes the first flight attendant (aka *skygirl*) on May 15th when hired by Boeing Air Transport (soon to become United Airlines). Her first flight was a 20-hour and thirteen-stop flight between Oakland, California and Chicago, Illinois; with responsibilities that included: ticket taking, being a tour guide, nurse, tool keeper, plane refueler (on occasion), baggage handler, waitress, safety consultant, while always smiling and nodding her head...pilot screwing became an optional service in the 1970's. And yes, she was single, not over 115 pounds, and no taller than 5 foot 4 inches!

Youth Hostels open in England, Wales, Northern Ireland and Scotland, with 75 operating by the end of the first year.

The Soviet Government creates the All-Union Society of Proletarian Tourism and Excursions (OPTE) to develop mass tourism, especially among Soviet youth.

Eastern Air Transport (aka Eastern Airlines) formed out of the former Pitcairn Aviation that had earlier secured some mail routes, begins offering passenger service. Captain Eddie Rickenbacker (1890-1973), World War I ace of aces, takes the helm in 1935.

The Greyhound Corporation formed from Motor Transit Corporation, that had earlier established buses in the U.S. Mid-West in 1926, begins service in regions across America.

Citing inefficient and expensive air mail delivery—and sweetheart government subsidies to boot, the U.S. Congress passes the McNary-Watres Act (aka Air Mail Act of 1930), which effectively shuts out smaller airlines from government postal contracts and gives Postmaster General Walter F. Brown the right to pick and chose winners and losers, who quickly dictates that only three airlines will run the mail: United Airlines, had the northern airmail route; Transcontinental and Western Air (TWA), had the mid-U.S. route; and American Airlines, the southern route. Talk about legacy airlines…

Trans World Airlines (TWA) becomes the first airline to require that its pilots have a flight plan, write a flight log, obtain flight clearance and complete a cockpit check list (See: 1937). Thank you TWA!

Mines Field (aka Los Angeles International Airport (LAX), opens for business, by 2010 LAX transported more "origin and destination" (aka non-connecting) passengers than any airport in the world!

Cleveland Municipal Airport (aka CLE) in Ohio becomes the first radio-equipped air traffic control tower in the United States.

A new era of sports tourism takes off with the inaugural World Cup (aka soccer or European football) in Montevideo, Uruguay.

1931

The first *nonstop* transpacific flight takes place October 3rd between Sabishiro Beach, Japan and Wenatchee, Washington. Clyde Pangborn and Hugh Herndon Jr., pilot their *Bellanca Skyrocket* 8,851 kilometers (5,500 miles) over 41 hours and 13 minutes in their historical flight, but were required to perform a "controlled crash landing" near Wenatchee, Washington. They both walked away okay and collected the US$25,000 prize offered by a Japanese newspaper. (See: 1928 - Charles Edward Kingsford Smith)

The first attempted aerial hijacking takes place in Arequipa, Peru on February 21ˢᵗ, when a few rebellious soldiers attempt to force Byron Rickards, an American pilot, to drop propaganda flyers over Lima to help their cause. He refuses and a ten day standoff ensues until the revolution is a *fait accompli*…he then flies them gratis to Lima to celebrate!

The State of Nevada finally legalizes gambling, *err*, sorry, *gaming* to appease the crowd. The Northern Club, which had been openly operating since the 1920's, receives the first official license. Today, gaming tax revenues make up over forty-percent of Nevada's state revenue.

The American Steamship and Tourist Agents Association (aka American Society of Travel Agents (ASTA) was founded on April 20th. (Strictly a coincidence I am certain to the aforementioned citation). Travel agency growth and the growth of airline passengers run together until they are finally economically decoupled (See: 2002).

Knute Rockne (1888-1931), Notre Dame's legendary football coach, dies in the crash of a Fokker Trimotor that causes a public outcry over the quality of passenger air service. Americans are always ahead of the curve when it comes to safety first—but always after the fact!

Northwest Airways introduces in-flight radios for their passenger's in-flight enjoyment.

Wiley Post (1898–1935), an American pilot and adventurer, becomes the first to circumnavigate the world using a single aircraft, a Lockheed Vega monoplane he calls *Winnie Mae*. He completes the eleven-stop, 25,099 kilometer (15,596-mile) voyage in eight days and 15 hours and 51 minutes that ended on July 1ˢᵗ. Post does it again in his tried and true *Winnie Mae* two years later even faster at seven days and 19 hours and 21 minutes—but solo this time!

1932
Robert Edison Fulton Jr (1909-2004), a true American legend, travels around-the-world on his custom-made Douglas twin motorcycle over eighteen months and through 22 countries, and writes *One Man Caravan*. Actually he really only drove the motorcycle over 40,000 kilometers (about 25,000 miles) from London to Tokyo; but this man lived an amazing life,

and in 1983 he produced a film compiled from his home movies, *The One Man Caravan of Robert E. Fulton, Jr. An Autofilmography*. See it if you can...

Warner Bros studio releases *One Way Passage*, starring William Powell and Kay Francis, about a couple that met in Hong Kong and carry on a shipboard love affair. One of the many reasons people travel—romance! But remember the wise words: *What sails on the water, does not have feet on the ground...*

American Luggage Works (aka American Tourister) starts selling luggage. In 1993 the company was bought by its main competitor Samsonite and remains the company's low-end product.

The Music Hall (aka Radio City Music Hall) opens in the heart of New York City.

The Hertz car rental company opens the first airport rental location at Chicago's Midway Airport (MDW). Airport tax, convenience fees and drop charges apply.

Linious "Mac" McGee (1897–1968), an Alaska-based aviator, buys his first seaplane (aka float plane) in Anchorage, Alaska. His company McGee Airways would become Alaska's Star Airlines and finally Alaska Airlines in 1944.

Dame Freya Madeleine Stark (1893-1993), inspiring English traveler, who "dared to go where no man would" and writer with literally 100 years of personal experience, pens her first travel manuscript, *Baghdad Sketches*.

The Oscar winning movie Grand Hotel is released to great fanfare. The lobby is so busy that Greta Garbo has to deliver the line, "*I want to be alone.*" And now she can be with the help of a computer in the Wi-Fi lobby (See: 2008).

Graham Greene (1904-1991), an English author, releases a wonderful novel about adventure on the Orient Express entitled *Stamboul Train*. He writes a few other travel books too, like: *Journey Without Maps* (1936), *The Lawless*

Roads (1939), *Travels with My Aunt* (1969)…he's kind of world-renowned, you should look him up!

Western Air Express introduces the first live in-flight television broadcast (aka media event') onboard a Fokker F-10. The show was cancelled as the affiliates did not receive ad revenues.

The first of the major international film festivals was held in Venice attracting Hollywood celebrities and paparazzi ever since (aka Film Festival tourism). The now more popular Cannes Film Festival did not begin until after World War II in 1946.

The Eastman Kodak company (See: 1888), brings to market the first 8mm amateur motion-picture cameras…and travel videos and pornos have never been the same!

The Air Line Pilots Association, International (ALPA), the North American airline pilots union is created. Today, the ALPA union represents over 66,000 pilots working for over 40 U.S. and Canadian airlines…the pilots united will never be defeated!

1933
The illusive term *Shangri-La* is coined in the novel *Lost Horizon* by British novelist James Hilton (1900–1954). It refers to a fictional utopia…and travelers have been looking for that Shangri La ever since (aka the grass is always greener syndrome)!

On October 10th, a Boeing 247 is destroyed in midflight by a nitroglycerin bomb. All ten people aboard are killed. This incident is the first proven case of air sabotage in the history of aviation.

The Great Depression, err, depresses, hotel revenues as hotels across America post the lowest average occupancy rate on record, just 51 percent. It is claimed that 50% of all hotels in America enter receivership (aka bankruptcy).

Henry Beck (1902-1974), a London-based draftsman, designs the new-look connect the dots London Underground map that becomes the accepted norm for global subway maps. He realized that real geography did not matter to the riders, only the topology of the railway mattered. The dumbing-down of geography has continued ever since...

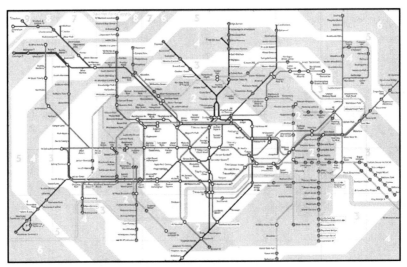

Modern-day Tube map.
(Courtesy Transport for London)

United Airlines offers USA coast-to-coast service on a Boeing 247 two engine ten passenger plane. It takes 20 hours with four refueling stops! Beats the alternative—three nights on a train!

Erwin George Baker (aka "Cannon Ball" Baker), an American racer, becomes the first person on record to drive (speed) coast to coast; driving his Graham-Paige model 57 Blue Streak 8 from New York City to Los Angeles, California in 53 hours and 30 minutes (an average greater than 50 mph (80 km/h) in a record that stood for almost 40 years. (See: 1971)

1934

The first diesel train, the 4-car *Pioneer Zephyr*, travels the 1,776 kilometer (1,104-mile) Denver to Chicago run at an average speed of 125 km/h in about 14 hours—cutting the travel time in half for wealthy ranchers taking their paramours to the big city. The *Zephyr* also has a significant role in the 1934 movie production of *The Silver Streak*.

Wally Byam (1896-1962), a life-long American road traveler, introduces the name *Airstream* to his improved RV trailers, "because that's the way they travel, like a stream of air." In 1936 he introduced the Clipper, a silver sleeper trailer pulled by a car and builds his Airstream Trailer Company in 1948; and also writes *Trailer Travel Here and Abroad*. The Wally Byam Caravan Club International (WBCCI) was formed in 1952.

Agatha Christie (1890-1976), an English writer, pens her popular mystery novel *Murder on the Orient Express*.

Walter and Cordelia Knott, two American berry farmers, open their roadside stand in Orange County, a suburb of Los Angeles, California and begin selling Boysenberry Pies; that begat a restaurant, that begat interactive berry displays, that begat rock gardens and waterwheels, that begat a gift shop, that begat a 12-foot-tall volcano, that begat a gold-mine shaft...you get the point of all that begetting, and Knott's Berry Farm now sees millions of visitors from around the world each year! Sensing a good location, Walt Disney builds his Disneyland (See: 1955) right nearby...

Helen Richey (1909–1947), an American aviation pioneer, becomes the first woman to be employed as an airline pilot for Central Airlines—later Pennsylvania Central Airlines (PCA). Sadly, Helen never flies commercial, as the all-male cockpit balks at her taking the controls. (See: 1973)

1935
The New York Convention & Visitors Bureau is founded to attract, well, conventions and visitors to The Big Apple.

The Kodak Company (See: 1888), begins offering amateur photographers their dream film—Kodachrome 35mm. It remains the film until it is sadly displaced in 2009 with the popularity of digital photography.

Pan Am's China Clipper service begins operations between San Francisco, California and Manila on October 25th. After getting the bugs out, Pan Am would later use three planes on the legendary route: the Sikorsky S-42, the Martin M-130, and the Boeing 314. The San Francisco-Honolulu-Midway-Wake-Guam-Manila (and then to Hong Kong) route took 59 hours and 48 minutes. The route was interrupted in 1941 with the onset of World War II.

The Moscow Metro opens in Russia with one 11 kilometer (6.8-mile) line and 13 stations. It later expands quickly to 182 stations along 300 kilometers (187 miles) to become the world's second busiest subway system with over 6.5 million daily riders—Tokyo is first!

The 20-foot Covered Wagon Tandem Axle recreation vehicle is introduced.

Jimmy Angel (1899-1956), an America bush pilot, discovers Angel Falls (aka *Salto Ángel*); the world's tallest, in Venezuela, by accident—literally. Angel Falls is so high at 979 meters (3,212 feet), that most of the water falling from it either evaporates or turns to mist before hitting the ground! The falls name was changed in 2009 to the indigenous Pemon name, *Kerepakupai Merú*. Historians argue whether or not Sir Walter Raleigh (See: 1603) was actually the first to have discovered the falls during his nearby Guiana expedition and trip up the Orinoco River.

The first all airways air traffic control (ATC) tower is erected at Newark International Airport (EWR). This regional airspace control tower—as opposed to just for the airport take-offs and landings—becomes the first of many to open across America, with towers in Chicago and Cleveland opening in 1936.

It did not take long after Jack Frye, a Transcontinental and Western Air (TWA) VP, states flatly that paying customers were going to "the competition primarily because of the pretty girls" that TWA's first airhostesses begin flying aboard their DC-2's. The race to the bottom begins... Trying to sell the avocation, Ruth Rhodes, TWA's first Chief Hostess, was quoted in 1937: *"Women haven't enough adventure in their lives. Flying through the air high above the earth, racing against time, absorbing the knowledge that after all, the world is one small place, was the most romantic thing a woman could do."* Indeed... On a side not, it seems that TWA, and the other airlines had a hard time keeping their hostesses in the air—they were in fact perfect marriage material! Haven't we all known a perfect "Glamour Girl of the Air"—and not so perfect ones too!?

The 21-passenger Douglas DC-3 enters service on December 13th and revolutionizes air transport and is called, "the most important aircraft in the history of civil aviation." By 1941, almost 80 percent of commercial airplanes in the United States were DC-3s. In total 16,079 DC-3's (both military and civilian) were built, and in 2000, a few hundred still worked the skies...

The *Spirit of Santa Monica* DC-3.
(Author Photo)

Starline Tours of Hollywood opens for business with the original and ever-so-popular Movie Stars Homes tour (aka celebrity tourism).

The world's first parking meter becomes operational on the streets of Oklahoma City in the United States—the first ticket was issued within a couple of weeks.

1936

The winter ski season expands when the world's first overhead chair lift is built at Sun Valley, Idaho—the first high-altitude ski resort in United States. Later, the first U.S.-based aerial tramway was installed at Cannon Mountain, New Hampshire in 1938. Alta mountain ski resort opens Utah powder in 1941 and the Aspen Skiing Corporation opens Colorado's snow in 1946. Snow itself is finally man-made in1952 at Grossinger's in New York.

A loose bus route system created by dozens of privately owned motor coach companies forms into the National Trailways Bus System (NTBS), an intercity bus line to give Greyhound Lines (See: 1926) a run for its money; it that later becomes Trailways.

William and Ethel Stuckey, Georgia pecan farmers, open their first Stuckey's roadside stand in Eastman, Georgia along U.S. Route 23, to sell pecans to snowbird motorists en route to and from Florida. Feeling the success and opportunity, they build their first restaurant a year later and by 1960 had over 350 locations across America. Every American child ever forced to take a summer family road trip knows Stuckey's!

Following wave after wave of worker protests and strikes in France, the left-center French Socialist government mandates vacations for workers for the first time, along with 48% wage rates and having their work week cut by 17%...how anti-capitalistic? Many reactionaries wonder aloud (often and especially on FOX TV), just how that country grew into the giant economic and industrial powerhouse it is today with such anti-business legislation?

United Airlines introduces the first in-air kitchen. Coincidently, the first mystery meat question is asked: "Is that stuff chicken or beef?"

The League of Nations officially defines a *foreign tourist* as someone travelling abroad for at least twenty-four hours. The United Nations later amends this definition in 1945, to include a maximum stay of six months.

William Heygate Edmund Colborne (Billy) Butlin (1899–1980), a Canadian entrepreneur with a good nose about working stiff aspirations, opens his first "holiday camp" in England as kind of predecessor to Club Med, called Butlins Holiday Camps. The idea of pre-paid all-inclusive tourism is hatched.

Victor H. Green (1892-1964c), an American writer, publishes his first black travel guide, *The Negro Motorist Green Book* (aka *The Green Book*), helping African-Americans navigate the bankrupt Jim Crow laws of America. In his introduction he notes his own demise with, *"There will be a day sometime in the near future when this guide will not have to be published. That is when we as a race will have equal rights and privileges in the United States."*And indeed, the last published annual edition was 1964 with the passage of the U.S. Civil Rights Act.

Eugene Fodor (1905-1991), Hungarian-American writer and soon to be Office of Strategic Services (OSS) spy, publishes *On the Continent—The Entertaining Travel Annual.* He would later form Fodor's publishing group in Paris in 1949. (Fodors.com)

The conception of the tradition of Spring Break (See: 1960c's) begins when a swimming coach of Colgate University in Hamilton, New York, brings his swim team south to Fort Lauderdale, Florida to practice their sport at the Olympic-sized Casino Pool—before the 1936 Olympic Games. It is reported that by 1954, as many as 20,000 U.S. college kids made their way to the Fort Lauderdale beach.

1937
The *Hindenburg* (aka LZ 129) the largest airship ever built at over 245 meters (800 feet) explodes on May 6th while attempting to land at the Lakehurst Naval Air Station in New Jersey. It is known forevermore as the Hindenburg Disaster with all thirty-five passengers dying in the fireball. The accident effectively kills airship flights...that and that little man in Germany named Hitler, who made travel to and from the Continent a tad dicey over the next decade! (In a side note for you *Indiana Jones* fans, in the film *Indiana Jones and the Last Crusade,* Indiana travels on the *Hindenburg.)*

Frank Capra (1897–1991), an American film director, releases his widely acclaimed adventure movie *The Lost Horizon.*

In an effort to better air safety, commercial airline pilots begin the mandatory pre-flight cockpit checklists like TWA had voluntarily started earlier (See: 1930).

Haw Par Villa (aka Tiger Balm Gardens), a sort of theme park *ala* mythical Chinese garden designed to celebrate Tiger Balm, opens in Singapore. It had a few rides; one called The Ten Courts of Hell...surely an apt name for a theme park attraction. It was rebranded in 1985 as Dragon World.

Ernest Henderson and Robert Moore, two American businessmen, purchase the Stonehaven Hotel in Springfield, Massachusetts—and the Sheraton Hotels company is born.

The travel magazine *U.S. Camera and Travel* begins arriving monthly and is bought by American Express in 1968 and in 1971 re-brands as the popular glossy *Travel + Leisure* travel magazine.

1938

It took twenty years of lobbying, but the British Parliament finally passes the *Holidays with Pay Act* of 1938 that mandates at least one week a year of paid vacations for all fulltime workers. The passage of this act legitimizes workers fundamental leisure needs. Some nations still to not have this basic acknowledgement—oh, sorry, just one, the USA!

Route 66, that 3,540 kilometer (2,200-mile) road from Chicago to Los Angeles is now fully paved. Now you could really "*(Get Your Kicks On) Route 66*", as Nat King Cole sang in 1946.

Route 66 sign.
(Author Photo)

The Civil Aeronautics Authority (CAA) is established to regulate airfares and routes in the United States.

As a response to growing unease in America about the developments in Europe, CBS airs the *World News Roundup* that ushers in modern news with a world-view POV.

The Black Hills Classic (aka Sturgis Motorcycle Rally) is first held in Sturgis, South Dakota. By 2000, and an estimated 750,000 bikers from around the world attended.

A Pan American Airways' *Hawaii Clipper* with fifteen passengers and crew aboard was allegedly hi-jacked on July 29th by Imperial Japanese Naval aviators and kept quiet in American circles. If this incident is true—and no one is talking—that flight would be the world's first passenger plane hi-jacking.

Another step forward in cocktail evolution occurs when Carlos "Danny" Herrera, a Mexican mixologist-extraordinare, serving tequila and *cerveza* at the Rancho La Gloria hotel in Baja, Mexico, creates the sublime (sorry) margarita for a non-tequila drinking patron. Thank you *senor* Danny... rocks no salt for me!

1939
Howard Hughes (1905-1976), noted American industrialist, acquires a controlling interest in TWA. In 1965 he sells his 6,584,937 shares netting US$546.5 million. Hughes fell in love with the aviation industry and truly loved to fly; he broke speed records—in 1935 going 566 km/h (352 mph) —and the around the world record—in 1938 taking just 91 hours (3 days, 19 hours) —at various times.

A roadside tourist attraction alluringly called *The Mystery Spot* opens outside Santa Cruz, California, where it is claimed the laws of physics and gravity do not apply. Check it out...if you need to kill some of your precious time—or the kids are acting up!

On March 25th, nine passengers fly aboard a Trans-Canada Air Lines flight, Canada's first ever country wide airline, that takes them from Victoria, British Columbia on the West Coast, to Montreal, Quebec via Lethbridge, Winnipeg and North Bay, Ontario. It is the first commercial flight to travel across Canada.

The New York World's Fair is held at Flushing Meadows with the promise of a better future through technology and the slogan *"Dawn of a New Day"* that is said to have inspired millions, including Walt Disney to create Disneyland (See: 1955). Exhibits included: the Westinghouse

Time Capsule, a futuristic car based city by GM, World Science Fiction Convention, the Jewish Palestine Pavilion, and Frank Buck's Jungleland, among others. The Polish and Czechoslovakian pavilions did not open as an ominous sign of things to come.

Interestingly enough, before the New York World's Fair opens, the newly formed union representing hotel workers—the Hotel Trades Council—negotiates a contract for hotel service employees that provided for a 48-hour, six-day work week for most workers (54 hours for waiters and busboys) and raised wages by an average of US$2.00 a week, setting these typical minimum weekly rates: maids $14.50, waiters $9.00 (waitresses got only $7.50!), bellman $4.00, elevator operators $19.00, and bartenders got $30.00—we have our priorities straight don't we!

The National Baseball Hall of Fame and Museum advancing sports tourism to a new level, opens in Cooperstown, New York at the height of the recession (and before World War II) as a way to get tourists to town. *"If you build it—they will come!"* And they did…

The first of seven *Road to…*movies, *the Road to Singapore,* starring Bing Crosby and Bob Hope opens.

On May 20th, twelve years to the day after Lindbergh's historic flight, Pan Am Airways B-314 *Yankee Clipper* departed Port Washington, New York for the first scheduled mail service across the Atlantic. Proving a success, passenger service quickly began, and on June 28th the *Dixie Clipper* left New York with 22 passengers en route to Horta, Lisbon, and a new era had arrived.

Quality Courts United, a hotel referral business with several suppliers located in Maryland opens for business that allows travelers to find hotels easier. The company evolves over the years into Quality Inn and what we know today as the Choice Hotels chain.

With the onset of hostilities in both Europe and the Pacific, travel-related innovations seem to come to a virtual crawl…and for good reason.

1940

The Boeing 307-Stratoliner, the first pressurized cabin and all-weather commercial airliner, begins service by TWA providing coast-to-coast travel in just 13 hours and 40 minutes...the pressurized cabin matters for many reasons, but mostly because it allows the plane to fly up to 6,000 meters (20,000 feet) avoiding turbulence!

The first Dairy Queen (aka DQ) restaurant opens in Joliet, Illinois. Today DQ has 5,700 stores in 19 countries!

The *RMS Queen Elizabeth*, the largest passenger ship ever built, is put into service by Cunard Line as a troop ship in February. In October 1946, she would serve paying customers.

On August 31st, a Pennsylvania Central Airlines DC-3 crashes near Lovettsville, Virginia killing all 25 aboard, making it the worst U.S. airplane accident to date...it also ushered in the beginning of formal investigations being conducted by the Civil Aeronautics Board.

1942

The Kodak company (See: 1888), does it again by introducing Kodacolor film, the world's first true color negative film.

Afro-American Newspapers publishes the *Travel Guide of Negro Hotels and Guest Houses*, which helped African-Americans stay out of trouble in racist areas of America.

1943

Jacques-Yves Cousteau (1910-1997), a French oceanographer, invents the *aqualung* breathing apparatus that allows divers to stay underwater. A new world is opened for man. Cousteau goes on to write the landmark *The Silent World* in 1956, and makes the oceans popular.

Franklin D. Roosevelt (1882 –1945), an American president, was the first president to fly on an airplane while in office, when he took the *Dixie Clipper*, a Pan Am-crewed Boeing 314 flying boat, to attend the 1943 Casablanca Conference in Morocco.

The Hockey Hall of Fame (aka *Temple de la renommée du hockey*) opens in Toronto, Canada. Hundreds of thousands of hockey fans visit it every year, especially Maple Leaf fans—because that is the only way they will ever see the Stanley Cup!

What the?... The German Baedekers guidebook company (See: 1829) publishes a guidebook for Nazi's visiting occupied Poland (apparently they are order to do so...) during World War II called *Das Generalgouvernement*. It lists Auschwitz simply as a "train station."

1944
Howard Hughes (See: 1939) and TWA President Jack Frye, together pilot a new Lockheed 1049 Constellation from Burbank, California to Washington D.C. in just 6 hours and 57 minutes—setting a new cross-country speed record on April 17th.

The Convention on International Civil Aviation of 1944 (aka the Chicago Convention), formalizes the *freedoms of the air*, a set of commercial aviation rights that grant airlines the privilege to enter and land in another country's airspace. This is an important step in the development of commercial passenger aviation as it begins opening the world to airlines to visit remoter nations that do not have airlines. There was concern from non-U.S. carriers and nations that U.S.-based carriers would dominate global air travel, but that of course did not happen. These freedoms of the air, are kind of like an Airline Bill of Rights, that included, among other things: the right to fly over a foreign country without landing there; the right to fly between two foreign countries while not offering flights to one's own country in return; and the right to rip off passengers with deceptive business practices...okay, I made that last one up—really, I did!

1945
Wilfred Thesiger (1910-2003), a British adventurer and avid boxer, walks through the so-designated Saudi Empty Quarter, and writes *Arabian Sands* in 1959 that highlights the Bedouins vanishing way of life—and creating the concept of Ethno Tourism.

The Air Line Stewardesses Association (ALSA) is established in the U.S., the first labor union representing flight attendants. The union is now known as Association of Flight Attendants (AFA) and represents over 55,000 flight attendants working at 22 airlines.

The International Air Transport Association (IATA) is morphed as the successor to the International Air Traffic Association (See: 1919).

The United Nations Charter is signed on June 26th in San Francisco, California by all but one recognized nation of the world—the Roman Catholic hierarchy of the Vatican holdout! Why is this important? Because it makes international law rather important to obey by all signatories, establishes an International Court of Justice (IJC) so real global bad guys can't continue being bad without paying the piper at some point, and lead quickly to the expansion of human rights (See: 1948). The preamble says it all, some get goose-bumps just reading it for all its hope and optimism:
"We the peoples of the United Nations determined: to save succeeding generations from the scourge of war, which twice in our lifetime has brought untold sorrow to mankind, and to reaffirm faith in fundamental human rights, in the dignity and worth of the human person, in the equal rights of men and women and of nations large and small, and to establish conditions under which justice and respect for the obligations arising from treaties and other sources of international law can be maintained, and to promote social progress and better standards of life in larger freedom, And for these ends: to practice tolerance and live together in peace with one another as good neighbours, and to unite our strength to maintain international peace and security, and to ensure, by the acceptance of principles and the institution of methods, that armed force shall not be used, save in the common interest, and to employ international machinery for the promotion of the economic and social advancement of all peoples, Have resolved to combine our efforts to accomplish these aims: Accordingly, our respective Governments, through representatives assembled in the city of San Francisco, who have exhibited their full powers found to be in good and due form, have agreed to the present Charter of the United Nations and do hereby establish an international organization to be known as the United Nations."

The inaugural around the world commercial airline service begins when an Air Transport Command, a military wing that ferries troops from here to there quickly, flies a Douglas C-54E *Globester* with 9-passengers from Washington, D.C. back to Washington, D.C—the perfect bureaucratic mission to nowhere! They flew 37,215 kilometers (23,147 miles) in 149 hours.

Pan Am begins using an in-plane convection oven to heat meals. Now the mystery meat burns your tongue too!

Having lost its Pacific air routes to Pan Am, American Export Airlines (AEA)—later called American Overseas Airlines (AOA) after being purchased by American Airlines—begins regular land plane passenger service between New York and England in October following the conclusion of World War II. The DC-4's would fuel in Gander, Newfoundland and then again at Shannon, Ireland after a long ocean flight.

According to the U.S. General Accounting Office (GAO) the intercity bus industry reaches its peak with 45 billion passenger miles—compared to just 7.5 billion in 1990, and just 2.6 billion miles by 2000! Mass transit is not in the cards in the U.S....a House of Cards?

Sheraton Hotel and Resorts (NYSE: HOT) is the first hotel corporation to be listed on the New York Stock Exchange.

1946
France and the United States sign the first of many bilateral reciprocal agreements covering commercial passenger airline service when they agree to the Five Freedoms Agreement on March 27th.

M.K. Guertin (1891-1970), an American businessman, who along with fifty-four liked-minded business associates, forms what is known as the Best Western chain out of an informal referral system. By 1963, it is "the world's largest hotel chain," and in 2002 there are over 4,000 global properties offering over 300,000 rooms in over 80 countries.

American Airlines begins operating the first automated booking system, the experimental electromechanical *Reservisor*. They lose the first reservation when Mr. Smith arrives late after a delayed flight attempting to make a connection!

Fred Pontin (1906-), a London businessman, originates Pontin's holiday company that specializes in offering half-board and self-catering holidays to working class Brits with the catchy slogan: "*All your want-ins at Pontins*". He has a life-long rivalry with fellow holiday packager Butlin's (See: 1936)

Westin hotels is said to debut the first guest credit card. (My best guess is this not a real credit card per se, but a card that guest may use to sign for things, or it may in fact be a merchant credit?)

The King David Hotel that was opened in 1931 in Jerusalem, is bombed on July 22nd by the militant Zionist group, the Irgun—whose members included former Israeli Prime Ministers Menachem Begin—leaving ninety people dead and forty-five wounded. The terrorist attack succinctly explains the modern-day truism that one man's terrorist is another's freedom fighter!

Warren E. Avis (1915-2007), an American entrepreneur, had a simple idea: car rentals should be available at airports; so he founded Avis Airlines Rent-a-Car to do just that. His first outlet opens at Willow Run Airport in Ypsilanti, Michigan. The fly-drive tourism model is invented!

President Harry Truman signs a bill authorizing the building of the National Air Museum in the Smithsonian Institution in Washington, DC, with US$50,000 in funds.

On April 26th, the Naperville train disaster occurs when the *Exposition Flyer* rams into the *Advance Flyer*, which wasn't supposed to be there, at 85 miles per hour (137 km/h) killing 47 passengers with 125 more seriously injured. This crash changes America's mindset about the safety of rail and with it any future potential advancements of high-speed rail in the United States; as from then on railway speeds everywhere and anywhere are limited to just 79 mph (127 km/h). High-speed rail RIP for America!

1947
Benjamin "Bugsy" Siegel (1905-1947), an American gangster, opens the first major Las Vegas Strip casino hotel, the 93-room Flamingo.

The Las Vegas Strip.
(Author Photo)

Chuck Yeager (1923-), an American test pilot, reaches the speed of Mach 1.07 (364.11 meters a second or 708 mph), and rings in the advent of the Jet Age.

Thor Heyerdahl (1914-2002), a Norwegian adventurer, sails his raft the *Kon-Tiki* watercraft for 101 days and 8,000 kilometers (4,300 miles) from Peru to Polynesia. He proves his point!

The Westin Hotel chain establishes *Hoteltype*, the first hotel reservation system.

TWA becomes the first airline to develop and use the quick-frozen precooked method of food preparation, packaging and shipping for in-flight meal service. Gee thanks TWA!

In what may be the first reported incident of Air Rage (See: 1998), an apparently intoxicated male passenger, becomes unruly on a flight from Havana, Cuba, to Miami, Florida, and physically assaults a fellow passenger. Was it gambling losses, bad food, too much alcohol, or just a bad joke—no one knows for sure.

United Airlines becomes the first airline offering passengers something to read in-flight when they begin publishing their *United Airlines Magazine* that would later change the name to *Hemispheres* in 1992.

AT&T, a U.S.-based telephone company, begins operating the *highway service*, a radio-telephone (aka digital) service between New York and Boston. It did not work so well...

Pan American Airways becomes the first airline to offer a regular commercial around-the-world (RTW) flight schedule departing San Francisco International Airport (SFO), California at 0:30 on Friday on a Constellation L749 *Clipper America,* and arriving in New York at 15:00 the next Friday; onboard westbound Flight #1 via Honolulu, Tokyo, Hong Kong, Bangkok, Calcutta, Beirut, Istanbul, Frankfurt and London. In 1959 it is the first airline to offer RTW 707 jet service.

The Roosevelt Hotel in New York City becomes the first to offer in-room television.

Howard Hughes (See: 1939), flies the Hughes H-4 Hercules (aka the Spruce Goose), the world's largest flying boat having the largest wingspan of any aircraft in history—to this day!—1.6 kilometers (one-mile) on November 2nd. It never flies again and is a museum piece adjacent to the Queen Mary in Long Beach, California. See Martin Scorsese's 2004 movie *The Aviator.*

If you, like many others, have ever wondered when airports began turning into shopping malls, well, the world's first duty-free shop was established at Shannon Airport in Ireland by Dr. Brendan O'Regan, an Irish entrepreneur. The duty-free idea is based on the premise that taxes are not levied on goods to be exported. Shannon Airport (SNN) was the perfect place also—a must refueling stop between Europe and North America.

The first aircraft, a modified Douglas DC-6 (aka C-118 Liftmaster), acting as Air Force One (the president of the United States' official airplane) came into duty under President Harry Truman. The Air Force One call sign began being used during World War II as the code phrase for the designated plane that the president was riding on, be it commercial or military; and the first official flight of Air Force One was in 1959 during the Eisenhower administration, a Boeing 707. (See: 1943)

Northwest Orient pioneers the "Great Circle Route" (Great circle routes have been used for centuries by ocean-going vessels, and now airlines, that utilize favorable wind conditions (and currents) for east and west journeys (aka trade winds.) to Asia with service from the U.S. to Tokyo, Seoul, Shanghai and Manila and back to the U.S.

1948

Temple Harndon Fielding (1913-), an American OSS propagandist and travel writer, establishes the Fielding Guides by publishing a hardcover guide to Europe. The travel guide company, referred to as *the bible* of adventure travelers and expats everywhere, offers a witty editorial bent that focuses on the unusual, unknown and unique.

Idlewild International Airport, built atop the Idlewild Golf Course in Queens, opens in New York City to relieve the air traffic at LaGuardia Airport (LGA), earlier built in 1939. The airport name is later changed to John F. Kennedy International Airport, in 1963.

The *Universal Declaration of Human Rights* is adopted by United Nations General Assembly on December 10th. Among other noble aspirations it promotes and recognizes basic human rights, like: the Right's of Movement by claiming that, *"Everyone has the right to leave any country, including his own, and to return to his country."* And the Right's of Leisure, *"Everyone has the right to rest and leisure, including reasonable limitation of working hours and periodic holidays with pay."* Amen…

Maurice & Richard McDonald, American brothers in the restaurant business, open the first McDonalds restaurant in San Bernardino, California. The rest is culinary (sic) history. By 1960 there were over 200 outlets, and by 2010 there are over 31,000 restaurants in 119 countries serving more than 58 million customers daily! By the way, the *Golden Arches Theory of Conflict Prevention*, which claims that no two countries that have a McDonald's outlet have ever gone to war together, is not true— the United States did invade Panama in 1989. Other examples also exist.

Dr. Leslie Gray, an American doctor, prescribes compound 1694 to a patient for an unrelated illness, but it seems to help her with her travel-related nausea (aka motion sickness). A use for Dramamine (aka dimenhydrinate) is discovered. Motion sickness can be caused by motion that is felt but not seen; caused by motion that is seen but not felt; or, caused when both systems detect motion but they do not correspond. It is estimated that up to one in three travelers are susceptible to motion sickness, be it from driving, sailing, or flying.

Over the course of a year, three separate planes disappear without a trace—a British South American Airways (BSAA) Avro Tudor IV, Star Tiger; another BSAA Avro Tudor, Star Ariel; and an Airborne Transport Douglas DC-3, in 1949—all helping to create the speculation behind the mysterious legend of the *Bermuda Triangle*. Late night TV has never been the same...

On July 17, a plane being operated by a Cathay Pacific company, the *Miss Macao*, with 23 passengers flying from Macau to Hong Kong, is hijacked in an apparent robbery attempt—pirates take to the air!—following a cockpit struggle, a crash kills all on board except one passenger, later identified as the hijacker! This incident is believed to be the earliest known actual mid-air airliner hijacking.

1949

The first nonstop around-the-world flight, a U.S. Air Force flight, takes place with four in-flight refueling (IFR) procedures over 94 hours and one minute.

Hilton Hotels becomes the first international hotel chain with the opening of the *Caribe* Hilton in San Juan, Puerto Rico. Never mind that Puerto Rico uses U.S. currency, votes in U.S. federal elections, and are U.S. citizens...it still is apparently a foreign country!? (And they wonder why we are a tad geographically-impaired!) On a serious note, Ramón "Monchito" Marrero, the *Caribe*'s bartender extraordinaire, becomes a living legend in 1954 when he conceives the sublime Piña Colada cocktail—after a Coco López promo. Thank you Ramon...and *I too like getting caught in the rain*!

The International Student Travel Confederation (ISTC) is created in Copenhagen, Denmark to make travel more affordable for students. The student ID card offering travel discounts quickly follows and 2010 they have 5000 offices in over 120 countries serving ten million student and youth travelers. (ISTC.org)

On October 17ᵗʰ, Northwest Orient Airlines becomes the first carrier in North America to offer complimentary in-flight alcoholic beverages. A drink to Northwest! (In an unrelated true story; Northwest also introduces plastic-lined airsickness bags for the first time this year!)

In the Dutch town of Lisse, the Keukenhof (aka the Garden of Europe) is opened to the public and is reputed to be the world's largest flower garden with in excess of 7 million flowers! An April must see!

Paul Frederic Bowles (1910 –1999), an American expatriate author, publishes his dark and brooding novel *The Sheltering Sky*. We all know Port and Kit's who travel (aka Escape tourists)…

1950
Gerard Blitz (1912-1990), a Belgian entrepreneur and yoga enthusiast, becomes a travel innovator with the establishment of *Club Méditerranée* (Club Med), the all-inclusive resort concept that he opens at *Alcudia*, a tent village in the Balearic Islands of Spain. He later opens Club Med's first ski resort in Leysin, Switzerland in 1957 and the first Caribbean resort in Guadeloupe in 1968. *Gentil membre* and *gentil organizateur* (GO's) became *de rigueur*—and those damn poppet beads too!

Ernesto Guevara (aka Che) (1928–1967), an Argentinean medical student cum revolutionary icon, begins his legendary 8,000 kilometer (5,000-mile) motorcycle trip across South America. His trip diaries of his various travel adventures over a couple year period were later marketed as *"Das Kapital meets Easy Rider"*—no kidding!—and now known around the world after its formal release in 1993 as *The Motorcycle Diaries*.

New York City's metropolitan area population exceeds ten million for the first time.

With the patronage of Hollywood stars and starlets like: Elizabeth Taylor, Frank Sinatra, Eddie Fisher and Brigitte Bardot, the golden age of Acapulco, Mexico begins as the south of the border hot spot. The Four Tops release their single *"Loco in Acapulco"* in 1988.

The International Air Transport Association (IATA) allows for the creation of "economy class" (aka Y class, coach class, steerage, or tourist class) in order to maximize airline industry income. It should be noted that it was a *fait accompli* as in 1949 Delta Airlines offered its first coach service with discounted-fares on night flights between Chicago and Miami in coach. Pan Am quickly followed, as did United, American, etc, etc…

Volkswagen introduces the world to the first Microbus (aka the world's first minivan), known technically as the *Volkswagen Type 1 Transporter* (aka the Hippie Bus). Father's across America collectively feared for their daughters virtues.

1951

Diners Club (aka Diners Club International) becomes the first real credit card. It is offered to 200 customers who can use it in any one of 27 restaurants in New York City. It is claimed that by the second year of operation Diners Club had 285 accepting establishments and 35,000 card holders paying US$3.00 a year for the privilege. References to credit cards however date back to 1890 when some European merchants offered them as perks to their better customers. What Diners Club did innovate was the "travel and entertainment" (T&E) card market that benefits frequent customers—and legal IRS deductions too.

Horizon Holidays, a British travel agency, creates the modern day equivalent of a package tour (air and ground portions included) by offering trips to the French island of Corsica.

The Serengeti National Park in Tanzania is established in the middle of the Maasai people's endless plain. It should be noted that earlier in 1929, the British government, the area's colonial master, did decide to make a smaller portion the Serengeti a *Game Reserve* in order to halt all the wanton killing of animals. Later yet, in 1959, German director Bernhard Grzimek produces the groundbreaking movie (read conservation documentary) *Serengeti Shall Not Die* that further solidifies the areas fragile and important natural habitat. The park is huge at 14,763 square kilometers (5,700 square miles).

With the bi-lateral agreement known as the Indo-Nepal Treaty of Peace and Friendship of 1950, King Tribhuvan of Nepal (1906–1955), finally opens borders allowing tourists to visit Nepal, and Sir Edmund Hillary waits in line for his visa and climbing permit!

Alfred Hitchcock (1899–1980), an English film director, releases his *Strangers on a Train* that effectively helps kill (sorry!) train travel in America.

Jean-Louis (aka Jack) Kerouac (1922–1969), an American novelist, writes his *tour de force* work *On the Road*—although it would not be published until 1957 after being turned down by a series of publishing houses—about a series of road trips taken by he and his friends across America.

CHAPTER TEN

The Era of Hyper-Mobility (1952 – 1986):
The era of great global destruction is over and man begins recovering and gets quickly back on his feet. The ability to travel much greater distances with ease and frequency begins with the wide acceptance and popularity of air travel. And beginning in the 1950s, the glory and predominance of ocean liners begins to wane when larger and larger, and faster and faster passenger airplanes began whisking more and more passengers across the ocean in less and less time. For obvious reasons, the speed of crossing the ocean became more popular than the style of crossing it, whether by Boeing 747 Jumbo, supersonic Concorde, or the double-decker Airbus A380. Between 1950 and 2005, international arrivals grow from 25 million to over 805 million! A new era of travel evolves when the journey itself is secondary to arriving at the destination—and getting there is *no longer* half the fun…

1952
The British engineered de Havilland DH-106 Comet becomes the first commercial jet airliner operated by British Overseas Airways Corporation (BOAC) (aka British Airways in 1972) when it flies between London and Johannesburg on May 2nd. The flight takes twenty-three hours and 38 minutes at an average speed of 805 km/h (500 mph). The jet age arrives! But this plane did not last long, and after a series of deadly accidents the fleet was taken out of service by 1954.

(I had a great photo inserted here of the first jet courtesy of Qantas Airways…but the ninny lawyers at the publishing house made me remove it out of obscure copyright concerns? Google Image it to see what it looks like.)

The U.S. Civil Air Administration (CAA) began requiring that all flight attendants (aka cabin crew) on all commercial aircraft be trained cabin safety professionals—not just waiters and waitresses.

Heinrich Harrer (1912–2006), an Austrian mountaineer (and really bad father), publishes Brad Pitts *tour de force* to be, his true life adventure tale *Seven Years in Tibet* chronicling his time in Tibet with the Dali Lama during World War II.

Following the urban air crash of American Airlines Flight 6780, a Convair CV-240 that crashes on approach to Newark Airport (EWR) hitting nearby into houses and businesses in Elizabeth, New Jersey, killing 30, the United States reacts by creating the Doolittle Commission. The Commission's report recommends laws in coordinating local urban zoning with federal airports to help keep airport approach and departure paths as clear and safe as possible. Fact is, most airplane crashes occur within the first or last 30-seconds of take off or landings—speed and height are rather important elements of flying!

For the first time in history—at least American Airlines history?—on August 28th American Airlines flies 10,000,000 passenger-miles, setting a new single-day mileage record for all airlines. Aviation quants have no real numbers in which to truly calculate the veracity of this press release claim. But that is a lot of people flying!

Kemmons Wilson (1913-2003), an unhappy American family vacation planner, opens his first Holiday Inn in the outskirts of Memphis, Tennessee. The chain is named after a Bing Crosby movie and revolutionizes the hotel industry by providing: free parking, in-room television sets, air conditioning, and swimming pools. Holiday Inn went international in 1961 and by 2010 there were over 2,500 Holiday Inn hotel brands worldwide.

Trans World Airlines (TWA) opens the first known First Class-only airport lounge when the TWA Ambassadors Club opens at Greater Pittsburgh Airport (aka Pittsburgh International Airport (PIT).

1953

After World War II and utter chaos and destruction of Japan, locals had trouble finding "meeting" places for their trysts, and *tsurekomi yado* (aka bring-along inns) started popping up in urban areas. These nicknamed *love hotels* (aka romance hotels, fashion hotels, leisure hotels, amusement hotels, and couples hotels) which were first sighted around Ueno, Tokyo, became a uniquely Japanese phenomenon in the 1950's in providing a private haven where young and old couples alike (prostitutes and johns too), could escape the confines and flimsy walls of their small urban family homes for some *amour*. Still operating today, it is estimated that on average 1.4 million Japanese couples visit a love hotel each day!

Edmund Hillary (1919-2008), a New Zealand mountaineer, and Tenzing Norgay (1919-1986), a Nepali mountaineer, appear to be the first to successfully climb Mt. Everest at 8,848 meters (29,029-feet)...and live to tell about it. Nowadays, anyone with an extra US$75,000 can take the Everest Highway and get to the top (aka ego tourism).

The idea of "house swapping" is created by Intervac International, a worldwide organization that facilitates exchanges of homes (aka home exchanges) for sometimes extended family vacations. Proponents like the idea because it is cheaper and more culturally-enriching as you live where the locals live.

Trans World Airlines begins offering the first non-stop eastbound scheduled transcontinental service aboard a Lockheed L-1049 Super Constellations. The flight from Los Angeles, California to New York City takes eight hours. Because of prevailing head winds, westbound transcontinental service continues to stop in Chicago to refuel. Bi-coastal long-distance relationships among creative wealthy jet-setters became all the rage...

United Airlines begins offering *men-only* "Executive" flights between Chicago and New York that include macho offerings like steaks, cigars, martinis and take home gifts for the little lady's too! It ceased operations in 1970 when the National Organization of Women (NOW) filed suit. The world was a very racist and sexist place not too long ago wasn't it...we have evolved like Darwin suggested. But then again it was not until 1968 that United started hiring male cabin crew members...

An organization known as the World Service Authority (WSA) begins issuing World Passports. Despite it being apparently accepted—at least once—in over 150 nations and the fact that it is a great idea...you still might want to keep your real passport just in case!

EAA AirVenture Oshkosh (formerly The EAA Annual Convention and Fly-In), America's largest annual gathering of aviation enthusiasts, holds the first "fly in" at Hales Corners, Wisconsin. This event has grown and grown each year with private planes from all over arriving for fun and games, and currently takes place at the larger Wittman Regional Airport (OSH) Wisconsin airport.

Gregory Peck and Audrey Hepburn star in *Roman Holiday*, a movie that takes you on a wild and romantic *Vespa* ride around Rome.

1954

The International Food, Wine and Travel Writers Association (IFWTWA) is established in, where else but Paris, France. It is the first prominent group of fellow writers and journalists from around the world who cover the growing hospitality and travel lifestyle fields...the perfect trade association set up to let all wannabe writing members benefit from some great allowable IRS tax deductions! (Please consult your tax advisor or accountant for legal details.)

Kalervo Oberg (1901-1973), a Canadian-American anthropologist, finally coins a phrase that we all understand when traveling—*cultural shock*. It was during an August 3rd talk to the Women's Club of Rio that he identified the four stages of "culture shock" that refer to the anxiety and feelings most travelers feel when arriving in strange places with strange people and equally stranger customs—*like Jersey*! Cultural shock explains the human psychological dimensions of surprise, disorientation, uncertainty, and confusion, etc., all felt when people are required to operate within a different and unknown cultural or social environment, such as a foreign country.

The gigantic 1,504-room resort we all know as the Fontainebleau Hotel (aka Fontainebleau Miami Beach) opens on oceanfront Collins Avenue in Miami Beach, Florida. Jerry Lewis plays a hotel employee in the 1960 comedy film *The Bellboy*.

DEET (aka *N*, *N*-Diethyl-*meta*-toluamide) insect-repellent, developed by the military earlier, is first commercially sold in America; proving once again that chemicals can be our friends. DEET becomes popular during the Vietnam War era in Southeast Asia by U.S. troops—and best friends who sleep outside by the pool in Thai resorts being introduced to all 3,500 species of mosquitoes while their friend is tended to by a British Army nurse.

A global tipping point is reached when worldwide ownership of radio sets for the first time out number newspapers printed daily.

The Travelers Century Club, an exclusive society of travelers (ala country collectors) whose sole membership requirement is that they must have visited at least 100 countries is founded by a tour operator in Los Angeles, California. (Hey to each his own, some travelers collect matches, others snow globes, these folks happen to collect countries!) Nation-state inflation immediately ensues with the club claiming (as of March 2010) that the world has 320 "countries." *Hmm*, the United Nations has only 192 member states (193 if you count Vatican City) and the CIA list only 227 sovereign entities! Seems someone wants to sell a lot of tours! (TravelersCenturyClub. org) Disclaimer, this author was once a member.

The Ramada Corporation enters the hotel business by opening their first property, a 60-room facility on U.S. Route 66 in Flagstaff, Arizona. *Ramada*, a Spanish word meaning "a shaded resting place," grew to have over 650 properties nationwide by 1976.

In what was the world's largest real estate transaction up to this date, the Hotels Statler Company was sold to Conrad Hilton of Hilton Hotel fame for US$111,000,000, and in the process creating the largest hotel company in the world.

1955
The Society of American Travel Writers (SATW) is formed to promote responsible travel journalism, networking opportunities, professional development, legal consultations, professional recognition, and travel discounts for members! Disclaimer, this author is *not* a member.

Walt Disney (1901-1966), an American dreamer and producer, opens his dream 510-acre dream-like park Disneyland in July in Anaheim, California. It took just one year to build at a cost of US$17 million! Priceless to everyone else…For-the-kids tourism (aka kiddy tourism) takes off. (Although it should be said that 75% of Disneyland visitors are adults!)

When they could not secure the rights to fly passengers directly from Miami to New York City, Delta Airlines pioneers the use of the hub and spoke system, by inconveniently taking passengers first to Hartsfield–Jackson Atlanta International Airport (ATL) and then onto New York City! Thank you Delta for introducing the new airline math: getting from point A to point B really meant going all the way to point Z first!

On November 1st, a United Airlines DC-6B, Flight #629, flying from Denver, Colorado to Portland, Oregon, was bombed, killing everyone on board . The dynamite bomb was planted by Jack Graham who placed the device in his mother's suitcase with the intent of collecting on her US$37,500 life insurance policy. It is the world's first airline bombing. Graham was arrested, confessed, tried, and judiciously killed to show every one that killing is wrong!

Orchard Place Airport (aka O'Hare International Airport (ORD) opens 27 kilometers (17 miles) from downtown Chicago. By 2005 it grows to be the busiest airport in the world with an average of more than 100 take off and landings an hour! The oft used quotes, "There are two certainties in life, taxes and changing planes at Chicago O'Hare," rings all too true…

The Trans-Mongolian Railway, a 2,237 kilometer (1,390-mile) rail line connecting the *Trans-Siberian's Ulan-Ude* station at Irkutsk, Russia with the *Chinese Railway system at Jining*, finally opens across Mongolia. It is now possible to go directly between Beijing to Moscow via the Trans-Siberian line that opened in 1916. The Communist conspiracy is complete—but it will take you eight grueling days to get there!

The Volkswagen van camper arrives on the American scene.

1956

The International Student Identity Card (ISIC) is created and offers discounts for traveling fulltime students (See: 1949).

The Soviet Union's Aeroflot airlines inaugurates the world's first sustained jet service with the introduction of the Tupolev-104 on the Moscow-Omsk-Irkutsk route. Czech Airlines follows the jet age and becomes the second jet airline in 1957.

Dwight Eisenhower (1890-1969), an American general and President, signs the Federal Aid Highway Act (aka National Interstate and Defense Highways Act) into law that provides 25 billion dollars over 20 years for the construction of more than 66,000 kilometers (41,000 miles) of Interstate highways. A little background here; while in Europe during World War II, then General Eisenhower viewed the ease of travel on the German *autobahns* (especially moving military conveys) and it became his transportation obsession when he became a politician. The U.S. interstate highway system began to meet the challenge of the growing number of automobiles on the nation's highways. It only goes to show you, travel broadens the mind! But then there is legendary road warrior and American commentator Charles Kuralt (1934-1997) and his take: "*Thanks to the (US) Interstate Highway System, it is now possible to travel from coast to coast without seeing anything.*"

Mike Todd (1909–1958), an American film producer, releases his adventure film version of the Jules Verne classic *Around the World in 80 Days*. The movie that was filmed in 13 countries went on to win the Best Picture Academy Award.

The Gale Storm Show (aka *Oh! Susanna*), starts airing on U.S. TV, the popular comedy series was based on a cruise director and her run in with travelers onboard a ship travelling around the world! Sound familiar? In all, 143 shows are produced over four years.

Despite the chances being almost *nil*, the Grand Canyon becomes the backdrop for a mid-air collision on June 30th between a United Airlines Chicago-bound flight and a Trans World Airlines Kansas City-bound flight. Apparently both pilots wanted to show their passenger the picturesque canyon when the mid-air crash occurs killing all 128 passengers and crew—the deadliest aviation disaster in history to date. The crash would become the catalyst for sweeping reforms (aka the Doolittle Commission) in the regulation of flight operations over the United States.

Atlanta Municipal Airport (ATL) officially becomes an international airport when an Eastern Airlines flight departs to Montreal, Canada. By 1999, ATL (aka Hartsfield–Jackson Atlanta International Airport) is the world's busiest airport by passenger traffic and number of landings and take-offs; leading to the old Southern joke that, upon one's death, *"regardless of whether you're going to Heaven or Hell—you will have to connect in Atlanta to get there."*

1957
Hotel Habana Riviera (aka Havana Riviera) a grand 21-story 350-room hotel built by Meyer Lansky (aka the Mob's Accountant) (1902–1983), opens in Havana, Cuba. Several hotels were built in Havana around this time, due to President Batista's 1955 Hotel Law 2070 that offered significant tax incentives and government loans to any developers building hotels in excess of US$1,000,000 in Havana. Needless to say, the mob came running with bags of ill-begotten gains building The Hotel Capri (Santo Trafficante, Jr.), and the Hotel Tryp Habana Libre (Conrad Hilton). And boy oh boy, are they all pissed off a few years later when Castro comes to town and takes over (See: 1959).

The International Air Transportation Association (IATA) begins setting guidelines for maximizing seat sizes on planes—to maximize seating capacity and airline incomes—and so the torture of economy-class seating begins.

J.W. Marriott (1900-1985), an American businessman, opens his first hotel, the 365-room Twin Bridges Motor Hotel (aka Twin Bridges Marriott Motor Hotel and Key Bridge Marriott) in Arlington, Virginia. Today Marriott International operates or franchises over 3,150 properties in 68 countries around the world. Original rates where US$8 a night!

Jay Pritzker (1922-1999), an American conglomerate organizer, opens his first hotel The Hyatt House in Los Angeles, California as the world's first fly-in (aka airport-based) hotel, located near the Los Angeles International

Airport (LAX). (See: 1929) By 2010, the Hyatt Hotels Corporation's global portfolio included over 444 properties.

The Soviet Union's *Sputnik I* rocks the world by becoming the world's first space satellite on October 4th. For the first time in the history of mankind, a manmade object is hurdled into the heavens and beyond, a feat of extraordinary imagination. Technically, the satellite traveled at the incredible speed of 29,000 km/h (18,000 mph) and took only 96 minutes to complete a single orbit of the blue planet we call home.

The 181-seat Boeing 707-120 becomes the first production jet airliner introduced into service on December 20th. The 707 was a civilian version of the U.S. Air Force KC-135 Stratotanker, which first flew on 15 July 1954. When Boeing halted production in October 1976, over 920 of the eight versions of the 707 had been built.

The Boeing 707.
(Author Photo)

The AirStream Caravanner is introduced to RV'ers—and land yachts are born.

A few sun-loving German's open a small hostel for fellow sun loving German's and what is believed to be the first holiday hotel in Benidorm, Spain; an up to this point, small Mediterranean coastal village that sports three sweet, although now very busy, beaches: *Llevante, Poniente* and *Mal Pas*. Nowadays, wide-bodied planes bring wide-bodied people here to fill the 240+ hotels at the spectacular rate of about 5 million visitors a year!

One British author, Giles Tremlett, speculates that the now all-too-popular Benidorm resort area as the "birthplace of package tourism" in his book, *Ghosts of Spain: Travels Through a Country's Hidden Past*. Maybe, *maybe not*!

The movie *An Affair To Remember*, starring Cary Grant and Deborah Kerr, a wonderful film about an onboard romance—and alter mishap—is released to the mortification of the Moral Majority. It remains a great love stories inspired by traveling hearts.

Arthur Frommer (1929-), and American lawyer-cum-traveler, publishes his revolutionary travel guidebook, *Europe on $5 a Day*. It is the civilian version of his semi-successful military day-guide book called *"Europe for GIs"* which had 5,000 copies printed. The Frommer's empire begins…and traveling on the cheap, *err*, budget-conscious, becomes the American way! By 2010 the company was publishing 350 individual guides and selling over 2.5 million each year.

The Odakyu Electric Railway begins operating the world's first high-speed rail line in Tokyo, Japan called *Romancecar 3000 SE*, with world record speeds of 145 km/h (90 mph). By 1963, the Japanese almost double their maximum passenger service speeds to 210 km/h (130 mph) on the Tokyo–Nagoya–Kyoto–Osaka route. The birth of high speed rail takes place.

1958
The era of jet envy arrives. The newly designed British de Havilland Comet 4 becomes the first jet to operate transatlantic passenger jet service, on October 4th and then Pan American World Airways inaugurated its trans-Atlantic 707 jet service between New York and Paris a few weeks later on October 26th. The Douglas Aircraft Company introduces the DC-8, another four jet engine commercial airliner less than a year later when Delta Air Lines flies it on September 18th, 1959.

A tipping point is reached for the first time since Columbus sailed the ocean blue (See: 1492) for trans-Atlantic travel when more travelers officially travel between Europe and North America by air, than by ship, when more than a million passengers flew the Atlantic in 1958, for the first time surpassing the total of Atlantic steamship passengers.

Prompted by the Doolittle Commission (See: 1956), the Federal Aviation Act establishes the U.S. Federal Aviation Administration (FAA) charged with among other things: developing an air traffic control system; regulating U.S. commercial space transportation; regulating air navigation flight inspection standards; issuing, suspending, or revoking pilot certificates; as well as developing and carrying out programs to control aircraft noise and other environmental effects of civil aviation. Two out of five isn't too bad is it?

A squirrel monkey named Gordo becomes the first mammal put in sub-orbital space on December 13th aboard a Jupiter rocket launched from Cape Canaveral, Florida. The monkey died after enduring a 40G reentry force! Never send a monkey to do a man's job, to loosely paraphrase Darwin.

The American Hotel Association (AHA) sells its license for its unsuccessful Universal Travel Card to American Express that becomes the American Express Card. Its first full year in operation ends with over 32,000 accepting establishments signed up and almost half a million cardholders. Green begat the Gold card (1966) which begat the Platinum Card (1984) which begat the Optima Card (1987) which begat the Centurion Card (1999) which begat Blue from American Express (2009) which all begat a lot of fee revenues for American Express.

The Sheraton hotels chain introduces *Reservatron*, the hotel industry's first automated electronic reservations system. They also introduce the first toll-free reservation number.

Trans World Airways publishes the first known in-flight magazine, the *Ambassador Magazine*.

John Houghtaling (1916-2009), an American bed salesman, invents the Magic Fingers Vibrating Bed, a mediocre hotel fixture for decades that for a quarter would let you escape for 15 minutes. As Jimmy Buffett sang: *"Put in a quarter / Turn out the light / Magic Fingers makes you feel all right."*

Ruth Carol Taylor, an American gal, is hired by Mohawk Airlines becoming the first African-American flight attendant in the United States. A trail-blazer...

*Melatonin (*aka N-acetyl-5-methoxytryptamine), the hormone that controls our circadian rhythm is identified as potentially helpful. Specific doses of it are claimed to help fight jetlag and restore the body's natural sleep patterns. Experts and studies disagree. Me, I enjoyed the American funny lady, Erma Bombeck's take: *"A drug called Melatonin has been used effectively on sheep, but how many sheep do you know who are frequent flyers?"*

A Cuban airliner is hijacked by the *26th of July Movement* and crashes killing seventeen of the twenty people on board. This may be the first politically-motivated civilian airline hijacking, although some claim it was a military flight?

On August 3rd, the nuclear-powered submarine *Nautilus* does what no ship has been able to do becoming the first vessel to cross the North Pole underwater.

Francis Albert Sinatra (aka *Old Blue Eyes*) (1915-1999), an American crooner, releases his ever-popular and upbeat album *Come Fly With Me*, designed as a musical trip around the world that includes the hits: *April in Paris, Brazil* and *On the Road To Mandalay*. The soundtrack to some folks lives...

David Warren (1925-2010), an Australian ham radio geek, invents the divinely-developed infamous black box (aka cockpit voice recorder (CVR). In an interesting side note, David's father had previously died in a plane crash in 1934. Many aviation neophytes always ask the big question: If the indestructible black box is so indestructible, then why don't they make the whole plane out of that same material?

The U.S. Supreme Court issues a decision in *Kent v. Dulles* (357 US 116)—it was a case where a former Communist Party member and U.S. citizen was denied the issuance of a U.S. passport—stating "The right to travel is a part of the 'liberty' of which a citizen cannot be deprived without the due process of law of the Fifth Amendment. In Anglo-Saxon law that right was emerging at least as early as the *Magna Carta* (See: 1215)" wrote Justice William O. Douglas in the majority opinion. He stressed "how deeply engrained in our history this freedom of movement is. Freedom of movement across frontiers in either direction, and inside frontiers as well, was a part of our heritage." The Court views the right to travel settled law. Now, about going to Cuba? (See: 1963)

1959

On May 28th, aboard the U.S. Jupiter AM-18 rocket, Able a rhesus monkey, and Miss Baker a squirrel monkey, became the first earthlings to successfully return to Earth after traveling into space. They owe all their success to those that traveled before them, especially Gordo (See: 1958) a fellow primate.

The first modern era show in Branson, Missouri, *The Baldknobbers Hillbilly Jamboree Show* opens to a warm clap. The next year, the Old Mill Theater opens and the Silver Dollar City, a faux frontier town including actors reliving the feud between the Hatfield's and the McCoy's entertains folk. By 2010, eight million—yes 8 million!—visitors head to the Ozarks for some Branson family fun. (See: 1894)

Fidel Castro (1926-), a Cuban politician, takes over as leader of Cuba and closes all foreign owned casinos and resorts giving Las Vegas tourism development a big boost.

In an effort to compete with the growing auto culture in Europe, the first multi-country Eurail Pass is sold to non-European residents in travel packages only sold overseas.

Johnny Cash (1932–2003), an American singer-songwriter legend, releases his classic hit *"I've Been Everywhere."* Many fans believe that he had too...

The Ecuadorian government establishes the Galápagos Islands as a protected national wildlife park and marine reserve, and limits the number of official residents (about 1,500 in 1959) and visitors. But by 2009, the combined effects of having over 160,000 annual visitors to this extremely fragile remote island chain located 960 kilometers (600 miles) off the Ecuador coast, along with the foot print left by the 38,000+ residents who are supported by the Golden Goose tourist revenues, have created serious ecological stress on the international attraction. It is always a fine line...

St. Lawrence Seaway in North America that permits ocean-going vessels from around the world to travel from the Atlantic Ocean as far as Lake Superior opens for business. The zebra mussels lay in wait.

> **The Travel Industry:** By now the travel industry and the infrastructure supporting it is firmly embedded into the European and United States economies; airports are functioning, airlines are flying new routes with faster planes, train stations are buzzing, rental car companies are expanding, travel agents are selling package trips to the ski slopes and sunny spots in the winter and to exotic destinations anytime, and hotel developments continue to grow. In fact, by 1960 there are over 2,400,000 hotel beds in the U.S. alone. Mass tourism has firmly taken root.

The Naismith Memorial Basketball Hall of Fame opens in Springfield, Massachusetts. Unlike the baseball and football halls, the basketball hall of fame celebrates international players. It is interesting how many great Los Angeles Lakers uniforms adorn the hall's walls—with more to come!

1960
When a handful of well-traveled students at Harvard University start handing out a 20-page mimeographed pamphlet about traveling through Europe called "The Bible of the Budget Traveler," the *Let's Go* guidebook series is not far off. And in 1961, *Let's Go Europe* is published as the first annual guidebook of the series.

In a semi-unrelated way, world-wide American Express offices rapidly become the *de facto* P.O. boxes (and meeting points) for traveling students.

The British Guild of Travel Writers (BGTW) is established for a growing group of travelers wanting to get reimbursed for their exotic vacations.

Jacques Piccard (1922-2008), a genetically endowed Swiss oceanographer, visits the Marianas Trench in a pressured bathyscape, called *Trieste*. At 10,916 meters (35,813) below sea level, it is the world's deepest darkest place.

What is now the Duty Free Shoppers (DFS) chain, created by two American entrepreneurs, Charles Feeney and Robert Miller, opens on November 7th in Hong Kong International Airport (HKG). (See: 1947)

A magazine know as *The Diners Club Magazine*, that was previously only sent to Diners Club (See: 1951) credit card holders, begins being published publically. It then evolved into *Signature*, which in 1987 turned into what we now know as *Conde Nast Traveler* magazine.

The super creepy, and wholly fictional Bates Motel opens in the Alfred Hitchcock (See: 1956) movie *Psycho*. The U.S. roadside motel business has a bad revenue summer.

Sensing the importance and growth of the travel and tourism industry in the United States, the U.S. Congress creates and funds the U.S. Travel and Tourism Administration (USTTA), a governmental agency designed to employ industry experts to help assist and promote the needs and development of the entire U.S. travel industry—and protect consumers too!

Merida's Teleferico opens in the Venezuelan city of Mérida and instantly becomes and still reigns, as the world's highest cable car and the largest in the world that extends over 20 kilometers (12.5 miles) from an altitude of 1,640 meters (5,400-feet) to Pico Espejo, at 4,765 meters (15,630-feet). It was not built by the Swiss—so you really don't want to go on it!

The first underwater park in the United States, the John Pennekamp Coral Reef State Park located at mile marker 102.5 on US 1 in Florida is founded at a popular tourist dive area to protect the undersea flora and fauna.

1961
The first ever high-jacking onboard a U.S.-based aircraft, a National Airlines Corvair 440 begins with the notorious words. "*I want to fly to Cuba!*" Although terrorist historians—a great and growing field of scholars by the way!—claim that since records have been kept, that between 1948 and 1957 there were just fifteen-reported hijacking attempts worldwide, but none involved aircraft previously originating in or flying to the United States proper.

The Orient Express takes its last Paris, France to Bucharest, Romania run.

Go: The International Travel Game, created by John Waddington Ltd. of England, is a Christmas hit in London. *Go* is basically a *Monopoly*-like game about travel where the winner must collect the most souvenirs. I know those travel types...

Isadore "Issy" Sharp (1931-), a Canadian businessman, opens and founds the Four Seasons Hotels and Resorts chain by opening the Toronto-based Four Seasons Motor Hotel.

Yuri Gagarin (1934-1968), a Soviet cosmonaut and one brave *hombre*, becomes the first person to ever orbit planet Earth once in a quick 108 minutes aboard *Vostok 1* on April 12th. His quote rings true: *"The Earth is blue...How wonderful. It is amazing."* Almost one year later on February 20th, 1962, John Glenn Jr. (1921-), a right stuff American pilot, becomes the first American to orbit Earth in *Friendship 7.* These remain remarkable feats for all of mankind...slipping *the surly bonds of Earth.*

Spring Fever: Spring Break (aka Easter Holiday or March Break), as we know it today, did not really begin until the 1960's, when the classic movie *Where the Boys Are* helped spread the new, and young folks began flocking to the beaches to "see-and-be-seen" of Florida, in what is now a well established annual rite of passage. The wild 70's brought drugs and free love to the Spring Break scene; and then Tom Cruise's 1983 movie *Spring Break* got America's corporations seeing the youth market potential. By 1985, Fort Lauderdale had an estimated 350,000 kids roaming the beaches and bars. Hot coastal destinations like Panama City, Daytona Beach, Fort Myers Beach, and South Padre Island, Texas, began seeing balcony diving, gratuitous PDA's, wet T-shirt contests, all-night parties and MTV film crews. Today, Spring Break has gone international, with students heading to the beaches of the Bahamas, Jamaica and Cancun, Mexico—where it is even hotter and the drinking age is only18!

Alan B. Shepard Jr. (1923-1998), an American astronaut, pilots the *Freedom 7 Mercury* capsule, America's first manned space mission into outer space on May 5th. Alan would later become the 5th person to ever walk on the moon in Apollo 14.

On a July 19th TWA 707 flight between New York and Denver, premieres the first in-flight full-length feature film—MGM and Lana Turner's *By Love Possessed*. It was only seen in the First Class cabin…a sign of things to come!

Eastern Airlines inaugurates *Eastern Air-Shuttle*, a revolutionary new service in the heavily traveled Boston-New York/Newark-Washington market corridor. The service operated hourly flights without reservations, guaranteeing each customer a seat.

It is speculated that Omani terrorists blew up a Dubai-based passenger liner *MV Dara* traveling between Bombay, India and Basra, Iraq on April 8th killing 238 people, mostly fellow Arabs.

John F. Kennedy (1917–1963), and American politician and President, challenges his fellow American's in his 1961 address to Congress boldly stating a national goal of "*landing a man on the Moon*" by the end of the decade. (See: 1969)

Angus Gilchrist Wynne, Jr. (1914-1979), an American real estate developer, wanting to emulate Walt Disney's success with opening Disneyland in California (See: 1955), develops and builds the first Six Flags amusement park outside Dallas, Texas, that he called Texas Under Six Flags. Wynne expanded on the concept opening Six Flags over Georgia, outside Atlanta in 1967, and Six Flags over Mid America outside St Louis in 1971. Always growing, Wynne purchases Los Angeles's Magic Mountain in 1979.

The U.S. Navy launches the world's first operational satellite-based navigation system called TRANSIT (aka NAVSAT for *Navy Navigation Satellite System*); it became available for limited commercial civilian use in 1967—or did it? It is still classified Top Secret!

It is known in Finland as the Koivulahti Air Disaster, when an Aero O/Y (aka Finnair) DC-3 flying between Kronoby, Finland and Vaasa, crashes on January 3rd, killing all twenty-five people on board. The disaster remains the deadliest aviation accident in the history of Finland. The pilot, a World War II fighter ace, and his co-pilot had both been found to have blood alcohol levels exceeding any acceptable limit. They simply should not have been flying.

The Portuguese luxury cruise liner *Santa Maria* with more than 900 passengers and crew aboard is hi-jacked on February 23rd by Portuguese rebels. U.S. and Brazilian warships intercept the ship and force the hijackers to surrender to Brazilian authorities (they sought political asylum) after a 10-day high seas drama.

So much for freedom of travel rights? On February 7th, the U.S. government embargos Cuba (aka Cuban Democracy Act) and makes it illegal for Americans to visit the island nation…it lasts a long time, too long— maybe 2011 is the year sanity will prevail? But, technically, Americans can go to Cuba—you just can't spend any money in Cuba! The ban is a perfect example of allowing a small minority group, but large campaign contributors, to hi-jack U.S. foreign policy beyond reason.

Life changes for a small Thai fishing village known as Pattaya on April 26th when the first group of about 100 American servicemen, who were fighting in the Vietnam War, arrived in Pattaya for some much needed R&R (aka I&I, for intercourse and intoxication). From this beginning, Pattaya became a popular beach resort which now attracts hundreds of thousands of visitors—disproportionally older white males at that. Sadly, the Thai whorehouse remains open.

1962
After a series of "*I want to fly to Cuba…*" hijackings, President Kennedy gets the Federal Aviation Administration (FAA) to begin using various federal law enforcement officers on designated high risk flights. In 1968, the Federal Air Marshal (FAM) service officially began as the FAA *Sky Marshal* Program. Initially, it was composed of six volunteers from the FAA's Flight Standards Division who were trained in firearms at Brownsville, Texas.

On a May 22nd a Continental Airlines 707 flight between Chicago and Kansas City, Thomas G. Doty, a down-on-his luck father, ignites dynamite in a lavatory in a desperate scheme to have his family collect his US$150,000 life insurance benefits—45 passengers and crew perish.

The Trans-Canada Highway between St John's, Newfoundland and Vancouver, British Columbia in Canada opens. It is 7,680 kilometers (4,800 miles) long from sea-to-shining-sea!

Trans World Airlines inaugurates the first fully automated Doppler radar system of navigation on scheduled trans-Atlantic flights. This technological advancement helps save the airlines money; also when the New York to London flights becomes the first trans-Atlantic flight (commercial or military) ever operated without a professional navigator aboard.

A hovercraft boat (aka air-cushion vehicle), that had finally been successfully developed in 1959, begins passenger service aboard a Vickers-Armstrong VA-3 between Boulogne, France and Dover, England.

Motel 6, the forerunner of budget brands, opens in Santa Barbara, California. Rooms cost US$6 a night—hence the company name.

The Hawaiian island of Maui begins seeing more Mainlanders visit when a series of fashionable beach front resorts open within a few years, starting with the Royal Lahaina, followed by the Sheraton Maui Kaanapali Beach Resort in 1963, and the Maui Hilton (aka Maui Kaanapali Villas) and Kaanapali Beach Hotel in 1964.

Dave Drum, a Montana businessman, sensing the need for comfortable, clean family-oriented road-side camping stops, opens his first Kampgrounds of America (KOA) in Billings, Montana. By 1972 over 600 KOA franchise campgrounds are scattered across America. The coming energy crisis of 1973 effects business in a big way as folks travel the highways and byways of America less. Oh, I remember them well...thanks grandma!

Pan American World Airways begins operating the first global computer reservation system called PANAMAC.

John Ernst Steinbeck (1902–1968), an illustrious American writer, pens *Travels With Charley: In Search of America* in which he uses a Spanish word *vacilando*; which is a wanderer for whom the experience of travel is more important than traveling for the purpose of reaching a destination. *Hmm,* maybe getting there *is* half the fun again?

Both American Airlines & Pan American World Airways install TV monitors in the First Class sections of their Lockheed Electra Aircraft.

Cultural Differences: Like America's new Spring Break tradition, the English Gap Year (aka *wanderjahr*) begins in earnest in the mid-1960's, as well-off Baby Boomers started taking a year off between their secondary studies and university traveling about and supposedly volunteering their time to help others. While *gap years* have a reputation for being available only to a rich few, nowadays, it means being resourceful enough to raise funds independently, rather than just relying on wealthy parents. The two key elements to the *gap year*—independent travel and volunteer work—have survived and continue to thrive. Interestingly, there is a huge cultural difference between the two new 1960's travel traditions: the North American version is done over a short time for purely hedonistic and selfish reasons; while the European version is done over an extend time spent helping others and learning about oneself at the same time.

Heinz Stucke (1940-), a German cyclists, leaves his home in Germany on a three-speed bicycle and has been cycling round the world ever since! At the time of this writing, Heinz is reported to have covered 539,000 kilometers (335,000 miles) and visited 192 countries…and claims to have never returned home. When he arrived in Portsmouth, England in 2006, he had his bike pinched—it was later returned. He has been shot at, beaten, hit by a truck, detained, chased by mobs and attacked by bees. The *Guinness Book of Records* calls him the "most travelled man in history" for the years between 1995 and 1999. Heinz, go home.

The first telephone conversation relayed by satellite between the U.S. and Europe takes place on July 13th. Pre-orders for satellite phones overwhelm the folks at Iridium Satellite—that is before they go bankrupt!

Pope John XXIII canonizes St. Bona of Pisa, a 12th-century pilgrim, as patron saint of air hostesses! Enough said.

Valentina Vladimirovna Tereshkova (1937-), a Soviet cosmonaut, becomes the first woman in space aboard *Vostok 5* on June 16th. Not being a member of the military, Valentina also becomes the first civilian in space!

1963

The Pro Football Hall of Fame opens in Canton, Ohio and proves to be a Mecca for NFL fans everywhere.

Hapiamg, a French company operating ski resorts in the Alps, launches the first drive toward developing vacation related "time-shares," that encouraged guests to *"stop renting a room—buy the hotel."* Real estate success being what it is, the concept catches on and is embraced by developers worldwide boosting the sales of surplus condominium units everywhere. By 2010, there are an estimated 5,425 timeshare resorts offering "vacation ownership" (aka fractional ownership) worldwide; with 1,604 such resorts holding 154,439 units in the U.S. alone. (It is claimed by the industry that over four million Americans currently own at least a week in a timeshare somewhere.)

The Convention on Offences and Certain Other Acts Committed on Board Aircraft (aka the Tokyo Convention) is a multilateral agreement that makes it an internationally agreed to offence of *"any acts jeopardizing the safety of persons or property on board civilian aircraft while in-flight and engaged in international air navigation."* The convention also, for the first time in the history of international law, recognizes certain powers and immunities of the aircraft commander who *"on international flights may restrain any person(s) he has reasonable cause to believe is committing or is about to commit an offence liable to interfere with the safety of persons or property on board or who is jeopardizing good order and discipline."* Who's not fine with that law?

The Semester at Sea (SES) program develops like the earlier study abroad program (See: 1879) at the University of Virginia with the multidisciplinary Global Studies being the focus of students.

The U.S. government begins legally restricting U.S. passport holders from traveling to Cuba. (See: 1958)

Theron Nuñez's, a Mexican writer, talks about the exchanges of culture that take place between travelers and the places they visit in his book called "*Tourism, Tradition, and Acculturation: Weekendismo in a Mexican Village.*" Later in 1977, he is quoted in Valene L. Smith's "*The Anthropology of Tourism*" (1977), as saying: "*As a host community adapts to tourism, its facilitation to tourists' needs, attitude, and values, the host community must become more like the tourists' culture. That is what tourists in search of the exotic and 'natural' vacation setting mean when they say a place has been 'spoiled' by tourism, i.e., those who got there before them and required the amenities of home. Anthropologists are often in the forefront of those who deplore the dilution and adulteration of traditional culture. However, the alteration of one culture by another has always been a fact of existence. Some societies have remained in relative isolation from others for long periods of time, but in this century virtually no community is immune from outside contact, and the tourist is more ubiquitous than any other kind of representative of other cultures.*" The exchange theory at play…

Kenneth Crutchlow, an Englishman *not* living in New York, wins a pint of ale in a bar bet after beating a fellow unnamed traveler (we think he was an Aussie) in a race around the world on public transportation going from London to London via Sydney, Australia and San Francisco, California. To make it more complicated, the rules were simple: no borrowing, no stealing, and no flying; and to keep it even fairer, they could only spend the money that they currently possessed on their person—Crutchlow had 10 pounds sterling and his rival about twenty bob. In the end, they were solely dependent on the kindness of strangers. It took Crutchlow 94 days! A remarkable tale told…

1964
Originally conceived five years earlier between American Airlines and IBM as an attempt to offer real-time integrated booking and ticketing systems, the Semi-Automated Business Research Environment (SABRE) system is finally launched with travel agents beginning to use these Global Distributions Systems (GDS). The SABRE system, and others like it: Amadeus CRS, Galileo CRS and Worldspan, allowed travel agents exclusive rights (a monopoly as it were) on booking customers airline

tickets, hotels and car rental services—that is until the advent of the online Internet websites (See: 1996). ...and yes, they did lose the first reservation after charging extra for calling an agent to book it.

The Boeing 727 becomes the first tri-jet introduced into commercial service in February. By the time production is halted in August 1984, over 1,800 narrow-body 727's in all models were delivered, making the Boeing 727 the best-selling airliner in history...that is until her younger sister, the Boeing 737 was introduced. In all, over 4 billion passengers have flown on a 727 worldwide.

The *Shinkansen* (aka the Bullet Train) of Japan becomes the world's first high speed train system with speeds of 210 km/h (131mph) on the Tokaido line between Tokyo and Shin-Osaka—a distance of 515 kilometers (320 miles) covered in just over 2 hours and 20 minutes door-to-door! By 2010, the Japanese operate over 2,459 kilometers (1,528 miles) of fast track at speeds now exceeding 443 km/h (275 mph) for the "old conventional" rail lines and up to a world record 581 km/h (361 mph) for the new maglev lines! It works, it's fast and it's safe—why can't we all do that?

Pre-empting the Americans with Disabilities Act of 1990 and earlier provisions in 1973, Travelodge hotels does the right thing and is the first hotel group to offer wheelchair-accessible rooms. The idea of accessible tourism is born and by 2003 someone in a wheel chair actually makes it to the top of Mount Everest.

Universal Studios begins offering their GlamorTram tours of the movie producing back lot with behind-the-scenes encounters. Thus begins the new era of pop-culture tourism whereby media raised and infatuated travelers visit their favorite imaginary places. Some call them secular pilgrimages of sorts and they include: Abbey Road in London, Graceland in Memphis, Strawberry Fields in New York City, movie studio tours, Tunisia (Star Wars location), New Zealand (Lord of Rings locations (aka Tolkien tourism), and Jim Morrison's grave in Père Lachaise Cemetery, Paris, among scores of others.

Flushing Meadows, New York is the home of the 1964 New York World's Fair for the second time (See: 1939) that is dedicated to *"Man's Achievement on a Shrinking Globe in an Expanding Universe.*" Fifty-one million visitors attend seeing America's vision of the Space Age.

Geraldine "Jerrie" Fredritz Mock (1925-), an American aviator, fly's her Cessna 180 around the world becoming the first woman to fly solo around the world—27 years after Amelia Earhart's failed attempt. Jerrie takes her time taking 29 days including 21 layovers to complete her mission.

> **Did You Know?** That University Bridge in Boston, Massachusetts is the only spot in the world where a boat can sail under a train under a car under a flying plane.

On May 7th, a Pacific Air Lines Flight 773 crashes in California, after a senseless passenger shoots both the pilot and co-pilot before killing himself and causing the plane to crash killing all 44 aboard. Still no sane gun laws, still no metal detectors…

George Millay (1929–2006), an American businessman, opens SeaWorld in San Diego, California—Shamu the orca was added in 1965. SeaWorld, along with Jacques-Yves Cousteau's (See: 1943) TV work help entertain and educate people about the ocean and critters in it. Millay later opens SeaWorld Ohio in 1970 and SeaWorld Orlando in 1973.

1965c -
Sylvan Nathan Goldman (1898-1984), an American businessman, who had earlier invented shopping carts in 1937, invents human-powered baggage carts (aka luggage carts), much to the chagrin of *rampies* everywhere. (See: 1970 - *Smarte Cartes*)

By now the *Gringo Trail* is a well-worn zigzagging circuit of Latin American destinations popular among adventurous backpackers heading south of the border (versus along the Hippie Trail from Europe to Asia (See: 1966). Natural beauty, tropical beaches and colonial cities along the trail included: Mexico (Oaxaca and the Yucatan Peninsula), British Honduras (aka Belize), Guatemala (Flores and Antigua), Ecuador highlands, Peru's Lost Cities (Machu Picchu and Cuzco), Bolivia (Lake Titicaca), Argentina (the Train to the Clouds (Salta), Patagonia, and Buenos Aires), Chile

(Santiago and Los Andes), and Brazil (Iguaçu Falls, Rio, Salvador and Amazonian).

1965

The Douglas DC-9, a twin-engine narrow-body jet plane enters service with Delta Air Lines. In all, 2,500 units of the popular medium range jet are built.

What we know today as the INTERNET is created by the Defense Department's Advanced Research Project Association (DARPA) as means to communicate in the event of a nuclear attack. Called ARAPNET, the word INTERNET was first used later in 1982. The global nervous system is now complete. Al Gore is nowhere to be found?

A comedy starring Jerry Lewis and Tony Curtis, about a character having an affair with no less than three international flight attendants at a time, called *Boeing Boeing* is released. But we all know that life is stranger than fiction for some…only three Tony?

Conceived by *haute couture* Euro-designer Emilo Pucci, Braniff Airlines introduces the

"Air Strip", whereby their all-women cadre of flight attendants risquély peeling off their uniform during the flight until they were finally dressed only in hot pant-like culottes and flimsy halter-tops. Apparently sex sells… the company's stock soars!

The NBC-TV series *I Spy*, a buddy-genre drama, first airs starring Robert Culp and Bill Cosby. The show which ran for three seasons (1965-68), breaks new ground for not only casting the first African-American as a leading actor in an American TV show, but also because it was the first American TV show to be shot internationally in places from Spain to Japan, and Acapulco to Morocco.

The Beatles go global with their hit single, including jet aircraft sounds, *"Back in the USSR"*…Who could have forgotten the lure of that first line: *"Flew in from Miami Beach B.O.A.C."*

Back in the USA, American singer-songwriter Roger Miller keeps the Greyhound road trip alive with the release of his single *"King of The Road."*

Hans Gmoser (1932-2006), an Austrian-Canadian mountain guide, starts taking clients heli-skiing to the Bugaboo Mountains of British Columbia, Canada, creating a new reason for winter travelers to head for the hills. Warren Miller, that great skiing promoter, would help launch the advent of heli-skiing to the world.

United Airlines launches its latest attempt to persuade passengers to join them with their *"Fly the Friendly Skies"* advertising campaign. Many unsatisfied customers are still waiting...

1966

The Thailand Entertainment Places Act of 1966 is one of the more modern laws regulating massage parlors, go-go bars, karaoke bars, bathhouses, and similar establishments of potential ill repute; and under this particular law, such establishments are required to be licensed. The law does not expressly permit or make illegal prostitution, but it does allow for "service providers" and "bath service providers." Anyway, it becomes law in Thailand and Sex Tours become a well-established, albeit seedier, side of the global travel industry.

The Soviet-launched *Venera III* reaches Venus and becomes the first human-made object to land on another planet. Think about that...

The Norwegian Caribbean Line's (NCL) *MS Sunward* cruise ship begins offering three-night and four-day fun ship cruises from Florida to Nassau, St. Thomas, San Juan and other Caribbean ports-of-call.

International Tourism Bourse (ITB) is a travel marketing event with a unique "made in Berlin" feel. From the first humble beginnings in run-down Berlin in 1966 with only five participating countries, this *über* Berlin-centric travel trade show to become the world's largest travel trade show with over 180,000 visitors obtaining travel information from over 12,000 exhibitors. It is an exhausting, tiring and unforgettable global village experience.

Caesars Palace Hotel, the famed Roman Empire-themed 680-room Las Vegas Strip hotel and casino, opens on The Strip in Las Vegas. A year later motorcycle daredevil Evel Knievel unsuccessfully jumps the hotel's water fountain. As Elvis sang back in 1964, *"Viva Las Vegas."*

The ultimate surfer documentary movie, *Endless Summer,* is released creating a whole genre of low-budget surf culture tourists roaming the world looking for the perfect wave.

That remote speck in the middle of the South Pacific Ocean over six hours away from any nearby continent called Easter Island (aka *Rapa Nui*) with those large *moai* statues, opens to tourists…willing to endure bad weather, severe turbulence and air sick as the only mode of transportation.

On October 12th, a bomb detonates in the passenger cabin of Cyprus Airways De Havilland Comet airliner over Greece killing all 66 people on board. No suspects.

On November 22nd, a DC-3 aircraft is blown up in mid-air over the south Arabia desert, killing all 28 people on board. The bomb was placed in the baggage area of the aircraft. No suspects.

The Boeing Company beats out competitor Lockheed Corporation for the plum U.S. Government contract to develop America's first supersonic transport. The design was for the Boeing 707 to have a variable wing which could be swung around tighter to the man cabin while flying at supersonic speeds…and we are still waiting!

Britain's Foreign and Commonwealth Office begins advising travelers about personal safety and security matters in foreign destinations. (See: 1914) (FCO.gov.uk)

The *Hippie Trail* that basically took well-off Baby Boomer backpackers from Europe to Nepal and India via what was then Eastern Europe, Turkey, Iran, Afghanistan and Pakistan, is officially christened. It is the 20th Century's edition of the Grand Tour. (See Rory MacLean's excellent 2008 edition of *Magic Bus: On the Hippie Trail from Istanbul to India.*) The Beatles even followed the route, albeit on charter jet, in 1968, and many more have followed in their footsteps. This movement of travelers basically gives rise to the market that we call the *Independent Travel* market.

1967

The year 1967 is designated the *International Tourist Year* by the United Nations.

By now it is estimated that 27% of all U.S. residents have flown in a commercial passenger airplane—by 2001 that number had grown to 80%! One hates to sound elitist, but when people wonder what happened to the "romance of travel"…it could be said that masses packed it up and took it with them!

Pan American World Airways becomes the first airline to make a fully automatic approach and landing in scheduled service. In pilot flight control jargon, that is *flying-by-wire* (FBW), versus the traditional manual *flying-by-stick* method. As the technological evolution of flying continues, American pilots, usually well-trained former military aviators, prefer the manual approach, while the rest of the world angles towards the less human error prone computer-addled techno-approach of flying-by-wire (aka fly-via-computer). Dave: *"Hal, we need to land now!"* Hal: *"But I am having fun Dave."*

Lou Adler, (1933-), a legendary American rock music promoter and lifelong L.A. Laker fan, produces the Monterey International Pop Music Festival, a three-day concert event attended by as many as 90,000 music fans that was held near the coastal town of Monterey, California. Performers included: Otis Redding, The Who, Jimi Hendrix, Janis Joplin, The Mamas & the Papas, Eric Burdon and The Animals, the Steve Miller Band, the Byrds, and Simon and Garfunkel, among others, and influenced the rise of *Festival Tourism*. The Isle of Man Festival on an island off the coast of England took place the following year, and the Woodstock Music Festival, that almost 500,000 music lovers walked, biked, rode, bussed, trained and flew to attend to took place in 1969. Since then, annual music festivals from the Glastonbury Festival of Contemporary Performing Arts (aka Glasto) to the World Festival of Sacred Music held in exotic Fez, Morocco, continue to attract global travelers.

The U.S. Navy introduces an early space-based version of the Global Positioning System (GPS) when it launches and activates the second TIMATION satellite that basically places accurate clocks in space. (See: 1736)

The first automated teller machine (ATM) (aka cash machine and automatic banking machine (ABM) is made operational first at Barclays Bank's Enfield Town branch in London, England on June 27th. This makes asking dad to send money so much easier. The machine was originally installed in a New York bank in 1961, but taken out due to lack of interest—not literally! (This technology has always marveled me, think about it: I put in my card in a foreign bank's ATM, let's say in Borneo, and ask for US$200, it digitally talks to the bank's main branch in Malaysia who notices that I am not a customer and bucks me to the regional Asian international settlement bank who knows that I am from the U.S. and sends a message to the global international settlement bank in Europe who contacts the New York Federal Reserve who contacts my bank's HQ in California who confirms that 'yes he have US$200' (plus bank fees and exchange rate) to withdraw then reversing the digital yes give him the money all the way back to where I am standing in Kuching and spits out US$200 worth of local currency (*ringgits*) inside ten seconds flat—less time than it took to read this! Maybe I think too much, but wow...)

The International and Universal Exposition (aka Expo '67) is held in Montreal, Canada. (1967 also marked the Centennial 100th anniversary of Canada's Confederation in 1867.) And despite minor setbacks like the Six Day War, Quebec separatist threats, a 30-day transit strike, Vietnam war protesters, anti-Castro Cuban protests, French President De Gaulle's insightful *"Vive le Québec Libre!"* speech, and a US$210 million operating deficit; Expo '67 is considered to be the most successful event ever, according to Canadian pundits, with over 50 million visitors attending and 62 nations participating.

The Boeing 737, a short-to-medium-range jet plane, begins service with Lufthansa Airlines on December 28th. With more than 6,300 delivered to date (and orders for 2,000 more as of March 2010), the 737 series are the best-selling commercial jetliner of all time. On average a 737 takes off somewhere every 5.5 seconds worldwide!

The 800-room ultra-modern Hyatt Regency Atlanta opens in Georgia introducing the world's first modern atrium hotel and ushering the modern era version of magnificent hotel lobbies.

Two former flight attendants, Trudy Baker and Rachel Jones, offer up their salacious flying-day memoirs in a series of fictionalized anecdotal (Names, dates and places changed to protect the guilty we're sure!) stories in *Coffee, Tea or Me*, ghost-written by Donald Bain. The sensational expose about fellow flight attendant's glamorous lifestyles in the air, and flat on the ground, proves popular with three sequels and a made-for-TV movie deal: *The Coffee Tea or Me Girls' Round-the-World Diary* (1969); *The Coffee Tea or Me Girls Lay It on the Line* (1972); *The Coffee Tea or Me Girls Get Away from It All* (1974); and the *Coffee, Tea or Me?* Movie, starring Karen Valentine and Louise Lasser aired on CBS-TV in 1973.

The McDonald's fast food chain officially goes international opening an outlet in Toronto.

John Denver, a Colorado singer, hits the right note of bitter sweet good-byes that all travelers know so well, with the release of his hit heart-wrenching single *"Leaving on a Jet Plane"* that he sings with Peter, Paul and Mary.

Homosexuals had always visited and frequented "friendly enclaves" (aka communities) of towns, especially in larger metropolitan cities, since the beginning of time (See the Greeks and Roman) looking for understanding, affection, and love; but after the Stonewall riots in New York City, gay and lesbian friendly communities opened up in areas like Greenwich Village, San Francisco's Castro, West Hollywood, South Florida's Wilton Manors, etc...and in 1970 the first Gay Pride march was held—the era of lesbian, gay, bisexual, and transgender (LGBT) (aka Gay tourism) had arrived—and it is big business too, representing about 10% of all travel and tourism revenues worldwide!

The Rossiya Hotel opens in Moscow, USSR as "the largest hotel in the world", the 21- storey 3,200-room massive cement block of a hotel was ravaged by a terrible fire in 1977 in which 42 guests were killed. In 1993, the MGM Grand Hotel in Las Vegas would claim the new title as "the world's largest hotel room," and in 2006 the Rossiya Hotel closed forever.

Greg Lowe invents the internal-design frame backpack (aka *rucksack*) that becomes a mega-hit among hostel-flopping, gap-year hippie trekkers throughout the world. This is *not* to be confused with the much-dreaded popular in America fanny pack (aka belly bag)!

1968

A Delta Airlines DC-8 is forced to fly to Havana, Cuba on February 21st and is the first successful hijacking of a commercial U.S.-based airliner since 1961.

The longest-ever hijacking ordeal takes place when 32 Jewish passengers on an Israeli *El Al* Boeing 707 flight originating in Rome (FCO), Italy are held for 40-days by Popular Front for the Liberation of Palestine militants who divert the flight to Algeria. The era of Middle Eastern terrorism begins in earnest.

On December 26th two Popular Front for the Liberation of Palestine gunmen attack an El Al jet at Greece's Athens (ATH) airport, killing one person. In disproportional, and some would say an escalating *tit-for-tat* response, three days later Israeli commandos raid Beirut airport in Lebanon and blow up thirteen Arab-owned airliners on the tarmac worth an estimated US$50 million. Who knew?

The first human orbiting of the moon takes place during *Apollo 8*'s mission that took place between December 21st and the 27th. The U.S. crew included: Frank Borman, James Lovell, and William Anders. Never has man traveled so far from home.

Following the lead of the successful *I Spy* television show (See: 1955), ABC-TV airs *It Takes a Thief* starring Robert Wagner as sophisticated playboy-thief working for an American secret Cold War-era spy agency. The dramatic show ran for three seasons (1968-70) and included mostly international destinations that amp up the intrigue level.

Stanley Kubrick (1928–1999), an American film director, shows in his film *2001: A Space Odyssey*, a Pan Am spacecraft flying space workers and tourists alike to a space station as effortlessly as shuttling airplane passengers shuttled between New York and Washington, D.C. Unfortunately, Pan Am is long gone before real space tourism eventually takes off. (See: 1990)

U.S. President Lyndon B. Johnson (1908-1973), in order to remedy America's out-of-whack growing (since 1950) balance of payments deficit, restricts non- essential official travel abroad and asks traveling consumers to voluntarily defer overseas travel outside the Western Hemisphere for two years! He also advocates legislation to encode those requests. It seems that Expo 1967 (See: 1967) was a big hit with more Americans visiting Canada, and less Canadians visiting the United States—along with that little Vietnam War expansion—helped foster the reaction. This is an interesting development because it pits vague notions of U.S. national security against consumer wants. The wants win! And so it goes…

1969

Neil Alden Armstrong (1930-), an American aviator, become the first human to walk on the moon during the U.S. *Apollo 11* mission on July 20th, saying to the world, "…*that's one small step for man, one giant leap for mankind.*" Armstrong, a civilian, was joined with Col. Edwin "Buzz" Aldrin (1930-), a fellow American engineer, on that day. Children around the world stared in awe at their black and white television sets.

A man on the moon – Apollo 11.
(Courtesy NASA Images)

Did You Know? That in all, just 12 people—all men--have walked on the moon's surface, in addition to Armstrong and Aldrin, they are: Cdr. Alan L. Bean and Cdr. Charles "Pete" Conrad, Jr., *Apollo 12;* Edgar D. Mitchell and Alan B. Shepard, *Apollo 14;* Lt. Col. James B. Irwin and Col. David R. Scott, *Apollo 15;* Col. Charles M. Duke, Jr., and Capt. John W. Young, *Apollo 16;* and Capt. Eugene A. Cernan and Dr. Harrison H. Schmitt, *Apollo 17.* The *Apollo* program brought out the best in man and his technical prowess (See: 1961).

The Soviet Union's Tupolev Tu-144 becomes the first truly supersonic airplane to fly. The Tu-144 so closely resembles Europe's Aérospatiale-BAC Concorde, that Russia is alleged to have come up with the design of the Tu-144 via industrial espionage. The world is stunned. The plane, derisively nicknamed *"Konkordski"* was limited to freight service only and is de-commissioned in 1985. (The Tu-144 is officially said to have flown its first flight on December 31ˢᵗ 1968, but no one really knows for sure in the West…it did however beat the Concorde into the air.)

The first Aérospatiale-BAC turbo-powered Concorde (aka 001, SST), made its maiden voyage on March 2ⁿᵈ at a cruising speed of Mach 2.04 (~2,170 km/h or 1,350 mph). This plane cut the travel time between London and New York to just two hours, 52 minutes and 59 seconds from takeoff to touchdown! Plans were to build 300 such planes, but in the end only 20 were ever built. The plane was decommissioned in October 2003.

A record 82 commercial airline flights are hi-jacked (aka skyjackings) worldwide in 1969, a record to this day. During the 10-year period between 1968 and 1977, there were 414 reported hijackings—an annual average of 41! This is an amazing statistic when you look back with the benefit of 20/20 vision.

Did You Know? It was unofficial official state policy in both the U.S. and Taiwan to encourage the hijacking of civilian and military planes from both Cuba and mainland China respectively until around 1973! In fact, of the 177 worldwide hijacking attempts between 1958 and 1969, 77% either originated in Cuba or were efforts to divert planes to Cuba—maybe that travel embargo wasn't such a good thing and should have been lifted long ago? (See: 1961)

On February 1th, an Israeli sky-marshal aboard an El Al Boeing 707 on the runway at Zurich International Airport (ZRH) in Switzerland foils a plot to seize the aircraft by Palestinian militants—the pilot is killed.

On August 29th, members of the Popular Front for the Liberation of Palestine hijack a TWA flight leaving Rome and force it to fly to Damascus, Syria. Passengers and crew are later released.

On December 11th, a North Korean agent hijacks a Korean Air Lines flight with 54 passengers diverting it to North Korea. Only thirty-nine of the passengers were ever released?

Eastern Airlines becomes the first U.S. airliner to install airport metal detectors. *Hmm…* coincidence?

The Student Air Travel Association (SATA) is established and offers special types of discounted airline tickets for certain international flights for qualifying students—conditions and limitations apply.…

Trans World Airlines follows Pan Am's lead (again!) by finally inaugurating an around-the-world service, albeit a tad late. (See: 1947)

The Master Plan for the Cancún Project is officially approved by the Mexican Government. There will be roads. There will be hotels. There will be wet T-shirt contests. The first hotels begin opening in 1974—Playa Blanca, Bojorquez and Cancún Caribe.

1970

The *Smarte Carte* company begins offering vending machine luggage carts under the corporate creed of "*helping people help themselves*" so passengers can help themselves at Salt Lake City, Minneapolis, and Los Angeles airports. (See: 1965c). In most international destinations these carts are offered free!

Geoff Crowther, Nicholas Albery and Ian King, three English squatters, publish the grass-roots *Overland to India and Australia* (aka the *Bible of the East)* that was produced with the help of scores of other Hippie Trail (See: 1966) travel notes. It sells for donations, and could be considered the original Internet user-generated content travel forum, *sans* the Internet of course!

Royal Caribbean Cruise Line's first cruise ship, *Song of Norway,* sails the Caribbean, followed by *Nordic Prince* in 1971 and the *Sun Viking* in 1972.

Hawaii as a tourist destination grows fabulously with the advent of the jet age. In 12 short years between 1958 and 1970, tourism grows from 170,000 visitors to almost 1.8 million—and would continue to grow with an estimated 7 million arrivals by 2010!

Hans Johannes Höfer, a German artist, unhappy with the lake of cultural insight offered by guide books while traveling in Bali, publishes the aptly titled *Insight Guide: Bali.* The Insight Guides series offers great colorful photos and longer essays describing the people, places and things in exotic lands in order to give travelers a "real understanding into the historical and cultural background of destinations." The reflective traveler begins to evolve, and they still are today.

A company in Scottsboro, Alabama calling itself *Unclaimed Baggage* starts doing business selling, *well,* unclaimed baggage that the airlines cannot find the owners of. By 2010, this small mom and pop part-time business has turned into big business with "over one million items passing through the stores annually." Which reminds me of the great comedian Henry Youngman's skit: "*Getting on a plane, I told the ticket lady, 'Send one of my bags to New York, send one to Los Angeles, and send one to Miami.' She said, 'We can't do that!' I told her, 'You did it last week!*"

Cecil B. Day (1934–1978), an American real-estate salesman-cum-hotelier, opens the first 8 Days Inn (aka Days Inn) on Tybee Island, Georgia, calling his hotels "budget-luxury," with franchising rights for the asking. (By the end of the decade there were over 300 outlets.) As an added luxury, guests got to keep the bibles. Amen brother Cecil…gee thanks!

Delivered earlier on December 13, 1969, the first Boeing 747 (aka Jumbo Jet) takes its maiden Pan Am flight on January 21st between New York-Kennedy (JFK) and London-Heathrow (LHR). How big were the 747 Jumbo Jets? The Wright Brothers' entire first flight at Kitty Hawk, North Carolina (See: 1903), could have taken place within the 150-foot economy section of a new 747-400. We've come a long way baby! Carrying as many as 450 passengers, it revolutionizes commercial air travel for decades. Personally, I prefer seat 1B, 1A is too cramped for me…

The Mighty 747.
(Author Photo)

Did You Know? That a Boeing 747 jumbo jet can carry more than 240,370 liters (63,500 gallons) of fuel on long flights and burns approximately 12 liters of gasoline per kilometer (5 gallons of fuel per mile)…or about 240 liters (60 gallons) a minute!

Airbus Industrie a European consortium of French, German, and later, Spanish and British companies, combine industrial might and resources to better compete with the American commercial airliner monopoly and the big three known independently as: Boeing, McDonnell Douglas, and Lockheed, forms. Two short years later, in 1972, the A300 makes its maiden flight. The A310 came out in 1980, the A320 in 198, and the rest is competitive history. The big bad three are no more, now just the big one, Boeing survives alone to compete neck to neck with Airbus, who in 2010 had over 5,100 Airbus aircraft in service! They called the company Airbus as Euro-speak way of making travel more egalitarian with planes now being thought of as glorified buses...some would argue with the "glorified" part.

Thor Heyerdahl (See: 1947), does it again and sails his *Kon-Tiki* reed boat from Morocco to the Caribbean. No one really knows why?

Yippie (aka Youth International Party) counterculture activists protest at Disneyland by taking over Tom Sawyers island hide-out, threatening Mickey Mouse, and hoisting their New Nation flag over Disneyland's City Hall. It was an E-ticket day!

On February 21st, the Popular Front for the Liberation of Palestine (PFLP) blow up Swissair Flight 330 just after takeoff causing it to crash near Zürich, Switzerland, killing 38 passengers and all 9 crew members.

Steven Stills, a member of the rock band Crosby, Stills, Nash (and sometimes Young), tells it like is for everyone traveling and feeling alone in his single *"Love the One You're With"* much to the chagrin of love-sick left behinds...

The first for money extortion hijacking in the United States occurred in June when Arthur Barkley held a plane hostage at Washington Dulles International Airport (IAD) demanding a ransom of US$100 million from the government. He didn't succeed in his not so thought out plan.

On September th (aka Skyjack Sunday), the Popular Front for the Liberation of Palestine (PFLP) forced themselves on five planes: TWA Flight 741, Swissair Flight 100, and BOAC Flight 775, with a total of 400 people on board them and fly them to Dawson Field in the Jordanian desert. A fourth plane, El Al Flight 219 flying over London, attack was foiled by onboard security. The fifth hijacked plane, Pan Am Flight 93, a giant 747, was too big to fly to Dawson Field and ended up in Cairo via Beirut! After freeing the passengers on September 11th, the PFLP hijackers then blew up the empty planes on the tarmac drawing widespread international condemnation that finally results in the instigating of more comprehensive air passenger screening systems during the 1970's, heretofore done only haphazardly and a tad inconsistently...like mandatory metal detectors!

Richard Nixon (aka Tricky Dick) (1913–1994), an American politician, coincidentally considering the above—mandates better airport security screening and orders sky-marshals (aka armed non-uniformed security guards) to be assigned to more than just a select few flights. By exercising the "Bikini Principle" of security (providing strategic coverage of the most important vulnerabilities), these twin actions prove to be effective; with the simple act of better passenger screening at airports, said by experts to cause a 45% decline in airline hijackings, and the increased use of sky-marshals, reducing another 28% of hijackings. *Hmm*, that's only a 73% reduction ...those aren't great odds according to my bookie!

The dramatic movie *Airport* opens about a suicide bomber and a Boeing 707 and other back stories. Three mediocre sequels were made over the next decade as audiences seem to like the tense disaster-in-waiting themes.

> **Sound Sleeps:** The coffin-like *capsule hotels* for overworked businessmen in Japan were created in the 1970's when Japanese architect Kurokawa Kisho modified a shipping container to make a space-saving one-man room complete with TV, radio and alarm clock.

1971

Trans World Airlines becomes the first airline to offer a non-smoking section aboard every aircraft—between rows 23 and 29! These non-smoking sections always baffled me as a youth...how did the smoke know not to go into those forbidden areas?

In a plan to increase regional tourism, the London Bridge is purchased and shipped from England to the Arizona desert. The bridge was purchased in 1968 by a Missourian entrepreneur named Robert P. McCulloch for US$2,460,000...he denies rumors that he thought he was buying the Tower Bridge, not the non-descript third generation London Bridge. But tourists do come to see it and after the Grand Canyon, it is the number two attraction in Arizona!

The 380-seat three-engine wide body McDonnell-Douglas DC-10 enters commercial service with American Airlines on August 5th to counter Boeing's 747 wide bodies and Lockheed's L-1011 Tri-Star. Just 386 are built in almost twenty years as the plane got some rather unfavorable safety reviews; probably the result of almost 8% of the delivered jets (30 of 386) being involved in some type of accident!

The U.S. insurance seller, the American Home Assurance Company, begins offering travelers "weather insurance policies" that guarantee three out of four days of their vacation as rain free, or pay the traveler a daily rain rate.

The U.S. Congress forms the national rail passenger system (aka Amtrak or National Rail Passenger Corp) to provide intercity passenger train service in the United States. Unlike Europe, and Japan where train travel has thrived, Americans preferred cars and planes, and needing a viable intercity train service, it was effectively nationalized. Since1971, Amtrak has received over US$50 billion in federal tax subsidies. (We do that a lot in America; we privatize profits and subsidize losses!) But by 2008, Amtrak had grown eight straight years and was providing service to more than 70,000 passengers riding on one of Amtrak's 300 trains per day—that's 28.7 million passengers a year. (And it should be noted, that per passenger mile, Amtrak is 30–40 percent more energy-efficient than either commercial airlines or personal automobiles, and some lines with electrified trains are even more efficient.)

Southwest Airlines makes its maiden voyage and begins its consumer-friendly low-cost service between three Texas cities: Dallas, Houston, and San Antonio on June 18th. The era of regional airlines is born anew along with the seeds for the no-frills low-cost airline business model to evolve (or *devolve* depending on your point of view) with the likes of WestJet, EasyJet, Ryanair and People Express to come.

Albert Einstein (1879–1955), a world-renown thinker, and his legendary *Theory of Relativity* were proven true when two jets flew around-the-world going in opposite directions and showed that every time someone flies their year actually grows, albeit by only a few billionths of a second, and by a tad more traveling west than east. Got that—me neither!? But then again he did say, "*I love to travel, but I hate to arrive.*" Now, that I understand…

American Airlines puts Wurlitzer pianos in some coach lounges of its 747's. Now that's entertainment baby; and by the way, "*what's your sign?*" (Note: There is no truth to the rumor that they were later removed because they made the planes too tail heavy.)

Earthwatch begins operations creating charity tourism that focuses volunteers to join in global conservation projects. To date, over 93,000 travelers have joined the fun. Like the idea behind the Gap Years (See: 1960c), nowadays, charity tourism takes on many forms: teaching English abroad, raising money for the building of schools or clinics, volunteering a morning or afternoon at orphanages or clinics while traveling nearby, and lending a helping hand after a natural disaster.

With Pan Am losing a civil discrimination lawsuit in *Diaz v. Pan American World Airlines Inc.*, male flight attendants are now hired. Equality at long last!

Ken Welsh, an English writer, publishes the down and dirty *The Hitch-hiker's Guide to Europe* in England. The antithesis of the more high-end travel books and glossy travel magazines today, it provided advice for penniless travelers. Some believe that it gave philosophical birth to a few now well established guides like Lonely Planet and Rough Guides. Ken's opening line remains a mantra for real travelers: "*Hitch-hiking is a game of chance. In this world where we expect things to run on time or to be in a certain place by three o'clock, it is a refreshing experience. Just because the ninth car doesn't stop doesn't mean the tenth will; nor the hundredth, nor the thousandth. But you'll get there.*"

Douglas Adams (1952-2001), another English writer, publishes his divinely inspired *Hitchhikers Guide to the Galaxy*, a science-fiction comedy said to have some connection to the above citation. Who can't relate to his great travel quote: "*I may not have gone where I intended to go, but I think I have ended up where I intended to be.*"

It was not a myth, there was (is?) indeed an unofficial race across America called the Cannonball Baker Sea-To-Shining-Sea Memorial Trophy Dash (aka the Cannonball Run), that unofficially ran 4 times in the 1970's (1971, 1972, 1975, 1979) with the fastest time reported for driving the 4,608 kilometer (2,863 miles) highway (and byway) route between New York City and Los Angeles, California being 32 hours and 51 minutes—an 87 mph average. (See: 1933)

Walt Disney World Resort (aka Disney World) opens on 25,000 acres of central Florida swamp lane near Orlando, Florida. People love it, a lot! Some ask how Walt got the idea for another Disneyland. Easy; early market surveys showed that less than three percent of Disneyland's visitors came from east of the Mississippi River—where 75 percent of Americans lived at the time. Walt was a smart guy...and nowadays you can take a pre-packaged vacation to experience nothing real.

The first Starbuck's opens in Seattle's Pike Place Market and by 2010 they have 17,000 stores in 49 countries! You can order an over-priced *venti hot skinny half-café non-fat no-whip extra shot cinnamon dolce latte* in El Salvador, Romania and Algeria too!

Ray Tomlinson (1941-), an American computer engineer, invents an e-mail program for the ARPANet that allows e-mails to be sent to users on other systems. He also invents the use of the @ sign too! Al Gore is nowhere to be seen—yet again!

Peter Morton and Isaac Tigrett, two American's with big plans, open their first Hard Rock Café (aka HRC), a cool eclectic place in London, England. It explodes worldwide so that now you can buy a black T-shirt and eat an over-priced burger in over 50 countries—and many do!

The most infamous of all U.S. hijackings took place on November 24th, when a mysterious man boarded a Boeing 727 Northwest Orient flight in Portland International Airport (PDX), Oregon headed to Seattle–Tacoma International Airport (SEA), Washington, under the name of Dan Cooper (aka D.B. Cooper?). He hijacked the plane, demanding a ransom of US$200,000 and four parachutes? His demands were met and he later bailed out with the money never to heard of or seen again. (Experts believe he died bailing out in a heavy rainstorm over the Cascades at at least

170 knots (310 km/h or 200 mph)...it was a 727 he jumped out of—not slow moving vehicle!)

1972

Wernard Bruining (1950-), a budding Dutch entrepreneur, opens *Mellow Yellow* as Amsterdam's first "coffee house" ushering in the era of The Netherlands effective and enlightened soft drugs policy. The place is rather famous they say and the advent of Drug Tourism takes place. When the annual Cannabis Cup festival begins in 1987, things get a little higher...

The United States Tour Operators Association (USTOA) is formed by the tour operating industry to prevent a wave of travel rip-offs and inform customers.

The first Eurail Pass (aka Europass) for traveling the marvelously inter-city connecting train systems of Europe begins being sold to non-residents for just US$40.00 for a one-month pass.

The United Nations Educational, Scientific and Cultural Organization (UNESCO) create the World Heritage Site honorary designation system that "catalogues, names, and conserves sites of outstanding cultural or natural importance to the common heritage of humanity." By 2010, some 911 sites—704 cultural, 180 natural and 27 mixed properties in 151 nation-states make up the World Heritage List. Thus begins the paradox of modern tourism: sites have to be protected and promoted at the same time. A double-edged sword to be sure... (See: 2001)

The *RMS Queen Mary*, now docked in Long Beach harbor, California, opens as a Hyatt hotel with 150-guest rooms (aka a floatel).

Just plain odd: according to the *Guinness Book of World Records*, Vesna Vulovic, a flight attendant from Yugoslavia, survived a fall of over 10,000 meters (33,333 feet to be exact!), when JAT Yugoslav DC-9 Flight 367 she was working on blew up in midair. All the other 27 passengers die! *What the...?* This is one record I hope no one breaks!

Ted Arison (1924-1999), the Israeli-born British-American businessman, sails his first cruise ship, the *Mardi Gras* (aka the *Empress of Canada*, *Olympic, Star of Texas, Lucky Star, Apollo and Apollon,* and sold for scrap in 2003) on his new Carnival Cruise Lines. The cruise industry is a crafty industry.

After more than 21-years of haggling and planning, the Bay Area Rapid Transit (BART) system opens in San Francisco-Oakland (aka the Bay Area), California, for passengers on the first of soon to be four major lines and 45 kilometers (28 miles) of track. It expands over the years and finally makes a direct line connection to San Francisco International Airport (SFO) in 2003—and cabbies lose their god-given right to rip off unsuspecting arriving tourists.

On January 28th, Garrett B. Trapnell (1938 -1993), an American con man, hijacks TWA Flight #2, a Boeing 707 flying between Los Angeles (LAX) and New York's Kennedy Airport (JFK), and threatens to ram it into a JFK terminal if his demands are not met—US$306,800 in cash, the release of Angela Davis, and clemency from President Richard Nixon. Insanely, Nixon gets his clemency...

Not coincidently, the FAA begins requiring all U.S. commercial passenger airlines to conduct mandatory inspections of both passengers and their bags. It seems as though we've heard this before—and will again!

On May 8th, Israeli Special Forces storm a hijacked Belgian Sabena airliner sitting on the tarmac at Lod Airport (aka Ben Gurion International Airport (TLV) and kill four Palestinian members of Black September who had hijacked the plane and stupidly flew it to Israel—six die.

On May 30th, the Lod Airport Massacre occurs when members of the Japanese Red Army, on behalf of the Popular Front for the Liberation of Palestine (PFLP)—early terrorists outsourced apparently!—kill 26 and injure 78 at Israel's Tel Aviv Lod Airport (aka Ben Gurion International Airport (TLV).

On October 13th, an Uruguayan flight crashes in the Andes of South America with 45 passengers and the surviving 16 passengers further their survival for 72 days by resorting to cannibalism. South of the border, it is called *El Milagro de los Andes* (aka the Miracle in the Andes) and a book, *Alive: The Story of the Andes Survivors* (1974), and movie *Alive: The Miracle of the Andes* (1993) are subsequently released to mixed reviews.

Not accidently (sorry!), according to the Geneva, Switzerland-based Aircraft Crashes Record Office (ACRO), with 18 major airplane crashes, 1972 remains the year with most fatalities, and 3,214 deaths in all—until 2001.

1973

Dr. Martin Cooper (1928-), an American engineer, who while working with Motorola, makes the first telephone call on a portable mobile phone on April 3rd outside Manhattan's Hilton Hotel on a brick-like device which weighed 40 ounces. As we know, radiotelephone systems (aka cell phones, mobile, hand held) have roots to 1940's technology. By 1990, an estimated 12.4 million people worldwide had cellular subscriptions...by 2010 it is claimed over 4.6 billion subscriptions are in use!?

Arno Peters (1916–2002), a German film maker, unveils his Peters Projection map that is claimed to recognize the world in a non-racist manner with true proportionality. Back in 1855, James Gall (1808–1895), a Scottish clergyman, published the same type of projection map in 1855! The equal-area cylindrical map is now known correctly as the Gall–Peters projection. Greenland really shrinks!

Beginning in 1973, Japanese tourists become the biggest visitors of the United States–after Canadian and Mexican day-trippers of course.

The legendary rock band *Led Zeppelin* leases the ultimate party plane, a Boeing 720B called *Starship 1* from teen idol Bobby Sherman. The plane became the ultimate symbol of rock n' roll excess later servicing the needs of Elton John, John Lennon, Peter Frampton, Deep Purple, and the Rolling Stones in 1970's.

Tony and Maureen Wheeler, an English-speaking husband and wife traveling duo, who after completing an overland journey from London through Asia and on to Australia, publish Lonely Planet's first guidebook *Across Asia on the Cheap*. From humble beginnings to today's cult-like following (aka the creation of guidebook personality) with 500 releases in eight languages, a TV show, a magazine and website, 75% of Lonely Planet was sold to the British Broadcasting Corporation (BBC) in 2007.

The Sydney Opera House opens in Sydney, Australia and remains one of the most recognized buildings in the world.

French carrier Union des Transports Aériens (UTA) introduces celebrity chefs in planning in-flight menus. Thank you, but it is still bad in the back of the Airbus.

Club tourism begins with opening of the Pacaha night club (aka discothèque) in Ibiza, Spain (aka Gomorrah of the Med) and is quickly followed by a slew of swinging night spots including: Amnesia (1976), Café del Mar (1980), and Privilege (1987) known as "the world's largest night club" with a capacity of 10,000 sweaty Euro-dancers. Club tourism destinations like London, Paris and New York City take hold with later arrivals on the scene being Berlin, Manchester, South Beach Florida and Las Vegas.

Both General Motors and long-established Airstream trailer company launch the first Class A motor home recreational vehicles (RV's), all tricked out and expensive too. By 1989 you could add another room with the invention of slide-outs. The term *boondocking* becomes popular with RVers, which means roughing it in a US$200,000 house on wheels.

On October 30th, the Bosporus Bridge in Istanbul, Turkey opens for traffic and literally connects the continents of Europe and Asia over the Bosporus for the first time in history. We are the world...or as Rudyard Kipling so eloquently said in his 1889 poem *The Ballad of East and West*:
"Oh, East is East and West is West, and never the twain shall meet,
Till Earth and Sky stand presently at God's great Judgment Seat;
But there is neither East nor West, Border, nor Breed, nor Birth,
When two strong men stand face to face, though they come from the ends of the earth!"

Venedict Yerofeyev (1938–1990), a Soviet-era Russian writer, pens his masterpiece version of Hunter S. Thompson's 1972 novel *Fear and Loathing in Las Vegas: A Savage Journey to the Heart of the American Dream*, with his own alcohol-induced *Moskva–Petushki* (aka *Moscow to the End of the Line)*. A good read.

223

Emily Howell Warner, an American pilot, on January 29th becomes the first woman employed as a pilot for a scheduled commercial airline for Frontier Airlines. It was a long time in coming—too long. (See: 1934)

The Sheraton-Anaheim is said to be the first hotel to offer free in-room movies. It doesn't last long…

The Society of Incentive Travel Executives (SITE) is established in New York City with a plan to educate business managers about "A modern management tool used to achieve extraordinary goals by awarding participants a travel prize upon their attainment of their share of the uncommon goals," (aka incentive travel). By 2010, incentive travel—giving away trips to employees—is a huge business that by some accounts exceeds 15% of all travel spending!

United States airports begin installing magnetometers, an instrument used to measure the strength of the magnetic fields, to help de-magnetize hijackers carrying concealed weapons as the FAA begins to search every bag. As Yogi Berra says, *"It's déjà vu all over again…"*

> **The Thing About Automobiles:** Since about 1920, when cars became popular with the middle class, the automobile has had an average speed in most countries of 35 to 40 km/h (20-25 mph) —derived by dividing all the kilometers that cars travel by all the hours they travel. Since 1973, this speed has only reduced. The sad fact is that cars will inevitably become cleaner modes of transportation, but not faster ones!

On February 12th, two Israeli F-4 Phantom jet fighters shot down a Libyan Air Lines 727 flight with 114 traveling between Tripoli, Libya and Cairo, Egypt, that had strayed off course due to bad weather killing 113 passengers and crew with five somehow surviving.

On July 23rd, a Japan Air Lines Boeing 747 Flight 404 is hijacked after takeoff from Amsterdam Schiphol Airport (AMS) and after a series of bizarre flights and several days of angst; the passengers are released in Libya.

On August 4th, 12 people are killed and 48 injured when Italian neo-fascists explode a bomb on a train in Bologna, Italy.

On August 5th, a Black September suicide squad attacks passenger terminals at Athens International Airport (ATH), Greece, killing three and injuring 55.

On December 17th, Palestinian terrorists bomb the Pan Am office at Leonardo da Vinci-Fiumicino Airport (FCO) in Rome, Italy killing 32 and injuring 68 onsite; then kidnapping seven Italian policemen and hijacking a Lufthansa Boeing 737 to Athens (ATH), Greece, before completing their crime spree and flying on to Kuwait killing a hostage.

> **The Energy Crisis:** The world enters a new era, an era of limits and unchartered territory, when the energy crisis of 1973 begins to affect the travel industry and transportation systems worldwide. It seems obvious now, with 20/20 hindsight, but the continued growth for growth's sake business model proves unsustainable and things must change. The day had to come; hotel guests are asked to conserve electricity (and water), airlines begin charging extra fuel surcharges, family road trips get more expensive, RV's go unsold, roadside motels suffer, inter-city and urban transit systems become electrified, and yet our automobiles keep getting bigger…

1974

The great Post World War II tourism boom bubble suddenly pops after almost 25 years of continuous double digit growth when the lingering effects of the so-called Energy Crisis (aka Arab oil embargo) hit incomes and prices everywhere.

Dave Kunst (1939-), an American on a mission, becomes the first man to walk around the world; starting out in Minnesota on June 20th, 1970 and returns four years, three months and sixteen days later on October 5th—wearing out more than twenty pairs of shoes in covering 23,250 kilometers (14,450 miles).

Under the guise of protecting United States commercial air carriers from international competition (read: lower costs and better service), the U.S, Congress passes what is dubbed as the Fly American Act that requires all Federal employees and their dependents to travel only by U.S. flag air carriers, no matter the price or convenience.

Cancun, Mexico becomes an instant resort destination (See: 1969) with the opening of five new hotel properties: the Cancun Caribe Hyatt, Playa Blanca, Las Glorias, Club Med and Camino Real. Spring break takes a south-of-the-border turn! Ah, the memories…

Pan American Airways becomes the first airline to install and operate fleet-wide, a FAA-certified Ground Proximity Warning System. No more crashes into mountains and hard landings!

With the launch of the cruise ship Queen Elizabeth 2, Cunard Cruise Lines ushers in the equalitarian era of single-class cruising by eliminating First Class, Steerage, and Tourist classes. First one to the dinner buffet table wins!

The Hong Kong Hilton becomes the first hotel to experiment with the idea of allowing guests direct access to alcohol and peanuts by introducing the first mini-bars in the hotel industry. Now you know where those US$10 bags of chips come from…

On February 22nd, Samuel Joseph Byck (1930–1974), an unemployed salesman, attempts to hijack a Delta Air Lines Flight 523 DC-9 flying out of Baltimore-Washington International Airport (BWI) to Atlanta. He intended to crash the plane into the White House in hopes of killing President Richard Nixon—stop if this sounds oddly familiar—he is shot and killed. The media and public do not learn until much later of his intentions because the Secret Service fears copycats—also a lot of folks just didn't like Nixon! But, as a direct result of this assassination attempt the Secret Service immediately took steps to provide manned-portable air-defense systems (MANPADS aka FIM-92 Stingers) on the White House roof to somehow shoot down a threatening jet flying into the White House! (Military experts acknowledge that these anti-aircraft weapons cannot obliterate a large-mass aircraft of course and would turn one large incoming plane into many only slightly smaller incoming objects enlarging the area of damage.)

On November 23rd, a British Airways DC-10 is hijacked at Dubai International Airport (DXB), UAE, by Palestinian Rejectionist (A new terrorist brand?) and eventually is flown to Tunisia where a German passenger was killed.

The World Tourism Organization (WTO) (aka UNWTO) is established as a subsidiary organ of the United Nations General Assembly to address the growth and specter of global and multi-national travel-related issues. The statistical World Tourism Rankings keeps track of all the comings and goings or global travelers. It is as dry as it sounds with more meetings—in Madrid, Spain!

A Cornell University research study attempts to answer the age-old question, "Why do travel destinations rise and fall in popularity?" The answer is basically that places are hyped by word-of-mouth and travel agent commissions (nowadays via blogs and travel porn magazines) and that after people start coming, investors naturally want to cash in on the lucrative tourism boom and a combination of the growth in tourist numbers and the development of tourist-oriented facilities, changes the nature of the original destination. There is indeed a destination life-cycle (grow/decline, ebb/flow), from authentically native, to *it* list, to must see, to passé; that more often than not leads to the sacrificial tourist killing of the Golden Goose by loving a place to death! (See: 1992)

1975
Hyatt Hotels introduces a hospitality industry first when it opens its Regency Club, a concierge club level that provides the ultimate in VIP services for frequent guests. Membership does have its benefits...

Braniff Airways introduces Atari video games onboard flights. Pong becomes a big hit in the cheap seats.

The Convention on International Trade in Endangered Species of Wild Fauna and Flora (aka CITES) goes into force as a multi-national agreement to ban the importation of wild animals and plants—and their by-products. This new law effects the travel collections of many travelers. In the past, obviously uninformed travelers would regularly return home with souvenirs including: baby alligators, baby turtles, tropical birds, whale baleen, ivory and other exotic pets, foods, traditional medicines, clothing, and jewelry made of tusks, fins, skins, shells and horns of endangered critters around the world. *Netsuke* collectors everywhere feel remorseful.

George Gerbner (1919–2005), an American media scholar, promotes the idea that our perception of the world out there is badder, meaner and nuttier, than it is in real life due to the mass media's coverage and that we only see the worst (disasters, war, terrorism, famine, destruction, sensational elements, etc) of it and believe it to be more dangerous than it really is. His work is embedded in his cultivation theory that examines the long-term effects of television on audiences. Some now call it the *Mean World Syndrome*, and many claim it one of the reasons why American residents travel internationally so little and have such a meager working knowledge of geography, history and international realities. Point taken…

The Helsinki International Travel Accord deals with specifically European rights and the rights of people to migrate freely. The tourism portions of the *Accord* encourage: a) tourism and tourism studies; b) preservation of artistic, historic and cultural heritages of signatories; c) lowering of fees and documentation needed for international travel; and d) other efforts to encourage cooperation on tourism among countries. These *Accords* were created during the Cold War to engage the Soviet Union more into European values.

Paul Theroux (1941-), an American writer and fellow traveler, publishes what many consider his best work, *The Great Railway Bazaar*. Who can forget one of his seminal quotes, *"I have seldom heard a train go by and not wished I was on it."*

Sean Connery and Michael Caine star in Rudyard Kipling's epic travel adventure tale, the John Huston-directed *A Man Who Would Be King*. Adventure never was so thrilling…

Bog Seger, the king of Detroit rock n' roll, belts out his rite of passage Hippie Trail hit single *"Katmandu."* Many pack their bags…

The Federal Aviation Administration (FAA) adopts rules regarding the use of X-ray machines to screen carry-on baggage for the first time. It has been two years since the last FAA innovation, they were due!

On January 19th, terrorists attack Paris-Orly Airport (ORY) in France, seizing ten male hostages in a terminal bathroom. Never ones to capitulate, the French eventually provided the terrorists with a plane and fly them to safety in Baghdad, Iraq.

On December 2nd, South Moluccan separatists (aka freedom fighters/ terrorists from an archipelago in Indonesia) seize a train in The Netherlands with 85 passengers for twelve days. Three hostages were shot before the terrorists eventually surrender. They pull the same stunt two years later on May 23, 1977, when 13 South Moluccan terrorists seize 85 passengers again on a train before Dutch Marines storm the train to end a 19-day siege, unfortunately two hostages were killed.

David Bianco and Martin Knowlton, two American travelers of a certain age, who are inspired by the youth hostel movement (See: 1912), establish the first Elderhostel, that offers older travelers learning experiences around the world with cheap accommodations in unused college dormitories during the off season.

Tor Sørnes (1925-), a Norwegian inventor, creates what is known as the hotel key card, those popular throwaway plastic credit card-sized room keys that did away with those bulky brass room keys. Ving*Card's* eliminate the awkward front desk key pickup and drop off encounters.

1976
The unmanned *Viking 1* lands on Mars after a 10-month journey from planet Earth. It is the first inter-planetary visit known to earthlings. It heroically went where no man had ever gone before—or since—and performed its mission for over six full years on Mars. As man reaches out into the universe, this was a big step!

The last legendary Orient Express run between Paris, France and Istanbul, Turkey takes place ending an era of romance on the rails.

The Aérospatiale-BAC Concorde enters service after almost a decade of development and delays as the world's first commercial supersonic service after years of trials. The inaugural Mach 2 flight takes place on January 21st when Air France flew between Paris, France and Rio de Janeiro, Brazil at the same time a British Airways flight flew between London, England and Bahrain. (See: 1969)

Voters in Atlantic City, New Jersey approve a ballot initiative allowing casinos. The race to bottom begins, and on May 26, 1978, two years later, Resorts Hotel and Casino Atlantic City opens to the gambling public in an effort to revitalize a rundown town and increase state tax revenues.

The *International Travel News* monthly travel magazine begins publishing.

And by the way, if you didn't already know, the Tourism Society of England redefines what tourism means again, "*Tourism is the temporary, short-term movement of people to destination outside the places where they normally live and work and their activities during the stay at each destination. It includes movements for all purposes.*" Okay, we got it, people travel, move on...

On June 27th, an Air France flight was hijacked with 258 hostages being taken by a joint German Baader-Meinhof and Popular Front for the Liberation of Palestine (PFLP) terrorist group and flown to Entebbe International Airport (EBB) in Uganda. The hostage ordeal was brought to an abrupt end when Israeli commandos rescued the passengers—3 died during the hostage-rescue mission—after a week of fruitless negotiations. *The Raid on Entebbe* became a movie of the week.

> **Baggage Roulette:** The odds that your checked baggage will be either lost (aka misdirected), damaged, or stolen when flying on a U.S. carrier is 1 in 150. My bookie likes that bet. Although it does happen four million times a year!

On August 1th, the Popular Front for the Liberation of Palestine (PFLP), this time joins evil forces with Japanese Red Army terrorists and attack a passenger terminal at Atatürk International Airport (ART) in Istanbul, Turkey, killing four civilians and injuring twenty.

On September 10th, a TWA airliner flying from New York (JFK), United States, to Paris, (CDG) France is hijacked by Croatian terrorists seizing 93 hostages. The terrorists surrender in Paris.

On October 6th, Cubana Flight 455 flying from the Barbados to Jamaica was brought down by a terrorist attack with all 73 people on board the Douglas DC-8 aircraft being killed. (Evidence later implicates several CIA-linked *El Condor* anti-Castro Cuban exiles as well as elements of DISIP, the secret police of Venezuela. Some terrorist experts refer to this act as state sponsored terrorism.)

1977

The Love Boat a fictionalized ABC-TV show about life on a cruise ship with lovable characters becomes an instant hit in the U.S. and runs from 1977 until 1986. It single-handedly helps invigorate and spur the growth of the cruise ship industry after disastrous time following the theatrical release of *The Poseidon Adventure* in 1972. There is no foundation to the rumor that the cruise industry helps in the funding or production of the TV show, nor does that life imitate art.

Freddie Laker (1922-2006), an English businessman, ushers in the *Laker Skytrain* service between England and the U.S. and the advent of budget, no-frills air travel. Laker Airways was earlier formed in 1966 to fly holiday charter flights using a couple of ex-BOAC Bristol Britannias. Laker's trans-Atlantic charters started in 1973 with a handful of leased DC-10's until he finally forms *Laker Skytrain*. By 1982 the airline had gone bust.

George Millay (See: 1964) (aka Father of the Waterparks) opens Wet 'n Wild, the world's first amusement park solely dedicated to wild and fun water rides in Orlando, Florida. The blue urine-indicator dye myth becomes real for many young adults.

John Edward Long, an American pilot, retires and makes a claim as "the pilot with the most flying hours in America" who from May 1933 to April 1977 flew 62,654 hours—a total of more than seven years of actually flying time.

Jimmy Carter (1924-), an American politician, who as President of the United States lifts the outright travel ban on U.S. passport holders visiting Cuba. (See: 1963) The restrictions are eased between 1977 and 1982 when Reagan reinstitutes the ban to return the favor of Miami-based financial contributors.

On March 27th, at the Los Rodeos Airport (aka Tenerife North Airport (TFN) in the Canary Islands, two Boeing 747's, a Pan American World Airways and KLM, one taxiing, the other taking-off, collide. In all, 583 passengers and crew die. Conditions for the accident precipitate when a bomb explodes in the passenger terminal at Gran Canaria International Airport (LPA) earlier, and due to a warning of a possible second bomb, that airport was closed, with all flights diverted to the smaller Tenerife airport creating cramped wing conditions. Aside from September 11th, this remains the deadliest accident in aviation history.

On October 13th, four Palestinians hijack a Lufthansa Boeing 737 and order it to fly around to a number of Middle East destinations for four days until it lands in Mogadishu (MGQ), Somalia. All the ninety hostages are rescued when the plane is stormed by German GSG9 counter-terrorist troops and British Army Special Air Service soldiers.

On the lighter side, ABC TV airs *Fantasy Island* a made for TV movie, that proving watchable, catches on as a weekly TV series and runs for seven years (1978-1984).

New York state launches their ubiquitous and world famous **I ♥ NY** tourism promotion.

1978
The Airline Deregulation Act passes in the U.S. as a way to cease government control over airline fares, traffic routes and market entry requirements. Yield management systems based on complex computer formulations begin being used by the major legacy U.S. airlines to maximize profitability. Yes, fares went down about 10% but not on less-traveled routes; yes, passenger loads increased and the era of bumping began; yes, new airlines entered the market place, but over 100 airlines went bankrupt (among them Pan Am, TWA and Eastern) over the years and labor strife became rampant; yes, direct flights decreased as the hub-and-spoke system expanded and

airline feeder systems (aka fortress hubs) took hold causing longer flight delays at major airports. Deregulation produced a mixed bag depending on your P.O.V.; but did help usher in the new *Don't ask, don't tell* culinary policy.

> **How much did you pay?** Every airline passenger hates finding out that their seatmate got a "great deal" and paid half as much as they did. So what gives? The Yield Management (YM) (aka revenue management or capacity management) system developed in 1985 at American Airlines, and now used universally by airlines, hotels and rental car companies, to basically change the prices of their goods in real-time based on "various factors affecting perishable demand." YM is basically a flexible supply-demand econometric equation that some call price discrimination (why should I pay more than you did?)—while others just think of yield management as a dirty word…

In an unrelated item, airlines begin cutting back on china and flatware in coach class, lose more baggage and are late more than ever.

Oliver Stone, an American filmmaker and all-around good guy, pens the screenplay *Midnight Express*, an Alan Parker-directed movie about a traveler to Turkey caught smuggling hash out of the country. Leisure travel to Turkey plummets! The movie arose from the true-life book published in 1977 by Billy Hayes called aptly, *Midnight Express*.

In another unrelated item, based on the theories of economist Julian Simon (1932–1998), airlines begin to provide rewards (incentives) for travelers to voluntarily give up their seats on overbooked flights rather than arbitrarily bumping random passengers. It works!

The Persian Gulf country of Bahrain begins operating the world's first commercial cellular telephone system.

Outside magazine's first issue hits the newsstands.

The revolutionary rock n' roll band The Clash at their power-punk best explain their angst about traveling to Jamaica in the song "*Safe European Home*" with the lyrics including:
"Well I just got back an' I wish I never leave now (Where'd you go?)
I was there for two weeks, so how come I never tell (Where'd you go?)
That natty dread drinks at the Sheraton Hotel yeah? (Where'd you go?)
They got the sun and they got the palm trees (Where'd you go?)
Yes I'd stay and be a tourist but can't take the gun play (Where'd you go?)
I went to the place where every white face is an invitation to robbery
An' sitting here in my safe European home
Don't wanna go back there again."

On February 19th, a real international FUBAR (F#$ked Up Beyond All Repair) evolves after a civilian passenger airliner is hijacked at Larnaca International Airport (LCA) in Cyprus by terrorists who had just murdered a leading Egyptian publisher at a nearby hotel. After being chased around the Middle East and being refused permission to land anywhere, the hijackers return to Larnica airport where the fun really begins. Egyptian commandos secretly land and attack the plane but end up in gun battle with Cypriot troops protecting the plane. In all, 15 Egyptian troops, seven Cypriot soldiers and a German cameraman are killed...no word about the condition of the original hijackers.

1979
Richard "Rick" Steves (1955-), an American entrepreneur and tour guide), publishes his first of soon to be many travel guides called *Europe Through the Back Door* (aka ETBD) based on a series of classes he taught at the University of Washington. Things go exceedingly well for Rick and he now publishes many guidebooks a year, hosts a public television series called *Rick Steves' Europe* and a public radio travel show, *Travel with Rick Steves*—a success story all around.

Dr. Sylvia Alice Earle (aka Her Deepness) (1935-), an undersea explorer and marine biologist, makes the world's deepest solo dive of 385 meters off Hawaii. She goes on to inspire kids to pay attention to Mother Earth and the oceans in particular and writes several wonderful books.

The first World Travel Market (WTM) is held at the Olympia in London, England as an *"opportunity for suppliers in travel industry to negotiate business contracts*"; and by 2009 WTM had an industry attendance exceeding 45,500 with over 5,120 exhibiting companies representing 187 countries and regions from around the world.

Sun City, a posh casino resort just a two hour drive from Johannesburg, South Africa, opens amidst great controversy in the nominal tribal homeland of Bophuthatswana as the policy of apartheid still reigns in the country until 1994. "*I ain't gonna play Sun City*," sings Jim Kerr of the band *Simple Minds* in one of the first travel-related boycotts ever (aka ethical consumerism or conscientious consumption) that historians believe helped contribute to the fall of the white regime.

The United States begins pursuing bilateral *Open Skies* agreements with other nations allowing for access to reciprocal markets, free market pricing competition, and the further expansion of U.S.-based routes.

One year after deregulation, the U.S. Congress enacts the International Air Transportation Competition Act to address some excessive concentrations of resources occurring among some larger airlines in the hope of helping to ensure international competition among all carriers. Good luck with that…

The first car telephone service was introduced in the 23 districts of Tokyo, Japan.

Originally built a year earlier by Sony engineers so that "Sony co-chairman Akio Morita, who wanted to be able to listen to operas during his frequent trans-Pacific plane trips" could in fact do that; the birth of portable media players (PMP) and the first cassette-based Sony Walkman TPS-L2 rocks the world—my world too.

Modern day bungee jumping is born when four members of the Oxford University Dangerous Sports Club leapt from the Clifton Suspension Bridge in Bristol, England. The silly lads live and the sport grows.

The inaugural 12,874 kilometer (8,000-mile) off-road endurance race known as the Paris-Dakar Auto Rally (aka The Dakar Series or The Dakar) is held. Participants and spectators die with regularity. The 2009 Dakar Series was held in South America!

Southwest Airlines sets up a rudimentary self-ticketing machine and by 1994 airline kiosks started appearing in all the major airports.

Qantas Airlines becomes the first airline to offer a Business Class, thus beginning three-tiers of class services and the era of road warriors begins.

The first frequent flyer program is created by Texas International Airlines. American Airlines AAdvantage quickly followed in May 1981 with a secret in-house program for its top 150,000 customers, followed by United Airlines Mileage Plus and Delta Airline's SkyMiles, also in 1981, and British Airways Executive Club was launched in 1982. Some call it a commercial bribery scheme that allows loyal business travelers (aka road warriors) the VIP perks of earned mileage awards at the expense of their corporate bosses who have to pay for the higher than average airline flight expenses.

Bryan Allen (1952-), an American hang glider, pedals his big-winged *Gossamer Albatross* across the English Channel. Interesting concept…

On November 15th, 12 people are injured in a bomb mishap aboard American Airlines Flight 444 flying from Chicago to Washington D.C.— although the bomb is a dud, smoke bothers a few folks and the incident is blamed on the infamous Unabomber.

On November 22nd, Islamic fundamentalists seize Mecca's Grand Mosque in Saudi Arabia, taking hundreds of religious pilgrim's hostage. After an intense battle that leaves 250 dead and over 600 wounded, Saudi and French security forces retake the Islamic world's most holy shrine.

On November 28th, an Air New Zealand McDonnell Douglas DC-10 on a sight-seeing flight over Mount Erebus in the Antarctic, flies a little too low and actually crashes into Mount Erebus killing all 257 passengers and crew on board.

1980c
Twin travel phenomenon begin to evolve within the travel industry by the early 1980's, one being the idea of *Voluntourism* (aka holidays that help) with travelers attempting to do good deeds while traveling; and the other closely related market segmentation is referred to as Work Travel (aka Work

and Travel) that begins being associated with younger travelers abroad, especially during their Gap Year (See: 1962), and as they take working holidays around the world obtaining student work visas when available.

> **The Shrinking World (aka globalization):** In 1950, the top 15 destinations around the world absorbed 88% of all international travel arrivals. By 1970, the proportion of travelers going to those top 15 destinations had decreased to 75%, and by 2005, those top 15 destinations represented just 57% of all international arrivals. Not only had the world shrunk but new travel destinations had emerged globally.

1980

The United Nations World Tourism Organization (UNWTO) designates September 27th as World Tourism Day! Nations everywhere give their citizens a paid day off…so fire up the BBQ and call some friends over for a beer, better yet, get on a plane heading off to exotic destinations.

Paul Fussell (1924-), an English professor of culture, pens *Aboard: British Literary Travelling Between the Wars* that for the first time delves critically into the psychology of travel writing and its use as escapism in certain circles by both the reader and writer.

A new breed of airline begins operating as Texas Air out of Houston, Texas. The Enron of Airlines of its day, it was designed as a holding company to gobble up as many operating airline assets as possible. In 1982 it took over Continental Airlines, Eastern Air Lines, People Express and Frontier Airlines quickly came into the fold. It is claimed that after just a few years in existence and only a handful of real employees, that Texas Air controlled over 20% of the entire United States airline passenger marketplace. By 1990 Texas Air was no more, *poof*!

McDonnell Douglas builds the MD-80, basically an improved version of the popular DC-9, a twin-engine narrow bodied jet, when it enters service as a Swissair flight in September. It is not very fuel efficient—it burns over 4,500 liters (about 1,000 gallons) of jet fuel per hour on a typical flight versus about only 3,000 liters (about 800 gallons) for a Boeing 737. By 2009, over 830 of the 1,200 built MD-80's were still in operation.

David J. Springbett (1938-), an English insurance salesman, becomes a true road warrior, when according to the *Guinness Book of World Records* he becomes the fastest person to fly around-the-world on scheduled commercial flights in 44 hours and 6 minutes—with the help of a few legs of supersonic travel on the Concorde!

The first commercial passenger flights between China and the U.S. since the 1949 Communist takeover begin with Air China (CAAC) and Pan Am getting the reciprocal routes: Pam Am is first to fly the New York to Beijing via Tokyo run on December 7th. Oddly, the first scheduled non-stop flight between the two countries by a U.S. carrier did not take place for fifteen years when on May 1, 1996, Northwest Airlines (NWA) flew between Detroit (DTW) and Beijing (PEK).

The Alton Towers theme park and resort built on the ruins of an old castle opens in Staffordshire, England.

Nicholas Ridley (1929–1993), an old crusty English conservative politician, coins the phrase "Not in my backyard" (NIMBY) and creates the anti-progress selfish philosophy of Nimbyism; as in: no new airports in my back yard, no new magnetic levitation trains (Maglev) in my backyard, no new highways in my backyard—no new nothing to advance mankind's needs and improve our transportation options.

Lightweight, waterproof and breathable travel clothes become a reality when the folks that invented Gore-Tex are given a patent. Suitcases just got smaller!

Willie Nelson, an American singer, gives everyone the first song for their homemade travel tunes cassette with the release of his hit single *"On the Road Again,"* that has us all: *"Goin' places that I've never been / Seein' things that I may never see again..."*

Ted Turner (1938-), an American corporate titan, launches his Cable News Network (CNN) 24-hour news network. From this day forward it is finally true that *the whole world is watching.* In 2010, CNN International can be seen in 212 countries—a truly remarkable global development: global news from everywhere and anywhere a camera can get to 24/7! It also gives rise to a phenomenon known as the *CNN effect*, which basically shows that some decision makers, by watching the news make real-time policy decisions based on what they see and hear on TV. In effect, CNN's coverage becomes a real-time intelligence agency for decision makers. CNN International debuts in 1985.

On August 1st, a right-wing Italian paramilitary group allegedly linked to rogue elements in the country's intelligence service detonates a massive bomb in the Bologna railway station in Italy, killing 85 travelers and injuring over 300 more.

On August 13th, an Air Florida flight flying from Key West to Miami is hijacked by seven Cubans and flown to Cuba. Six other U.S. flights are hijacked to Cuba over the next month with all the passengers being freed without incident. But in an odd *tit-for-tat*, three passengers are killed when Cubans hijack an aircraft in Peru and demand that it be flown to the United States!

On October 26th, a neo-Nazi made bomb explodes at the *Oktoberfest* festival in Munich, Germany leaving 13 dead and 27 wounded. Is nothing sacred?

Eighty-four gamblers and employees die in nasty little fire at the (old) MGM Grand Hotel in Las Vegas. The 2,814-room hotel was built by the lowest bidder of course according a time-honored U.S. construction tradition and no water sprinklers were ever installed—ah, capitalism. The good news…the fire did create an immediate international reaction (Because it was seen live on CNN!) that called for the implementation of fire safety improvements worldwide.

The satirical comedy *Airplane!* feature film is released to a wide audience.

1981
People Express Airlines is launched following the lead of the *Laker Skytrian* (See: 1977) as a cut-rate no-frills economy-class focused airline in the United States. People Express take it a step further and develops the *ala carte* pricing that really evolves thirty years later by charging passengers for

extra services including meals and for checked baggage. By 1986, People Express had grown to be the fifth largest U.S. airline carrier and was acquired in 1987 by Texas Air Corporation (See: 1980).

> **Did You Know That?** Less than 2% of the world's population actually moves hundreds or thousands of kilometers (or miles) away from where they were born. In fact 98% of us will die within 80 kilometers (50 miles) of where we were born!

The U.S. space shuttle *Columbia* takes off and lands after two days beginning a new more functional stage of the USA's NASA space program.

Stephen Ptacek, a green aviator, flies a solar-powered aircraft called the *Solar Challenger* 262 kilometers (163 miles) across the English Channel in five hours.

Benjamin L. Abruzzo (June 9, 1930 – February 11, 1985), an American ballooning enthusiast, make the first crossing of the Pacific Ocean by balloon in his Double Eagle V on November 13th...it is also the longest balloon trip ever.

The Lyon-Paris high-speed train service (aka TGV) begins operating with trains traveling at speeds of 270 km/h (168 mph) cutting the journey time between the two French cities from 4 hours 30 minutes to just about two hours.

As if you needed yet another reason to visit Edmonton, the world's largest shopping mall, the West Edmonton Mall (WEM), opens for business. In 1985, they added the first ever indoor waterpark too. WEM reigned the largest until 2004.

IBM introduces the IBM 5100 Personal Computer (PC) with high-tech specs including: 4.77 MHz Intel 8088 and 16 KB of memory. Over 250,000 are sold in the first month at US$1,565 for a bare-bones model. The rest is history, thank you IBM!

The Explorers Club (See: 1904) of New York City, previously an all men's adventure club, inducts the first female members.

The first truly international cell phone service begins operations when those Nordic darlings: Sweden, Denmark, Finland and Norway, create the Nordic Mobile Telephone System.

In a lawsuit brought against Southwest Airlines in *Wilson v. Southwest Airlines*, it was argued ineffectively that Southwest's business model required that their female flight attendants dress in provocative uniforms! The era of hot pants sadly ends.

Japan Airlines is the first commercial airline to try something new in training pilots when it begins using computerized flight simulators. The military-trained flyboys are not happy!

Ronald Wilson Reagan (1911–2004), an American actor turned politician, union-busts the air traffic controller union. After months of failed negotiations with the federal government fires, seeking among other things: a reduced 32-hour work week, a simple pay raise and a better retirement packages, the Professional Air Traffic Controllers Association (PATCO) and its 13,000 members go on strike. Two days after the walkout, Reagan fires summarily 11,000 of the controllers who did not return when ordered and declared a lifetime ban on their rehiring by the FAA. Unions have been floundering in the U.S. ever since this act of collective bargaining bad faith.

The new Singapore Changi Airport (SIN) opens 17.2 kilometers (10.7 miles) from Singapore's commercial downtown, complete with people movers, a Skytrain system, rooftop garden, and of course the requisite duty-free mall.

1982
On December 12th, a not so peaceful anti-nuclear protestor holds eight tourists hostage in the Washington Monument in Washington D.C. before he is shot dead by a police sniper.

The late great and powerful Pan Am discontinues its much-celebrated around-the-world Flight #1 that it began in 1947. A sad day...but the next day Pan Am begins regular service between Los Angeles (LAX), California to Sydney (SYD), Australia, and the longest non-stop flight in the world at 11, 979 kilometers (7,487 miles). A really long day...

Tim & Nina Zagat, an American couple and practicing attorneys, write their first *Zagat* restaurant guide covering New York City eateries. By 2003, their *Zagat Survey* guides that uses a 30-point scale and consumer reviews covers eateries in over 70 cities worldwide. An early TripAdvisor.com (See: 2000).

Walt Disney (See: 1955) opens is high-tech EPCOT Center (aka Experimental Prototype Community of Tomorrow) near Disney World Resort in Orlando, Florida.

The steamy summer movie *Summer Lovers* starring Darryl Hannah and Valerie Quennessen arrives on the big screen in United States showing how things are done abroad—and bookings to the Greek Islands sky-rocket!

The Weather Channel (TWC) launches on cable TV as a 24/7 channel offering traveler's regional and international weather forecasts. It makes packing a lot easier.

Gosh, it didn't look like that in the brochure? The travel tourism industry spends more than US$6 billion dollars a year on their massive propaganda advertising campaign to inform, bamboozle, persuade and sell. Deciphering their semantic code can be tricky, here are a few helpful translations:

- a direct flight = is not a nonstop flight
- 1 brochure mile = 5 real miles
- 1 brochure minute = 5 real minutes
- based on double occupancy = cost twice for the same room
- airy rooms = no air conditioning
- arbitration clause = forget your rights, no lawyers allowed—for you!
- booking fee = they charge you extra to buy their stuff
- carefree locals = bad service…if you get any
- choppy air = a pilot's bad joke…expect heavy turbulence
- code-sharing = the reason you are sitting on an small plane on an unknown airline
- explore on your own = good luck finding something to do, bring lot's of cash
- gentle breezes = batten down the hatches a typhoon is coming
- heart of the city = located in an iffy area of town near a slum
- historic section of town = rundown and dilapidated area awaiting gentrification
- inclusive tour = that does not include meals, alcohol or gratuities
- in-room entertainment = a CD player…you brought CD's right!
- majestic location = a long way from anything atop a hill
- mass transit nearby = a bus stop 5 brochure minutes away
- near hotel amenities = a 7/11 next door
- nominal fees = outrageous nickel and diming for everything
- ocean view room = yes, on your tip toes out the bathroom window
- old world charm = the bathroom is outside
- rustic accommodations = bring toilet paper, DEET spray and mouse traps
- TBA = to be arranged because we really don't know yet
- undiscovered = you bet and for good reason too…
- wildlife nearby = the dumpsters are busy with birds and critters
- *a la carte* menu = everything cost extra

Rough Guides enters the travel guidebook market place with the publication of *Rough Guide to Greece,* as an alternative to either the budget-conscious traveler or the high-brow culture vulture with the slogan: *Make the Most of Your Time on Earth.*

It is called the Jakarta Incident when British Airways Flight 9, a 747 flying between London (LHR) and Auckland (AKL), New Zealand, with a few stops in Bombay, Madras, Kuala Lumpur, Perth, and Melbourne on June 24th flew into a cloud of volcanic ash thrown up by the eruption of Mount Galunggung 180 kilometers (110 miles) south-east of Jakarta, Indonesia and all four engines fail...but they are restarted. Aviation experts then battle over the significance of this engine fail that effects travel near volcanoes (See: 2010).

Graceland, the former home of the one and only *King of Rock and Roll,* Elvis Presley (1935-1977), opens to the public as a museum in Memphis, Tennessee. After the White House in Washington D.C., it is the most visited private residence in the world. Paul Simon releases his hit album and title hit single *"Graceland"* in 1986.

1983c
With the Federal Express's continued success and growth as a cheap and reliable international courier service, the good old days of when an intrepid adventurer with a valid passport getting a cheap last-minute airline ticket to some foreign land by allowing a bonded courier company to use their baggage allotment, sadly begins declining fast.

1983
Hector Ceballos-Lascurain, a Mexican environmentalist, coins the term eco-tourism. The term eco-tourism means many things to many people, but at its core is responsible tourism based on sustainable development in countries visited by travelers. It remains in 2010 one of the fastest growing sectors within the travel and tourism industry globally as travelers want to know they are doing no harm at the least and positively contributing to sustainable local development at best.

Holiday Inn becomes the first hotel group to launch its own rewards program in January. (See: 1975 - Hyatt Regency Club) Marriott follows with its Honored Guest Awards in November.

Tokyo Disneyland Park opens in Japan.

The Gay and Lesbian Travel Association (IGLTA) is created in the United States and by 2000, self-anointed pink money" (aka gay and lesbian money) represents an estimated 10% of the U.S. travel industry and a US$64 billion international annual market as of 2010. (See: 1967)

The movie *National Lampoon's Vacation* is released and folks laugh as Ellen Griswold ridicules Clark, her husband, for being distracted trying to find attractions such as "the world's largest ball of twine" on their way to their actual destination, a fictional amusement park called "Wally World." *Ha ha…*

Bill Kimpton, an American hotelier, launches the first boutique hotel group in the U.S. when he opens his second San Francisco hotel, the Hotel Vintage Court (his first opening was San Francisco's Bedford Hotel in 1981). Kimpton Hotels jump-starts America's urban hotel scene toward high style, personalized service, and individual design in the small- to medium-size hotel business. These hotels are hyped in glossy travel magazines as "design hotels" or "lifestyle hotels."

There is a report that on March 3rd and 4th, a Cubana de Aviación Ilyushin Il-62M commercial airliner strays off course and dangerously close to "important American buildings." No other information is available identifying the buildings, the city, nor the flights involved. But what is known is that the FAA bans the airline from U.S. airspace two-weeks later—maybe a small dot to connect later?

On July 23rd, eight people are killed and over fifty injured when a suitcase bomb planted by Armenian terrorists explodes near a check-in desk at Paris-Orly Airport (ORY) in Paris, France.

On September 1st, in a case of Cold War jitters and uncertainty, a Soviet fighter shoots down a civilian Korean Air Lines Flight #007, a 747-jumbo jet, killing all 269. The world reacts with anger and dismay

On September 23rd, Gulf Air Flight 771 flying from Abu Dhabi International Airport (AUH) in Abu Dhabi, United Arab Emirates to Jinnah International Airport (JHI) in Karachi, Pakistan, crashes after a bomb planted by Abu Nidal in an extortion attempt explodes in the baggage compartment killing 117 passengers and crew. He gets paid they say…

1984

The Sambódromo (aka Sambadrome) is open in Rio de Janeiro, Brazil for the annual Carnival samba dancing competitions. It is a 700 meter stretch of the Marquês de Sapucaí Street that is converted into a permanent parade ground seating for 90,000 of the craziest party-goers you will ever want to meet. Never has so much beauty been put on parade!

The Jinjiang Amusement Park, China's first, opens outside Shanghai. Let the good times roll…

Redmond O'Hanlon, (1947-), an English writer and wild traveler, publishes *Into The Heart of Borneo.* His other books about his travels to the truly wild regions of the world include: *In Trouble Again: A Journey Between the Orinoco and the Amazon* (1988), and *No Mercy: A Journey Into the Heart of the Congo* (1997). He single handedly re-vitalizes the Ethno Tourism vein of traveling to visit indigenous peoples and tribal folk in some of the more remote regions of the world.

Dr. Ralph Crawshaw, an American physician, who after traveling and seeing how much needed to be done in places less fortunate than ours, creates the non-profit Health Volunteers Overseas (HVO) organization that sends doctors, dentists and fellow medical practitioners to over 50 developing nations to help out. That is truly wonderful; but what inspires so many travelers is his take on seeing the world and bringing it home, *"Travel has a way of stretching the mind. The stretch comes not from travel's immediate rewards, the inevitable myriad new sights, smells and sounds, but with experiencing firsthand how others do differently what we believed to be the right and only way."* Hear, hear…

Bruce McCandless II (1932-), a U.S. astronaut, becomes the first person ever to float freely and untethered in space. It is amazing to think about it, all that blackness and silence.

Choice Hotels becomes the first chain to offer no-smoking rooms.

Richard Branson (aka Sir) (1950-), an English businessman, shakes things up in the stogy world of commercial aviation entering the business by launching his Virgin Atlantic Airways and beginning service to North America.

Airfone introduces the world's first in-flight air to ground telephone system on American Airlines, for US$4.99 per minute! *"Hi mom, guess where I'm sitting right now?"* And the best thing about it—outgoing calls only!

According to the International Association of Cybercafés (IAC) and Yahoo!, the first cyber café (aka Internet café) is opened by Eva Pascoe at London's West End Cafe Cyberia. Over the years, over 30,000 such cafes open in over 170 countries from Timbuktu, Mali to Kathmandu, Nepal.

On June 5th, Sikh separatists seize the holy Harmandir Sahib (aka the Golden Temple) in Amritsar, India, where hundreds—some would say thousands—die when Indian forces retake the holy shrine.

On August 2nd, Tamil Tiger terrorists blow up a Madras Municipal Airport (MDJ) terminal in India, killing at least thirty people and injuring dozens more. The bomb was intended to blow up a Sri Lankan airliner.

On December 3rd, Kuwait Airways Flight 221 is hijacked en-route to Pakistan from Dubai by Iranian backed Lebanese Shi'a terrorists. The aircraft was forced to land in the Iranian capital city of Tehran, after two American USAID workers had been killed. The terrorists surrendered to the Iranian authorities and are later released.

The National Geographic Society (See: 1888) builds on its trusted and respected name and enters the travel magazine market with the launching of *National Geographic Traveler*.

The USA TODAY International is launched on July 10th...now you can know more about nothing from everywhere!

Eclipse chasing (aka umbraphiles) becomes vogue among those that love the celestial bodies with travelers jetting off (or chartering boats) to remote geographical areas to best catch lunar, solar, partial and full eclipses. The best ones occur every 16 months in various locales around the globe.

1985

Robert Ballard (1942-), an American oceanographer, locates the *RMS Titanic* on the ocean floor. See the movie…

Dick Bass (1929-2006), an American ski resort developer, becomes the first person to climb the designated Seven Summits (all of the tallest peaks on each of the seven continents) and co-authors *Seven Summits*. Bass was also the developer of Utah's Snowbird Ski and Summer Resort in 1971.

> **The Seven Summits:** Kilimanjaro (Africa), Vinson Massif (Antarctica), Kosciuszko (Australia), Everest (Asia), Mont Blanc (Europe), Mount McKinley (North America), and Aconcagua (South America). (*Note*: Mount Elbrus has a claim for Europe's highest peak, but is considered in Asia by most geography experts.)

This is a terrifying story so you may not want to read it…but on February 19th, China Airlines Flight 006 making its normal daily non-stop flight run between Taipei (TPE) and Los Angeles (LAX), experiences an engine blowout and takes a sudden roll at 12,192 meters (40,000-feet), and then just as suddenly plunges over 9,100 meters (30,000-feet) while experiencing 5-g-forces and speeds exceeding design limits of the aircraft before the captain somehow is able to recover from the dive…all in under 150 seconds! The plane landed battered and bruised at San Francisco International Airport (SFO) with not deaths. Absolute hell…Orson Welles may have been right when he said, *"There are only two emotions on a plane: boredom and terror."*

On June [th], members of the Red Army Faction detonate a bomb at Frankfurt am Main Airport (FRA), Germany, killing three people.

On June 15th, a TWA Boeing 727 Flight 847 flying between Greece and Italy is hijacked en route by Lebanese Hezbollah terrorists and forced to fly to Beirut International Airport (BEY), Lebanon. One hundred and fifty three passengers and crew are held for seventeen days, during which one American hostage was murdered. The hostages are eventually released after the U.S. Government pressures the Israelis to release 700 Lebanese and Palestinian prisoners. This event leads to the creation of the elite U.S. Delta Force.

On June 23rd, an Air India 747 Flight 182 operating on the Montréal-Pierre Elliott Trudeau International Airport (YUL), Canada to Indira Gandhi International Airport (DEL), India route is destroyed by a bomb over the Atlantic killing all 329 aboard. Sikh terrorists are blamed for the attack, which is the worse single terrorist incident to date… The incident remains the largest mass murder in Canadian history. The explosion and downing of the carrier occurred within an hour of the related explosion at an India Air baggage center in Tokyo (NRT), Japan, killing two that were intended to be stowed aboard India Flight 301 bound for Bangkok International Airport (BKK), Thailand, with 177 passengers and crew on board. Sadly, a well thought out plan…

On August 12th, Japan Airlines 747 Flight 123 traveling domestically between Tokyo and Osaka explodes and crashes into Mount Otsuka, of the 524 aboard, only four survive. As of 2010 this remains the worst single-aircraft air disaster in aviation history.

On September 25th, Palestine Liberation Organization (PLO) commando squad kills three Israeli tourists aboard a yacht in Larnica marina, Cyprus.

On October 7th, an Abu Abbas-led faction of the Palestine Liberation Front (PLF), boards and sea-jacks the Italian cruise ship *MS Achille Lauro* carrying more than 400 passengers. One passenger was killed, Leon Klinghoffer.

On November 23rd, an Egyptair aircraft is held hostage by Palestinian terrorists at Malta International Airport (MLA), Malta, with 98 hostages. All together 60 people died, most of them when Egyptian commandos stormed the aircraft in an ill-conceived rescue operation.

On December 27th, twin suicide attacks occurred against El Al Airlines passengers at Rome's Leonardo da Vinci-Fiumicino Airport (FCO) and Vienna International Airport (VIE) by the Abu Nidal terrorist group resulting in 18 deaths and over100 injured.

The Australian Government begins providing citizens with travel notices and up-to-date bulletins about travel destination countries. (SmarTraveller. gov.au) (See: 1914)

A sign of things to come? *The Canadian Geographer* magazine publishes an article by a Professor Zach Mieczkowski, which for the first time examines the impact of projected future climate change on the climates of tourism destinations, and creates the *tourism climatic index* (TCI). Basically, this discussion opens the door about the relationship to weather and tourism spending (or no spending) during summer peak and winter peak times as it relates to the weather. Al Gore is still not in the building...

1986

Jeana Yeager (1952-) and Richard Glenn "Dick" Rutan (1938-), an American aviatrix and aviators respectfully, co-pilot *Voyager,* the first aircraft to circumnavigate the globe non-stop without refueling. It takes them nine days to travel the 40,211 kilometer (28,000-mile) circle.

Carlo Petrini (1949-), an Italian editor and food lover, who in a response to the opening of a McDonald's fast food restaurant at the foot of the Spanish Steps in Rome, Italy, starts the *Slow Food Movement,* and begins to protest the spread of fast food chains worldwide. Their simple goal is to preserve traditional and regional cuisines and enjoy meals slowly with loved ones... familial and paramours!

The hi-fidelity Bose Company applies their noise-cancellation technology to develop the headphones now common on flights.

Reinhold Messner (1944-), an Italian mountaineer, becomes the first climber in the world to scale all 14 of the 8,000-meter peaks...he may be alone in his pursuits.

Midwest Airlines offers passengers freshly baked (sure!) chocolate chip cookies aboard its flights. In an unrelated story, TV's *Sesame Street's* Cookie Monster begins flying more frequently...

London's *The Economist* magazine introduces what is dubbed the Big Mac Index, a method of comparing prices and currencies around the world and "seeks to make exchange-rate theory a bit more digestible." If the price of burger is cheaper here than there, life is better here, or vice versa!

Joe Jackson, an English musician, releases his live *Big World* album that is about his travels around the world, with songs including: *"(It's A) Big World"*, *"Shanghai Sky"*, *"The Jet Set"*, and *"Fifty Dollar Love Affair"*.

The Jules' Undersea Lodge opens in Key Largo, Florida and quickly becomes the only underwater hotel in the U.S. when guests have to scuba dive to get to their rooms!

The NetJets program of fractional aircraft ownership begins for wealthy travelers. Gee, now you too can take your own Gulfstream V to Rio for the weekend.

On April 2nd, a TWA Boeing 727 flying between Rome (FCO) and Athens (ATH) has a bomb explode while in flight—a small one—planted by a suspected Palestinian terrorist group, killing four passengers and injuring nine others. The aircraft does land safely.

On May 1st, a Cargese holiday camp on the French island of Corsica is seized by Corsican separatist rebels, who kill two tourists and injure three.

On September 5th, a Pan Am Boeing 747 Flight 73 is seized by Arab terrorists at Karachi's Jinnah International Airport (KHI) in Pakistan, beginning a 16-hour siege with over 400 hostages. Thinking they were under attack, the terrorist kill 17 hostages before they are stormed by Pakistani security forces. In all 22 travelers are killed.

Because a cowardice Jordanian man planted Semtex explosives in his pregnant fiancés bag (nice guy!)—detected by airport authorities I should add—the security question, *Did you pack your own bags?"* becomes *de rigueur*.

Hijacking History: Airplane hijacking have been around since planes first flew, but they have peaked from an era of almost common daily occurrences:
1948-1957: there were 15 hijackings worldwide;
1958-1967: there were 48 hijackings worldwide;
1968-1977: there were 414 hijackings worldwide;
1988-1997: there were 180 hijackings worldwide;
1998-2007: there were less than 25 hijackings worldwide.
By the way, according to the Rand Corporation, 85% of all hostage deaths in airplane hijackings since 1968 have occurred during rescue attempts!

CHAPTER ELEVEN

Post-Modern Tourism (1987 – 1996):
The reality of Post-modern tourism evolves which shows our travel tendencies irrevocably intertwined with our progressive instincts and civilized modernity. As Buckaroo Banzai said: *"No matter where you go, there you are."* Travel consumption patterns become thoroughly mixed with wealth and consumerism, our attitudes about leisure (and ourselves), with technological innovations, and pop-culture. The average travel consumer is media saturated 24/7 in this everything-all-the-time world; as a cynical edge about travel evolves. "We're *not* tourists—ugh, bite your tongue!—*we are travelers!*" People become jaded with a *"been there, done that, what's next"* attitude. Travel is somehow now less than the *"way it used to be."* And so the commercialization of travel adventure begins to accelerate as people anchored to desk jobs dream of getting away and become more thrill-seeking in their leisure pursuits. Travel is no longer undertaken just to travel or to just go on a vacation—it must mean something to us and add to our modern cultural identity. Robert Young Pelton, a North American adventurer and travel commentator, may have said it best, *"The more civilized a society is, the more outrageous their adventures."*

1987
The Travel Channel begins broadcasting as the first all-travel-focus cable channel on February 1st. At the time of launch it is owned and operated by TWA. That focus is soon lost.

In February, British Airways, now a profitable concern is privatized and comes off the dole—again we witness profits privatized and losses socialized.

At the height of the "greed is good" Reagan decade, MGM Grand airlines begin flying the lucrative Los Angeles International Airport (LAX) to John F. Kennedy International Airport (JFK) route using only all–First Class configured planes. Air One Airlines, Regent Airlines and a few other copy-cats also enter the market. By 1994, the private jets took over this cross-country celebrity business.

National Rental Car introduces the Emerald Club, the first true car rental frequent user program in March. Although, Hertz was the first car rental company to join an airline frequent flyer program being one of the first partners in American Airlines AAdvantage program back in 1981.

Tim Cahill (1944-), an American adventure travel writer, publishes his hilarious *Jaguars Ripped My Flesh: Adventure is a Risky Business*. That same year Tim and co-driver Garry Sowerby set a world record driving from Ushuaia, Argentina to Prudhoe Bay, Alaska along the Pan American Highway in 23 days, 22 hours and 43 minutes. He pens *Road Fever: A High-Speed Travelogue* in 1989 chronicling the epic road trip. Tim sums up his trip saying, *"A journey is best measured in friends, rather than miles."*

American Airlines and Citibank revolutionized the way we earn miles by co-introducing the first mile-earning credit card. The basic concept, one mile for every dollar charged, still is the rule. It allows even non-frequent fliers to chase the illusive free trip miles. By 2010, it is said there are over 12,000 ways to earn miles—while not flying.

Steve Martin and John Candy, two North American comedians, star in the classic travel buddy road comedy movie *Planes, Trains and Automobiles* is released. Silliness reigns.

Robert Plath, an overworked and tired Northwest Airlines pilot, comes up with *Rollaboard* by affixing wheels to his suitcase in his garage, the first luggage with wheels (aka Bellman Busters). Available initially to only the airline industry, he began mass-marketing his *Travelpro* Rollaboard in 1991. Thank you Bob!

Alan John "A. J." Hackett (1958-), a New Zealand madman, popularizes the Vanuatu ritual of land diving into bungee jumping by taking a dive off the Eiffel Tower in Paris, France further advancing the pseudo-sport of bungee jumping and extreme tourism at the same time.

The era of airline frugality begins when American Airlines bean counters (aka accountants and actuaries) calculate that by simply eliminating one olive from their First Class salad service that they will save the airline US$40,000 annually!

On May 29th, Mathias Rust, a 19 year old West German pilot, shocks the world, and embarrasses more than a few Kremlin generals, when he lands his Cessna 172 plane in Red Square, Moscow, amid the blank stares of locals. When asked why he did it, he is quoted as saying he just wanted to build an "*imaginary bridge to the East.*" (At the height of the Cold War, we suddenly realize that the Soviet's are a paper tiger!)

1988
The European Travel Monitor (ETM), a continuous collection and surveying of data as it relates to the travel behavior of Europeans, begins collecting and surveying. Sensing a good thing and markets to conquer, ETM expand with the World Travel Monitor that covers all overseas markets. You can never have too many statistics can you?

Northwest Airlines officially bans smoking on all North American flights, the first major U.S. airline to do so. (See: 1971) It should be noted that at about this time, a FAA federal regulation took effect that barred lighting up on flights of less than two hours. Later, in 1995, Delta Airlines becomes the first airline to ban smoking on all flights.

Northwest Airlines tests the first in-seat video system and launches an arms race in the in-flight entertainment (IFE) airlines war that continues with the rollout of personal video-on-demand and live TV shows in-flight... on some airlines on some flights. Travel experts have noticed the direct co-relationship between the development of IFE and the declining space available for passenger's feet to rest!

The U.S. Congress passes the Indian Gaming Regulatory Act allowing for Indian tribes to open gambling establishments on tribal lands. Finally justice is served and the First Nations people are allowed to get all our money!

Alison Stancliffe, an English activist, establishes Tourism Concern, a non-profit to further the tourism industry in the developing world as an agent of good and necessary for economic development. The philosophy being about shared benefits, mutual respect as stakeholders and the pursuit of low impact sustainable green tourism.

The well-respected medical journal *The Lancet* (26 August 1988), publishes an article entitled "Air Travel and Thrombotic Episodes: The Economy Class Syndrome," introducing the effects of the single worst complaint among airline passengers—the seats are too small!

The National Geographic Society adopts the Robinson projection map as a better representation of Earth. (See: 1922)

On April 5th, Iranian-backed Shia hijackers divert a Kuwaiti Boeing 747 with 1222 passengers and crew to Mashad, Iran, before flying on to Cyprus. The negotiations last for 15 days until the hijackers are granted asylum in Algeria and release their hostages unharmed.

On July 3rd, at the height of the Iran-Iraq War, in which the U.S. was funding and arming Saddam Hussein's Iraq, the cruiser *USS Vincennes* fires a surface-to-air missile and *mistakenly* shoots down an Iran Air Airbus 300 Flight 655 killing all 290 religious pilgrims aboard. (After lengthy International Court of Justice (ICJ) proceedings, the U.S. Government pays US$61.8 million—US$213,103.45 per passenger—in compensation to the families, but has never admitted responsibility, nor apologized to Iran.)

On December 21st, a Pan Am Boeing 747 flight bound for New York (JFK) from London (LHR) explodes midair over Lockerbie, Scotland, leaving 270 dead. Libyan secret agents are found guilty of the act and planting the bomb believed to have been placed on the aircraft at Frankfurt Airport (FRA) in Germany.

The *MS Sovereign of the Seas* launched by Royal Caribbean International, ushers in the new era of mega-cruise ships that can host over 3,400 passengers. The *Freedom*-class launched in 2006 with *MS Freedom of the Seas*, and then the designated *Oasis*-class cruise ship with the launching of *MS Oasis of the Seas* in 2009, both *house* over 8,500 passengers and crew—with sadly only 18 lifeboats each with a 370 capacity...anybody ever heard of the *SS Titanic* (See:1912)? It seems that old adage about cruise ships being only for the old, newlyweds and almost dead, is no longer true—because everyone takes cruises nowadays. Flu shots, get your flu shots...

A specially designed Boeing 747-400 sets a new around-the-world record of 36 hours 54 minutes on January 30th.

On April 22nd, MIT's *Daedalus '88*, the first human-powered craft flown from the island of Crete to Santorini in the Mediterranean Sea successfully takes flight flying the 115 kilometer (71-mile) route in 3 hours and 54 minutes...except for the last 7 meters when it crashed into the sea, *oops!*

The Seikan Tunnel opens for railway traffic between the two Japanese islands of Honshū and Hokkaidō, and at 53.85-kilometers (33.46 miles) it is the world's longest. A remarkable and gigantic engineering accomplishment, the tunnel that was constructed both under budget at US$3.6 billion and according to schedule.

The first, and only, 26-day 13,679 kilometer (8,500-mile) long Trans-Amazon Adventure Rallye (sic) is held in South America with 71 driving teams starting in Cartagena, Columbia, racing down a course west through the Amazon basin and over the Andes to Ecuador, then south through Peru and Chile, and finally east ended in Buenos Aires, Argentina. Eleven teams finished.

On July 11th, the *City of Poros,* a cruise ship operating in Greek waters with over 470 happy day-tripping island-hopping passengers, was stormed by Palestinian gunmen and hit with a barrage of gunfire that killed four from France and one each from Denmark, Sweden and Hungary, as well as two Greeks, 99 others were injured.

On April 28th, metal fatigue lead to an Aloha Airlines Boeing 737-297 Flight 243 between the Hawaiian islands of Hilo and Honolulu in Hawaii, suffering extensive damage...and the loss of a flight attendant who was blown out of the plane. No other deaths occurred.

Aloha Airlines Flight 243's aftermath.
(The Honolulu Advertiser - 18 January 2001)

Pico Iyer (1957-), an English writer and global observer, publishes his smart and witty *Video Night in Kathmandu* and continues to set a high standard for modern travel reportage. Who can forget the insightful travel truism, *"We travel, initially, to lose ourselves; and we travel, next, to find ourselves."*

P. J. O'Rourke (1947-), an American humorist, pens *Holidays in Hell: In Which Our Intrepid Reporter Travels to the World's Worst Places,* that some claim is the beginning of the bad idea of war tourism (aka Dark Tourism); where tourists seek out man's inhumanity to man sites around the world, like: Killing Fields of Cambodia, war zone graves in Bosnia, the Korea DMZ, concentration camps, and the proliferation of torture museums around the world. (See: 1988)

Global Tourist Enclaves (aka tourist ghettos): Are areas that developed of time, usually close to major internationally famous tourist destinations, that cater to the conspicuous consumer wants of visitors versus the daily needs of the locals. A few of the more notorious hangouts include:

Thamel, Kathmandu, Nepal
Aguas Calientes, Machu Picchu, Peru
Koh Pi Pi, Thailand
Calle Santander, Guatemala City, Guatemala
Pub Street, Siem Reap, Cambodia
Sudder Street, Kolkata, India
Kuta Beach, Bali, Indonesia
Magalluf-Palma Nova, Mallorca, Spain
Sultanahmet, Istanbul, Turkey
Dubai, United Arab Emirates
Everest Base Camp, Nepal

1989

The Tiananmen Square massacre takes place in Beijing, China, that leaves an estimated 3,000 Chinese citizens dead and hundreds more institutionalized in those infamous reeducation prison camps. Organized tourist travel to China plummets as many travelers begin wondering about traveling to nation-state's that show such little regard for human rights. A Chinese travel boycott is maintained among a number of conscientious independent travelers to this day.

The West German (aka Germany) Love Parade begins to take place annually in Berlin gathering hundreds of thousands from around the world.

A San Francisco, California-based non-profit organization called Global Exchanges begins offering Reality Tours. The idea of reality tourism is to give concerned citizens their own fact-finding tour of politically and economically troubled regions of the world to empower them to act upon their return. These tours are more political in nature and are conducted by churches, unions and educational institutions.

The Mirage Hotel opens in Las Vegas with 3,039 rooms, ushering in a new era of casino mega-resorts in Sin City. Las Vegas tourism had been sagging until Steve Wynn opens the US$630 million Mirage casino/hotel and reinvigorates the Vegas allure sparking a hotel construction boom that propels Las Vegas to become the most-visited city in the United States.

Freie University in Berlin, Germany establishes the Historical Archive on Tourism (HAT) (aka Historisches Archiv zum Tourismus) housing material on "tourism" as a special sort of travelling sub-genre, like guidebooks, private photo albums, tourist flyers, promotion posters and the like dating back as far as 1600. I guess someone has to...

On September 19th, a French UTA airliner explodes in mid-air over Niger, killing all 170 people aboard. The French government issued warrants for the arrest of four Libyans.

On August 18th, a Qantas Boeing 747, flies non-stop from London (LHR) to Sydney (SYD) and sets a world record for a four-engine jet having flown 17,703 kilometers (11,000 miles) in 20 hours...one really long flight for the people stuck in the middle seats!

The first big company alliance with the commercial passenger industry takes place when Northwest and KLM Royal Dutch Airlines agree to code sharing and other exchanges on a large scale. Collusion, *err*, alliances, become all the rage as United Airlines forms Star Alliance in 1997, followed by American Airlines **one**world in 1999, and Delta's SkyTeam in 2000. If you aren't colluding, you aren't competing!

Peter Mayle (1939-), an English ad-man turned French vacationer, pens *A Year in Provence*, much to the chagrin of the French locals...

The Berlin Wall, built in 1961 separating East Berlin from West Berlin, the communist world from the capitalist world, finally falls on November 9th—with the world becoming a better place.

Travel becomes a competitive sport when the world's first around-the-world (RTW) travel competition called the Human*Race* takes place in November. Andrus J. Valvur (1954-), an American humorist and former Pan Am flight attendant, and William D. Chalmers (1958-), a North

American writer, win the around-the-world event in 17 days traveling from San Francisco to New York—*the long way*! Travel writers dub them, among other things, *"the world's greatest travelers."* Chalmers later writes the gonzo-tale *A Blind Date with the World* about the epic adventure in 2000.

Raid Gauloises (aka The Raid), a multi-sport, multi-team adventure race conducts its first international event in New Zealand, and remains the grand daddy of international adventure races.

1990c
After the collapse of Communism and the fall of the Berlin Wall (See: 1989) and the 1989 Velvet Revolution in Czechoslovakia, Americans begin coming in swarms to Prague. By 1993, *The New York Times* estimates that more than 30,000 Americans were living in Prague, comparing it to the expat generation living in Paris in the 1920's. (According to the U.S. Department of State, there was a substantial rise in the number of American-born expatriates since 1990, growing from about 1.5 million to 4.5 million by 2005, and eventually growing to about 6 to 8 million by 2009.)

1990
The McDonnell Douglas MD-11, the world's only modern large, wide-cabin tri-jet takes its maiden flight on January 10th. Personally, I always prefer 4 engines, but some call me old fashion.

Marianna Torgovnick, an American English professor, publishes *Gone Primitive: Modern Intellects, Savage Minds,* a look into how writers, *ala* travel writers, present foreign cultures in many derogatory and stereotypical ways.

The Los Angeles, California Metro system's Blue Line opens for passengers. The plan is to take passengers *"from the mountains to the sea"*…by 2036—maybe! (See: 1887)

McDonald's opens a restaurant in Moscow, USSR—capitalism finally prevails!

People of Jewish decent have been visiting the state of Israel since 1949 (and Palestinians have been doing the same); but 21st century Western-immigrants who had earlier escaped the tyranny of East Europe begin visiting those newly-freed nations in the hopes of rediscovering their roots and with ethnic reunions back home, taking in their old heritage, residential memories and traditional festivals. Diaspora Tourism is born, which is different from Genealogy Tourism when travelers are looking for their family-tree records.

Tom Van Sant, an American artist, designs the first high-resolution picture of a cloudless Earth by piecing together over 2,000 satellite images in the 3-year Geo*Sphere* Project. A remarkably beautiful map that hangs above my desk.

What is it about Northwest Airlines? In 1990, three Northwest Airlines crew members were sentenced to jail for flying from Hector International Airport (FAR), North Dakota to Minneapolis-Saint Paul International Airport (MSP) while drunk! Again in 2001, Northwest Airlines fires a pilot who failed a breathalyzer test after flying from San Antonio's Horizon Airport (LID), Texas to Minneapolis-Saint Paul (MSP). Is it that people need to brace themselves for the Minneapolis scene, or that Northwest hires unrepentant frat boys? (One other incident occurred in July 2002, when two American West Airlines pilots were arrested because they had been believed to be under the influence prior to their scheduled flight.)

Growing out of a small bonfire ritual celebrated on the summer solstice nights in San Francisco in the late 1980's, the first international *Burning Man* festival takes place in Black Rock Desert, a remote and largely unknown dry lake bed about 100 miles outside of Reno, Nevada. Known as fun in the sun and an experimental society, the 2010 event had 51,454 participants from many countries.

Stephen Hawking (1942-), an English theoretical physicist, reading a few proposals from fellow colleagues relating to time travel and conjectures that it should be banned because, "If time travel were as common as taking a Sunday picnic in the park, then time travelers from the future should be pestering us with their cameras," and there ought to be a law, he further proclaimed, making time travel impossible. Hawking proposed "Chronology Protection Conjecture" to ban time travel from the laws of physics in order to "make history safe for historians," I think I understand?

Megan Epler Wood, an American educator, organizes the International Eco-Tourism Society (TIES) conference that is created as the world's first international non-profit dedicated to ecotourism as a tool for conservation and sustainable development. Doing good and having fun begins catching on. They also define ecotourism as, *"Responsible travel to natural areas that conserves the environment and improves the well-being of local people."*

Toyohiro Akiyama (1942-), a Japanese journalist, becomes the world's first space tourist when he takes a Russian *Soyuz TM-11* spacecraft to the *Mir* space station and spends a week with the cosmonauts and returns on a regularly scheduled *Soyuz TM-10* flight. Space tourism became a reality sooner than expected, when the Russia Space Agency, short on cash for another space voyage, came up with pay-for-flights into space notion and took Toyohiro on a trip of a lifetime for seven days, 21 hours and 54 minutes in space for a cool US$28 million paid by his network sponsor the Tokyo Broadcasting System (TBS). (*For the record*: Dennis Anthony Tito (1940-), a wealthy American engineer, becomes the first space tourist to *pay his own way* in 2001 when he spends eight days in orbit flying out the International Space Station (ISS) on *Soyuz TM-32* and then returning on *Soyuz* flight TM-31 (See: 2001).

John Urry, an English scholar and author, introduces the term post-tourism to the discussion as a further evolutionary branch of *homo touristicus*; stating that a post-tourist per se is someone inhabiting the post-modern world of consumption and distraction and does not actually need to leave the confines of his own habitat to sight-see (aka virtual tourism) via modern communication technologies of prefabricated manufactured experiences! (See: 2035c) Others claim *"...that changes in the production and consumption of tourism have actually taken place during the past thirty years, with tourism becoming a manifestation of and metaphor for the disappearance of absolute values, beliefs and structures as well as the postmodern fluidity of social life."* Well, I don't know about that and what about the spirit and authenticity of travel?

1991

RIP: Pan American World Airways (Pan Am) (1927-1991), after 64 years of innovation and international service they go bankrupt on August 11th. It was the end of a very fond era for some.

The Westin Hotel chain becomes the first hotel chain to provide in-room voice mail service.

Virgin Atlantic Airways begins offering seat-back video in all classes.

The Global System Mobile (GSM) cellular phone system is introduced in Europe.

> **An Odd Fact:** If you have ever wanted to know what was the largest number of people ever to fly aboard a Boeing 747 was...it was exactly 1,088 passengers who braved a 1991 flight from Ethiopia to Israel on an *El Al* 747-charter flight! They were Jewish refugees.

Where in the world do you want to go? Well, you can now be a "virtual tourist" anywhere with the first online webcam (aka streaming video) courtesy of the kids at the University of Cambridge who pointed the first webcam at the Trojan Room coffee pot. By 2010, webcams are everywhere and with the introduction of Google Earth (See: 2005), the virtual world is complete.

Dennis Porter, an American writer, speculates in his book Haunted Journeys: Desire and Transgression in European Travel Writing, that a tremendous amount of self -doubt and guilt exist in the works of travel writers, as he psychoanalyses the works of Boswell, Diderot, Bougainville, Stendhal, Flaubert, D. H. Lawrence, T. E. Lawrence, Barthes, and V. S. Naipaul to name a few. One wonders what Naipaul was thinking when he said, "I travel to discover other states of mind." Hmm...sounds like he beat Porter to the punch!

The World Tourism Organization (WTO), by committee we're sure, produces an official definition of tourism as being: "The activities of a person traveling to a place outside his or her usual environment for less than a specified period of time and whose main purpose of travel is other than the exercise of an activity from within the place visited." Gee, now we know.

Wichita State University develops the annual Airline Quality Rating (AQR) system that is an "objective method of comparing airline quality of domestic airlines based on 15 performance criteria," including: timeliness, mishandled baggage, denied boarding, customer service, comfort and food; and obtaining data from airline experts, customer surveys and government data. The airlines are not amused. (www.aqr.aero/pastaqr.htm)

With the breakup of the old Soviet Union into modern day Russia and creation of 14 new republics, the world's largest airline Aeroflot disbands... In 1990, before the breakup of the Soviet Union, Aeroflot was in fact the world's largest airline that carried about 140 million passengers on over 5,400 planes in their fleet. Pravda, the state-controlled newspaper once was quoted as saying "...flying Aeroflot is about as safe as playing Russian roulette." The airline experienced at least 36 official domestic crashes and at least 33 official hijackings in 1990 alone!

PBS launches the children's TV game show, Where in the World is Carmen Sandiego?, that runs for five successful years. The show is created as a direct response to survey after survey showing that Americans have an alarmingly low level of geographic knowledge. Many residents of the United States continue to ask: Where is Puerto Rico anyway?

Air France adamantly denies an NBC News documentary that alleges that the airline spies on its First Class travelers—specifically, traveling hi-tech executives from America—by bugging their seats and placing hidden cameras above their seats as "an elaborate industrial espionage campaign run by the French secret service." The CIA and NSA are shocked!

1992

The U.S. military's Global Positioning System (GPS) (aka NAVSTAR GPS (NAVigation Satellite Timing and Ranging Global Positioning System) (See: 1961 & 1967) originally created to target nuclear warheads is opened to civilian use for commercial navigation purposes in 1983, is opened further to the public when President Bill Clinton allows the now popular system to be changed from precision of civilian GPS units from 300 meters

(1,000-feet) to just 20 meters (65-feet). Little did Bill know that this decision would affect the lives of untold numbers of couples, all habitually deadlocked on whether to ask for directions when lost? Indeed, the era of MapQuest and TomTom begins without TomTom and MapQuest—they would both first appear online in 1996. Consider the social and cultural ramifications on Western society if the GPS technology had been available sooner: Would The Odyssey have been taken so long? Columbus might've actually found the illusive Spice Islands? Amelia Earhart might have really made history? The Civil War may even have turned out differently? And what did we do with this marvelous technological breakthrough—play a high-tech game called Geocaching! Personally, I love the technology, but feel sad and think about Ray Bradbury's great quote when he claims that, "Half the fun of travel is the esthetic of lostness." No more lostness...

The 171 kilometer (106-mile) Rhine–Main–Danube Canal opens and finally completes the transcontinental Rhine-Main-Danube Waterway system that allows vessels to travel over 3,500 kilometers (2,200 miles) inland from Rotterdam on the North Sea all the way south to the port of Sulina on the Black Sea.

Euro Disneyland (aka Disneyland Paris) opens outside Paris, France on April 12th. Sacrebleu!

A California statewide ballot-initiative called *The Such Effective Worker Scheme*, that would have offered California-based employers incentives to give their workers longer vacations of up to six weeks, sadly, fails to qualify for the ballot as they could not get enough signatures from qualified voters.

Pittsburgh International Airport (PIT), in Pennsylvania, pioneers a revolutionary concept in that guaranteed airport terminal passengers "street pricing" in its shops and restaurants. That means no price gauging! The idea did not catch on...but, knowing they could price gauge, brought in major chains to other airports and has led to the "mallification" of U.S. airports.

Mary Louise Pratt, an American social linguist, publishes *Imperial Eyes: Travel Writing and Transculturation,* a critical study of Victorian-era travel writing and the lies told by the writers of the day in the name of their narrow colonial mindset.

High-tech roller coasters and inverted coasters were pioneered at Six Flags Great America and literally turns theme parks' biggest attractions upside down— and spawned a new generation of stomach-churning scream machines.

The *"Lonely Planet effect"* (aka guidebook effect) begins getting discussed as a travel-related phenomena occurring on three levels: 1) that by traveling with a certain guidebook, be it *Lonely Planet, Frommer's, Fodor's*, etc., you inevitably keep running into the same travelers time and time again who are also following that particular book's advice (aka guidebook personality disorder); 2) that by following the advice of "off-the-beaten path" guidebooks, too many people are inundating places that don't have the tourist infrastructure to handle the popularity (aka the *loving-it-to-death syndrome* (LDS); and 3) that just by getting mentioned in a popular guidebook it almost guarantees (sometimes undeservedly) business success in and of itself.

On September 30th, a spokesman for Al-Gama'a al-Islamiyya (Islamic Group), a militant Muslim group, warns tourists not to enter certain parts of the country, which includes some of Egypt's most famous pharaonic temples and tombs. This begins a new type of violent campaign against tourists (the repressive regimes largest source of revenue) visiting Egypt, and over the next five years over 33 separate attacks occur; leading up to the massive attack that kills 71 in Luxor (See: 1997).

On May 2nd, a tourist was killed by Islamic Jihad terrorists at an Israeli Red Sea resort of Eilat.

On October 21st, a British female tourist was shot during an Islamic terrorist attack on a tourist group in Beirut, Lebanon.

In an effort to thwart undesirables from entering the United States, U.S. Customs & Immigration began collecting Passenger Name Record (PNR) data for all inbound international flights. This policy is strictly enforced after the 2001 9/11 attacks; and European Union nations balk over privacy issues and the pre-departure screening of all U.S. bound passengers. The

U.S. unilaterally threatens to turn back flights unless they comply, that would impose a financial burden on the airlines—they comply. In 2008, the program is further enhanced to the point that the Homeland Security is "pushed" data from the airline reservation systems a full 72 hours before a flight departs.

1993

Catherine A. Lutz and Jane L. Collins, two American scholars, publish *Reading National Geographic*, a critical survey and evaluation of the contents and editorial slant of the illustrious yellow National Geographic monthly magazines. After extensive research about the magazines methods and narratives, choice of photographs and ultimately topic selections, the authors conclude that the magazine is but a middlebrow attempt to justify U.S. foreign policy and culture at home. And that it may indeed help perpetuate the *Mean World Syndrome* (See: 1975) held by most Americans. (My friends growing up always wondered a few things too, like why weren't there any photos of white bare-breasted women?)

ValuJet issues the first e-ticket for travel in October, and the new era of paperless tickets begin. It is also claimed that Southwest Airlines becomes the first airline to issue e-tickets in 1994. It also claimed that a family from Washington State bought the first paperless tickets ever sold via the Internet from Alaska Airlines in December 1995. Damn press releases...a great idea no matter who did it first; but early on it was tough getting a refund or getting credited for frequent flyer miles—because you could not show an actual receipt!

The MGM Grand opens in Las Vegas and immediately becomes the world's largest hotel with over fourteen restaurants and some 5,009-guest rooms.

Virgin Airlines cancels its massage service on Tokyo-bound flights after a "cultural misunderstanding"—in which it is believed that a baffled Japanese businessman complained after not having a *happy ending*!

The U.S. Federal Aviation Administration (FAA) begins mandating that all commercial passenger planes based in the U.S. to have traffic collision avoidance systems (TCAS) onboard. Thank you FAA.

On February 26th, a bomb explodes in the parking garage of the World Trade Center in New York City, killing six people and injuring more than 1,000 others. Did anyone learn from this? Dot…dot…dot…

A White House scandal erupts that is sometimes referred to as *Travelgate* by ill-informed pundits. In May 1993, seven employees of the White House Travel Office were let go without cause—they were all former Reagan and Bush appointees. Federal law informs that all Executive Branch employees work at the strict pleasure of the President, and can be let go at any time without cause. There was no scandal according to all subsequent investigations, but you probably never read that.

1994
The ultra-modern Kansai International Airport (KIX) opens on a man-made typhoon-proof and earthquake-proof island 38 kilometers (24 miles) from downtown Osaka, Japan, complete with express train services to downtown subway connections and high-speed ferry service to Kobe. (With the opening of KIX in 1994, a new era of mega-international airports begin sprouting up around the world, including new or improved airports opened in: 1994 - Frankfurt am Main Airport (FRA); 1995 - Denver International Airport (DEN) (See: 1995); 1998 - Hong Kong International Airport (HKG), and Dubai International Airport (DXB); 2001 – Seoul's Incheon International Airport (ICN); 2004 - Guangzhou Baiyun International Airport (CAN); 2006 - (New) Bangkok International Airport (See: 2008).

The notion that tourism facilities need to go green and be more environmentally conscious expands, especially in Europe, when the Green Key labeling system is created in Denmark and starts evaluating and rating campsites.

The Business Travel Coalition is created with a mission "to bring transparency to industry and government policies and practices so that customers can influence issues of strategic importance to their organizations." Practically speaking this consumer group supports corporate buyers, not personal consumers.

First proposed in 1802 by Albert Mathieu, a French mining engineer, the 50.5-kilometer (31-mile) Channel Tunnel (aka the Chunnel or *Le tunnel sous la Manche*) becomes a reality and opens fixed-link quick-train service between England and France. It takes 8-years and a cost of US$17 billion to build. About nine million cars and passengers use the tunnel a year with high-speed passenger rail travel time down to 2 hours and 15 minutes on the Paris to London route, and less than 2 hours on the London to Brussels route.

On December 24th, an Air France Flight 8969 Airbus A-300 with 232 passengers and crew was seized by Algerian Islamic terrorists after takeoff from Algeria and diverted to Marseille Provence Airport (MRS), France. French CIGN counter-terrorist troops stormed the aircraft and killed all the terrorists, 16 passengers suffered minor injuries.

The Internet becomes a travel industry marketing tool when TravelWeb. com becomes the first online hotel catalog. Promus (Holiday Inn brand) and Hyatt Hotels are the first hotel chains to establish a website on the Internet—and some complain that they haven't updated it since! It may be true that computer geeks with an affinity for alphabet-soup fare codes could access flight information as early as the mid-1980s, but this seems to be the year that the travel industry started to see and feel customers surfing the net to shop for their travel industry goods.

Due to advances in avionics technology, the U.S. FAA allows commercial air passenger pilots' greater freedom for "Free Flight" over the crowded skies, instead of always being maneuvered by air traffic control (ATC) ground personal. It saves time, money and fuel.

Ralph Nader (1934-), an American consumer advocate, publishes *Collision Course: The Truth About Airline Safety* an eye-opening and revealing expose of the industries standards and practices, including: ageing fleets, cutting maintenance corners, overcrowded airports, overcrowded skies, overworked and inexperienced pilots, overtaxed and antiquated air traffic systems oh my…not a recommended read for frequent flyers!

Robert Young Pelton (1955-), a Canadian-born adventurer, publishes *The World's Most Dangerous Places* that includes interesting data and advice on about 26 rather troubled and violent countries or regions of the world. He follows up this book with *Come Back Alive* (1999), and *The Adventurist, My Life In Dangerous Places (2001).*

Billed as the world's first Internet café, *Cafe Cyberia,* opens in March in London, England's fashionable West End. Since then, estimates say that over 20,000 Internet cafes were opened in more than 100 countries in the next decade. (The first Internet café I ever saw was the Binary Café that operated in downtown Toronto, Canada, it opened in June 1994 and closed quickly due to lack of interest.)

David Spade and Helen Hunt perform in a NBC-TV *Saturday Night Live* sketch playing two flight attendants working for Total Bastard Airlines… they happily wish there disgruntled passengers a fondly dismissive *"Buh-bye."* Art does imitate life.

Attempting to clamp down on Sex Tours and the exploitation of underage sex workers, Australia passes *Crimes (Child Sex Tourism) Amendment Act,* and the becomes the first country to introduce laws that provide jail terms for its citizens and residents who engage in sexual activity with children in foreign countries. Canada passes a similar law in 1997.

On July 26th, a train carrying backpackers is attacked by remnants of the genocidal Khmer Rouge who kidnap and kill three tourists, from England, France and Australia.

On December 11th, Philippine Airlines Flight 434 a Boeing 747 flying between Manila's Ninoy Aquino International Airport (MNL) and Tokyo's Narita International Airport (NRT), Japan, experiences a small explosion that kills one passenger. In the ensuing investigation, what is labeled the *Bojinka plot* is uncovered that was Khalid Shaikh Mohammed's plan to blow up twelve airliners and their estimated 4,000 passengers as they flew on flights between various Asian airports to the United States. The plan was to become operational in January 1995 before the Filipino police followed the trail and made the needed arrests. More dots to connect…

1995c

By now the so-called *Banana Pancake Trail* (aka The Lonely Planet Express) is a well-established "off-the-beaten-path" route among Western backpackers traveling through the Southeast Asian nations of Thailand, Cambodia, Laos, Vietnam, Singapore, Malaysia, Indonesia and The Philippines. It is a newer version of the Gringo Trail (See: 1965c) and the Hippie Trail (See: 1966), that developed after the Vietnam War hostilities ended.

1995

Denver International Airport (DEN) opens on the outskirts of Denver, Colorado replacing the older Stapleton International Airport, nearly US$2 billion over-budget and 16 months behind schedule. It is the first new airport built in the U.S. in over a decade—with no new opens planned on the horizon.

The Rock and Roll Hall of Fame and Museum opens in Cleveland, Ohio.

United Airlines, follows Pan Am's lead again, and on December 14th introduces its RTW air service with a Los Angeles-London-New Delhi-Hong Kong-Los Angeles route. They go the wrong way in my book...west to east is easier on the body!

After PC's Travel software program is launched a year earlier, the first general travel booking website Travelocity.com, owned by SABRE, is launched marking the beginning of online travel agencies (OTA).

Air France introduced the first 180-degree flat-bed seats (sic) in its First Class compartments. Four years later, British Airways becomes the first airline to install actual beds in their Business Class cabin.

Transparency International (TI), a non-governmental organization (NGO), that attempts to publicize international corruption, produces the first of its annual Corruption Perceptions Index that compares the level of corruption in various nations of the world. Burma, Nigeria, Pakistan, Russia and Haiti annually top, err, bottom the list! (TI does *not* however offer a "Traveler's Bribe Paying Index" (aka the Going Rate Price List) of bribes, inducements, commissions, finder's fees, consulting fees, dash, presents, *cadeau*, sweetener, or *baksheesh*, etc., altogether necessary for travelers to pay their way out of pseudo-legal gambits and cultural indiscretions (aka *faux pas)* when the old *Dumb Tourist Routine* fails and they wish not to spend an unpleasant evening at the Hotel Bread & Water (aka the Black Hotel Inn, hoosegow, jail or poky).

The U.S. Travel and Tourism Administration (USTTA), the agency designed to promote the needs and development of the entire U.S. travel industry (and consumers), succumbs to election-year politics and is defunded.

Unlike other nations that have created a Ministry of Tourism & Trade, or a Department of Tourism, the Reagan-era mantra that the private sector can better promote its own interests prevails, despite travel and tourism making up as much as an estimated 10% of our entire economy!

The American Express travel company establishes the World Monuments Watch as a non-profit organization designed to preserve and protect (and ironically promote) some of the world's noteworthy cultural and architectural heritage sites similar to the United Nations World Heritage Site (See: 1972 and 2005).

The first *Eco-Challenge*, an adventure race that pits international teams against each other racing non-stop, 24 hours a day, over a rugged 500 kilometer (300-mile) course, takes place in Utah, United States. Inspired by the *Raid Gauloises* adventure race (See: 1989), the event is conducted annually in different parts of the world until 2002.

Before Sunrise, an American movie starring Ethan Hawke and Julie Delpy, shows that magic can happen anywhere, anytime, anyplace, when a couple of independent travelers who met on a train share an intimate getting-to-know-you better evening on the streets and in the cafés of Vienna, Austria. The sequel, *Before Sunset* takes place in Paris a decade later and is released in 2004.

The *Schengen Agreement* is reached between the territories of twenty-five European nations. The agreement establishes a sort of United States of Europe when it comes to travel arrivals and departures; with the Schengen area operating very much like a single state for international travel purposes with border controls for travelers travelling in and out of the area, but with no other internal border controls. That means you can land in Munich, train to Paris, fly to Athens, boat to Italy and no one will ask to see your passport!

John Clouse (1926-2008), an American attorney and avid travel junkie, is recognized by the 1995 edition of *The Guinness Book of Records* as "the world's most traveled man," having personally visited every one of 317 nations on a list. That is one amazing travel collection of passport stamps. By the way, John was married six times, apparently five of them weren't very good travelers! The folks at *The Guinness Book of Records* (aka *Guinness*

World Records) rested this category in 1999 because no one expert or group could decide on a standard as to what a "country" was! (See: 1954)

On August 16th, A Concorde sets a new speed record for a round-the-world flight when it returns to New York's JFK airport after a journey lasting 31 hours and 27 minutes, after making stops in Toulouse, Dubai, Bangkok, Guam, Honolulu and Acapulco.

On March 20th, 12 traveling civilians are killed and thousands more injured in a Sarin nerve gas attack perpetrated by the Aum Shinrikyo cult on Tokyo's Kasumigaski subway. After the attack it is revealed that in June 1994, seven people died and 150 were injured in a gas attack in Matsumoto, Japan, also perpetrated by the same group, but widely revealed so as to not cause mass panic.

In July, the Kashmiri militant group al-Faran, kidnaps five Western tourists trekking in the beautiful Jammu and Kashmir regions of India. One was sadly later found beheaded in October, while the four others were never seen again.

1996
Jon Krakauer (1954-), an American adventure writer, publishes *Into Thin Air* about a really bad Everest expedition. A harrowing read…

After first getting the bugs worked out on Northwest Airlines over a five year period beginning in 1990, the U.S. FAA and FBI begin implementing the Computer Assisted Passenger Prescreening System (CAPPS) (aka CAPPS I) as an air passenger vetting program. Along with the automatic creation of a PNR (Passenger Name Record) for each passenger being supposedly cross-checked on numerous government held "No Fly Lists", and identifying your threat level as to whether or not you: a) booked a one-way flight, 2) booked to fly at the last minute or on a flight that day, c) paid cash for your ticket, or d) were flying to any of a number of high risk and suspect areas; the CAPPS system would classify you as "high risk" and would then designate you as a Secondary Security Screening Selectee (SSSS). When you get that seal of unapproval on your boarding pass (about a 14% chance)—SSSS—you basically got extra personal attention by both the airlines and security screening authorities.

The No Fly List: Prior to September 11, 2001, the FBI had only 16 people deemed "no transport" because they "presented a specific known or suspected threat to aviation." Following 9/11 hysteria, the list had grown to more than 400 names by November 2001 according to the FAA. In mid-December 2001, the lists were expanded and bifurcated: the "No Fly List" contained 594 people to be denied air transport, and the new and improved "Selectee" list held the names of 365 people who get special treatment. CBS's *60 Minutes* revealed in October 2006, that the March "No Fly List" had exponentially expanded and contained more than 44,000 names. By April 2007, the Terrorist Screening Center agency administering the list held 700,000 records. The Transportation Security Agency (TSA) claims as of the summer of 2010 to have only 8,500 names on the active "No Fly List." (The ACLU estimated the list to have grown to over 1,000,000 names and continues to expand.) Who to believe and what to believe on "national security" issues has always been a crap shoot!

Alex Garland (1970-), a British novelist, pens the backpacker cult novel *The Beach* about a mythical hidden Thai utopia that turns into cult book— and a really bad movie. For a better version, see William Golding's 1954 must-read *Lord of the Flies*.

Federico F. Peña (1947-), an American politician, who while serving as the Secretary of Transportation, calls an airline "safety summit" after a series of airline accidents rocks public confidence in the U.S., and declares a goal of zero accidents; which is later changed to the more realistic goal of cutting the rate of fatal accidents by 80 percent. Because we all know *accidents do happen*! By the way; The actual drop in the accident rate was about 65 percent; dropping to one fatal accident in about 4.5 million departures in 2007 compared to the almost alarming one in nearly 2 million in 1997. Maybe Mr. Nader was right (See: 1994)?

On April 19th, eighteen Greek tourists were gunned down near the Egyptian Pyramids by Islamic terrorists attempting to continue to disrupt the country's tourist industry.

On August 26th, a Sudan Airways Airbus A310 en route from Khartoum to Jordan is hijacked and diverted to London's Stansted Airport (STN) in England by six Iraqi dissidents. After some heart-felt negotiating with British authorities, the hijackers happily release all 193 hostages unharmed.

On November 12th, Saudi Arabian Airlines Flight 763 Boeing 747 en route from New Delhi (DEL), India to Dhahran (DMM), Saudi Arabia, collided in mid-air with Kazakhstan Airlines Flight 1907 Ilyushin Il-76 en route from Shymkent (CIT), Kazakhstan to New Delhi (DEL), over a northern India village. All 349 people on board both flights were killed.

On November 23rd, an Ethiopian Airways Boeing 767 is hijacked en route from Addis Adaba (ADD), Ethiopia to Nairobi (NBO), Kenya and attempted to be diverted to Australia, but runs out of fuel and crashes into the Indian Ocean killing 123 people; but 52 people survive including the two hijackers!

In a sign of things to come for travel agents, Delta Air Lines becomes the first change the historic travel agent commission structure from 10 percent per ticket to a capped payment of just US$50. (See: 1997)

C H A P T E R   T W E L V E

The Advent of Travel 2.0 (1996 – 2001):
Pre-packaged tourism evolves into dynamic tourism with more and more traveler consumers, especially independent travelers, now empowered by the technological advances of the era. Travelers and tourists alike, now have at their fingertips (aka a mouse click away), a truly remarkable breath of online research potential with the proliferation of website offerings and travel information, be it for planning a trip, using GPS mapping sites, buying goods via e-commerce, checking fellow user-generated peer reviews, reading blogs, participating in collaborative community bulletin boards and forums, using wikis and professionally-written guidebooks, eye-balling video-sharing sites, writing moblogs (aka mobile blogging), along with a multitude of social media platforms—all often offered in real-time. Never before has so much been available to so many!

1996
The first web-based e-mail service @hotmail.com (now owned by Mircosoft) comes into use for travelers wanting to access their e-mail from anywhere. Yahoo! launches a similar service in 1997 followed by Google's Gmail in 2007. The first e-mail abroad was sent home on July 15th, and read:

To: dad@corporatejob.com
From: wdc@hotmail.com
Re: I miss you all something terrible
Message: "Hey Dad, Learning about cultures in Greece. Miss you all… please send money!"

Both Cheaptickets.com and Expedia.com launch websites offering online consumer travel-related purchases. The brick and mortar antiquated travel agent industry begins its slow decline as travel consultants become the new catch-phrase in selling their expertise.

Internet Travel Network (ITN) becomes the first website to sell airline tickets, book hotel rooms and rent cars online.

American Online creates the first instant messaging (IMing) service known as AOL Instant Messaging (AIM). Now can get pinged from 10,000 miles away!

The first digital camera, as we know them today with Compact Flash (CF) storage cards, was the Kodak DC-25—ironic isn't it! Within a few short years, point-and-click digital cameras were also able to record broadcast quality video. And so ends the traveler's nightmare of film being fogged in x-ray machines, the fear of losing film and the expense of developing your film. Now we all have millions of really bad photos and really short home movies sitting on our computers...

American Airlines establishes the Travelocity.com online travel agency as a subsidiary of its Sabre Holdings Corporation. By 2010, Travelocity grows to become the sixth-largest travel agency in the U.S. and number one online seller.

Microsoft creates Expedia.com online travel agency that is currently owned by Barry Diller's InterActiveCorp, which also owns Citysearch. com, Hotels.com and TripAdvisor.com.

The first annual Bonaire Dive Festival takes place among scuba diving enthusiasts from around the world on the island of Bonaire (aka Divers Paradise). Scuba Tourism is now a big business with enthusiasts flying off to remote corners like: Egypt's Red Sea, India's Andaman & Nicobar Islands, Indonesia's Bunaken National Marine Park, Mexico's Cozumel, and scores of other popular places.

Karen Guthrie and Nina Pope, two Scottish art students, create, write and perform one of the Internet's first online travel diaries called *Hypertext Journal: A journey to the Western Isles,* (Actually they thought it was a piece of performance art but what do we know?) as they followed in the footsteps—reconstructed a past adventure (aka retro-tourism)—of Boswell and Johnson's famed 19ᵗʰ century tour (See: 1775), all the while interacting with followers (aka their audience) online. Yep, they answered questions via e-mail and blogged too. It had to begin somewhere didn't it, and yet again art imitates life!

San Francisco's Nob Hill Lambourne hotel becomes the first hotel to offer Internet access in all rooms. No word on whether it was dialup or broadband…

A website called travel.com begins offering US$20.00 per month per banner ads for sale! And so it begins…

1997

Bill McMillion (1942), an American writer, publishes his *"Volunteer Vacations: Short Term Adventure that will benefit you and Others"* and pushes Volunteer Tourism (aka Charity Travel) to a more popular level.

United Airlines takes the lead and begins the creation of the Star Alliance, the first ever multi-airline alliance (See: 1989), comprised of international airlines including: United Airlines, Lufthansa, Air Canada, SAS and Thai Airways. The idea is to create a system of seamless international travel on the world's busiest routes, sharing airport gates and ground infrastructure, pooling sales and marketing operations, and maybe just maybe even offering flyers a more convenient system in which to fly. The Star Alliance now has 28 airline members serving 1,172 international destinations—and a 29% global market share!

Swissair installs the first interactive video-on-demand (VOD) in-flight entertainment (IFE) system on its aircraft. Finally, the choice of how to kill time is yours!

Dr. Michael Fay (1957-), an American conservationist, decides to walk the entire Central African corridor of over 1,930 kilometers (1,200 miles) on a fifteen-month journey collecting data for the Wildlife Conservation Society—and survives! Who said adventure isn't there for the taking anymore?

Lonely Prince Edward Island is finally connected with the opening of the Confederation Bridge, a 12.9 kilometer (8-mile) long fixed link, with Canada's mainland and New Brunswick.

The Gore Commission on Aviation Security report is released in February and gives the federal seal of approval to a number of pressing aviation security issues, including: surface-to-air missile threats; the expanded use of the automated passenger profiling system known as CAPPS (See: 1996); the continued use of covert adversary screening testers (aka Red teams); increased use of Israeli-created behavioral profiling techniques; bag matching; and the expansion of trace element and explosives detection systems (EDS); instigating airline employee background checks; the increased use of terminal dog teams; and increasing the minimum wages, non-existent standards and short training of airport security screeners. All good commonsense ideas; at least in theory!

The cable news station CNN self-proclaims the *Seven Natural Wonders of World* to include: the Grand Canyon (USA), the Great Barrier Reef (Australia), Harbor of Rio de Janeiro (Brazil), Mount Everest (Nepal), Aurora Borealis (aka Northern Lights), Victoria Falls (Zambia/Zimbabwe) and Parícutin volcano (Mexico). *Hmm*...I'd take Iguazu Falls (Brazil/Argentina) over Victoria Falls any day!

Glorious and amazing Iguazu Falls.
(Author Photo)

Proving that there is no travel niche to small, Storm Chasing Adventure tours starts selling storm chasing tours to explore severe weather, be it "explosive supercell thunderstorms, stunning vivid lightning, large hail, massive wall clouds, and violent tornadoes" in Tornado Alley. Weather tourism is born!

Donald Ross, an American English professor, seeing a proliferation of travel writing on his local Barnes and Noble bookshelves, organizes the first international travel writing conference, "Snapshots from Abroad" at the University of Minnesota and attracts over one hundred scholars. The conference aside from being a great travel story outlet, leads to the foundation of the International Society for Travel Writing (ISTW) and a new scholarly journal called *Studies in Travel Writing*. He also writes his survey of American travel writing, *American Travel Writing, 1850-1914* later in 1998.

What, Me Worry? The Dirty Dozen Biggest American Travel Concerns*:

#1- Can't get time off work;

#2 - Being pick-pocketed;

#3 - Losing their passport;

#4 - Why go anywhere else, we have it all here;

#5 - Food poisoning;

#6 - Terrorist attack;

#7- It might be dirty there;

#8 - Sun exposure;

#9 - Language and communication difficulties;

#10 - Violent crime;

#11- It will be too expensive;

#12 - Drinking the water.

*According to a WorldsGreatestTravelers.com website survey (Nov/2010).

On Sept 18th, Muslim fundamentalists in Cairo, Egypt fire bomb and machine gun a bus of German tourists killing nine.

On November 17th, Muslim fundamentalists brazenly attack tourists at the Temple of Queen Hatshepsut near Luxor killing 62 tourists and injuring scores more. The so-called "Luxor Effect" works and tourism to Egypt drops 70% within a year causing significant harm to the economy.

United Airlines leads the pack of U.S. based passenger carriers by cutting travel agent commissions to 8 percent from 10 percent. (See: 1996) The decline of airline commission business model of revenues and the travel agent business begins. It is estimated that this year is the high water mark for travel agents with an estimated 34,500 agencies in the U.S. and 130,000 worldwide—and in just a decade, U.S. agencies would be reduced to just over 15,000 by 2009.

Art goes mobile when the New York Guggenheim museum chain expands with opening of state-of-the-art Frank Gehry-inspired Guggenheim Museum Bilbao, Spain, and with the opening of the Deutsche Guggenheim Berlin in Germany. The Guggenheim Hermitage Museum at the Venetian Hotel in Las Vegas had a seven year run between 2001 and 2008. The Guggenheim Abu Dhabi is scheduled to open in 2012. The Peggy Guggenheim Collection had previously opened along the Grand Canal of Venice, Italy in 1979.

1998
On July 6th, a changing of the guards occurs and a tradition ends when Hong Kong's Kai Tak Airport (old HGK) is closed at 01:28 with the lights of its 13/31 runway being switched off, as operations of the new Hong Kong International Airport at Chek Lap Kok (new HKG) commence with the first commercial flight landing at 06:25. It was an amazing runway to land on…

The National Geographic Society adopts the Winkel Tripel projection map as a new way of looking at things replacing the Robinson projection (See: 1988 and 1922), which replaced the…technology and perspective are always evolving. This is a high-math issue beyond the scope of this book to explain—you're on your own.

Indira Ghose, a Swiss-based English professor, writes a rather political interpretation of women traveling the world in her fresh *Women Travelers in Colonial India: The Power of the Female Gaze.*

Malaysia became the first country to utilize radio-frequency identification (RFID) passports (aka E-passports), that allows card reading computers to quickly scan and verify valid passports. The U.S. begins issuing E-passports in 2007. Biometric passports remain on-deck until November 2005 when Germany issues the first one with facial images and finger prints named ePass.

An odd trend begins to emerge when a 130-year old jail in Lucerne, Switzerland is converted into the Jail hotel Löwengraben, complete with Alcatraz Bar! The trend continues when the Charles Street Jail in Boston, Massachusetts, is converted into the 300-room Liberty Hotel in 2007. No word if they have solitary cells for those who really "want to be alone."

The K2 Big Wave Surf Challenge, an international competition with US$50,000 at stake, sends surfers from around the world off in search of the biggest wave they can find; with Taylor Knox, a 26-year old Californian surfer, claiming the prize money after successfully finding and riding an *El Nino*–inspired 52-foot gargantuan wave off Mexico's Todos Santos islands. Dude, how epic was that?

The mega-resort known as Atlantis Paradise Island (aka Vegas-by-the-sea) opens for business in The Bahamas.

Air rage (See: 1947) becomes a national phenomena, when news report after news report reveal a disturbing national trend in the *not so friendly skies* above the United States, with Federal Aviation Administration statistics backing up the growing menace and reporting 283 incidents of disruptive behavior—compared to just 121 incidents reported five years earlier. One Air Transport Association official claims the incidents are vastly underreported by air carriers and may exceed 5,000 a year saying, "*Planes are more crowded, and passengers are less comfortable.*" The British FAA equivalent claims a 400 percent increase in violent attacks during the past three years. Really! It is indeed hard to believe that the unrealized romantic travel adventure expectations of surviving rush hour traffic anxiety; being time-stressed; inadequate parking; crazy check-in procedures; surly over-worked and under-paid service employees; long lines at check-in counters; more long lines and expressed fear at security theater checkpoints; taking off your shoes, belts, coats and…who knows what else; rude fellow passengers; cramped terminal seating; over-stuffed overhead bin space; smaller and smaller airplane seats; lack of in-flight meals; maddening gate and tarmac delays; more flight delays; lack of nicotine; and alcohol don't mix! Odd…

Rob McGrath, an American developer, invents the concept of a destination club (DC) tourism that allows members (who pay upfront fees and annual dues) access to a selection of luxury vacation homes, spas and private chefs around the world—subject to availability. His company is called Private Retreats, later *Tanner and Haley;* and by 2009, the club claims 3,250 members with over 400 vacation homes in located 35 locations worldwide.

Space Adventures, Ltd. a Virginia, U.S.-based travel agency whose specialty is, well, space, is founded. They become Dennis Tito's (See: 2001) travel agent to space—and who said commissions were headed south?

The Akashi Kaikyo Bridge (aka Pearl Bridge) that links the Japanese city of Kobe to Iwaya on Awaji Island opens as the longest suspension bridge in the world at 3,911 meters.

The Aviation Medical Assistance Act passes the U.S. Congress (aka the Good Samaritan Act) and protects third parties from civil liability when helping out during an in-flight medical emergency.

Priceline.com opens for business with its *Name-Your-Own-Price* (NYOP) system…it also revives the career of Canadian actor William Shatner. Only in America would someone buy something that they don't really know what it is—with a strict no-cancellation and no-refund policy!? It boggles the mind…

NBC-TV's *Today* show starts a segment entitled *Where in the World is Matt Lauer?* that features co-host Matt Lauer out of the studio visiting some international destinations for a week. The series runs out of gas by 2008.

The travel romance movie *How Stella Got Her Groove,* starring Angela Bassett and Whoopi Goldberg, that takes place on the beaches of Jamaica, opens to mediocre box office; but has boyfriends and husbands everywhere wanting to know the truth about their ladies road adventures. Female sex tourism draws an estimated 80,000 North American and European cougars to Jamaica for sex (aka rent-a-rasta) every year! The Kuta Cowboys of Bali, Marlboro Men of Jordan, and Beach Boys of Cancun, round out the field of global gigolos. Men are shocked, just shocked I tell you!

On August 25th, a group calling themselves Muslims against Global Oppression, kills three and injures 25 in a bomb attack at a Planet Hollywood restaurant in Cape Town, South Africa.

On December 28th, Yemini Islamic militants (or are they catch and release kidnapers?) become active against western visitors in their nation and seize a group of tourists, including: 12 Britons, two Americans and two Australians. Four die during an ill-conceived rescue attempt.

> **Did You Know?** By the year 2002, more Americans visited theme parks, an estimated 280 million a year, than national parks!

1999

Following the Star Alliance formation (See: 1997), American Airlines forms the **one**world airline alliance with fellow international carriers British Airways, Cathay Pacific, Finn Air and Iberia Airlines. By 2010, the alliance grows to include 11 international carriers serving over 870 global destinations—and a 23% market share.

National Geographic Society begins marketing a digital cartographic database *National Geographic Atlas of the World*.

The world's tallest hotel, the 321 meter (1,060-feet) Burj al-Arab (aka Arab Tower) opens on its own man-made island in Dubailand (aka Dubai). What will they think of next; an indoor ski slope, an underwater hotel, the world's tallest building, the world's largest shopping center, allowing guest to kiss on the beach?

United Airlines leads the airline pack by reducing travel agent commissions paid from 8% of the ticket price to just 5%. (See: 1997) Some travel agents start charging their clients service fees—about 80 percent of airline tickets are sold through travel agencies at this time—but with the growing popularity of online booking, the end is near for traditional travel agents—creative destruction at work.

Bertrand Picard (1958-), a Swiss psychologist, and Brian Jones (1947-), an English balloonist, co-pilot their *Breitling Orbiter 3* hot air balloon nonstop around-the-world from March 1-21. They write *Around the World in 20 Days,* about the first nonstop balloon circumnavigation of the globe that took 19 days, 21 hours and 55 minutes to complete.

Westin Hotels scored an overnight sensation when the hotel chain introduces the pillow-top mattress shrouded in three high-thread-count cotton sheets and topped with a down blanket, duvet, comforter and five goose-feather pillows (aka Heavenly Beds). Other major lodging chains quickly beefed up their own boudoirs.

Tummy Tuck Tourism, a type of medical tourism, becomes vogue among the rich and famous and celebrities among us, as an opportunity to multi-task as they fly off to safari for a month (or winter in South America) they make a short 2-3 day visit in between to have cosmetic surgery—liposuctions, rhinoplasty, face lifts, tummy tucks, and breast augmentations. All better by the time they return looking tanned, rested, rejuvenated and—hey, "There's something about you that looks different Louise?"

Northwest Airlines (aka North*worst* Airlines) somehow makes an error in commonsense, judgment and bad for business move, when it strands a plane full of passengers on the tarmac for eight solid hours, without food, water, working toilets, and honesty. The gross inhumanity causes some to sue the airlines for "false imprisonment and breach of contract;" and leads to the idea of an Airline Passengers Bill of Rights (See: 2006) In the end, nothing really happens expect some feel-good voluntary Customer Service Initiative put forth by the airline industry itself.

Community-based tourism (CBT) offering travelers authentic living experiences by having them live (and work) *within a local community learning about everyday life begins taking shape. These, usually 2-3 week trips, take travelers to small* remote villages in developing countries like: Ecuador, Kyrgyzstan, Ethiopia, and Swaziland among others.

Ralph Nader (See: 1994), founds the Six-Footers Club in an effort to represent the interests of all tall passengers flying in cramped seats on airlines in the hope of "increasing coach class leg room to tolerable levels." Don Quixote had nothing on Saint Ralph.

On January 17th, four Dutch and two British citizens are kidnapped in Yemen; and later released. On January 27th, three Germans are kidnapped in Yemen; and later released. On July 14th, four Belgians and one Brit are kidnapped in Yemen; and are later released. On October 26th, three Americans are kidnapped in Yemen; and are later released. It is just business (aka an Express Kidnappings).

On March 1st, about 100 Rwandan Hutu guerillas (aka Interahamwe soldiers) hacked to death eight tourists visiting a gorilla preserve in Bwindi National Park, Uganda.

On April 27th, the Intercontinental Hotel in Athens, Greece, is blown up by Revolutionary Nuclei far-left militants resulting in one death. (Despite the militants calling the hotel about the bomb and them not being taken serious?)

On December 24th, an Indian Airlines Flight 814 Airbus A-300 flying between Kathmandu's Tribhuvan International Airport (KTM) Nepal and Delhi's Indira Gandhi International Airport (DEL) is hijacked by Islamic militants taking 200 passengers and crew hostage and flying to a few spots in Pakistan and then to Dubai (DXB), ends up on the grounds Kandahar, Afghanistan. The hijackers demands for the release of 36 Kashmiri militants held in Indian prisons is met and the hostages are subsequently released safely, although one passenger is stabbed and few are injured in scuffles.

George Monbiot (1963-), an English environmentalist, on July 29th calls for an end to leisure air travel in an op-ed piece in *The Guardian* (London, England), saying that, "*...flying across the Atlantic is as unacceptable, in terms of its impact on human well-being, as child abuse!*" And so begins the next chapter in travel—green travel, or simply not traveling at all...

2000

New Age sites around the world, from Sedona and Machu Picchu, to Stonehenge and Uluru are crowded on January 1st as Millennium Madness takes place—one year prematurely!

JetBlue Airways introduces live (via satellite) in-flight television fleet-wide and in all cabins. Now you can get commercials in the air too, oh wait, they already do that!

Ken Burton, a Canadian skipper and RCMP sergeant, sails a 20-meter twin-hulled aluminum catamaran Nadon named *St. Roch II* through the Northwest Passage in a record 21-days while encountering no ice blockages.

The Greater Metropolitan area of Tokyo's population exceeds 35 million people.

Bangkok, Thailand's *Skytrain* system opens with 23 stations and a total length of 23.5 kilometers. *Tuk-tuk* rides take a back seat to new air-conditioned rides zooming above the city sights.

The Oresund Bridge, a 15 kilometer (9-mile) bridge opens linking the two Nordic countries of Denmark and Sweden.

Davo Karnicar, a Slovenian skier, tames Mount Everest when he takes a five hour uninterrupted ski run down the world's tallest mountain, taking extreme adventure tourism to a whole new level—8,848 meters to be exact!

Joe Robinson, an American adventure writer, begins his campaign *Work to Live*, that is the movement pushing people to *work to live* versus just living to work (aka the U.S. is a vacation-starved nation) in his travel adventure magazine known as *Escape*.

Malcolm Foley and John Lennon, two American writers, release their book that uncovers the topic of *Dark Tourism* (See: 1988), about travelers who support niche-markets including: disaster tourism, war tourism, and graveyard tourism, among others.

Following the lead of the other two American legacy airlines, Delta Airlines forms the Sky Team alliance with a few friendly airlines including: Air France, Aeroméxico and Korean Air. By 2010, the Sky Team had 13 carrier members serving 898 international destinations and a #3 market share of 21% of the global air passenger market.

Starbucks, the Seattle-based coffee company, opens an outlet *inside* the walls of the 600-year old Forbidden City in Beijing, China. Is nothing sacred—apparently not when about seven million visitors a year walk by? I order a *café Americano*.

The First World Hotel located in the theme park Genting (aka City of Entertainment) about an hour outside Kuala Lumpur, Malaysia, opens and instantly becomes the new reigning champion of the title of the world's largest hotel with 6,200 rooms. Take that MGM Grand in Las Vegas! (I urge everyone to Google *Hilbert's Grand Hotel Paradox*" to truly boggle your brain.)

American Airlines (AA) begins offering "more room in coach" seats in only a few rows for the highly discriminating passengers—for an extra charge of course. (In 2003, AA would get rid of those extra inches to get more cows in the seats! Moo…)

Tens of millions of consumers finally get to voice their views, opinions, rants and raves on where to stay, what to do, where to eat, etc., after TripAdvisor.com establishes its Zagat-like Internet ratings forum. Internet democracy is created (See: 1982). But in just a few short years, hoteliers learn to game the system by posting fake reviews puffing up their own properties while slandering their competitors. In an unrelated story, the hotel bed bug outbreak emerges around the world. (By 2010, TripAdvisor.com would have over 30 million monthly visits and generate over $340 million in annual ad revenues!)

The U.S. Federal Aviation Administration releases a report that claims that over 95% of all the passengers involved in U.S. plane crashes between 1983 and 2000, survived…*hmm*, okay.

On May 25th, Philippine Airlines Flight 812 Airbus A330 with scheduled domestic service between Francisco Bangoy International Airport (DVO) and Manila's Ninoy Aquino International Airport (MNL), with 278 passengers and 13 crew members is hijacked by an apparent plane robber who demands that all the passengers place their valuables in a bag. He then demands that the pilot descend and depressurize the aircraft so that he could escape with a homemade parachute, but he panics seeing the sky and ground below him after opening the aircraft doors, when a pissed off flight attendant simply pushes him out the door at an altitude of about 1,800 meters! He died. No word on the flight attendant's legal or financial status!

An innovative California-based company called Great*Escape* Adventures Inc. begins promoting an around-the-world travel adventure competition in October designed to test hardened globetrotters travel savvy and cultural skills in an event called *The Global Scavenger Hunt*™ that will annually crown *The World's Greatest Travelers*™. Finally an annual international competition for real travelers! (GlobalScavengerHunt.com)

Who wants to be The World's Greatest Travelers?
(Courtesy GreatEscape Adventures, Inc.)

2001
The first in-flight e-mail transmission takes place onboard an Air Canada flight on January 17th between Montreal and Toronto, Canada. *"Mom, guess where I am sitting."*

Dennis Tito (See: 1990), becomes the world's first space tourist that paid his own way when he visits the International Space Station (ISS) for seven days. The air and hotel costs set him back a cool US$20 million—with no miles offered or room service available!

The World Health Organization (WHO) reports that the long discussed *economy-class syndrome* (aka travelers' thrombosis), does indeed take place during long air flights potentially causing serious medical damage, including death with the condition known as deep vein thrombosis (DVT).

Over 60 million Hindu pilgrims attend the Kumbh Mela festival in India along the sacred Ganges River, when unusually significant planetary positions that repeats only once every 144 years, attracts a record turnout of humanity attending the world's largest act of faith.

The Centre for Tourism and Cultural Change (CTCC) is established at Leeds Metropolitan University in England that focuses *not* on the management (aka hospitality schools) or business of tourism and *not* on the environmental or development aspects of tourism, but on the dynamic cultural context in which tourism changes people—understanding others, as well as ourselves.

Michael Palin (1943-), an English comedian and traveler, gives rise to what is known in the travel business as the *"Palin effect"* (aka booking bump), when television viewers, after seeing one of his many travel shows, start booking trips to those locations. I love Michael's travel quote, *"Travel, at its best, is a process of continually conquering disbelief."* Indeed…

Bernard Schweizer (1962-), a Swiss-born American English professor, writes her post-colonial perspectives on travel *Radicals on the Road: The Politics of English Travel Writing in the 1930s.*

Borge Ousland (1962-), a Norwegian polar explorer, becomes the first person to cross both the North and South Poles alone. He completed the Antarctica leg in 1996. The "why" once again remains an elusive unanswered question?

Five American-based airlines: American, Continental, Delta, Northwest and United, come together to fulfill a mission to develop a travel website to sell their wares and create Orbitz.com, an online travel booking company that effectively cuts out already marginalized travel agents and counters Expedia.com and Travelocity.com (See: 1996) success. Some argue collusion; some claim antitrust issues; others anti-competitive behavior, but no one listens. The Big Three is complete…

Anthony Michael "Tony" Bourdain, (1956-), and American chef, publishes his captivating *A Cook's Tour: Global Adventures in Extreme Cuisines,* which covers the culinary delights of the world. Later in 2007, he follows it up with the equally witty *No Reservations: Around the World on an Empty Stomach.* Eating has never been so good…or so funny!

Sensing that many world heritage sites are being exploited, the UN's World Heritage Committee (See: 1972) creates a Sustainable Tourism Programme that has stakeholders focus on the managing, preserving and protecting the world's great heritage sites to help counter the *Loving-it-to-Death Syndrome* and save the goose that laid the golden egg. (aka sustainable tourism)

The *Loving-it-to-Death Syndrome* Counter-Attack: Below are some of the more successful sustainable tourism strategies designed to counter over-crowding and other negative tourist impacts at fragile *must-see* sites:
Better training of local conservation employees.
Raising public awareness as to site fragility.
Non-political control and management by committee.
Timed and limited number of tickets sold.
Two-tiered pricing (locals and foreigners).
Tourist taxes to pay for conservation efforts.
Limiting areas accessibility (roping off).
Closing a site periodically.
Creating and deploying facsimiles and replicas.
Long-term planned restoration projects.
More private-public partnerships.
Better zoning and development controls.

Steve Jobs (1955-), an American success story, introduces what he calls, *"the Walkman of the 21st Century,"* in giving the world the portable iPod. Thank you Steve; what's next, a phone that takes photos and movies, sends e-mail, text message, use as a GPS, play games, play your music, watch TV, rent movies, and surf the net anywhere?

On April 22nd, Chechen militants take 120 hostages in Istanbul, Turkey, including four Russians and 16 Swiss. All are eventually released unharmed.

On May 26th, the Abu Sayyaf group in the Philippines, kidnaps 20 foreigners, including three Americans. One of the Americans is beheaded, and the bulk of the hostages are held for more than a year.

On June 2nd, the Abu Sayyaf group in the Philippines kidnaps 200 more foreigners, but Filipino (and American) security forces intervene and free all but five of them.

> *"Travel has never been so urgent, even necessary, as it is today."*
>
> - Pico Iyer – travel writer

CHAPTER THIRTEEN

Travel in the Post-9/11 World (2001 – 2010):
The tragic events of 9/11 changed everything in the American mindset—
indeed the Barbarians (sic) were at the gates. Rightful fear, scary paranoia
and willful ignorance, helped usher in an era of collective national *insecurity*
and create the climate for a whole new set of risk management challenges
facing travelers both domestically and internationally; but nowhere more
than within the United States itself, where a new national obsession with
security becomes synonymous with unrealistic expectations—never a
pleasant combo!

2001
On September 11th, four U.S.-based commercial jetliners are hijacked *en
masse* by four al Qaeda suicide squads. Two jets (American Airlines Flight
11 and United Airlines Flight 175, both Boeing 767's) are crashed into
the World Trade Center Towers; a third jet (American Airlines Flight 77
a Boeing 757) is crashed into the Pentagon in Washington D.C.; and the
fourth jet (United Airlines Flight 93 a Boeing 757) is crashed by passengers
revolting against the hijackers, into a Pennsylvania field in an effort to foil
the terrorists unknown mission. In all, it is the worst day on American soil
since the Civil War with over 3,000 deaths in total, including nationals
of over 70 countries. The terrible, evil, attacks rattle all Americans and
civilized citizens around the world, and create the conditions for the new
U.S.-led multi-front and extended War on Terror.

On September 11th, American and Canadian air traffic controllers implement
Security Control of Air Traffic and Air Navigation Aids (SCATANA),
effectively grounding all in-flight aircraft and face the difficult situation
of how to safely re-route and land 6,500 planes carrying close to a million

people. Canada took in 226 diverted trans-Atlantic flights that had already been airborne.

Beginning on September 14th, when North American air carriers start flying again, passengers are suddenly faced with in-flight hunger pangs beginning on America West and TWA, who said it would stop serving meals on all flights due to 9/11 security measures—metal flatware is now prohibited. Other airlines follow their lead and eliminate all free coach-class meals to save costs—under the guise of security issues. Schedule and price quickly become the bottom-line factors with passengers booking flights.

Within a week after 9/11 U.S. stocks had lost more the US$1.4 trillion in value.

The phrase *Flying while Muslim* is introduced into the vocabulary.

On September 22nd, President George W. Bush asks the U.S. Congress for US$15 billion in emergency assistance to help the aviation industry (aka a bailout) that provides airlines with US$10 billion in federal loan guarantees and credits, plus an additional US$5 billion in reimbursements for direct losses. (It should be noted that airlines were already swimming in a sea of red ink before 9/11 due to the twin effects of the dot.com bubble recession and out-dated business model practices.)

On October 7th, the U.S., along with some NATO allies, attack and invade Afghanistan in an effort to root out the planner of the 9/11 attack.

On October 26th, the infamous *USA Patriot Act* is signed into law that is designed to make it easier for domestic law enforcement agencies to detect and apprehend terrorists, but is roundly criticized for diluting basic and fundamental U.S. Constitutional rights, and other legal issues, including: privacy concerns, the unwarranted wiring-tapping of phones and e-mails, allowing for domestic spying on U.S. citizens, Fourth Amendment due process rights, eliminating judicial oversight of law enforcement agencies.

November 2nd marks one full year of continuous human presence in orbit around the Earth in the International Space Station (ISS).

On November 4th, a Sibir Airlines Flight 1812 Tupolev-154 flying at 36,300 feet from Israel's Ben Gurion International Airport (TLV) en route to Russia's Novosibirsk Tolmachevo Airport (OVB) explodes in the skies over the Black Sea killing all 78 aboard after being hit by a Ukraine Air Force military missile exercise.

On November 12th, American Airlines Flight 587 Airbus A300, crashes after takeoff at John F. Kennedy International Airport (JFK), killing 265 people total—and scaring many flyers wrongly in the U.S. into thinking about the prospects of terrorism again—it was a pilot navigation error.

On November 19th, the U.S. Congress passes the Aviation and Transportation Security Act of 2001 that: creates the new Transportation Security Administration (TSA) to oversee airline safety; expanded the use of federal flight deck officers (FFDO's) (aka sky marshals) on flights; limited airline insurance causality claims to a US$100 million limit; required airport screeners to be naturalized citizens; imposed strict fines on the airlines for any security breaches and/or violations; requires the hardening of cockpits and new in-flight security procedures; and implements *Vision 100* that ask all Americans to keep their eyes and ears open to obvious tell-tale terrorist signs.

CBS begins airing the reality-TV show *The Amazing Race* for the first time that pits casted teams-of-two against other selected teams who travel the globe performing stunts in various locals. Real traveler's wince in horror while they watch with one-eye open; the show becomes a commercial and critical hit. Armchair tourism soars.

An idiot loser (aka the Shoe Bomber, Richard something...) is to blame whenever you have to take off your shoes at all U.S. airports. And the security screening process becomes increasingly inconsistent, leading some experts to dub it "America's security theater."

RIP Trans World Airlines (TWA) (1930-2001).

By the end of 2001, an estimated 13% of the global fleet of commercial passenger airplanes is grounded. People had simply stopped flying. (Again, this crisis was already beginning before the 9/11 attacks with growing global economic uncertainty cause by the dot.com bubble bursting.)

2002

Fear in America hits a fever pitch after 9/11 when Louis Armstrong New Orleans International Airport (MSY) in the U.S. is closed and evacuated for over five hours in February due to an unidentified package—found to contain a delicious gumbo! The absurdity of America's new security theater knows no bounds.

The World sets sail as the first ever floating residential community with 165 units (aka apartments at sea) that will allow its tenants to travel around-the-world without leaving home! Monthly association fees are a cool US$20,000. The perpetual traveler is born.

To help counter the *Loving-it-to-Death Syndrome* (See: 2001) overtaking many international man-made and natural treasures, the Travel Industry Association of America (TIAA) and National Geographic Traveler magazine team up to create the Geotourism Charter, a list of 13 principles to help sustain the integrity of those special places.

The Norwegian Cruise Line (NCL) begins offering e-mail and Internet access on *Norwegian Sun.*

Perception vs. Reality: In 2002, just 31 American residents were killed in terrorist related incidents while traveling abroad with odds being 1 in 9.3 million; yet the odds of dying from skin cancer/ melanoma was 1 in 38,000, and the odds of dying in an auto accident was 1 in 6,000!

Air Canada bans British author Salman Rushdie from its flights because of the extra security required for him to fly due to the *fatwa* against him for writing his novel *The Satanic Verses* (1988).

Great*Escape*2002: The Global Scavenger Hunt, the inaugural around-the-world travel adventure competition and global fundraising event crowns Victoria Rivers living in Vancouver, Canada, and teammate Joan Harvard of Texas as *The World's Greatest Travelers* in the first annual travel adventure event. The event also featured what may be the first mobile real-time daily international travel event blogging (aka moblog or mobile blogging).

Feeling the heat of competition from low-cost airlines, American West and Alaska Airlines eliminate the much hated Saturday-night-stay rule (aka the airlines Golden Gotcha Rule) that required travelers wanting the cheapest fare, to be required to spend a Saturday night at their desired destination. (This was a form of collusion by the legacy airlines (United, American, Delta, Continental and US Airways) to offer a schizoid two-tiered price structure that cost U.S. business travelers billions over the years.) Air Canada followed in 2004 and Delta Airlines followed in 2005, thereby effectively killing the much dreaded rule—except of course on monopoly routes.

The Ritz Carlton Doha, is believed to be the first hotel offering the services of an on-call Technology Butler to assist weary (and extremely frustrated) road warriors attempting to get connected while traveling—be it dial up services, broadband, DSL, or Wi-Fi.

Leonardo DiCaprio plays a con man-cum-Pan Am pilot in the art imitates real life film version of *Catch Me if You Can*, as we follow his journey through the very friendly skies.

Travelblog.com arrives on the web scene as a place for ordinary travelers to share their extraordinary travel stories. People like it and by 2010 the site is home to over 150,000 members. Look at it as a modern day version of Aunt Millie sharing her slides from her trip to Myrtle Beach.

On July 2nd, Steve Fossett (1944–2007), a wealthy American adventurer, completes a circumnavigation of the globe in the 180-foot-tall *Spirit of Freedom* balloon, on his sixth try.

The Cape Town Conference on Responsible Tourism in Destinations, attended by 280 delegates from 20 countries, decrees that travelers have certain environmental, economic, and social responsibilities to adhere to when they travel. I agree with the responsible traveler's creed, honest I do, but geez they are taking all the fun out of travel.

The Bibliotheca Alexandrina (aka Library of Alexandria) reopens in Alexandria, Egypt after being closed for 1,631 years!

On January 31st, a lone U.S. tourist is killed on Mount Pinathibo in the Philippines by Islamic militants.

On October 12th, a car bomb, set by al Qaeda-linked militant Islamic group Jemaah Islamiyah (JI), explodes outside a tourist-filled nightclub in Kuta, Bali, Indonesia killing almost 200 while injuring another 300 people. Tourism to Bali plummets.

On October 23rd, fifty Chechen militants seize the Moscow's downtown Palace of Culture and hold over 800 hostages for five days before the security forces use gas to end the siege. The gas and subsequent assault kills all the Chechens along with 124 hostages.

On November 28th, Islamic suicide bombers attack the Paradise Hotel in Mombasa, Kenya, killing 12 and wounding 40; and on the same day, an Arkia Airlines 757-300 charter leaving Mombasa bound for Israel with 272 passengers was attacked by two Russian-made Strela-2M's surface-to-air missiles—they miss.

Wi-Fi Internet connections start appearing in hotel lobbies and airport terminals around the world and in 2005, Sunnyvale, California becomes the first city to offer city-wide free Wi-Fi. (See: 2008)

The annual Global Geographic Literacy Survey conducted by National Geographic and Roper that surveyed citizens in 9 nations with 56 geography-related questions, revealed that only Mexicans scored worse than U.S. residents. Despite 9/11, over 83% of Americans could not locate the country they were at war with (Afghanistan) on a map of the world— but then again, 11% could not locate the U.S. itself on that same map! The same 2006 survey found that six in 10 could not find Iraq—whom we had been at war with by now for three years—on a map of the Middle East. In another study, the United States scored 117th out of 193 countries on a test of global geographic knowledge...

Delta Air Lines begins to no longer pay commissions for tickets issued by travel agents. (See: 1999) Within a few weeks, all the other major U.S. airlines follow suit. Travel agents are reduced to booking pre-package tours and cruises, and begin charging travel agent consultant fees to a new generation of online consumers who would rather pay wholesale than retail.

2003

We celebrate the 100th anniversary of the Wright Brothers flight on December 17th. My, how time flies…

The European Community starts offering the Eco-label seal of approval to any tourism accommodation operator in the EU, be it small farmhouse to large hotel chains that show a turn towards sustainable green habits. The era of *greenwashing* begins.

An Argentina company begins offering twice-weekly commercial airline service to the last frontier of mass tourism—the Antarctica. The service takes 70 passengers from Ushuaia, Argentina to Seymour Island on Antarctica. (In 2001 just 15,000 people visited Antarctica, and then 37,506 tourists visited it in 2007 and over 80,000 by 2010.)

A Texas-based clothing-optional specialty travel company takes travelers on the "First Ever Nude Airline Flight" to Cancun, Mexico. Enough said…

The sinking island-nation of Vanuatu opens the world's first underwater post office to mail postcards from in an effort to highlight their global warming plight.

Cimex lectularius (aka bed bugs) begin arriving at some of New York City's most luxurious hotels! The international flea circus hits the road and comes to the U.S.

> **Did You Know?** The top eight reasons Americans travel were:
> Shopping – 32%
> Visiting family & friends – 19%
> Sun & beaches – 11%
> National/state parks – 10%
> Theme/amusement parks – 8%
> Gambling & entertainment – 7%
> Sporting events – 6%
> Golf/tennis/skiing – 4%

Three Australian comedic writers, Australians Tom Gleisner, Santo Cilauro and Rob Sitch, publish the fictitious guidebook called Molvania as a cheeky parody about how guidebooks use stereotypes and cheap clichés in their writings. The book sells well and they publish a sequel, *Phaic Tăn: Sunstroke on a Shoestring* in 2004.

The severe acute respiratory syndrome (SARS) epidemic (aka Yellow Pneumonia (sic) hits Southeast Asia hard and the World Health Organization (WHO), issues a global health alert on March 15th. Southern China, Hong Kong, Vietnam, Singapore, Taiwan, and Toronto, Canada are the hardest hit areas. In all, there are 8,096 known infected cases and 774 confirmed human deaths. According to the New England Medical Journal, during the SARS epidemic, awareness of the of acquisition of infection on a commercial aircraft reached its zenith on one flight operating between Hong Kong and Beijing, when 16 of the 120 passengers on the flight developed proven SARS from a single carrier. Man has created the perfect disease proliferators for a global pandemic—airports and airplanes!

Just when you thought adventure was lost, David Hempleman-Adams (1956-), an English adventurer, became the first person to ever fly solo across the Atlantic Ocean in an open wicker-basket balloon! He finished the flight on September 29th after 83 hours and 14 minutes aloft.

The British television station *Sky1* begins broadcasting *"Mile High"* a comedy/drama series about the lives of several flight attendants living in London. The show has a three year run until 2005.

In order to promote tourism, Las Vegas begins rebranding, not as family friendly entertainment city, but as Sin City—again—and begins using the *"What Happens Here Stays Here"* slogan *Lost Weekend*-style in luring adult spenders back to Sin City for adult fun and games. A new era of Debauchery Tourism that includes excessive drinking, glamorous nightclubs, exotic shows, gambling, wild pool parties, and sexual fantasies, begins at the height of the American Empire—but paid for on credit.

A Northwest flight attendant pleads guilty to spiking a crying 19-month old little girl's apple juice with *Xanax*—she was caught by a vigilant Dutch mother—and serves four months!

A revolutionary new website called Skype.com goes online that allows for voice (and now video) calls from anywhere over the Internet. Travelers can figuratively reach out and touch their loved ones while 10,000 kilometers away. Phone sex takes on a whole new meaning...which begs the question: How can you miss someone when you see them every day? (aka *Absence makes the heart grow fonder*...or was that Absinthe?)

Evan Prodromou and Michele Ann Jenkins, two wonderful folks, launch Wikitravel.com "a Web-based collaborative travel guide project" in July. Thank you and thanks all you *Wikitravellers* for the 50,000+ guides and articles.

The U.S. Congress passes the PROTECT Act of 2003 that prohibits U.S. citizens or permanent residents (PR) "to engage in international travel with the purpose or effect of having commercial sex with a person under the age of 18, or any sex with a person under the age of 16; or facilitating such travel", following the Australian lead (See: 1994). Always working that special relationship between U.S. and Britain, the British parliament quickly passes similar legislation known as the Sexual Offences Act of 2003. Laws are good, appropriate behavior even better.

On odd story: In September, Charles D. McKinley, a cash-strapped American, had himself shipped by airfreight from New York to his parents' house in Dallas to save the cost of a plane ticket. Is this a trend or one-off?

A tourism industry backlash begins when twin concerns about the mass tourist effects on regional environment and indigenous cultural heritages being destroyed, rock the Mayan Riviera (aka Cancun) where mass tourism development has officially run amok (See: 1969) with more than 150 hotels with over 30,000 rooms and 400 bars and restaurants crowding the area... and hordes of Spring Break *gringos* too!

On May 16th, Islamic militants en route to their own private heavenly-ordained 72-virgin orgy, mount five simultaneous suicide bomber attacks on tourist centers throughout the seaside city of Casablanca, Morocco, killing 42 and leaving more than 100 injured while.

On August 5th, Islamic militants target the Marriott Hotel in central Jakarta, Indonesia with a car bomb that kills 12 and wounds 150 guests.

Did You Know? That according to airline industry analysts, frequent flyer junkies (aka mileage whores) take about a million extra wholly unnecessary trips a year (aka mileage runs) just to add miles to their buck up their airline status (aka mileage dementia), and that the inflated costs of the airline tickets that they (aka business travelers/road warriors) purchase to earn those extra personal miles—some call it a form of non-taxable corporate bribery—costs U.S. businesses an estimated 8% of all business travel expenses—about US$10 billion in 2009! It is also believed that this small group of business travelers makes up as much as 25% of all airline revenue.

On October 2nd, the Abu Sayyaf Group militants of the Philippines kidnap six foreign tourists in Sabah, Malaysia; five are later found dead with one escaping death.

The U.S. Transportation Security Administration (TSA) presents a plan to expand air passenger screening in the wake of 9/11, (See: 2001) by introducing the CAPPS II passenger vetting process that among other changes CAPPS I (See: 1996) by having the government, not the airlines, screen passengers, and also includes: the screening of all passengers, not just ones checking bags; would expand Passenger Number Record (PNR) information data fields to include street address, date of birth, home telephone number, place of employments, that would be cross-checked against government databases (which would as a by-product include the apprehending of federal deadbeats, those with any type of outstanding warrants, and illegal aliens—or maybe overdue library books or a late video rental); having computer algorithms then assign each PNR a color-coded risk score indicating the "screening level" for each passenger—and 5% are said to be automatically assigned secondary searches. After privacy advocates and civil libertarian groups angrily opposed the program, and then when Senator Edward Kennedy is denied boarding due to a false positive, the program is killed and replaced with the Secure Flight program (See: 2009). Many non-politically correct-types ask out loud, "Why can't we simplify the whole screening process and just racial profile—we know who the bad guys are?"

Joel Henry, a bored French traveler, creates the Laboratory of Experimental Tourism (Latourex), whereby he expands the parameters of why we travel and where we travel (aka counter tourism) by creating alternative and creative methods of both choosing travel destinations (sometimes at random) and what you will experience upon arrival. It makes some recall that great Kurt Vonnegut Cat's Cradle line, "Strange travel suggestions are dancing lessons from God." Only in France…

2004

Nervure, the French journal of psychiatry, describes outbreaks of the aptly labeled *Paris Syndrome* (aka *Syndrome de Paris*) being diagnosed as a transient psychological disorder among tourists visiting Paris, France. It is found to occur when language barriers, cultural differences, inflated expectations, disorientation, jet lag and surly waiters mix, among mostly Japanese tourists (about 20 a year succumb and require treatment), visiting Paris. It is closely approximates other travel-related syndromes including Culture Shock (See: 1954); Jerusalem syndrome (See: 1930); and the original grand-daddy of travel ailments the Stendhal syndrome (See: 1817).

The first commercial high-speed Maglev line in the world opens between downtown Shanghai, China and Shanghai Pudong International Airport (PVG) on the 30.5 kilometer (19-mile) Shanghai Maglev Train (aka

Shanghai Transrapid). The line took four years to build and has a top operational commercial speed of 431 km/h (268 mph).

In reaction to 9/11, the U.S. Border Control and Immigration Office begins photographing and fingerprinting all travelers entering the U.S. by air or sea from non-visa waiver countries.

The 2nd international around the world travel adventure competition Great*Escape*2004: The Global Scavenger Hunt that has teams of two visiting ten nations across four continents, crowned Vicki Sheahan of Dallas, Texas and Alicia Blier of Los Angeles, California, *The World's Greatest Travelers*™.

The Patagonian Expedition Race (aka the race to the end of the world), an annual 10-day endurance multi-discipline adventure race takes place for the first time—picking up where the Eco-Challenge left off. (See: 1995)

The 2,592-passenger *RMS Queen Mary 2,* the largest, tallest and longest ocean liner ever built becomes operational as the flagship of the Cunard Line.

EuroTrip, an American comedy is released to side-splitting yuks and applause in the U.S., when four American buddies cross Europe looking for beer and babes and the predictable stereotypical cultural *faux pas* prevail.

Canada begins prosecuting individuals under the sex tourism law when *Donald Bakker* is charged in Canada for having sex with underage girls in *Cambodia*, the oldest of whom was 12. That is not what the Dead Kennedy's were singing about in their 1980 song entitled, *"Holiday in Cambodia."*

To better manage safety and reduce costs of the over 33,000 commercial air passenger flights a day flying over the skies of Europe, the European Union creates the Single European Sky ATM Research (SESAR) and begins overhauling and updating the continents antiquated and fragmented air traffic control system and better prepare for future growth by bringing together all the stakeholders. The U.S. attempts to do the same with the development of the NextGen system (See: 2008).

Life is stranger than fiction for a change. The Terminal, a movie directed by Steven Spielberg starring Tom Hanks, is a real life story about a man bureaucratically trapped in an international airport terminal in legal limbo. The film is inspired by the 18-year stay of Mehran Karimi Nasseri (1942-), an Iranian refugee, in Terminal 1 of the Charles de Gaulle International Airport (CDG) in Paris, France from 1988 to 2006. Talk about having the terminal blues…

The end of an era occurs when American Airlines stopped selling their lifetime AAirpass, which is supposed to give the purchaser a "lifetime" of First Class travel anywhere, anytime on any American Airlines flight for a fee—the last one sold went for a reported US$3 million! It is estimated by insiders that American Airlines sold 500 such passes. (By the way, Steven Rothstein is pissed, and he's suing American Airlines to the tune of US$7 million, because back in 1987, Rothstein plunked down US$250,000 for the all-access AAirpass, and two years later he antes up US$160,000 for a companion pass, but American Airlines apparently pulled Rothstein's pass for some "technical reasons.")

On December 26th, the Indian Ocean tsunami that followed an 8.7 magnitude earthquake wreaks havoc on Sri Lanka, Indonesia, India, Thailand, and other South Asian nations, causing a death toll that exceeds 230,000 in fourteen nations, including 9,000 tourists visiting those countries.

On February 26th, suicide bombers attack a 10,192-ton SuperFerry in the Philippines with over 900 passengers, killing 126 travelers.

On March 11th, Islamic militants of North African origin, explode ten bombs on numerous commuter trains in Madrid, Spain, killing 191 people and injuring 1,900 more.

On June 24th, Chechen separatists are blamed, when two Russian civilian aircraft crash within minutes of each other outside Moscow, killing all 90 passengers and crew aboard the planes.

In October, after more than seven uneventful years, with no noteworthy violent incidents aimed at foreign tourists visiting Egypt, Islamic fundamentalist terrorists bomb resorts in the Red Sea villages of Taba and Ras Shitan killing 34 persons and gravely wounding another 100.

A Japanese charter airline announced an all male flight-attendant flight called "Men's Flight" to a Japanese resort town of Miyazaki in order to attract female flyers.

Wealthy urban Gen X couples, who upon finding out they are pregnant, have one last fling of togetherness as a couple and begin taking babymoons. Some go to Cancun or Vegas, while the more adventurous couples head for the Thai hills and Laos.

Ellen Simonetti, an American blogger, is fired by Delta Airlines for documenting her life and work experiences as a Delta Airlines flight attendant on a blog called "Queen of Sky: Diary of a Dysfunctional Flight Attendant". Not once during her year and a half of blogging did she mention who she worked for, but that did not seem to work to her advantage. So much for free speech! (And by the way, in an unrelated story, there is no truth to the falsely reported rumor that Delta actually means "**D**on't **E**xpect **L**egroom on **T**his **A**irline.")

The world's longest regularly scheduled commercial passenger flight becomes the Singapore Airlines Flight SQ21operating between Newark Liberty International Airport (EWR) and Singapore International Airport (SIN). The nonstop Airbus 340 flight covers 15,345 kilometers (9,535 miles) in 18 hours and 50 minutes.

A company called Vocation Vacations begins offering clients the opportunity to "test-drive" different jobs while on vacation to help people regain their passion for life—with a new job! Only in America…

2005
Google.com launches the incredible Google Earth allowing anyone a high-resolution satellite view of the world. The tools for being a "virtual tourist" are complete.

The third around the world travel adventure competition, Great*Escape*2005: The Global Scavenger Hunt takes place over 23 days and crowns Lisa Hunt of Chicago, Illinois and Helen Qubain of Belgium *The World's Greatest Travelers*™ for 2005.

Reality Tours and Travel, the brainchild of Chris Way and Krishna Poojari, begin offering "slum tours" in Mumbai, India that they claim is "designed primarily to show the positive side of the slums and break down its negative stereotypes." The tours are attacked domestically and internationally and criticized as voyeuristic, being poorists (sic), and as treating humans as animals in a zoo for roaming tourist buses. Like all trends, other like-minded tours begin taking place in the *favelas of South America, the shanty townships of Africa, garbage dumps of Manila...like we don't have enough street people in our own urban cities!*

Fact or Fiction? Road warriors (aka business travelers) who claim they fly one million miles a year? Let's do the math: 1 million miles divided by 500 mph = 2,000 hours of actual flight time, which equals 250 days a year flying 8 hours a day. It's a myth! Maybe the accrued one million miles with their frequent flyer programs, credit cards miles, along with hotel and car rental points, but flying, nope.

United Airlines no-frills low-cost Ted airlines begins selling playing cards for US$5 per pack and makes a killing too, because flyers are always looking for new ways to kill time when flights are late—and Ted flights are seemingly perpetually late. Ted dies an unannounced quiet death in 2008.

EC 261 (aka the European Airline Passenger Bill of Rights) goes into effect within the European Union and applies to any European Union airline flying to or from a member state. The legislation expands compensation from airlines to passengers that cover not only denied boarding situations (aka bumping) of 250Euros for flights less than 1,500 kilometers; 400Euros for intra-community flights of more than 1,500 kilometers and for other flights between 1,500 and 3,500 kilometers; and 600Euros for flights longer than 3,500 kilometers, along with necessary meals, refreshments and hotel accommodation if needed; but also offers financial compensation to paid passengers for cancelled and long-delayed flights over and above meals and refreshments and required hotel accommodation, including reimbursements, rightfully paying for all additional flights and delays, as well as compensating for lost and delayed baggage. *Hmm*, nope, that could never happen in North America. By the way, little known fact—clearly not made public here in North America—this law applies to *any* carrier departing from any country within the European Community! Speak up disgruntled travelers…and keep clicking your heels too.

British Airways becomes the first major airline in September to establish a carbon-offset program (for a fee of course) for passengers with a heavy conscious about their frivolous travels. Delta Airlines begins the same program in 2007.

Northwest Airlines saves US$2,000,000 annually by eliminating free in-flight pretzels. No word on how much they made by reselling them back to their passengers?

The British Broadcasting Company (BBC) airs a travel series called *Round The World In 80 Treasures*, a 10-part documentary visiting the eighty greatest international man-made treasures, from Machu Picchu to Xi'an's Terra Cotta Warriors. The documentary touches on a disturbing new trend occurring, at least being openly discussed, within the travel industry—the *"Loving-it-to-Death Syndrome"* (See: 2001) whereby too many people are visiting our most precious sites with that wear and tear ironically leading to their demise through over-use (aka carrying capacity)!

According to the U.S. Environmental Protection Agency (EPA), the chance that an airliner has dangerous levels of disease-causing pathogens in its drinking water is 1 in 7!

Foreign Policy magazine begins offering travel advice in the form of annually publishing their *Failed State Index* (aka most dangerous places in the world list) (See: 1994) of places to be avoided based on the score of 12 rather dreadful social, political and economic indicators. This year's winners, err, losers, included: Ivory Coast, Yemen, Haiti, Dominican Republic and Columbia, among others.

The facts and figures speaks for itself as vacation time in the United States continues to dwindle among the working population (the only industrialized nation that does not mandate paid vacations) and are reduced to an average of 4.1 days (aka *nano*-vacations) down from six nights about 25 years ago before the Reagan era—which begs the question, *"Are you better off today?"*

Fisherman's Wharf, Macau's first theme park opened amidst a casino building boom that by 2007 has Macau gambling revenues exceeding Las Vegas!

The 60-meter tall Nann Myint (aka Bagan tower) opens on the vast historic plain of Bagan in Burma allowing visitors to see a bird's eye view of the over 2,000 temples and monuments of the 11th to 13th century. Some call it sacrilegious.

Hong Kong Disneyland opens.

Ellen Patricia MacArthur (1976-), an English yachtswoman, became the fastest solo sailor to circumnavigate the world when she clocked in at a time of 71 days and 14 hours and 18 minutes on her 50,660 kilometer (27,354-nautical mile) voyage aboard her 75-foot trimaran *B&Q/ Castorama*.

Ugh, the sign of flights to come? On November 10th, a new Boeing 777-200 Worldliner sets a new world record for the longest non-stop flight by a commercial jet, flying 22 hours and 42 minutes and 20,255 kilometers (12,586 miles) from Hong Kong (HKG) to London (LHR).

A depressing series of events in 2005 begins for travelers on April 7th, a fringe extremist group dubbing itself the Abdullah Azzam Brigades (aka Islamic Brigades of Pride) delivered bombs driven by a motorcycle-driving suicide bomber right into the heart of the historic Cairo shopping bazaar called Khan al-Khalili killing two tourists, a French woman and an American man, wounding 18 others.

On April 30th, two veiled Islamic women committed suicide after opening fire on a tour bus in Cairo, Egypt, wounding two passengers.

On July 7th, a series of al-Qaeda associated militants coordinated suicide attacks on London's Underground (aka The Tube) and a double-decker bus during the morning rush hour with four bombs being detonated; fifty-two travelers were killed in the attacks and around 700 were injured.

On July 23rd, associates of al Qaeda claim responsibility for setting off three bombs at the Egyptian Red Sea resort city of Sharm el-Sheikh, killing 88 and wounding over 200.

On October 1st, two suicide car bombs explode at the Jimbaran Beach Resort and in the tourist ghetto Kuta in Bali, Indonesia, killing 26 tourists and injuring another 100.

On November 9th, three alleged Iraqi suicide bombers attack three tourist hotels in downtown Amman, Jordan: the Grand Hyatt Hotel, the Radisson SAS Hotel, and the Days Inn, killing at least 60 people and injuring 115 others.

Somalia pirates on the high seas are unsuccessful in their attempt to seize the cruise ship *Seabourn Spirit*, but set off a wave of attacks in the Gulf of Aden which lies between the Red Sea and the Arabian Sea off the coast of Somalia. It becomes one of the most dangerous places in the world for ships of any kind.

The Transportation Security Administration (TSA) begins the Registered Traveler Pilot Program that is a private-public program designed to vet and assess airline passenger security threats (aka not let bad guys on planes and make it easier for good guys to get on planes). Passengers will voluntarily pay for the privilege of filing in mountains of paperwork about their personal life, then submit to a rigorous background check before getting cleared (aka Security Threat Assessment (STA)—or arrested, served, or chased by a creditor!—you get a Registered Travelers biometric smartcard and are then supposed to get through security lines quicker; although cardholders are still required to: remove their coats and shoes, take out laptops, are not allowed any beverages, must still undergo baggage x-ray and personal metal detector screenings, as well as not being exempt from random secondary screenings...*sounds like a good deal!*

2006

The Qingzang a high-altitude railway opens that run trains 1956 kilometers (1215 miles) from Xining, China to Lhasa, Tibet. The line runs across 550 kilometers of permafrost and through the Tanggula Pass at 5,072 meters (16,640-feet) making it the world's highest rail track. The Chinese really wanted this line to complete their power grab on isolated Tibet.

American Airlines, Delta Airlines and Northwest Airlines all stop providing flyers on domestic flights with pillows and blankets. And it is about time too…

Snakes on a Plane, one of the worst travel movies of all time runs to limited audiences.

The International Cruise Victims (ICV), a nonprofit organization, is created to offer support and assist to cruise ship passengers who have been affected by crimes. Statistics vary, but crime on the high seas is a serious issue with 12 million Americans taking cruises every year.

Beijing Happy Valley, an amusement park, with over 40 rides and other attractions opens in the Chinese capital city.

British secret police uncover a terrorist plot to board at least 10 airlines traveling between England bound for Canada and the U.S., with a plan to detonate liquid explosives once aboard. Over 1,700 flights out of British airspace are cancelled and airline passengers carrying liquids onto commercial aircraft in Europe and North America are limited to this day, as the U.S. Transportation Security Administration quickly rolled out the *"3-1-1 for carry-on"* rule (aka 3.4 ounce containers in a 1 clear quart baggie, 1 bag per passenger)…breast milk exempted.

Its official, air travel can create pandemics. A September 2006 Harvard study *"provides evidence that air travel plays a significant role in the annual spread of influenza…"* (See: SARS 2003)

Female sex tourism (aka romance tourism) is explored in the book *Romance on the Road* by Jeannette Belviveau who exposes the darker side of females, especially cougars, on the prowl in developing nations. *Et tu* sister?

Anousheh Ansari, an Iranian-born U.S. citizen, becomes the first female space tourists on September 18th when she takes a Russian Soyuz TMA-9 to visit the International Space Station (ISS) for 10 days.

The National Transportation Safety Board reports that since 1997 airplane crashes have been decreasing to the level of safety of just three deaths per 10 billion passenger miles! My bookie tells me those are really good odds…

A British website called Guests Behaving Badly (GBB) begins offering hotels a five-tiered database registry in which to check on potential customers who may have indulged in prior inappropriate hotel behavior—being too loud, not paying bill, vandalism, smoking in non-smoking rooms, and stealing towels! It is a hotel industries *no-stay* blacklist.

The Coalition for Airline Passengers is formed by angry airline passengers with the goal of getting an Airline Passengers' Bill of Rights American-style—not European-style—through the U.S. Congress. (See: 2005) (FlyersRights.org) Then in 2008, the Airline Association for Passenger Rights (AAPR) was created to join the fight.

In the feature film *Last Stop for Paul*, two buddies travel the globe spreading the ashes of their dead friend in odd places he always wanted to visit—but obviously didn't! Proving what every real travel junkie already knows, and what Mark Twain (See: 1866) probably said best: "*Twenty years from now you'll be more disappointed by the things you didn't do, than by the ones you did.*"

On April 24, an Islamic group sets off three powerful bombs targeting two restaurants and a market in Egypt's Red Sea resort town of Dahab killing 23 people and seriously injuring more than 85, including tourists from 13 countries.

On September 4th, a lone-gunman fires on a group of foreign tourists visiting the ruins of an ancient Roman amphitheater at Hashemite Square in downtown Amman, Jordan, killing a British man and wounding seven others.

The Lonely Planet company publishes their *Guide to Micronations*, about places so small they may only exist in the minds of their creators. In an unrelated story, The Century Club (See: 1954) immediately recalibrates their list of nation-states!

U.S. Transportation Security Administration "Red team investigators" (aka undercover TSA agents) test airport screeners by smuggling fake bombs through security check points. And alarmingly find that security screeners at LAX failed to identify 75% of the fake bombs, while Chicago O'Hare screeners missed 60% of the bomb components! (Facts and figures in the past have been revealed to show that "Red team" system attacks have been identified more often in the past than today after heightened 9/11 security checks; with a series of tests conducted in 1978 showing only 13% of the fake bombs being missed by security screeners, and 23% of the fake bombs being missed in a 1987 test.) My bookie says those are really bad odds...

United Airlines (UA) emerges from Chapter 11 bankruptcy on February 1st after dumping its US$5 billion in employee pension obligations on the backs of the U.S. taxpayers—the largest such default in U.S. corporate history. Reason #136 why many fliers so dislike the old legacy airlines and United Airlines in particular (it routinely scores lower than the IRS in most Customer Service Satisfaction surveys) and why some say that they will never fly on UA again!

2007
Fantawild, mainland China's largest amusement park, opens just two hours from Nanjing.

Barrington Irving (1983-), a Jamaican-born 23-year-old pilot, becomes the youngest person ever to fly solo in a single engine plane around the world and also becomes the first African–American to do it taking 96 days and 150 hours of flight time to get the 43,132 *kilometer* (26,800 miles) circumnavigation done.

Taiwan High Speed Rail (THSR) a line that runs along the west coast of Taiwan between Taipei and Kaohsiung begins operating with trains traveling the 345 kilometer (214-mile) line at speeds of 300 km/h (186 mph) making the old four hour plus trip in less than 90 minutes door-to-door.

Dear old Iris Peterson (1922-), an American flight attendant, finally retires from the not so friendly skies as a United Airlines flight attendant with 60 years worth of personal experiences. First hired in 1946, she is 85—and

#1 on seniority list. Didn't we all have Iris at one time or another? A fond bye-bye and thank you Iris, we hope you enjoyed your flight!

The private/corporate jet industry numbers speak for themselves, since 9/11, the annual worldwide sales of private jets has more than doubled to US$19.4 billion with 70% (or 10,000) of the 14,000 business jets worldwide, operating in the U.S. The rich speak with their wallets and abandon the public air carriers creating an even larger disparity between the haves and the have-yachts! These corporate jets not only pollute more, dodge security requirements, and overtax the air traffic control system (the F.A.A. estimates that private planes account for 16% of the air traffic control system's overhead but contribute only 3% of the fees.), but they also manipulate the tax codes to allow us taxpayers to subsidize their Lifestyles of the Rich and Famous-like travel costs too—seems fair! Where's the Monopoly game's luxury tax card when you need one?

U.S. air passenger traffic reaches an all-time high with all air carriers (domestic and international) flying a total of 769.4 million air passengers; of which 160.7 million (21%) will fly to international destinations outside the United States. On average, 2 million people a day take flights on over 30,000 daily scheduled flights in the United States alone.

The New York City Taxi and Limousine Commission, with the "intention of providing useful information to riders" have turned New York City's yellow cabs into loud and confusing vehicles full of unwanted advertisements, entertainment delivery systems with the occasional buried bit of useful information.

The U.S. Department of Homeland Security's data-mining test program (aka searching for bad guys without a known suspect) called Analysis, Dissemination, Visualization, Insight and Semantic Enhancement (ADVISE), takes the place of the previous program introduced as Total Information Awareness (TIA), that wanted to track and cross-check names, address, credit card information, telephone, e-mail contacts, itineraries, hotel and rental car reservations–and was killed by the U.S. Congress in 2003 as being a tad too invasive. No word on its effectiveness or data parameters. (But, in an unrelated story, it is also revealed that another U.S. government program called Automated Targeting System (ATS), that keeps records on Americans who travel internationally (in and of itself an issue to many!) kept additional personal data relating to: items carried during their journeys, the books that travelers carried, racial or ethnic origin, political opinions, religious or philosophical beliefs, trade union membership, and other data about the traveler's health, traveling partners, sexual orientation and whom they associate with while traveling. These remarkable privacy invasion revelations did not go over well…

Most Visited Tourist Attractions? ForbesTraveler.com compiled a 2007 list that showed the top ten as:

#1 - Times Square, New York City – 35 million (visitors a year)

#2 - Mall & Parks, Washington D.C. – 25 million

#3 - Disney World, Orlando – 16.6 million

#4 - Trafalgar Square, London – 15 million

#5 - Disneyland, California – 14.7 million

#6 - Niagara Falls, Canada/U.S. – 14 million

#7 - Fisherman's Wharf, San Francisco – 13 million

#8 - Tokyo Disneyland, Japan (1983) – 12.9 million

#9 - Notre Dame, Paris – 12 million

#10 - Disneyland Paris – 10.6 million

(One would think that both Tiananmen Square in Beijing and Red Square in Moscow would get enough visitors annually to merit inclusion on this list?)

The Airbus A380 SuperJumbo, the world's largest commercial jetliner (ending the Boeing 747's 38 year reign) and most expensive commercial airplane ever produced that carries a US$320 million list price, finally took off on its first historic journey as the Singapore Airlines scheduled flight with 455 paying customers on a 7 1/2-hour flight between Singapore (SIN) and Sydney (SYD), Australia. The A380 is capable of carrying up to 853 passengers. The plane has 50 percent more cabin space than a later model Boeing 747. Think about that…853 people standing in the aisles trying to disembark!

Jason Lewis (1967-), an eccentric English adventurer, who has spent the last 13 years of his life walking and pedaling around the world in a bid to become the first to cross the world under his own steam, finally finishes his

74,842 kilometer (46,505 miles) journey across five continents, two oceans and one sea. He originally thought it would only take him three and half years to complete! (The record attempt has not been without controversy. Last year Colin Angus, a Canadian explorer, appeared to have beat Lewis to the post. However, although Angus did circle the globe, his achievement has not been officially recognized by Guinness World Records because he did not cross the equator in his 43,000 kilometer circumnavigation.) Both of you guys—get a life you ego trippers!

An English company begins selling The London Star Map, London's first ever celebrity map showing where the rich and famous live including: J K Rowling, Paul McCartney, Richard Branson, and David Bowie, among others; along with famous music landmarks and film locations. Celebrity tourism runs amok abroad. (See: 1935)

Traveocity.com voluntarily pays US$182,750 to settle a complaint brought by the U.S. Treasury Department, which said the company had violated the U.S. embargo of Cuba by booking travelers to the island nation.

What are nicknamed pop-up hotels begin, err, popping up, with the idea of a travelpod (aka prefab mobile hotel room—a trailer or converted shipping container)…the concept is to give folks attending events such as Burning Man or Glastonbury and other seasonal or temporary events, better accommodation options.

The theatrical release of *A Map For Saturday* shows travelers from around the world answering that age-old question: *"What would it be like to travel the world?"* We all know that when we are traveling—everyday is a Saturday!

The U.S. begins the United States Visitor and Immigrant Status Indicator Technology (US-VISIT) program for vetting and processing all foreign visitors coming to the United States from non-visa waiver nations, which includes an in-person appointment to the U.S. embassy, the collection of data and biometric data (finger prints and photographs) and US$140 in visa costs. In a tit-for-tat, other nations start imposing the same conditions on U.S. residents visiting their nations. By 2009, even Visa Waiver Program (VWP) countries "must pay operational and travel promotion fees" of US$14 when applying for an Electronic System for Travel Authorization

(ESTA)—a pre-approved electronic visa now required by all getting on a plane headed to the United States. And the travel industry wonders why visitor growth to the U.S. is so sluggish. (In 2001, the U.S. State Department issued 7.6 million nonimmigrant visas, but only 5.8 million in 2009.)

A new trend begins to emerge in the hotel industry when the Beverly Hills Peninsula and Raffles Hotels & Resorts chain, begin offering "24-hour check-in check-out" service (aka you have the room for an entire 24 hours—not check in at 3PM check out at 10AM)...travelers everywhere rejoice.

Aircraft Crashes Record Office (ACRO), a Geneva, Switzerland based office that compiles statistics on aviation accidents, reports that 2007 was the safest year in aviation history since 1963 in terms of number of accidents with only 136 registered accidents (compared to 164 in 2006), resulting in 965 deaths (compared to 1,293 in 2006). Now you know!

The American Society of Civil Engineers created a new list of the Seven Wonders of the Modern World (read man-made building projects).

The Seven Modern Wonders: The Empire State Building (New York, USA), The Itaipu Dam (Brazil and Paraguay), The CN Tower (Toronto, Ontario, Canada), The Panama Canal (Panama), The Channel Tunnel (France and United Kingdom), The North Sea protection works (The Netherlands), and The Golden Gate Bridge (San Francisco, California, USA).

For the first time in U.S. hotel history, the average daily rate (ADR) for a single hotel room breaks the US$100.00 mark at US$103.87. In 2007, there are an estimated 4.4 million hotel rooms in over 50,000 properties in the U.S.—almost double the number 50 years earlier.

The United Nation's World Health Organization releases the WRIGHT Report (aka the WHO Research into Global Hazards of Travel), a study collecting data in the harmful effects of travel on travelers. The Report covers deep vein thrombosis (DVT) (aka Travelers Thrombosis or the Economy Class Syndrome (ECS) issue acknowledging that it is a concern for a few passengers. Seems those extra long flights that passengers sit semi-immobilized, dehydrated, in seats almost too small, not to mention those 28-inch pitches, covered in infectious pillows, bad recycled air, eating approachably poisonous foodstuffs, and enduring psychological distress caused by sometimes rude and disrespectful service employees, and fellow passengers who might be contagious with infectious diseases, is something they should look at closer…

The World Economic Forum begins publishing that annual Travel and Tourism Competitiveness Index (TTCI) that rates nations travel and tourism environments. Switzerland is the perennial number one ranked nation with the U.S. falling each year in the polls.

Chuck Thompson, a travel writer, who was an editor atMaxim and Travelocity.com, publishes his irreverent exposé called Smile When You're Lying: Confessions of a Rogue Travel Writer, claiming that traveler writers lie…the world sits in stunned silence!

Reformed sinner and recovering travel writer Mark Ellingham, the founder of the Rough Guides (See: 1982) and the man who encouraged a generation of travelers, claims that "binge flying" makes travel the new tobacco because the aviation industry currently accounts for an estimated 5.5 per cent (and growing) of all CO_2 carbon emissions.

An Argentinean researcher has found that Viagra reduces jetlag in hamsters…where does one begin; there are just too many jokes available for this headline.

UNESCO and leading language scholars estimate that there are 6,000 used, working and unique languages in the world; with sadly linguistic extinction happening more and more often.

On June 30th, a car bomb is driven through the terminal doors at Glasgow International Airport (GLA) and was the first terrorist attack to take place in Scotland.

On July 2nd, a suicide bombing attack takes place at the Queen of Sheba temple in Marib, Yemen, killing eight Spanish tourists and leaving another twelve wounded.

Did You Know? Although travel seems an everyday occurrence for the people of the West (albeit more expensive, uncomfortable and degrading than ever before), it is not for the other 90% of the world's citizens. In fact, in 2007 the travelers from just 5 nations (USA, England, France, Germany and Japan) with only 10% of the global population make up 50% of all global tourists. But that is changing quickly...

On December 2th, a group associated with Al-Qaeda guns down a family of four French tourists in Aleg, Mauritania.

According to frequent flyer guru Randy Petersen, airlines have awarded more than 19 trillion frequent flyer miles since they started (See: 1981), yet more than 73% of those miles, 14 trillion miles, have gone unredeemed; there is a reason air carriers make it so hard to cash in your miles—it works!

Full body scanner airport screening machines (aka virtual strip searches) using either backscatter x-ray technology or millimeter wave technologies, begin popping up at U.S. airports under Transportation Security Administration (TSA) mandate as a "voluntary alternative" to "a more invasive physical pat-down during secondary screening"...despite there being no clinical trials as to any possible DNA fragmentations or other possible long-term effects of the public safety—many wonder if it is now all just security first instead of that old mantra safety first?

As a reaction to all the global problems confronting us (climate change, Asian economic boom, political instability, water shortages, food scarcity, Pan-Islamic fundamentalism, environmental degradation, terrorism, economic recession, etc...) doomsday tourism (aka catastrophe tourism) is created whereby travelers that can afford it, attempt to see rapidly disappearing natural resources and world heritage sites around the world—before it is too late! Last-chance hot spots include: Galápagos Islands, Great

Barrier Reef, Maldives, Mount Kilimanjaro, cruises to Antarctica, glaciers of Patagonia, etc…

2008

Due to the twin effects of the global recession and bad airline management, U.S. air carriers begin à la carte pricing techniques (aka nickel-and-diming passengers to death) with not so hidden additional fees, charging airline passengers for things that used to be included in ticket prices (like fuel!), instead of raising ticket prices. US Airways leads the new movement by charging passengers US$2 for non-alcoholic beverages. Spirit Airlines charges US$4.90 as a "passenger user fee?" American Airlines follows by charging US$15 for each bag! And Jet Blue begins charging US$2 for headsets to listen to the free entertainment and US$7 for a pillow and blanket set. And within a few short years, airlines frequently charge for over three dozen "extra" services, including: making a reservation by phone; requesting a seat assignment; priority boarding (rather undemocratic some feel); special dietary meals; all snacks and beverages; entertainment access; lap children; unaccompanied minors; changing a reservation; extra-coach leg room; exit row seats; for the privilege of maybe being able to fly stand-by; for getting a refund when the fares decrease; for curbside check-in; for access to airline lounges; for earning frequent flyer mileage and worse, redeeming them; for airport counter check in, etc, etc…Using the bathrooms is still free—but stay tuned! By 2009, "ancillary fee revenue" (aka user fees) are said to account for as much as 29% of all revenue on some airlines—US$7.8 billion. One wonders if an extra destination fee will be coming next…

Beijing Capital International Airport (PEK) opens the new terminal making it the world's largest airport in anticipation of the 2008 Beijing Summer Olympics. According to China's *People's Daily*, 97 new airports will be built in China over the next 12 years and that the number of Chinese airports serving more than 30 million passengers a year will increase from the current three to 13 by 2020. In 2008, there are only 7 airports outside China catering to 30 million passengers a year. (Transportation experts are concerned that no new modern airports will ever be constructed again in the United States (See: 1994) as a result of both lack of political vision and Nimbyism (See: 1980). We can see the future…

Steve Hunt and Bart Hackley, both of California, are crowned *The World's Greatest Travelers*™ after beating 15 other teams and winning the 2008 version of the around the world travel adventure competition known as Great*Escape*2008: The Global Scavenger Hunt.

Arr, Somalia pirates unsuccessfully chase the 11-deck-high 30,000-ton Oceania Cruises' *M/S Nautica* with over 1,000 passengers and crew aboard near the mouth of the Gulf of Aden; but in April that same year pirates were successful in hijacking the French three-masts sailing ship *Le Ponant* that was on a repositioning sailing with no passengers. Ransom was paid and the 30-crew members were released.

People's Alliance for Democracy (PAD) (aka Yellow shirts) use massive people power demonstrations in Bangkok, Thailand and force the closure of Suvarnabhumi International Airport (BKK) stranding an estimated 240,000 foreign tourists with no flights in or out for seven days in November. (In an unrelated story, Patpong area massage parlors do record business in November 2008!)

Two Harvard professors, Paul F. Nunes and Mark Spelman, define the term "scarcity of place" to explain a growing global phenomena-to-be in which skyrocketing demand for travel leads to actual scarcity among tourism destinations; be it in capacity, actual space, or infrastructure overload (aka no vacancy sign), in their Harvard Business Review article "The Tourism Time Bomb".

US Airways removes all in-flight entertainment systems on domestic flights to reduce weight and save on fuel. Passengers sleep increases.

The U.S. Government Accountability Office (GAO), releases for the first time that an estimated 85.5 million U.S. passports are in circulation, representing just 28 percent of the U.S. population. Millions have been issued due to new U.S.-mandated Canada and Mexico cross-border rules as well as new ports-of-landing cruise ship requirements.

A U.S. Joint Economic Committee reported that flight delays cost the U.S. economy over US$41 billion a year—not including spewing an estimated additional 7.1 million metric tons of carbon dioxide into the atmosphere.

The airlines are to blame as just 6% of the delays are said to be caused by either weather or security-related issues.

By now the Wi-Fi Lobby has replaced the nature of the common lounge in the grand hotel lobbies of the world. Instead of meeting and mingling with other like-minded international travelers, nowadays travelers are isolated and alone oddly connected to their cyber-space social networks back home on their laptops, instead of being in the moment and open to allowing for serendipity and spontaneity to invade their lives. Digital pixilated connections have replaced real human connections. A wall of technology begins to make travel somewhat superfluous. (And by the way, how can absence make the heart grow fonder when we are never really missed with real-time Skype video chats, IM's and Flickr shares?)

Due to a down turn in the U.S. economy and the rising cost of gas, the term "staycation" begins appearing in nightly TV news broadcasts showing middleclass Americans deciding to spend their allotted vacation time staying at home instead of traveling. Being too poor to travel is another way to say it.

Take Back Your Time, a Seattle-based organization, started a campaign advocating three-week annual paid vacations, which they claim 69% of Americans agreed to in a 2008 poll—in the same poll 52% of respondents took 5 days or less vacation time off in that last year! By the way, America remains the only country in the industrial world that does not mandate vacation time—137 other nations have such a law! A National Vacation Matters Summit was held in 2009. (Timeday.org)

Ludovic Hubler, a French adventurer (but of course!), allegedly completes his 5-year hitchhiking trip around the world; which, according to his press release, had him traveling over 170,000 kilometers through fifty-nine countries on 1,300 different vehicles—all while spending nothing on transport!

Represents the most worldwide air passengers since the beginning of commercial flight with over 4.882 billion passengers flying on over 29 million flights a year—920 million flying internationally! The air passengers in the United States represent just 16% of worldwide air passengers—and decreasing annually! Dot...

The EU-US Open Skies Agreement begins allowing any airline of the European Union and any airline of the United States to fly between any point in the European Union and any point in the United States.

> **Did You Know?** That there is an online search, discover and booking process; and that Google.com maintains their research shows that an estimated 24% of wannabe online travelers don't know where they actually want to go to when they start the process, and that on average those future travelers conduct 12 web-based searches and visit 22 separate sites—before finally booking (aka making a purchase).

The U.S. Department of Transportation Inspector General questioned the feasibility of the much needed implementation of a new air traffic control system known as the U.S. Next Generation Air Transportation System (NGATS) (aka NextGen) (See: 2004). The system calls for a combination network-centric satellite-based air traffic management (ATM) systems, along with the introduction of real-time onboard avionics technology that empowers pilots better. The new system would cost an estimated US$75 billion and be completed by 2025. It would not only double (some say triple) the systems current technologically obsolete (read: radio and lights), overloaded and wasteful (that cost the U.S. economy $40 billion per year) capacity; but also allow planes to fly faster, closer and more direct routes to their destinations, saving U.S. travelers time (and money) and reducing energy costs—and potential flight mishaps. Seems no one has the guts to raise taxes!

Virtual tourism arrives with the launching of the spectacular website world-heritage-tour.org that uses 360° panographic interactive images to allow any armchair traveler with a computer and mouse to enjoy hundreds of the world's greatest sites. Truly amazing!

The Luthan Hotel & Spa opens in Saudi Arabia as the world's first female-only hotel in order to protect their modesty within the Islamic code. It follows the La Femme beach resort near Cairo, Egypt, that opened in 2006 that also imposes the female-only restrictions, and may be the beginning of an Islamic-world trend (aka Halal tourism).

On March 20th, Emirates Airline begins allowing passengers the use of their own cell phones on flights…Hmm, seems that they don't electromagnetic interfere (EMI) with the aircraft's navigation system after all! That said, polls continue to show that 63% of U.S. airline passengers opposed personal cell phone use on planes—they would rather pay the US$5.99 to use the Airfone to make a call to mom, "Hello mom, guess where I am?"

Thomas Kohnstamm, an American author, publishes the memoir Do Travel Writers Go to Hell?, which touches on his alleged experience writing a guidebook for the Lonely Planet in Brazil. The revelations create some controversy about writers and guidebook ethics. Many literary critics long ago pronounced the "death of travel writing" as all but brainless art in the Internet era of self-importance—Kohnstamm just proves the point.

On January 18th, a Yemeni al-Qaeda gunmen opened fire on a group of tourists, killing two Belgian women.

On September 20th, Islamic militants bomb the Islamabad Marriott Hotel in Pakistan killing at least 54 and wounding upwards of 260, with most of the victims being Pakistanis.

On November 26th, ten Kashmiri terrorists laid a 60-hour siege on two luxury Mumbai hotels—the Oberoi-Trident and Taj Mahal Palace & Tower—killing at least 174 people and injuring 230 more in the outrageous financial district massacre. It is India's own 9/11-like event and the whole world watched it live.

2009

Zoe Littlepage of Houston, Texas and Rainey Booth of Pensacola, Florida, second place finishers in 2008 event, are finally victorious winning the around the world travel adventure competition Great*Escape*2009: The Global Scavenger Hunt and are crowned *The World's Greatest Travelers*™.

Boeings 787 Dreamliner, a twin-engine mid-sized wide-body airliner made of composite materials flies on December 15th and is awaiting final FAA approval as they get the bugs out—and almost 1,000 planes to build.

On December 23rd, the 333 meter (1,093-foot) high Rose Rayhaan by Rotana (aka The Rose Tower) opens as the world's tallest hotel with 482 rooms in Dubai, UAE. Those crazy dessert kingdom developers do it again!

Kurt Wachtveitl (1937-), a Thai-based hotelier, retires after 41 years running the one and only Thai Chao Phraya River establishment known simply as the Oriental (aka Mandarin Oriental, Bangkok) (See: 1876). During his legendary tenure, the hotel reigned unmatched for service around the world and he revolutionized the hotel industry by training his staff to "anticipate guest needs before they even know that they want it," that included: Princess Diana, Mick Jagger, Sean Connery, Neil Armstrong, Elton John, Michael Jackson, and Elizabeth Taylor, among thousands of others. Remembering those glorious days spent looking for my bathroom in the Norman Mailer suite, I bid you a fond *adieu* Mister Kurt.

In November, the Dutch airlines KLM became the first commercial passenger airline to perform a passenger-carrying flight using biofuels.

Mic Looby, an Australian author and former *Lonely Planet* guidebook writer, publishes his novel *Paradise Updated*, a witty satire about the inner workings of a guidebook company. Fictionalized to protect the innocent no doubt!

The Mexican tourism industry, the nation's third largest revenue maker after oil and expat remittances, suffers from a triple blow: the global recession keeps high spending American's away, the gang violence and drug wars have travel agents booking vacationers elsewhere, and the new swine flu (aka *H1N1*) outbreak hits Mexico City hard closing much of the city to residents and travelers alike.

Those Northwest Airlines pilots are at it again (See: 1990), this time Northwest Flight 188 from San Diego (SAN) to Minneapolis-St. Paul International Airport (MSP), with pilots appreantly distracted and military jets ready to shoot them down, overshoots the airport by 240 kilometers (150 miles) winding up in *Wisconsin*—before turning around to land safely at MSP. Hmm...distracted! What was happening in the cockpit boys?

Australia's Great Barrier Reef Marine Park established in 1975, today receives 1.9 million tourist visits a year—that's 5,200 visitors a day *every day*—with the dinghies, divers, resort goers, charters, and super yachts, all beginning to take a toll on the reef's rich biodiversity.

After a local Emirati woman complained about a public kiss in a romantic restaurant, a British couple visiting the manufactured desert play land of Dubai are arrested and convicted of inappropriate behavior. Not the first time…boy that is a buzz-kill in the supposed "tax-free tourist Mecca of the world."

Marriott Corporation began subsidizing (US$2 million to a Foundation) a 1.4 million acre rainforest preserve in Brazil in a voluntary carbon offset program, that clearly emphasizes the importance of conservation to the tourism industry. Now if they could just get their customers to reduce water usage, waste by-products (reduce, reuse and recycle) and energy consumption, we will be getting somewhere!

A travel agency in France, *Pierre et Vacances*, begins offering sun worshipping travelers heading off to remote beaches Sunshine Insurance with rain-spoilt holidays now worth up to 400 euros (US$556)! Now that's a guarantee!

An economic study done by Oxford Economics, showed for the first time a clear link between business travel (BT) and revenue and profit increases: For every dollar invested in BT, businesses experience an average US$12.50 in increased revenue and US$3.80 in new profits due to face-to-face client meetings. The mantra being—what's good for travel is good for business too!

On February 22nd, Islamic militants detonate a bomb in a tourist-filled area around Khan el-Khalili and near Al Hussein Mosque in central Cairo, Egypt, killing French tourists and wounding 17 other French nationals and three Saudi tourists.

On March 15th, a Yemeni suicide bomber detonates himself near Korean tourists posing for pictures; four South Koreans and their Yemeni tour guide were killed and four other foreigners along with an "unspecified number of Yemenis" were wounded.

On July 17th, Islamic militants bomb the JW Marriott Hotel and the Ritz-Carlton hotels in downtown Jakarta, Indonesia, killing seven tourists, three Australians, two from The Netherlands, and one each from New Zealand and Indonesia.

On November 27th, Chechen separatists were thought responsible for a bomb detonating on a track and derailing the Nevsky Express travelling from Moscow to St. Petersburg, Russia, killing 26 people and injuring another 90 more.

On December 25th, a Christmas Day attempt by a Nigerian-born Al-Qaeda zealot to blow up Northwest Airlines Flight 253 flying from The Netherland's Amsterdam Airport Schiphol (AMS) to Detroit, Michigan (DTW) using plastic explosives sewn into his underwear, ushers in a new era of traveler paranoia and airport security theater. The man, who will shamefully go unnamed here, was known to intelligence services, begging the question: *How did he get on that plane?*

After eight straight years of declining foreign tourist visits to the United States and an estimated US$140 billion in lost revenue along with an estimated US$23 billion in lost tax receipts since the 9/11 attacks and America's border control reaction, the U.S. Congress passes the Travel Promotion Act designed to promote the United States as a tourist destination. No word on how the program is at the time of working, but the U.S. Customs and Border Protection (CBP) lines keeps getting longer…

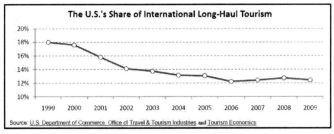

A lingering trend.
(Courtesy U.S. Dept of Commerce)

The Transportation Security Administration (TSA) begins administering *Secure Flight*, an airline passenger pre-screening program that in effect transfers the responsibility for passenger watch list matching away from the carriers to the TSA in order to prevent individuals on various U.S.

Government *No Fly List*'s (aka blacklists) from boarding any aircraft. It will also help assist in threat assessments and assign passengers to the Selectee List that gives them special additional attention and screening—one would hope! *Secure Flight* supplants CAPPS I (See: 1996) and CAPPS II (See: 2003) passenger pre-screening programs. (In an unrelated matter, a special CNN investigation found that of the 28,000 commercial airline flights that daily take to the skies in the United States, that fewer than 1 percent are protected by on-board armed federal air marshals—just 280 flights of 28,000 a day!)

After a series of passenger complaints and endless armrest battles, United Airlines starts charging obese passengers for second seats and Air France follows in 2010 by beginning to charge obese passengers 75% for an additional seat when, "*people who arrive at the check-in desk and are deemed too large to fit into a single seat will be asked to pay for and use a second seat.*" Despite the obesity epidemic in the Western world, where an estimated one in four adults are considered obese, the real problem may not be that fat people are too big to fit into airline seats, but that airline seats may be just too small to fit a large segment of the population comfortably.

> **Did You Know?** On any given day, more than 87,000 flights are in the skies over the United States (3,625 flights are in the air at any given hour); but only one-third are commercial carriers—others are private, military and freight flights—an average of 190,000 daily flights (7,916 an hour). Globally, there are 54,317 scheduled international flights a day!

The busy sky routes of North America.
(Courtesy FAA)

The Amazing Race spinoff series begins, *Around the World For Free*, in which someone attempts to travel around the world without any money and only the help of interactive online supporters. (See: 1963) The second season in 2010 airs on CBS-TV.

The U.S. FAA issues one of its largest ever fines, a US$10.2 million gotcha, on Southwest Airlines for flying planes without inspecting the bodies. Yikes!

George Clooney stars in *Up In The Air*, a Jason Reitman-directed parable of a corporate road warrior (aka business traveler) and loyal mileage collector (aka frequent flyer mile junkie) who is more comfortable traveling where he is never alone than being at home where he is.

Rick Steves (See: 1979), publishes his thoughtful and enlightening book *Travel as a Political Act*, and is immediately vilified as anti-American by many non-travelers for bringing foreign ideas back from over there! It seems that many believe that travel should *not* help us raise our consciousnesses, encourage debate into finding solutions to common problems, or show empathy towards others. *Nuff* said…you go Rick!

2010

In April, the Icelandic volcano *Eyjafjallajokull* erupts and creates havoc over European airspace as planes are grounded and travelers around the world are stranded. It is estimated that over 95,000 flights worldwide are cancelled effecting over five million people (with some travelers encountering visa issues after arriving at destinations unexpectedly) and causing losses of an estimated US$200 million within the airline industry.

Zoe Littlepage of Houston, Texas and Rainey Booth of Pensacola, Florida, successfully hold off all competitors in Great*Escape*2010: The Global Scavenger Hunt and are again crowned *The World's Greatest Travelers*™— the first repeat travel adventure competition champions.

Ever wonder why it seems to take less time to get home from a trip? Apparently others have too, and a scholarly study explains all those time-space-mind vagaries with their aptly titled "going-home effect" theory; that states that the physical area and familiar signposts surrounding our home is wide, and so we perceive that we're home before we are actually home; that and the fact that we over-estimate how long it takes to get places. Got it!

On August 2nd, history is made when a graduate student from the University of Toronto in Canada, flying a human-powered wing-flapping craft (aka an ornithopter) called Snowbird, sustains itself in the air for 19.3 seconds while traveling about 130 meters. Daedalus and Icarus live!

A Carnegie-Knight News21 longitudinal aviation accident research program reveals the four primary reasons for airplane accidents in which deaths occur as: runway mishaps, ice buildup on aircraft, faulty aircraft maintenance, and overtired pilots. Good to know—*I think*!

The Airbus plane manufacturing company forecasts that 29,000 new passenger planes will be sold over the next 20 years!

The U.S. Government Accountability Office (GAO) releases a report concerning the airport security anti-terrorist program officially known as Screening of Passengers by Observational Techniques (SPOT), which apparently costs US$212 million annually (and an additional US$1.2 billion over the next 5 years!) and employs some 3,000+ so-called behavior detection officers (BDO's) at 161 airports. (It is the U.S. version of the system used by the Israelis for passengers boarding El Al Airlines flights.) The findings: not a single terrorist has ever been caught—hundreds of wacko nutcases, illegal aliens, and drug smugglers—but not one single terrorist! It does beg the question, is there a point to all this expensive security screening—or is that the point?

Australia's Millennium House publishes the world's largest book, a six-by-nine-foot atlas titled Earth, Platinum edition…it cost US$100,000.

Angelina Jolie and Johnny Depp star in the theatrical release *The Tourist*… we're not sure what it has to do with travel or tourism, but we like them. (But not together it seems—the movie bombs!)

In yet another case of real life imitating art, a Malibu, California, resort opens the Biggest Loser Resort, a play on the NBC TV show of the same name that is based on weight-challenged contestants losing the most weight. Ugh…

Those crass Dubai developers do the impossible again when they open Ice Land (not Iceland that would be a registered trademark infringement!), and bring the icy-snow-covered Alps to the hot desert of the Arabian Peninsula, complete with five snow clad mountains to luge down!

In October, Virgin Galactic's space tourism rocket, *SpaceShipTwo* took its first solo glide flight and flew freely for 11 minutes before landing at an airport. Now, if they can just get those pesky rockets to fire maybe the US$200,000 tickets sold to ride *SpaceShipTwo* can get used.

In November, Yves Rossy (1959-), a Swiss aviation enthusiast, becomes the first man to fly with a jet-fitted 2-meter wing attached to his back—he loops and soars at 299 km/h (186 mph) to 2,400 meters (7,900-feet). Landing continues to vex him!

The Mecca Metro, an 17.7 kilometer (11-mile) elevated subway, opens to help ease the travel of Hajj pilgrims between the holy sites of Mina, Arafat and Muzdalifa in the Islamic holy city of Mecca, Saudi Arabia.

The US$40 billion cruise industry is rocked after a fire a aboard Carnival's *Splendor* strands the floating city with over 4,500 passengers and crew some 321 kilometers (200 miles) off the coast of Baja, Mexico. Horror stories of caviar-class passengers making do with Spam and Wonder bread while forgoing daily massages, threaten the industry.

Hilton Hotels settles a corporate espionage suit with rival Starwood Hotels over Hilton's attempting to compete against Starwood's chic "W" chain with their own "Denizen" luxury brand. Stolen documents, insider trade secrets, and excessive fat cat finger-pointing all lead Hilton to shell out US$75 million to halt the legal action…without admitting any guilt of course!

On April 15th, Antonio Tajani, the European Commissioner, attracted international attention when an article in London's *The Sunday Times*, reports that he has a plan to declare tourism as a human right, saying that, "Travelling for tourism today is a right. The way we spend our holidays is a formidable indicator of our quality of life." *Amen…*

Chapter Fourteen

The Future of Travel, the Tourism Industry, and *homo touristicus* is Unwritten:

Man as *homo touristicus* has come a long way from primitive hunter gathers, to city folk and traders, warriors and conquerors, and into a thoughtful and adventurous traveler, and finally a space tourist.

As can be so plainly seen in the presentation of our historic timeline and the evolution of travel and *homo touristicus*, man has always been evolving and changing his travel focus as his transportation methods have evolved in parallel with him; and no doubt as he survives and thrives well into the future, will his travel options continue to expand. Indeed, *what is the next wave?*

More mega-infrastructure projects, *ala* The Chunnel (See: 1994) are assured as man is a builder and problem-solver extraordinaire. But what other quantum leaps of technology (aka The Spike) will force a paradigm shift that will revolutionize the travel tourism industry?

The future *is* unwritten as they say…but let's read the proverbial tea leaves, look into our crystal ball and play a highly speculative game of looking over the horizon to catch a glimpse of the good, the bad, and the ugly, of what is sure to come…

> *"The future is already here, it's just unevenly distributed."*
>
> - William Ford Gibson, an American writer

2011

U.S. flyers become mad as hell and they are not going to take it anymore, about both the perceived safety and invasions of privacy issues present with TSA airport screening procedures. After pilot and flight attendant unions question the long-term safety of the X-ray full-body scans; and passengers become incensed over the thought of invasive body scan images (aka virtual strip searches) of them lingering online somewhere along with aggressive pat-downs searches (aka official airport sexual assaults)—significantly change their travel habits and a trend of decreasing passenger volume begins. (Many experts and pundits begin to wonder aloud why the TSA seems to be wasting so much time, resources and money, only looking for would-be weapons—knitting needles, tweezers and 5-ounces of toothpaste—instead of Muslim-looking men between 18 and 40?)

U.S. carriers that operate newer planes with seatback in-flight entertainment systems, begin joining forces with movie studios who know a captive audience when they see it, and start previewing new release films on flights and getting passengers to fill out evaluation forms—as an offset for watching them for free. The airlines have a new gimmick to lure passengers.

The U.S. embargo on tourism to Cuba ends.

2012

Medical tourism, especially for residents of the United States, whose health care system is broken, will significantly increase sending would-be patients to India, Thailand, Cuba and Argentina for medical procedures that will cost 30-70% less in out of pocket expenses.

The continued expansion of air carriers finding new profit centers (aka revenue streams) will include passengers paying extra for convenient flight times (6AM-9AM or 4PM-7PM); as well as for departing and arriving at conveniently-located airports (LAX versus Ontario, or Heathrow versus Gatwick).

The Transoceanic Highway (aka Southern Interoceanic Corridor), a 5,440 kilometer (3,400-mile) highway, running east-west through Brazil and Peru (and parts of the Amazon and over 4,850 meter (15,908-foot) Andes mountain passes) will for the first time link the Atlantic and Pacific Oceans in South America, opens after decades of work.

The Boeing 787 Dreamliner finally enters commercial passenger service (See: 2009).

Both overworked employees and recession-weary unemployed Americans begin eschewing staycations in favor of nano-breaks—one night away vacations to local hotels and spas.

Westin and Hyatt Hotel chains simultaneously begin offering guests free Wi-Fi services. Other major chains quickly follow the leaders.

Overwhelmed by available Internet information and social media, wannabe travelers begin asking *"who can they trust?"* Expert travel consultants become a growth industry, as people no longer want to decide anything about where they go or what they do.

Airlines collectively begin methodically loading passengers from the back to the front of the plane based on simple mathematical and logical formulas. A *duh* moment had by all…

For the first time in human and economic history, the world is home to over 10 million "ultra-high net worth individuals" (aka millionaires), that drive the travel industry towards private jets, more First Class airline seats, hotel suites, spa expansions, and casino revenues. It is estimated by travel economists that over 30% of all travel industry revenues come from this one-percent of travelers.

Beijing Capital International Airport (PEK) surpasses Hartsfield–Jackson Atlanta International Airport (ATL) to become the world's busiest airport.

After a former-mountaineer opens his Northern Base Camp Hotel, China allows for tourists to visit *Everestland*, a small theme park built after completing paving of the 110 kilometer (66-mile) road to the north-slop base camp of Mount Qomolangma (aka Mount Everest) at 5,200 meters (17,060-feet). Thousands each summer will make the trip.

First there was the shoe bomber (See: 2001) and we had to take off our shoes, then all liquids were banned (See: 2006), then the underwear bomber (See: 2009) and we had to go through full-body scanners; now as a result of the unsuccessful efforts of the so-called Bum Bomber, who was recently caught with hidden plastic explosives up his rectum while on a suicide mission to down an Airbus A-380 Super Jumbo between Los Angeles and Singapore, U.S. passengers are exposed to random anal cavity searches (aka anal probes). There is a general feeling that the TSA may have finally crossed the line! Travel in the U.S. takes a precipitous downward drop in air passengers, falling 25% in the first weeks of the TSA's new screening procedures.

Either Chinese or Islamist computer hackers—no one really knew!—gain access to European air traffic control systems and repeatedly shut down the system resulting in chaos in Europe and the ripple effect hits Asia and the U.S. as well—planes are flying, landing and taking off on visual flight rules *(*VFR*)*.

2013
Westin and Hyatt Hotel chains simultaneously begin offering guests "24-hour check-in check-out" privileges (See: 2007). Other major chains quickly follow the leaders.

The online booking of leisure travel in the U.S. exceeded US$100 billion for the first time.

Hotel Disconnect, the world's first techno-free hotel opens in the West End of London, England. The hotel is an electronics and high-tech free zone (aka slow tourism) that offers guests (mostly lovers) a disconnected rest from their hectic 24/7 digital electronic worlds to enjoy luxuriating in hot baths, warm beds, and room service—orders are made with pen and paper.

In an attempt to increase ancillary revenues, United Airlines starts charging a US$10 fee to get your checked bag *back*!

Xbox360 3-D comes out with the Virtual Vacation system that allows for armchair staycation travelers to take inter-active and virtual-reality immersion vacation-like experiences in the privacy of their own homes.

Do You Understand Me? Inc., comes out with an iPhone-7G app that allows for any traveler in any country to use any dialect by immediately translating voice data from one language to another. No more lost in translation games of charades with strangers in strange lands, sadly.

The last Siberian tiger (aka *Panthera tigris altaica*), is killed by a man called Vladimir Vladimirovich, in the wild after a decade of foreign travelers (aka ego-maniacal hunters) being routinely allowed to hunt for them via helicopters in the lawless Siberian national parks of Eastern-Russia.

China, using its massive cash reserves starts subsidizing U.S. air travel to China, in one instance, charging just a token US$199 for a round trip from the U.S. (to cover fuel costs) to their gambling city Macau (See: 2005). Las Vegas revenues take a dive.

2014
The Black Sea resort town of Sochi, that enjoys humid subtropical Mediterranean-like climate, will be the first Russian city to host the Winter Olympics. The Arabian-desert kingdom of Dubai wins the bid to host the 2018 Winter Olympics as they actually have snow—albeit man-made and inside—but bans the couple's figure skating competition.

Emirates airlines starts offering US$399 no-nonsense roundtrip fares from anywhere in the world they fly to Dubai in an effort to increase declining tourism to UAE.

The Galactic Suite Space Resort opens as the first modular space habitat (aka an orbital resort) ever built called *The Moon* and begins taking reservations—they still have that two-night minimum stay requirement however! Talk about a room with a view.

The Shanghai Disneyland Resort opens in China and is connected to the city by a Maglev transit system.

The U.S. Congress passes the *Airline Passenger Bill of Rights Act of 2014*, that among other things: puts real teeth in airline carriers for lying to, stranding, delaying and mishandling airline passengers (See: 2005); establishes truth in pricing guidelines that include all the taxes and fees in price advertisements—that also includes the flight's on-time rate;

provides for fee refunds to passengers for baggage handling when the airlines mishandle those bags; creates an airline passenger ombudsman to investigate all passenger complaints; and requires that all provisions of the *Airline Passenger Bill of Rights* apply to all code share and international partners.

Door-to-door seamless travel systems become a reality in most European and Asian cities, with cheap, clean, and easy to navigate subway-to-high speed railway to another city subway-links being built everywhere to supply their citizens (and visiting travelers) with ultra-modern infrastructure, along with safe and reliable modes of transportation. Freeway expansions continue apace in the United States.

Finally surrendering to their domestic war on drugs, a Mexican referendum passes in Mexico that legalizes all drugs; this leads to a new boom of drug tourism south of the border. It makes Amsterdam look like amateur hour. Anything you want is available for a price.

2015

As the Asian air sector continues to grow in volume and frequency (currently about 20% of global arrivals to maybe as much as 33% of global volume by 2020), there will also be more travel-related issues occurring within this sector, including hijackings and airplane crashes.

Virgin Galactic's rocket ship, *SpaceShipTwo* (See: 2010) will begin regular service for space tourist willing to pay the price of a ticket.

The 41 kilometer (25-mile) Qatar-Bahrain Friendship Bridge across the Persian Gulf opens.

The European commercial jet builder Airbus delivers their first carbon fiber-reinforced polymer built passenger jet, the A350-XWB (as in *extra* wide body), albeit three years late. The A350 was built to compete directly against the all composite fuselage Boeing 787 Dreamliner (See: 2009).

The Peruvian Ministry of Tourism begins auctioning off the limited number of daily park passes to Machu Picchu online as "scarcity of place" begins overwhelming the sacred park.

Due to continued economic stagnation in the leading Western nations (Japan, United States, England, Italy and Spain), globalism recedes as populist nationalism and chauvinistic xenophobia begin taking root in declining Western economies. The travel and tourism industry contracts 20%.

All major European and Asian cities have integrated mass transit systems linking airports directly to their downtown areas. The U.S. continues with freeway expansions.

Western-based conscientious consumption trends have Generation Xers significantly reducing their airplane flying in order to reduce their carbon foot prints.

The Chinese state-owned civilian aircraft builder Commercial Aircraft Corp. (CAC) delivers the first mid-range passenger jet, the Comac C919 to Air China—almost 2 years ahead of schedule and under budget. The passenger plane will compete directly against the Boeing 737 and Airbus A320 in the Chinese market.

The U.S. Customs and Border Protection begins instituting Operation Exit, already established in every other nation in the world, and begin processing all departing international passengers and matching data with their incoming travelers lists. Finally, we know who is coming—and going!

Hong Kong International Airport (HKG) becomes the world's second busiest airport after Beijing Capital International Airport (PEK). Asian airports rank 1, 2, and 3 in the world, with Tokyo International Airport (HND) rounding out the list.

As London-area hotel rooms become more and more scarce (aka "scarcity of place"), hotel room scalpers begin hawking already pre-purchased hotel rooms at Heathrow International Airport (LHR) to weary arriving travelers. This also begins to take place in destinations like Hong Kong, New Delhi and Rome.

Due to numerous U.S. Open Skies agreements (See: 1979), foreign carriers are finally allowed to carry passengers from city to city within the U.S., that quickly puts shoddy service and out-dated business model U.S. airlines out of business. Why fly U.S. carriers with bad service, surly crews and nickel-and-dime-you corporate attitudes, when you can be pampered by Singapore Girls, Thai ladies, and Emirates gals, making minimum wage? Outsourcing comes to America…

2016
Rio de Janeiro, Brazil, hosts the Summer Olympic Games marking for the first time in the history of the games that they are played in South America.

RIP United Airlines (1934-2016)

The U.S. Congress suspends funding of the NextGen air traffic control system remodel project as too costly. (See: 2008) in favor of a private-public scheme and hand out US$10 billion in sweet-heart speculative government contracts to Halliburton, the Carlyle Group, and Bechtel.

Due to severe fresh water shortages, protesters in China demand the closure of all the nation's 2,000 golf courses ending the golf tourism business in China. The Communist Party agrees. Japan's 2,500 golf courses come under scrutiny for the same reason.

After a series of Gulf of Mexico oil rig explosions beginning in 2010, the U.S. Environmental Protection Agency (EPA) closes 50% of the working rigs as a public pollution nuisance and business entrepreneurs quickly turn them into a community of off-shore luxury hotels connect with high-speed ocean racers and helicopters.

The Korean company Samsung Construction and Trading builds the first new airship since the 1930's called *Aircruise One,* that can take 100 passengers from London to New York City in just 36-hours and from Los Angeles to Shanghai in less than four days with their slogan, *"Slow is the new fast."* The airships once in port are tethered and serve as a floating hotel for the guests.

China cancels all outstanding undelivered orders of Boeing and Airbus passenger jets, settling on only buying and using their home-made Comac

C919 (See: 2015). The global aviation passenger jet business is thrown into chaos as billions are lost and the number one market is now off-limits.

The Louvre Museum of Paris begins operating a reservation only ticket system due to excessive tourist volume. You must now apply online to get a reservation time. The Eiffel tower quickly follows suit.

2017
RIP American Airlines (1934-2017)

In an effort to cash in on much needed tourism revenue, and responding to a sophisticated Western-based adventure junkie market, Israeli travel agents (former Mossad agents) begin offering "live action" underground battle zone trips (aka Leisure Soldier Tours) to the basket-case failed state nations of Somalia, Congo and Sudan, to officially play paintball against paid guerilla groups—but unofficially, with real guns of their choice and live ammo! The Government of Canada is outraged…the governments of Myanmar, Columbia and Afghanistan quickly jump on the bandwagon offering organized battles of their own.

2018
RIP Delta Airlines (1929-2018)

2020
According to the United Nations World Tourism Organization, international tourist visits are expected to double to over 1.6 billion by 2020 in a travel explosion, led by the rise of middle class Chinese and Indian global travelers.

The U.S. Federal Aviation Administration reports that 1.2 billion passengers flew on U.S. carriers last year, up from 741 million in 2007!

For the first time, French residents retiring to live in Tunisia exceeds one million.

The long-delayed (originally slated to open in 2006) Hydropolis Underwater Hotel and Resort opens off Jumeira Beach in Dubai after a decade of engineering and environmental difficulties—not to mention billions of recycled petro-dollars! Travelers still are uncertain about coming to Dubai since the crackdown on kissing tourists began. (See: 2009)

The Southern Corridor of the Trans-Asian Railway (TAR) (aka Iron Silk Road) running from Singapore across Asia to Istanbul, Turkey (and Europe), via Malaysia, Thailand, Burma, Bangladesh, India, Pakistan and Iran, opens for business.

The Trans-African Highway (TAH 4), running north-south from Alexandria, Egypt 10,288 kilometers (6,392 miles) to Cape Town, South Africa finally opens after decades of construction interrupted by war, famine, geography, climate, nationalism, religious fundamentalism, corruption, Apartheid and hopelessness, with the final paving of what is known as "the road to hell" in northern Kenya.

High speed rail will arrive in the United States, including routes: between the San Francisco Bay area to Los Angeles (with spurs to San Diego and Sacramento); Los Angeles to Las Vegas (and Phoenix); Boston-New York City-Washington D.C. (Baltimore and Philadelphia spurs); the Houston-Dallas-San Antonio (with spurs to New Orleans and Austin) areas; and the opening of the Cascadia Maglev running between Portland, Oregon to Vancouver, British Columbia, via Seattle, with spurs to Eugene (in the south) and Whistler (in the north).

In an unrelated story, airline passengers flying the Los Angeles (LAX) to Las Vegas (LAS) route, Los Angeles (LAX) to San Francisco (SFO), and the Boston (BOS) to New York (JFK and LGA) routes, fall by more than 80%!

A mile long cruise ship (aka a city at sea) be launched that will travel at 10 knots and have ferries to shuttle the 50,000+ passengers to and from shore.

The 56 kilometer (35-mile) Gotthard Base Tunnel opens through the Swiss Alps cutting travel time between Munich and Milan (via Zurich) by more than 75%.

With only four types of commercial passenger aircraft flying the friendly skies (Airbus A350 and A380, and Boeing 787 and 737), air carriers unite and create a single standard size for all carry-on's to prevent carry-on abuse.

A Korean entrepreneur opens Biodiversity Farms, the first heritage zoo that is entirely composed of the reconstructed DNA from extinct species *ala Jurassic Park* (1993) without the dinosaurs. Visitors can see live polar bears, Siberian tigers, dodos, mountain gorillas, panda bears, snow leopards, black rhinos, orangutans, albatross, and Tasmanian Devils, among dozens of other functionally extinct critters.

Due to the recent fear caused by the spreading global pandemic that began in Asia, international air travel contracts by 30% for the second year in a row. People just don't want to take the chance of getting sick.

As the Colorado River dries up due to global warming, Arizona tourist areas and the golf vacation industry of the Southwest collapse. Soon, Tucson, Phoenix and Scottsdale are ghost towns. Which opens up a new tourist site called Survival City.

A rise in sea level precipitated by global warming combined with an aging retired U.S. baby boomer population that just wants to keep living in luxury, has more people living permanently on cruise ships that have been converted into seagoing condos. (See: 2002)

The last snow disappears completely from Mount Kilimanjaro. Hemingway would have been sad...

2020c

A 14 kilometer (8.7-mile) bridge-tunnel combo, resembling the Chesapeake Bay Bridge-Tunnel, will open across the Strait of Gibraltar between Spain and Morocco, linking Africa with Europe for the first time.

A 14 kilometer (8.7-mile) bridge-tunnel combo (aka the Bridge of Horns) will open across Red Sea between Djibouti and Yemen, linking Africa with Asia for the first time.

The Pan-American Highway that runs continuously between Alaska and Chile from North to South America via Central America will finally be completed with the final 87 kilometer (54-mile) stretch through the Darién Gap between Panama and Columbia opening for traffic.

The 26 kilometer (16-mile) Sunda Strait Bridge, a road and railway connection across the Sundra Straight between the islands of Sumatra and Java in Indonesia opens.

Due to continued unabated global climate changes, many international travel destinations are severely and adversely effected. (See: 1985) The continued bleaching of coral reefs in Australia, the Red Sea, the Caribbean, and around Indonesia, have dramatically affected the dive destination business. Decreasing natural snow cover in winter sport destinations like the Swiss Alps, Utah and Colorado Rocky Mountain ski resorts, and in British Columbia, have all required a shortening of their ski seasons to just two-months a year due to lack of snow. The continued rising sea levels have made tourism to places like the Maldives, Tahiti, the Caribbean, and other low-lying beach island resorts all but a lost cause. The lack of predictability of sunny summer conditions has severely impacted the traditional summer peak times of traditional vacation sun, sea and sand get-a-ways like San Diego, Hawaii, Cancun, Costa del Sol (aka Costa del Concrete), Goa, and the Greek islands, Tunisia, the French Riviera, Morocco and the Dalmatian Coast. In Australia, the weather is just too darn hot. Hurricane season becomes unpredictable in the Caribbean. The economic ripple effect of decreased travel and tourism spending pushes millions into unemployment and thousands of tourist facilities into or near bankruptcy, cascading the rapid decline in leisure-based tourism.

U.S. government-owned Scramjet (aka supersonic combustion ramjet) technology cuts diplomatic flight time from Beijing to Washington D.C. to just two hours.

A second round of war tourism booms, when U.S. and NATO veterans begin going back to visit the places they fought, including: Bosnia, Iraq and Afghanistan.

2030c
A bridge and tunnel combo for rail and truck traffic will open across the Bering Strait between Alaska and Russia linking Asia with North America for the first time…err, since (See: 10,500c BCE)

For the first time, U.S. residents retiring and living in Mexico, exceeds five million.

The Disney Corporation opens Equ-resort, a 100% self-sufficient eco-friendly floating botanical city that sits in equatorial waters of the Pacific Ocean.

The 128 kilometer (79-mile) Japan–Korea Undersea Tunnel crossing the Korea Strait is opened connecting Japan with United Korea and linking Asia and Japan for the first time.

The first space hotel, powered entirely by solar energy, opens in low-orbit. A three-night minimum stay is required at booking for the promise of incomparable star-gazing!

The 1,000[th] Airbus A380 Double-decker jumbo jet (See: 2007) is delivered to Southwest Airlines (they now fly 10 such planes, mostly on their busy LAX to MEX route) in less than 23 years of production; besting the Boeing 747's record of delivering their 1,000[th] 747's after 24 years! In a side note, there are now more than 2,025 Jumbo 747's still flying!

2035c
Making all transportation systems obsolete, *homo touristicus* begins traveling via teleportation (aka Star Trek's teletransporter) after finally conquering a few unresolved technical issues like putting Humpty Dumpty back together again. Matter being matter—it is indeed moveable! Travelers reach nirvana.

Or will we have stopped wanting to travel by now because 24/7/365 holographic 3-D cameras *ala* CTV and Google Earth 3-D, have made the world already ubiquitous?

Or, *maybe not*…to be continued!

Acknowledgements:

I am a very thankful guy because I have a lot to be thankful for…

Thank you Pamela.

About the Author:

A father of two and scholar at heart, William D. Chalmers was educated in Canada, the U.S. and England, and has lived in Europe and South America. He has stepped foot in over 100 countries—okay, a *few* toes—and is a reformed Cold War-era Summit Junkie. He is also the winner of the 1989 Human*Race,* an around-the-world race using public transportation—collecting the $25,000 prize after circumnavigating the globe in just 17 days. *National Geographic Traveler* magazine erroneously dubbed him, the *"World's Greatest Traveler"* in April 2002. He is the author of the gonzo travel tale *A Blind Date With the World* and is a regular contributor to the op-ed sections on the weighty social issues of the day, including the *Los Angeles Times, San Francisco Chronicle* and *Times of India.*

For the last decade he has served as the Event Director for *The Global Scavenger Hunt™,* an around-the-world travel adventure competition that tests the travel savvy and IQ of participants and annually crowns *The World's Greatest Travelers™* following a three-week international event that includes exciting *sight-doing* activities and *trusting strangers in strange lands.* The event serves as a travel-a-thon to help raise charitable funds to build co-ed elementary schools and support micro-financing loans in at risk nations.

Bibliography:

Aerial Age Weekly.

Aron, Cindy A. (1999) *Working at Play: A History of Vacations in the United States.* (Oxford University Press)

Barry, Kathleen. (2007) *Femininity in Flight: A History of Flight Attendants.* (Duke University Press Books)

Bell, Barbara Nicholson. (1999) *Thomas Cook and the Grand Tours.* (Unknown)

Bell, Claudia & John Lyall. (2001) *The Accelerated Sublime: Landscape, Tourism, and Identity.* (Praeger)

Boorstin, Daniel J. (1983) *The Discoverers.* (Random House)

Bottomley Renshaw, Mike. (1997) *The Travel Agent.* (Sunderland)

Bowen, Brent D., & Dean E. Headley. (1996-2010) *Airline Quality Rating Report* (Wichita State University)

Buckley, R. (2006) *Adventure Tourism.* (CABI)

Burkart, A.J., & S.A. Medlik. (1974) *Tourism: Past, Present and Future.* (Heinermann)

Center for Defense & International Security Studies. (2010) *Terrorism Programme Database.* (cdiss.org)

Chalmers, William D. (2000) *A Blind Date With The World.* (Writers Club Press)

CIA World Factbook.

Clayton, Peter & Martin Price. (1988) *Seven Wonders of the Ancient World.* (Barnes & Noble Books)

Cocker, Mark. (1992) *Loneliness and Time: The Story of British Travel Writing.* (Pantheon Books)

Coryate, Thomas. (1611) *Coryate's Crudities.* (Gibson Square Books)

Cousineau, Phil. (2000) *The Art of Pilgrimage: The Seeker's Guide to Making Travel Sacred.* (Conari Press)

Davies, R.E.G. (1987) *Pan Am: An Airline and Its Aircraft* (Orion Books)

Dickinson, Bob & Andy Vladimir. (1997) *Selling the Sea: An Inside Look at the Cruise Industry.* (John Wiley & Sons, Inc.)

Dickerson, Thomas A. (2006) *Travel Law.* (Law Journal Press)

Doganis, Rigas. (1992) *The Airport Business.* (Routledge)

Doubleday, Nelson, editor. (1967) *Encyclopedia of World Travel Volume 1 & 2.* (Doubleday & Company)

The Economist.

Encyclopedia Britannia

Federal Aviation Administration.

Feifer, Mazine. (1985) *Tourism in History: from Imperial Rome to the Present Day.* (Stein & Day)

The Globe and Mail.

The *Guardian*.

Greene, Graham. (1936) *Journey without Maps*. (Penguin)

Harper's Weekly.

Heil, Scott & Terrance W. Peck, eds. (1998) *The Encyclopedia of American Industry, 2nd ed*. (Gale Research)

Hester, Elliott. (2001) *Plane Insanity: A Flight Attendant's Tales of Sex, Rage and Queasiness at 30,000 Feet*. (St Martin's)

Hill, Charles. (2000) *Fix on the Rising Sun: The Clipper Hi-Jacking of 1938—And the Ultimate M.I.A.'s*. (1st *Books* Library)

The Honolulu Advertiser.

Hudman, Lloyd E., & Richard H. Jackson. (1994) *Geography of Travel and Tourism*. (Delmar Publishers, Inc.)

Hudson, Kenneth. (1972) *A Social History of Air Travel*. (Adams & Dart)

Inglis, Fred. (2000) *The Delicious History of the Holiday*. (Routledge)

International Herald Tribune.

Iyer, Pico. (1988) *Video Night in Kathmandu*. (Vintage Departures)

Iyer, Pico. (1994) *Falling Off The Map*. (Vintage Departures)

Iyer, Pico. (1997) *Tropical Classics*. (Alfred A. Knopf, Inc)

Iyer, Pico. (2000) *The Global Soul*. (Vintage Departures)

Klein, Ross A. (2002) *Cruise Ship Blues: The Underside of the Cruise Industry*. (New Society)

Leed, Eric J. (1991) *The Mind of the Traveler: from Gilgamesh to Global Tourism.* (Basic Books)

Lloyd, Martin. (2003) *The Passport: the History of Man's Most Travelled Document.* (Sutton Publishing)

Löfgren, Orvar. (2000) *On Holiday: A History of Vacationing.* (California)

Los Angeles Times.

Löschburg, Winfried. (1982) *History of Travel.* (Hippocrene Books)

Lowenhein, Oded. (2007) *The Responsibility to Responsibilize: Foreign*

Offices and the Issuing of Travel Warnings. (International Political Sociology, 1, 203–221)

Lundberg, Donald E. (1974) *The Hotel and Restaurant Business.* (Cahners Books)

Lundberg, D.D., M.H. Stavenca & M. Krishnamoorthy. (1995) *Tourism Economics.* (John Wiley & Sons)

MacCannell D. (1973) *The Tourist: A New Theory of the Leisure Class* (MacMillan)

Maclean, Rory. (2008) *Magic Bus: On the Hippie Trail from Istanbul to India.* (Penguin Books)

Mak, James. (2003) *Tourism and the Economy: Understanding the Economics of Tourism.* (University of Hawaii Press)

Marks, Jason. (1993) *Around the World in 72 Days: The Race Between Pulitzer's Nellie Bly and Cosmopolitan's Elizabeth Bisland.* (Gemittarius Press)

Merari, Ariel. (1998) *Attacks On Civil Aviation: Trends And Lessons.* (Volume 10, Issue 3 Autumn, pages 9 – 26)

Mintz, Sidney. (1996) *Tasting Food, Tasting Freedom: Excursions into Eating, Culture and the Past.* (Beacon)

Mouchard, Christel. (2007) *Women Travellers: A Century of Trailblazing Adventures, 1850-1950.* (Flammarion)

Nader, Ralph (1994) *Collision Course: The Truth About Airline Safety.* (McGraw Hill)

NASA.

The New York Times.

Nunes, Paul F., & Mark Spelman. (2008) *The Tourism Time Bomb.* (Harvard Business Review, June)

O'Hanlon, Redmond. (1984) *Into the Heart of Borneo.* (Vintage Departures)

O'Hanlon, Redmond. (1988) *In Trouble Again – A Journey Between the Orinco and the Amazon.* (Vintage)

O'Hanlon, Redmond. (1997) *No Mercy: A Journey Into the Heart of the Congo.* (Vintage Departures)

O'Rourke, P.J. (1988) *Holidays In Hell.* (Atlantic Monthly Press)

Ostrovskii, I., & M. Pavlenko. (1998) *Intourist 1929 - 1999.* (VAO Inturist)

Oxford English Dictionary.

Palin, Michael. (1989) *Around the World in Eighty Days.* (KQED Books)

Palin, Michael. (1997) *Full Circle.* (BBC Books)

Park, Mungo. (1799) *Travels in the Interior Districts of Africa*. (Duke University Press)

Paquet, Laura Bryne. (2007) *Wanderlust: A Social History of Travel*. (Goose Lane)

Pearce, Douglas. (1989) *Tourist Development*. (Longman Publishing)

Pelton, Robert Young & Coskun Aral. (1995) *The World's Most Dangerous Places*. (Fielding Worldwide, Inc.)

Pelton, Robert Young. (1999) *Come Back Alive*. (Doubleday)

Perrottet, Tony. (2001) *Route 66 A.D.: On The Trail of Ancient Roman Tourists*. (Random House)

Pickles, Shelia, editor. (1990) *The Grand Tour*. (Harmony House)

Prescott, Jerome. (1996) *100 Explorers*. (Bluewood Books)

Polo, Marco. (1298) *The Travels*. (Penguin Classics)

Raghubir, etal. (2010) *Spatial categorization and time perception: Why does it take less time to get home?* (Journal on Consumer Psychology, Summer)

Roberts, David. (2001) *Great Exploration Hoaxes*. (The Modern Library)

Ross Jr, Donald James. (1998) *American Travel Writing, 1850-1914*. (Bruccoli Clark Layman)

Rugoff, Milton, editor. (1960) *The Great Travelers*. (Simon & Schuster)

Setright, LJK. (2003) *Drive On! A Social History of the Motor Car*. (Granta)

Shaffer, Marguerite. (2001) *See America First: Tourism as a Ritual of American Citizenship*. (Smithsonian Institute Press)

Short, John Rennie. (2003) *The World Through Maps: A History of Cartography.* (Firefly)

Shrady, Nicolas. (1999) *Sacred Roads: Adventures from the Pilgrimage Trail.* (Harper)

Smith, Myron J. (2002) *The Airline Encyclopedia, 1909–2000.* (Scarecrow Press)

Smith, V. L. (1977) *Hosts and Guests: the Anthropology of Tourism.* (University of Pennsylvania Press)

Soule, Thayer. (2003) *On the Road With Travelogues: 1935 - 1995 A Sixty-Year Romp.* (Authorhouse)

Speke, John Hanning. (1863) *Journal of the Discovery of the Source of the Nile.* (Dover Publications)

Stanley, Henry M. (1878) *Through the Dark Continent.* (Dover Publications)

Swinglehurst, Edmund. (1982) *Cook's Tours: The Story of Popular Travel.* (Blandford Press)

Tregaskis, Hugh. (1979) *Beyond the Grand Tour.* (Ascent Books)

Twain, Mark. (1869) *Innocents Abroad.* (Signet Classics)

Urry, John. (1990) *The Tourist Gaze: Leisure and Travel in Contemporary Societies.* (Sage Publications)

USA Today.

U.S. Department of Commerce.

U.S. Department of State.

U.S. Department of Transportation.

Vancouver Sun.

Verne, Jules. (1873) *Around the World in Eighty Days.* (Bantam Classics)

Wall Street Journal.

Washington Post.

Wikipedia.com.

Wikitravel.com.

Wilford, John Noble. (1981) *The Mapmakers.* (Alfred A. Knopf)

Wilson, Colin. (1996) *The Atlas of Holy Places and Sacred Sites.* (Dorling Kindersley Ltd.)

Witney, Lynne. (1996) *Grand Tours and Cook's Tours: A History of Leisure Travel: 1750-1915.* (William Morrow & Company)

World Travel & Tourism Council.

Yapp, Peter, editor. (1983*) The Traveler's Dictionary of Quotations: Who Said What, About Where?* (Rutledge & Kegan Paul)

An Index - The Evolution of *homo touristicus* through the ages:

2850c BCE - Religious tourism
1829c BCE - Sports tourism
1390c BCE - New Age/Sacred tourism
            - Mancations
800c BCE - Spa tourism
500c BCE - Medical tourism
462 BCE - Heritage tourism
190c BCE - Beach Resort tourism
75c BCE - Wine tourism
333 - Christian tourism
294c - Buddhist tourism
633c - Hajj tourism
980c - Honeymoon Tourism
1064 - Group tourism
1260 - Road warrior/business travel
1370c - Day trips
1461 - Shopping/mall tourism
1480 - Bookstore tourism
1506 - Museum tourism
1591 - Annual festival tourism
1608 - Grand Tours
1638 - Casino tourism
1650 - Winter tourism
1693 - Round-the-world travel
1750c - Archaeological tourism
1760 - Adventure tourism
       - Extreme tourism
1769 - Cultural tourism

1775 - Buddy road trip tourism
1780 - Resort tourism
1784 - Restaurant/culinary tourism
1798 - Annual exhibition tourism
1802 - Hotel tourism
1807 - Railway tourism
       - Riverboat tourism
1817 - Ocean cruises
1832 - Convention tourism
1836 - Safari/wildlife tourism
1840c - Summer vacations
        - Romance/female sex tourism
1841 - Photo tourism
1843 - Amusement park tourism
1844 - Pleasure cruise tourism
1847 - Zoo/aquarium tourism
1853 - Garden tourism
1863 - Package tourism
1864 - Winter tourism
1867 - Urban exploration tourism
1872 - National park tourism
1879 - Study Abroad tourism
1880 - Golf tourism
1884 - Literary tourism
1887 - Snowbird tourism
1889 - Retro tourism
1896 - Olympic game tourism
1897 - Aboriginal tourism
1898 - Birth tourism
1900 - Pleasure cruises
1901 - Hawaiian tourism
       - Extreme tourism
1903 - Ski tourism
1906 - Patriotic tourism
1908 - Aviation tourism
1912 - Student travel
       - Rural tourism
1916 - RV tourism
1919 - Water/Boating/Nautical tourism

1927 - Motorcycle tourism
    - Celebrity tourism
1930 - Cuban tourism
1932 - Film Festival tourism
1936 - Spring Break tourism
1939 - Roadside tourism
1945 - Ethno tourism
1946 - Fly-Drive tourism
1949 - Escape tourism
1953 - House-Swapping vacations
    - Ego tourism
1955 - Kiddy tourism
1960c - Gap Years
1962 - Volunteer travel
    - Campground tourism
1963 - Time-share vacations
1964 - Accessible tourism
    - Pop-culture tourism
1966 - Cruise ship tourism
    - Surf culture tourism
    - Sex tourism
    - Independent travel
1967 - LGBT/Gay tourism
    - Music tourism
1971 - Charity travel
1972 - Drug tourism
1973 - Incentive travel
    - Club tourism
1980c - Work travel
1983 - Eco-tourism/Responsible tourism
    - Volcano tourism
1984 - Eclipse-chasing tourism
1988 - Dark tourism
    - War zone Tourism
1989 - Reality Tours
1990 - Sustainable tourism
    - Diaspora tourism
    - Space tourism
1996 - Scuba Tourism

1997 - Weather tourism
1998 - Destination Club tourism
1999 - Tummy Tuck Tourism
    - Community-based tourism
2000 - Disaster tourism
2001 - Armchair tourism
2002 - Geo-tourism
    - Perpetual traveler
2003 - Debaucherism tourism
    - Experimental tourism
    - Counter tourism
2004 - Babymoon tourism
2005 - Poverty/Township/Slum/Ghetto tourism
2007 - Doomsday tourism
2008 - Halal tourism
2008 - Staycation
2008 - Virtual tourism

An Index - The Evolution of *homo touristicus* from A-Z:

Aboriginal tourism (1897)
Accessible tourism (1964)
Adventure tourism (1760)
Amusement park tourism (1843)
Annual exhibition tourism (1798)
Annual festival tourism (1591)
Archaeological tourism (1750c)
Armchair tourism (2001)
Around-the-world travel (1693)
Aviation tourism (1908)

Babymoon tourism (2004)
Beach Resort tourism (190c BCE)
Birth tourism (1898)
Bookstore tourism (1480)
Buddhist tourism (394c)
Buddy road trip tourism (1775)

Campground tourism (1962)
Casino tourism (1638)
Celebrity tourism (1927)
Charity travel (1971)
Christian tourism (333)
Club tourism (1973)
Community-based tourism (1999)
Convention tourism (1832)
Counter tourism (2003)
Cruise ship tourism (1966)

Cuban tourism (1930)
Cultural tourism (1769)

Dark tourism (1988)
Day trips (1370c)
Debaucherism tourism (2003)
Destination Club tourism (1998)
Diaspora tourism (1990)
Disaster tourism (2000)
Doomsday tourism (2007)
Drug tourism (1972)

Eclipse-chasing tourism (1984)
Eco-tourism (1983)
Ego tourism (1953)
Escape tourism (1949)
Ethno tourism (1945)
Experimental tourism (2003)
Extreme tourism (1760)

Film Festival tourism (1932)
Fly-Drive tourism (1946)

Gap Years (1960c)
Garden tourism (1853)
Genealogy Tourism (1990)
Geo-tourism (2002)
Golf tourism (1880)
Grand Tours (1608)
Group tourism (1064)

Hajj tourism (633c)
Halal tourism (2008)
Hawaiian tourism (1901)
Heritage tourism (462 BCE)
Honeymoon tourism (980c)
Hotel tourism (1802)
House-swapping vacations (1953)

Incentive travel (1973)
Independent travel (1966)

Kiddy tourism (1955)

LGBT/Gay tourism (1967)
Literary tourism (1884)

Mancations (1390c BCE)
Medical tourism (500c BCE)
Motorcycle tourism (1927)
Museum tourism (1506)
Music tourism (1967)

National park tourism (1872)
New Age (1390c BCE)

Ocean cruises (1817)
Olympic game tourism (1896)

Package tourism (1863)
Patriotic tourism (1906)
Perpetual traveler (2002)
Photo tourism (1841)
Pleasure cruise tourism (1844)
Pop-culture tourism (1964)
Poverty/Township/Slum/Ghetto tourism (2005)

Railway tourism (1807)
Reality Tours (1989)
Religious tourism (2850c BCE)
Responsible tourism (1983)
Resort tourism (1780)
Restaurant/culinary tourism (1784)
Retro tourism (1889)
Riverboat tourism (1807)
Roadside tourism (1939)
Road warrior/business travel (1260)
Romance/female sex tourism (1840c)

Rural tourism (1912)
RV tourism (1916)

Sacred tourism (1390c BCE)
Safari/wildlife tourism (1836)
Scuba Tourism (1996)
Sex tourism (1966)
Shopping/mall tourism (1461)
Ski tourism (1903)
Snowbird tourism (1887)
Spa tourism (800c NCE)
Space tourism (1990)
Spring Break tourism (1936)
Sports tourism (1829c BCE)
Staycation (2008)
Study Abroad tourism (1879)
Student travel (1912)
Summer vacations (1840c)
Surf culture tourism (1966)
Sustainable tourism (1990)

Time-share vacations (1963)
Tummy Tuck tourism (1999)

Urban exploration tourism (1867)

Virtual tourism (2008)
Volcano tourism (1983)
Volunteer travel (1962)

War zone Tourism (1988)
Water/Boating/Nautical tourism (1919)
Weather tourism (1997)
Wine tourism (75c BCE)
Winter tourism (1650)
Work travel (1980c)

Zoo/aquarium tourism (1847)